BROOKINGS PAPERS ON
Economic Activity

William C. Brainard and George L. Perry, Editors

1997

Kathleen M. Bucholz, Production Associate
Kevin R. Foster, Assistant to the Editors
Tyree W. Harris Jr., Statistical Associate
Tanjam Jacobson, Editorial Associate

BROOKINGS **B** INSTITUTION

WASHINGTON, D.C.

BROOKINGS PAPERS ON

Economic Activity

William C. Brainard and George L. Perry, Editors   **1997**

Purpose *Brookings Papers on Economic Activity* contains the articles, reports, and highlights of the discussions from conferences of the Brookings Panel on Economic Activity. Financed today in part by grants from the National Science Foundation, the panel was formed to promote professional research and analysis of key developments in U.S. economic activity. Prosperity and price stability are its basic subjects.

The expertise of the panel is concentrated on the "live" issues of economic performance that confront the maker of public policy and the executive in the private sector. Particular attention is devoted to recent and current economic developments that are directly relevant to the contemporary scene or especially challenging because they stretch our understanding of economic theory or previous empirical findings. Such issues are typically quantitative, and the research findings are often statistical. Nevertheless, in all the articles and reports, the reasoning and the conclusions are developed in a form intelligible to the interested, informed nonspecialist as well as useful to the expert in macroeconomics. In short, the papers aim at several objectives— meticulous and incisive professional analysis, timeliness and relevance to current issues, and lucid presentation.

Articles appear in this publication after presentation and discussion at a conference at Brookings. From the spirited discussions at the conference, the authors obtain new insights and helpful comments; they also receive searching criticism about various aspects of the papers. Some of these comments are reflected in the published summaries of discussion, some in the final versions of the papers themselves. But in all cases the papers are finally the product of the authors' thinking and do not imply any agreement by those attending the conference. Nor do the papers or any of the other materials in this issue necessarily represent the views of the staff members, officers, or trustees of the Brookings Institution.

Correspondence Correspondence regarding papers in this issue should be addressed to the authors. Manuscripts are not accepted for review because this journal is devoted exclusively to invited contributions.

Editors' Summary

THE BROOKINGS PANEL on Economic Activity held its sixty-third conference in Washington, D.C., on March 27 and 28, 1997. This issue of *Brookings Papers on Economic Activity* includes the papers and discussions presented at that conference. In light of the great increase in U.S. immigration and trade since the 1960, the first paper estimates the impacts of these two factors on the labor market outcomes of U.S. natives. The second paper examines the effects of systematic monetary policy on the economy, disentangling these effects from the effects of other shocks, such as OPEC oil price increases. The third considers public resistance to the indexation of long-term contracts, using survey data from the United States and from Turkey—a country with high and variable inflation. The fourth examines to what extent and by what means families are able to smooth year-to-year variation in the earnings of the household head. The fifth paper addresses recent criticisms of the procedures used by the Bureau of Labor Statistics in accounting for quality change in the Consumer Price Index. And the sixth assesses the performance and prospects of Brazil's stabilization and economic reform under the Real Plan.

OVER THE PAST two decades, the United States has experienced high rates of immigration and a rapid growth of imports from less developed countries (LDCs). Over this same period, the earnings of less skilled U.S. workers have declined markedly relative to the earnings of other U.S. workers. In the first paper of this volume, George Borjas, Richard Freeman, and Lawrence Katz analyze how these trends in immigration and trade have affected relative wages in the United States and, in particular, the extent to which they have contributed to the large decline in the relative wages of less skilled, low-paid U.S. workers. Such questions underlie ongoing policy debates in this country and have been the subject of considerable economic research in recent years. The authors summarize the main facts on trade, immigration and relative wages, evaluate recent research in this area, and present their own model quantifying how immigration and trade impact the U.S. economy.

The authors first analyze immigration, which began to surge soon after 1965 amendments to the immigration laws, reversing a long downward trend in the proportion of the population that is foreign-born. The authors calculate that between 1970 and 1996, the foreign-born share of the population nearly doubled from a low of 4.8 percent to 9.3 percent. Its composition changed sharply too. Whereas in 1970, 68 percent of the foreign-born had come from Canada and Europe (down from 84 percent in 1960), by 1990 only 26 percent had come from these regions. The destination of immigrants was concentrated. In 1990, 75 percent of them lived in the six main immigrant-receiving states: California, New York, Texas, Florida, New Jersey, and Illinois. Over 33 percent lived in California alone. This wave of immigration represented a sizable shock to the labor supply in these regions.

The authors, along with most others who have studied relative wages, mainly use educational attainment as a proxy for skills, and also provide results using place in the income distribution as a skill proxy. Although not all immigrants are poorly educated, the authors show that they have been increasingly concentrated in the lower educational categories. By 1995 in California, with its large immigrant population, 90 percent of workers with fewer than nine years of schooling and 68 percent of workers with fewer than twelve years of schooling were immigrants. The authors also document that immigrants are widely employed in services and trade, as well as in manufacturing and agriculture; native workers in most sectors have faced competition from immigrants.

Borjas, Freeman, and Katz demonstrate why it is difficult to determine the effects of immigration on relative wages, reviewing several earlier studies along the way. They first point out the pitfalls of simply looking at the relative performance of high-immigration states like California. Doing so would be valid only if, across areas, immigrant flows were uncorrelated with economic conditions, and natives did not themselves migrate in response to immigration to an area. However, neither condition is met. To deal with this, the authors first turn to regressions that control for forces that could be expected to change regional wage structures over time. But even with regressions that use education-specific supply shocks as the measure of immigrant penetration, and that net out relative wage changes that occur at the national level, as well as the impact of state economic activity on all natives residing in a state, they still cannot identify consistent effects of immigration on relative wages. They infer that immigration is not a major determinant of the regional structure of wages for natives.

In light of this negative finding, the authors consider whether native internal migration diffuses the effects of immigration from particular regions to the country as a whole. The experience of California, the major immigrant-receiving state, provides a clue that this mechanism may be important. From 1950 to 1970, before the surge of immigration, the fraction of U.S. natives who live in California rose rapidly. The fraction barely changed from 1970 to 1990, even though California's share of the total population kept growing. Over this period, its growth shifted from in-migration of natives to immigration. The authors suggest the flow of immigrants to California displaced the native net migration that would have otherwise occurred and thus diffused the economic effects of immigration from California to the rest of the country.

The authors support this suggestion with a cross-state regression that explains the change in a state's native population growth by the change in the state's immigration growth. This regression gives a substantial negative coefficient on the change in immigration growth. The authors go on to examine the response of native flows by particular skill groups, allowing for both the initial skill distribution of each state's work force and the rate at which this distribution was changing before 1970. Their results indicate that immigration does not alter the distribution of skill groups within a state. The response of native migration roughly counterbalances the immigrant shock by skill groups.

Having established that the effects of immigration on relative wages must be examined for the economy as a whole, rather than across regions, Borjas, Freeman, and Katz turn to an analysis of aggregate factor proportions in which they estimate the effects of trade and immigration simultaneously, recognizing that both can be analyzed as competing with native factors of production. They postulate a general constant elasticity of substitution aggregate production function, using skilled and unskilled labor as inputs. With this production technology, the relative wages of the two types of labor depend on the relative supplies of each, and the size of the effect depends on the elasticity of substitution. Immigration and the labor embodied in trade thus affect relative wages by affecting the relative supply of each type of labor. To keep their analysis tractable, the authors use broad skill groupings of workers—such as high school dropouts versus others, or workers above versus workers below the twentieth percentile in the income distribution. They apply wage elasticities based on previous studies to the labor supply changes coming from immigration and trade to calculate the effects of these changes on relative wages for these skill groups.

The authors discuss some potential criticisms of this general model. The model assumes that the global economy is not so integrated that only world, rather than national, demand and supply conditions affect relative wages by skill class; they cite numerous studies supporting this assumption. To deal with ambiguities in assigning natives, immigrants, and foreign workers who produce U.S. imports to comparable skill groups, they use alternative educational categories and define skill categories by position in the native earnings distribution, as well as by education. They also discuss circumstances under which the full effect of trade on wages may not be captured by the labor content in the flow of traded goods, but argue that their estimates are unlikely to greatly understate trade effects by ignoring them.

The authors provide a range of results arising from the many alternatives they consider. For the effects of immigration, their main findings are robust across these alternatives. The important effects are concentrated on high school dropouts, the least skilled group in the native population. With their preferred relative wage elasticity of -0.322, the inflow of immigrants since 1979 accounts for 44 percent of the decline in the relative earnings of native dropouts from 1980 to 1995. Using the place of workers in the earnings distribution rather than educational attainment to define skill groups provides somewhat lower, though still pronounced, estimates of the effects of immigration on low-wage workers. This difference arises mainly because with the earnings-based classification, the proportion of natives who are in the group remains unchanged, whereas with the educational classification, the share of natives who are dropouts declines over the same interval. Comparing higher skill groups, such as high school and college graduates, the effect of immigration on relative labor supplies is too small to have an important effect on relative wages under any of the alternative estimates.

Turning to trade, the authors show that, under plausible assumptions about production technologies, trade with developed nations has had little effect on the skill distribution of labor supplies. They therefore concentrate on the effects of trade with less developed countries, which may have had substantial effects on the relative supplies of low-skill workers. In this analysis, they acknowledge the difficulty of measuring the relative labor content of goods involved in LDC trade: they can infer the output affected by trade at the level of three-digit industries; but within each industry, trade may supplant not the average firm, but relatively less efficient firms that use relatively less skilled workers. To deal with this possibility, they provide estimates using three alternative assumptions. In the low impact assumption, LDC imports displace production from firms that use the contemporary average skills and productivity of their industry. In the middle assumption, which the authors prefer, the imports displace production from firms that use the skills and productivity of the average firm in their industry as of ten or fifteen years ago. In the high assumption, LDC imports displace production that uses the skills and productivity of the industry's average firm in 1970. In all cases, exports are assumed to expand production using average current skills and productivity for the industry.

To evaluate trade effects, the authors first calculate the labor embodied in LDC imports and exports, disaggregating by industry and by country of origin or receipt and using the three alternative estimates of labor input by industry described above. The estimates are substantially affected by the alternative used. Using the high alternative—assumptions that the authors regard as extreme—growth in LDC trade accounts for 27 percent of the decline in the relative wages of high school dropouts. Under their preferred middle alternative, the growth in trade with LDCs since 1979 accounts for only 8 percent of the decline in relative wages of dropouts. The effect of trade on wages is a little more than half this large under the low alternative.

The authors draw several broad conclusions from this study. Considering the entire U.S. work force, the effects of immigration and trade flows on relative skill supplies have not been substantial enough to account for more than a small part of the overall widening of the wage distribution, nor more than a modest part of the growing college-high school wage differential. They have been more important in contributing to the relative wage decline of high school dropouts since 1980. For this group, using the authors' preferred alternative for measuring trade impacts, immigration and trade together account for roughly half of the decline, with immigration by far the more important of the two.

MANY OBSERVERS have come to believe that monetary policy is the major, if not the dominant, source of economic fluctuations. Each of the four major recessions since 1965 has been associated with a monetary tightening. Yet a considerable body of recent research attributes relatively little of the overall variation in output to monetary shocks. This research, based on vector autoregressions (VARs), makes a sharp distinction between monetary policy innovations and the endogenous response of policy. In a typical specification, for example, policy is credited only with the economy's response to innovations—movements in the federal funds rate that cannot be forecast by other economic variables included in the system. Using this VAR methodology minimizes the chance that policy will be credited with causing movements in output when, in fact, policy is responding to output or to other variables that are causing the output fluctuations. However, it also does not credit policy with economic responses flowing from normal policy reactions to events. The standard VAR models are silent on the importance of endogenous responses of policy to the economy's behavior. Nor do they provide a basis for predicting the consequence of changing the policy rules governing monetary behavior. In the second paper of this issue, Ben Bernanke, Mark Gertler, and Mark Watson attempt to assess the importance of the endogenous component of monetary policy by restricting the way policy interacts with the economy, while not restricting other coefficients in the model. The authors focus on the role of oil prices in their analysis, both because oil prices have been subject to large exogenous shocks and because such shocks compete with monetary policy in statistical explanations of economic fluctuations.

The authors begin with a brief review of earlier work that assesses the importance of monetary policy and oil shocks, documenting that essentially all recessions of the past thirty years have been preceded by both oil price increases and a tightening of monetary policy. In order to distinguish the endogenous and exogenous movements in oil prices

and monetary policy and to disentangle the effects of these two variables, the authors estimate a five-variable VAR on monthly data that
includes, in order, real GDP, the GDP deflator, an index of spot commodity prices, an indicator of the state of the oil market, and the level
of the federal funds rate. Ordering the macroeconomic economic variables ahead of oil prices and the federal funds rate corresponds to the
plausible assumption that the effects of the latter on the economy lag
by at least one month. The authors try four alternative measures of the
state of the oil market and find that the simplest—the nominal price of
crude oil—implies anomalous responses of both output and prices to a
shock. The other three measures give more sensible impulse response
functions, implying that output falls and prices rise following a shock.
In general, responses are modest in magnitude and statistically insignificant. In the authors' view, the most sensible results come from a
measure constructed by James Hamilton, which ignores oil price increases that do not exceed the maximum value achieved in the preceding
twelve months. A 10 percent shock to this measure results in a modest
0.45 percent cumulative loss in GDP over four years. They note, however, that the economic and statistical significance of oil price shocks
is larger in the more elaborate models that they estimate subsequently.

Most observers believe that the reductions in output that have followed oil price increases are too large to be explained by oil alone, and
that part of the output decline reflects the contractionary response of
monetary policy. Indeed, in the basic VAR model an unexpected increase in the price of oil, using any of the measures, results in monetary
tightening; part of the subsequent reduction in output is hence attributed
to the reaction of the monetary authority. The authors quantify this
response by means of a technique previously used by Christopher Sims
and Tao Zha. This amounts to "shutting down" the response of the
federal funds rate as estimated by the VAR, so that the federal funds
rate follows the path that it would have taken in the absence of the
exogenous shock to oil. The authors here assume that the other coefficients of the model are invariant to this hypothesized change in
policy behavior, and note that this assumption is subject to the Lucas
critique. Although they are sympathetic to Sims's view that this may
not be a major problem for deviations from historical behavior that are
neither too large nor too protracted, they suggest that the relevance of
the critique is much stronger for financial markets than for other sectors

of the economy. This leads them to propose a modification of the Sims-Zha procedure that assumes that financial markets quickly reflect changes in the policy rule, forming rational expectations of interest rates in the changed environment. They assume that equations other than those relating to interest rates are invariant to the change in rule.

To implement these ideas, Bernanke, Gertler, and Watson let the federal funds rate affect macroeconomic variables such as output and prices only indirectly, through its effect on short- and long-term interest rates. Because they rule out other possible channels of influence for monetary policy, such as the exchange rate and the "credit channel," they regard their results as a lower bound on the importance of monetary policy. They also follow the common practice of assuming that the other macroeconomic variables in their system are causally prior to market rates—that is, interest rates cannot affect output and prices within the month. For most of their analysis they also treat the federal funds rate as causally prior to market rates, in effect assuming no response of policymakers to movements in market rates within the month, on the grounds that market rates contain no information about the economy that is not already present in the other macroeconomic variables.

In order to incorporate the expectations theory in the rate equations, as is required in their method, the authors decompose short and long rates into two parts: expectations of future values of the funds rate and a term premium. Rather than estimate the weights on future expected funds rates, they assume the weights appropriate to a fixed discount rate of 4 percent. Given this assumption, it is easy to decompose any predicted change in the market rates into its two components. For example, to simulate the effects of an oil price shock under a counterfactual policy regime, they first specify an alternative path for the federal funds rate and calculate the change in the expectations component of interest rates implied by this modified behavior. With the time path of the expectations component of market rates determined, they can then trace out the impulse responses of each of the other variables, including the term premium itself. Because the term premium varies even with their rational expectations assumption, market rates do not move one for one with expectations.

Bernanke, Gertler, and Watson report a number of policy experiments with their seven-variable model. They first show that the basic system incorporating short and long rates gives familiar predictions of the responses of output and prices to a federal funds rate innovation. The response of market rates is interesting: the short rate term premium is significantly negative immediately following a funds rate innovation, indicating that short rates respond less than implied by the expectations hypothesis. This discrepancy quickly disappears for short term rates, so that the expectations theory seems to be a reasonable approximation of reality. However, expectations about future short rates explain relatively little of the movement in the ten-year government bond rate, and there is some evidence that the long rate "overreacts" to short rates.

The most extensive exercise is the decomposition of the impact of oil shocks into direct effects and indirect effects that reflect endogenous monetary policy. The authors provide a base case that includes the estimated endogenous response of monetary policy and two scenarios intended to show how differently the economy would have performed in the absence of the policy response to the oil shock. One of these scenarios follows the Sims-Zha procedure, simply setting the funds rate at the value that it would have had in the absence of the oil shock, with the market rates following in accord with the unconstrained reduced-form estimates. The second, "anticipated policy," scenario applies the authors' methodology described above. Short and long term premiums are assumed to respond as estimated, but the expectations component of rates is made consistent with the counterfactual course of the federal funds rate. Both scenarios exhibit the qualitative behavior one might expect in the absence of policy tightening—that is, higher paths for output and price. The effects of induced policy seem large; in their absence, most of the output loss from the oil shock disappears and higher rates of inflation persist instead of turning down after a couple of years, as they do in the base case. The two scenarios show roughly similar departures from the baseline. However, market interest rates are systematically lower in the anticipated policy scenario than in the Sims-Zha scenario. When the endogenous response of the term premium is also shut down, so that market rates do not respond at all to the oil shock, endogenous policy is given less credit but is still responsible for two-thirds to three-fourths of the total output decline. The authors find similar results when they consider shocks to commodity prices or output rather than to oil.

The authors conduct these counterfactual simulations for each of the three major oil price shocks followed by recessions. They find that the 1974–75 decline in output is largely due to nonoil commodity prices, which rose sharply before the recession, rather than to the oil price shock. In contrast, the oil price shocks in 1979 and 1990 and their associated endogenous policy responses do appear to explain the subsequent declines in output. In order to check the plausibility of their findings, the authors compare the impulse response of the economy to an oil shock and to a pure federal funds shock of a magnitude that mimics the effect of the oil shock on rates. The response of output is virtually identical in the two scenarios. The authors see this as support for the view that policy responses are the dominant source of the real effects of an oil price shock.

The importance that Bernanke, Gertler, and Watson attribute to policy, once they recognize the impact of endogenous policy responses, is in sharp contrast to the small role that they and others attribute to policy innovations alone. They conclude that analysts who focus only on policy innovations miss much of the contribution of monetary policy to stabilizing the economy.

ECONOMISTS HAVE LONG been puzzled by the scarcity of price indexation in long-term contracts. History is replete with episodes in which inflation or deflation have wreaked havoc by producing unforeseen and major redistributions of wealth between debtors and creditors. In the post–World War II period inflation has been pervasive and variable, and in most countries the public has displayed a strong antipathy to it. Yet, except in a few countries with extreme experiences, people have not taken the apparently simple expedient of tying their long-term financial commitments to a price index. In the third paper of this issue Robert Shiller briefly reviews the reasons why indexation might be expected to be the norm rather than the exception, discusses its historical precedents, and reports on an extensive survey of individuals in the United States and Turkey, two economies with quite different inflationary histories, in an effort to illuminate the puzzling absence of indexation.

It would be easy to understand the absence of indexation if inflation were predictable and stable. But, Shiller argues, throughout history price levels have been notoriously unstable over long periods of time. To illustrate this fact, he computes the standard deviations of ten- and twenty-year changes in price levels for sixteen countries during the postwar period. For the twenty-year change, half of the countries have had standard deviations of over 500 percent, with six over 10,000 percent. Even the United States—the country with the third least variable price level, after West Germany and Japan—has a standard deviation of 60 percent. It does not take big surprises in the annual inflation rate to dramatically change the real value of a long-term contract. The power of compounding means that a 2 percent higher average annual rate of inflation lowers the real value of a twenty-year bond by one-third at maturity. Inflation uncertainty clearly makes long-term debt very risky in real terms.

Shiller suggests that indexing is virtually costless and hence, given historical experience and the entreaties of a long list of distinguished economists, he finds it puzzling that indexation has not become commonplace. He briefly describes the limited experience with the indexation of long-term contracts in the United States, where the first inflation-indexed federal government bonds were issued in January 1997, and describes the few short-lived private initiatives to issue similar bonds. Indexation in labor contracts appears to wax and wane depending on the rate of inflation. And Shiller finds little indexation in other private long-term contracts, such as alimony, child support, or private pensions. In his view, the U.S. experience is largely one of missed opportunities.

Shiller sees Turkey as a natural candidate to complement his study of the United States. Inflation in Turkey has been highly variable and has not been below 20 percent per year since the late 1970s. Although indexation for long-term contracts is common in many countries that have extremely high and variable inflation rates, in Turkey it is rare. While in major Turkish cities prices for real estate, apartment rentals, and the like are routinely quoted in U.S. dollars or deutsche marks, in small towns and rural areas such prices are typically given in Turkish lira. The Turkish government had never issued indexed debt before 1997. Nor is indexation important in other types of contracts. Shiller reports on interviews with divorce lawyers, bond dealers, and labor union officials, who state that indexation is almost never used for alimony, child support, corporate bonds, or labor contracts. Instead, debt and labor contracts are for the short term, and the courts are used to modify support payments, much as in the United States. Shiller's interviewees judged that dollarization is used in about 10 percent of alimony and child support settlements, particularly for the wealthy, but that corporate bonds and labor contracts are never dollarized. They also suggested that fluctuation in the exchange rate is one important reason why dollarization is not common.

The centerpiece of Shiller's paper is a summary and analysis of his survey aimed at finding out public attitudes about inflation and indexation. Shiller sent questionnaires to 800 individuals in the United States and 400 in Turkey, all randomly selected from local telephone books. The response rates were 38 percent for the United States and 25 percent for Turkey. A great deal of care went into survey design; early versions of the questions were refined after preliminary informal interviewing in New Haven, Connecticut; and two different questionnaires were used for the U.S. sample, with different orderings of answers and, in some cases, with different wording, to minimize the effect of framing.

The survey asks an array of questions intended to check out the importance of plausible explanations for the absence of indexed contracts. These include the inability of individuals to understand indexed contracts and to do the mathematics required to make intelligent comparisons between different types of contract; math anxiety and aversion to complicated contracts; skepticism about the accuracy of official price indexes; exaggerated belief in the possibility of off-setting inflation by substituting less expensive for more expensive items; the absence of risk aversion; inaccurate beliefs about the magnitude of inflation risk; misperceptions about who is hurt by inflation; and skepticism about the government's behavior and the likelihood of its changing the rules.

Readers will have different views about which of the rich tableau of responses are most interesting or most surprising. For the most part, there is a remarkable similarity between U.S. and Turkish responses. Shiller finds that most of those surveyed do not seem confused about inflation or how indexation works, and do not have great difficulty in making the calculations necessary to compare indexed with unindexed plans. While there is a suggestion of money illusion on the part of some respondents, a much more important misconception is underappreciation of the uncertainty of inflation. Individuals give low estimates of inflation uncertainty relative to historical variation, particularly in Turkey. Another interesting theme is that people tend to think of inflation not as the cause of arbitrary redistributions from creditors to debtors, but as an event that harms virtually everyone. They seem to believe that real incomes are eroded by high inflation, to the detriment of debtors, creditors, firms, and individuals alike. Shiller suggests that this may explain why it seems too much to ask that noncustodial parents automatically increase child support payments if inflation picks up a lot, and why workers find it reasonable that the real values of their pensions decline with inflation. He observes that this belief is consistent with experience; for fourteen of the sixteen countries he considers, unusually high inflation is correlated with unusually low rates of real output growth. Respondents also tend to believe that price indexes are not a reliable measure of how individuals will be affected by inflation, particularly when it is high, and they have some mistrust of the government's construction of such indexes. He concludes that the lack of enthusiasm for indexation has no single cause, but that a wide variety of thoughts about inflation lead to the belief that indexation is not a good idea.

Shiller is an unabashed proponent of indexation and provides a catalogue of ways in which the government could promote public acceptance of indexed debt. The boldest would be to eliminate long-term government nominal debt, replacing it entirely with indexed debt. He believes that if that were done, indexed debt would become the standard throughout the economy. Courts could routinely index alimony, child support, and personal damage settlements, but Shiller believes that in many of these cases it would be better to index to an income aggregate rather than to the CPI. Ironically, he does not see a strong case for institutionalizing indexation in labor markets, the one arena in the U.S. private sector where formal indexation has at times been significant. Nevertheless, he believes that government encouragement of most forms of indexed contract could lead to significant social benefits.

FOR YEARS the press has been full of stories about corporate downsizing and restructuring and increased foreign competition, all of which are said to contribute to a decreased sense of job security on the part of American workers. Such heightened anxiety about job loss is consistent with workers' actual earnings experiences. While the typical worker in the U.S. labor market has always experienced considerable year-to-year variation in earnings, earnings variation has trended up since the early 1970s. Peter Gottschalk and Robert Moffitt (*BPEA, 2:1994*), for example, have estimated that the transitory component of the earnings of household heads rose by more than 40 percent from the 1970s to the 1980s. In the fourth paper of this issue Susan Dynarski and Jonathan Gruber reexamine the evidence on earnings variation and estimate the extent to which various mechanisms—including offsets from the incomes of other household members, cushions provided by tax and transfer programs, and dissaving out of wealth—insulate consumption from shocks to the earnings of household heads. They regard the consumption variation arising from earnings variation as the indicator of the welfare loss of households.

The authors begin by reexamining the importance of earnings variability during the period 1970 to 1991 for a nationally representative sample of households with male heads aged twenty to fifty-nine. Drawing on the Michigan Panel Study of Income Dynamics (PSID), a longitudinal survey which follows a cross-section of families over time, they extend the sample period used by Gottschalk and Moffitt and shift the focus to total labor earnings, rather than just wages and salaries. To measure an individual's transitory earnings in a given year, Dynarski and Gruber use regressions for the household head's earnings that include time dummies to remove variations that reflect aggregate fluctuations and a number of individual characteristics: education, martial status and change in that status, change in family size and in the proportion of the family comprised by children, and change in a measure of family "food needs." Controlling for these variables is presumed to remove the predictable changes in income over the individual's life cycle, as well as changes in income that are permanent. The removal of aggregate fluctuations allows the authors to focus on the smoothing of idiosyncratic shocks. The residual from the estimated equation for an individual is taken as a measure of that person's transitory income in a particular year; and the mean of squared residuals across individuals is used as the measure of aggregate transitory variation in a given year. The authors also run the earnings equation including individual fixed effects. Two findings from this analysis stand out. First, earnings variation has a strong countercyclical component, with peaks in the recessions of the mid-1970s, the early 1980s, and the early 1990s. Second, confirming Gottschalk and Moffitt's earlier findings, annual earnings variation has a strong upward trend; over the entire period, the variation of the transitory earnings of male heads of household rose by 76 percent.

How important fluctuations in the earnings of the head of household are to household welfare depends not only on the magnitude of those fluctuations but also on the size of changes in taxes, transfers, and unemployment insurance, changes in income from other members of the household, and the availability of saving or borrowing to spread the effects of income shocks across many periods. To estimate the combined effectiveness of these mechanisms in mitigating the effects of shocks, the authors directly estimate the response of changes in household consumption to shocks to the head of household's income, including the variables that they use in estimating transitory income. The inclusion of these variables implies that the coefficient on head's earnings itself should be interpreted as the response of consumption to transitory income. Hence the authors take a zero or small coefficient on change in head's earnings as evidence that one or more of the mechanisms for smoothing consumption are important. If the response of consumption is small, the growing variation of transitory earnings in recent years may, in fact, have little impact on the welfare of households.

Dynarski and Gruber recognize that their measure of transitory income does not achieve a clean distinction between transitory and permanent variations in income. If shocks to the level of income are transitory, the errors in the authors' differenced equation should be negatively correlated. If, however, errors in the differenced equation are independent over time, the authors' estimates of transitory income correspond to permanent changes in the level of income and their effects on the lifetime budget constraint of the household would be much larger. But they argue that this ambiguity is unimportant, since they look directly at the consequences for consumption of earnings fluctuations.

The authors make use of two data sources to estimate the consumption response to transitory earnings: the PSID, which includes a set of high-quality indicators of earnings and labor force attachment, but has limited information on household consumption; and the Bureau of Labor Statistics's Consumer Expenditure Survey (CEX), which contains a more complete accounting for consumption, but has samples for only two points in time. Earnings reported in such recall surveys include substantial measurement error. In the case of the PSID, for example, it is estimated that 15 to 30 percent of the cross-sectional variation in earnings and 20 to 25 percent of variation in first differences of earnings is measurement error.

Such errors lead to a downward bias in ordinary least squares estimates of the response of consumption to income, and hence to an overestimate of the extent to which households can shield their consumption from earnings fluctuations. The authors deal with this difficulty by means of an instrumental variable technique, which only uses the variation in current earnings that can be predicted by a variable that is independent of the measurement error. Their instrumental variable is the change in "imputed earnings," calculated as the number of hours worked in the previous year times the current wage rate. They argue that change in this variable is likely to be a good instrument, with errors uncorrelated with the errors in the change in current earnings.

The authors' results suggest that households are able to shelter consumption significantly from adverse shocks to the head's earnings. In the case of the PSID, the response of both food and housing (the two available consumption variables) to changes in the head of household's earnings is quite small. The combined elasticity is only 5 percent using ordinary least squares. Estimates using instrumental variables are larger, but still imply a total elasticity of less than 20 percent. Allowing for fixed individual household effects makes little difference. Using the CEX data, which cover a much wider range of consumption items, leads to broadly similar conclusions, but some interesting details emerge. The instrumental variable estimates of elasticities for food and housing are somewhat smaller than for the PSID, and the elasticities for medical care and insurance, vehicle maintenance and fuel, utilities, and entertainment are smaller still. The main surprise is the low estimate for entertainment. In accord with expectations, the authors find for both data sets that the elasticity of expenditures on food away from home is significantly greater than the elasticity of demand for food at home.

In contrast to the low elasticities for expenditures on most nondurables, the CEX data show that durable expenditures, comprising only 11 percent of consumption on average, have a larger absolute response than all nondurables taken together. For the instrumental variables estimates, the implied elasticity is eight times larger than it is for nondurables. The authors note that this result conforms to the view that a portion of durables purchases should be regarded as saving, providing future consumption of durable good services. Hence the variation in current consumption and utility is overstated by the change in current expenditures.

Dynarski and Gruber recognize that their own measure of transitory income may include some permanent components. They observe that changes in hours are more likely to be transitory than changes in wage rates. Therefore they rerun their equations using these two sources of earnings variation as explanatory variables. For the PSID sample, the results show a striking difference between the two components, in accord with their priors. The response of food and housing consumption to wages is much larger than their response to hours. For the CEX data, the results are less clear. Food and housing, in fact, respond more to hours than to wages. However, both aggregate nondurables and durables have a larger response to wages, and overall the authors believe that the presumption that wage changes have a larger permanent component is confirmed. They find it striking, however, that even in the case of wage variation, most of earnings variation is smoothed: consumption changes by less than 30 cents for each dollar change in earnings from this source.

How important are the various potential sources of smoothing? Both the PSID and the CEX measure the wife's labor earnings and provide either observations on taxes and transfers or the information necessary to calculate them. This enables the authors to directly estimate the response of each to changes in the head's earnings. As in the consumption equations, change in head's earnings is instrumented by imputed income. Dynarski and Gruber find relatively little offset for lost earnings of the head through increased earnings of the wife, but find that transfers and taxes are important. The PSID data indicate that changes in government transfer income off-set about 12 percent of earnings variation, and taxes, including both income and payroll taxes, off-set about 35 percent of earnings variation. The CEX estimates are somewhat smaller: 5 percent and 26 percent, respectively. Taken together with the authors' estimates of the consumption response, these findings imply that 25 to 40 percent of the year-to-year changes in the head of household's earnings is smoothed by household saving; if durable goods expenditures are regarded as saving, the smoothing attributed to saving is about 15 percent greater.

Variations in the household head's earnings that arise from unemployment may be harder for households to smooth than variations arising from other sources, both because unemployment is likely to have a large effect on earnings and because it may be unplanned, resulting from involuntary rather than voluntary separation. To explore this possibility, the authors use unemployment as an instrument for earnings in their consumption equations. Lacking data that distinguishes layoffs from quits and information about unemployment duration, they use a dummy for the transition from employment to unemployment for a sample of households where, ex ante, the head appears to be regularly employed and where the spell of unemployment is so long that it is not likely to have been planned. Using this constructed variable, they find that for most components of consumption the results are similar to those for general downward movements in earnings. Curiously, the estimated effect on durable goods expenditures is substantially smaller than the earlier estimates. The authors also examine how unemployment-related changes in earnings are off-set by spousal income, taxes, and transfers. Their only consistent finding is that unemployment insurance off-sets more of earnings variation from this source than most previous research has estimated. From 50 to 55 percent of each dollar of earnings loss due to unemployment is compensated by increased income flows, and only 20 to 25 percent of each dollar loss is reflected in dissaving.

How plausible is the proposition that households have sufficient wealth to provide this amount of smoothing? By matching households in the PSID and CEX samples with households from the Census Bureau's Survey of Income and Program Participation for the two years that contain information on asset holding and net worth, Dynarski and Gruber show that the median household has liquid assets equal to about 35 percent of the income loss from an unemployment spell, and that 36 percent of households have assets that are greater than their entire income loss. If one includes illiquid assets, wealth appears more than adequate to finance the degree of consumption smoothing that they estimate.

Even though the median household appears to have sufficient wealth to cover a substantial fraction of the income loss from unemployment, many households do not, and these might be expected show much larger reductions in consumption when the household head becomes unemployed. Grouping the households into three categories of educational attainment—high school dropouts, high school graduates, and college graduates—the authors find dramatic differences in wealth and hence, presumably, the capacity to smooth adverse income shocks. The median household headed by a high school dropout with a job separation has gross liquid assets amounting to only 5 percent of the resulting income loss; by contrast, the median household headed by a college graduate has gross liquid assets of 1.2 times the income loss, and over three-quarters of these household have total assets greater than 25 percent of the income loss. Thus education may serve as a good proxy for wealth. When the authors estimate the consumption response to unemployment by educational group for the PSID, they find that the effects are much larger among households headed by high school dropouts, whereas there is essentially no effect of such shocks on the consumption of the highly educated. Using the CEX, the results for nondurables expenditures are similar, but somewhat muted. However, there is an enormous difference in the response of durables purchases across household types: there is essentially no change in purchases by households headed by the college educated and a drop of over 50 cents on the dollar for households headed by high school dropouts.

The finding that the typical household is especially able to smooth earnings shocks arising from variation in hours suggests that, for the entire economy, consumption variation should be less cyclical than income variation. Dynarski and Gruber find that this is so. However, they also find some anomalous results for the aggregate. Most striking, the growth in earnings instability over time is much lower for the college educated than for lower educational groups, yet the growth in consumption variation is much greater for the college educated. This, along with somewhat different timing in the change in aggregate income and consumption variation, leads the authors to conclude that the upward trends in both earnings and consumption variation are not causally related.

Dynarski and Gruber believe that their findings raise important issues for policy design. It is clear that the tax and transfer system plays an important role in consumption smoothing, in particular, for the unemployed. Any reform of the system should be attentive to this role. Second, while government insurance is helpful, it is far from sufficient to off-set the differential abilities of households to smooth consumption. For a substantial part of the population, the costs of even transitory earnings loss are likely to be severe.

THE CONSUMER PRICE Index (CPI), published monthly by the Bureau of Labor Statistics (BLS), is at the center of discussions about monetary policy and is used to adjust many private contracts and government programs for inflation. At the federal government level, the brackets of the personal income tax and the payments under social security and other retirement programs are indexed to the CPI. In recent years, a number of economists have questioned whether the procedures used by BLS in computing the CPI adequately capture quality changes in goods and services, including the quality changes inherent in new products, and whether they properly allow for the substitutions that consumers make in the goods and services that they buy. If, as this questioning suggests, the CPI has a substantial bias, it is not a suitable guide for policy and provides inappropriate adjustments of contracts for inflation. Last year, the Advisory Commission to Study the Consumer Price Index, which was formed in response to these concerns, presented its final report, in which it estimated that the CPI has had an upward bias averaging 1.1 percent a year. While there is agreement about some sources of bias identified in the report, and the BLS is already making efforts to correct them, there is much less agreement about the 0.6 percent a year that was estimated to come from insufficient quality adjustment. In the fifth paper of this volume, Brent Moulton and Karin Moses first appraise the advisory commission's estimates of quality bias and then analyze the quality allowances implicit in the BLS procedures for replacing items in the monthly surveys that provide the raw price data for the CPI.

The commission estimated that for nineteen out of twenty-seven CPI item categories, price increases were overstated because quality change was underestimated. Moulton and Moses observe that the information the commission brought to bear in making these estimates differed widely across categories. In six of the nineteen categories, it reviewed existing studies of bias for specific items and drew inferences about related items in the category. In another four categories, it conducted original research or presented back-of-the-envelope calculations of likely bias. In the other nine categories, it simply described potential sources of bias and offered estimates of their magnitudes. The authors summarize the commission's estimates for all twenty-seven categories and discuss a number of them in detail, explaining why they find some persuasive but are doubtful of others.

For two major components—appliances, which includes home electronics, and medical care—Moulton and Moses accept the commission's conclusion of upward bias arising from inadequate allowance for quality changes. They regard the commission's estimates for personal computers, television, video equipment, and related items as well documented and note that the BLS is improving the sampling of new products and developing hedonic methods to adjust for quality in these areas. They also agree that BLS methods are likely to underestimate quality improvements in medical care, although they are wary of the commission's estimates of the bias for this category because they were based largely on extrapolation from studies of only two medical conditions. They note that the BLS has recently changed its methods to address some of the issues in pricing medical care, but add that difficult measurement issues remain and will continue to be the subject of BLS research.

The authors criticize the commission's estimates of bias in several other categories. The commission attributes a bias of 20 percent in the pricing of fresh fruits and vegetables over the period 1967–96 to the failure of the CPI to properly value increased seasonal availability and variety. The authors provide their own model, based on assumed price elasticities, to show that the increased consumption of new seasonal items would have to be implausibly large to be consistent with such a high bias estimate. For the shelter category, which has a huge weight (28 percent) in the overall CPI, they use detailed information, such as changes in apartment size, to question the commission's estimate of a 0.25 percent a year bias in prices. In fact, they conclude that a small downward bias is more likely. For new vehicles, the commission estimates a bias of 0.6 percent a year, based on treating the entire increase in the lifespan of cars as an unmeasured quality improvement. The authors note that many improvements that are related to durability have been explicitly accounted for, so that allowing separately for increased lifespan would double count some amount of quality changes.

In the apparel category, Moulton and Moses question the commission's reliance on Robert Gordon's study of Sears catalogue prices to estimate CPI bias. They note that the catalogue study only measures price changes for items that remain identical from year to year, whereas CPI research finds that price changes are correlated with the introduction of new fashions or varieties. Gordon's methodology essentially attributes all price increase associated with the introduction of new fashion lines to quality improvement. As evidence that this effect is important, they observe that Gordon's price index for women's apparel, where fashion changes are most common, did not change from 1984 to 1993, although the indexes for men's, boys,' and girls' clothing rose between 14 and 17.5 percent over the period. The authors also provide evidence that the commission overstates the quality effects arising from the introduction of credit card machines at gas pumps and from the delay in bringing cellular phones into the CPI sample. In the latter case, they apply demand elasticity estimates from Jerry Hausman to the consumer expenditure share of cellular phones to calculate a bias of about 0.02 percent a year in the overall CPI from this delay. In their view, the fact that ignoring one of the most important new products in recent years biased the CPI by only this amount casts doubt on many of the larger numbers in the commission's report.

In the overall scheme of collecting monthly price data for the CPI, changes in the items sampled take place through three distinct avenues. Essentially new items, such as video-cassette recorders and cellular phones, that do not readily fit existing item categories, are usually introduced during the *major revisions* of the CPI, when market basket weights for all items are recalculated and item classifications are revised. Between major revisions, one-fifth of individual items and outlets are scheduled to be replaced each year by regular *sample rotation*. And on an unscheduled but frequent basis, items that become unavailable to data collectors from one month to the next are replaced by *item replacement* procedures. In the second half of their paper, Moulton and Moses describe the item replacement procedures used by the BLS and estimate how much quality change has been implicit in their application. Their analysis does not encompass the sample changes that take place with regular sample rotation, where there is little presumption of quality change, nor with the introduction of essentially new items in major revisions.

Item replacement is quantitatively important. Each month, some 80,000 sample prices are collected, providing the raw data for that month's CPI. But about 30 percent of the items that were due to be in the sample throughout a given year become unavailable at a particular outlet and are replaced with items deemed to be similar by the data collector. On the basis of information about the replacement item, one of several available procedures is used to introduce it into the CPI calculations. The choice of procedure determines the implicit quality change that accompanies the replacement. To take the simplest case, if a replacement item is deemed not to be identical to the item it replaces, a procedure may be chosen that ignores all of the difference between the last price of the old item and the price of the new item when it enters the sample. In this case, all of the observed price difference is implicitly taken to be quality change and no price change is recorded in the CPI. In general, some portion of the observed price difference is treated as an implicit quality change and the remainder appears in the CPI as a price change in that month.

By examining the actual raw price data collected for old and replacement items and which procedure was applied to each replacement item, Moulton and Moses tabulate how much of the price difference observed in the raw data was treated as quality change and so ignored in calculating the CPI. Two final steps in their analysis are important to their quantitative results. First, in addition to aggregating over all observations, they also aggregate over subsets of observations truncated to remove outliers—that is, raw price changes that appear to be too large to represent quality change in an item and may instead arise from an inappropriate substitution of a dissimilar item by the data collector. They consider two truncations: eliminating all observations when a raw price increases or decreases by a factor of 5 or more or by a factor of 2 or more. Second, in processing the raw data they use both arithmetic aggregation, which parallels the procedure used in aggregating price changes in the CPI, and logarithmic aggregation, which, under many assumptions about the generation of the data, is more appropriate for measuring quality effects captured by BLS procedures.

The authors present an extensive analysis of data for 1995 and also report some results from earlier studies based on data for 1983 and 1984. For 1995, using all the data and arithmetic aggregation, they calculate that BLS procedures for item replacement led to the CPI rising by 1.76 percent less than it would have if all of the recorded price difference on replacement items had been recorded as price change in the CPI.

To answer the different question—how much quality change is implicitly being allowed for by these procedures?—the authors reason that calculations using the truncated data to remove outliers or using logarithmic aggregation may be more appropriate. Outliers may well arise from inappropriate substitutions, which should not be counted as quality change. This problem is minimized with logarithmic aggregation, since with many observations, large positive and negative outliers should roughly cancel out. With arithmetic aggregation, their estimates of the quality change allowed for are 1.10 percent and 0.54 percent, using the less and more stringently truncated samples, respectively. With logarithmic aggregation, their estimates of quality change allowed for are

0.44 percent with the full sample, and 0.40 percent and 0.28 percent with the two truncated samples. Though the range is substantial, each of these estimates indicates that BLS procedures for item replacement have been capturing a noticeable amount of quality change in the market basket that makes up the CPI. However, these calculations do not address the issues raised in the first part of the paper, which concern the possibility of significant bias from other aspects of the methodology that the Bureau of Labor Statistics uses to calculate the CPI.

BRAZIL'S ECONOMIC PERFORMANCE over the years has been volatile, even by Latin American standards. It has enjoyed extended periods of rapid growth and has also stagnated for long stretches. It has long accommodated double-digit annual inflation rates, but has also experienced destabilizing bouts of hyperinflation. On many occasions, Brazilian governments have tried special stabilization plans aimed at curbing runaway inflation while maintaining growth. Most recently, the Real Plan of 1994 has brought inflation down from triple-digit rates in 1993-94 to expected single-digit rates this year, while continuing real expansion of the economy. In the sixth paper of this issue, Rudiger Dornbusch examines Brazil's past performance, assesses the potentials and risks of the Real Plan, and suggests how Brazil can improve its growth prospects.

Dornbusch's historical review emphasizes the bouts of inflation in Brazil's past and its governments' attempts to deal with them. Thoroughgoing indexation of wages and price contracts, promoted both by law and by long practice, is a central feature of the economy. It normally makes inflation easy to live with, but also makes it very costly to bring inflation under control when it becomes disruptive. This has led Brazilian economists to seek "heterodox" policies that would coordinate a stop to the wage-price spiral through incomes policies, while simultaneously controlling demand. However, in Dornbusch's view, Brazil's low pain threshold is another key feature of the economy and it explains why heterodox programs such as the Cruzado Plan of 1986 and its numerous successors failed. Rather than applying restrictive demand policies to reinforce incomes policies, policymakers saw the initial respite provided by the incomes policies as occasions to stimulate demand.

Against this background, the Real Plan avoided reliance on an incomes policy and instead created the real as a new currency linked to the dollar. At the outset, wages were converted to reais at a level that required no catchup to past price inflation, and were indexed to inflation going forward. This, together with an initial appreciation of the real, abruptly stopped the triple-digit inflation. Many dimensions of economic performance have since improved, and the new policies have been politically popular. Inflation has continued to slow, with the consumer price index rising by only 10 percent in 1996. Real output has grown and real wages have risen rapidly, especially for the poorest workers. In a country with extreme disparities between rich and poor, the ratio of the wages of the richest 10 percent to those of the poorest 10 percent dropped from 72 to 49 between 1993 and 1995, reversing the trend toward growing inequality that had persisted since the 1960s.

While applauding these achievements, Dornbusch finds other aspects of Brazil's economic performance troublesome. A sizable real appreciation of the currency heads his list of concerns. He warns that worldwide, large real appreciations have almost invariably ended in external crises when events have hampered the rollover of debt and the ability to finance current account deficits. Just how much appreciation has occurred and how much is tolerable are both matters of dispute. Estimates of the extent of Brazil's real appreciation differ widely, depending on what measure is used. Dornbusch cites a number of alternatives, ranging from a modest 6 percent by taking the industrial price index for São Paulo relative to Brazil's trading partners, to near 50 percent by comparing the rise in the ratio of consumer prices to wholesale prices in Brazil, a ratio often taken as a proxy for the price ratio of nontradables to tradables.

He also notes that although Brazil has started on economic reforms, it still has a long way to go. Many of these reforms would require real depreciation in order to sustain employment growth. Capital markets and foreign trade have already been substantially liberalized, and imports and capital inflows have expanded. Other reforms, such as privatization, firm restructuring, and government downsizing, could eventually improve productivity and permit higher real wages. But, as with trade reform, they are likely to require lower real wages in the short run in order to reemploy the workers released by the reforms and the rise in imports.

Dornbusch is also concerned that, under the Real Plan, Brazil's expansion has been driven by too much consumption. To help curb inflation, the government has allowed real interest rates to rise to very high levels. This has encouraged capital inflows, but investment as a share of GDP remains relatively low. The current account deficit, which was modest to start with, is growing and is projected to reach 5 percent of GDP in 1998.

Dornbusch offers a colorful description of the conflict faced by policymakers who have the social objectives of high real wages and employment levels but are constrained by the size of the sustainable foreign deficit—a conflict that may soon, if not already, confront policymakers in Brazil. He describes an outcome that meets the external constraint with full employment but an unacceptably low real wage and labels it the IMF equilibrium. An outcome with full employment and a high real wage he calls the Latin equilibrium, because it involves overborrowing to evade (for a time) the foreign deficit constraint. And he sees a temporary retrenchment that maintains a high real wage but accepts unemployment for a time as typical of the year before an election, just before an expansion starts. For Brazil, he envisages two potential alternative responses: trade protection or borrowing in the hope that time will somehow resolve the conflict, perhaps through a surge in productivity that reconciles real wages and competitiveness.

Despite his misgivings about the present course of policy, Dornbusch does not expect Brazil to suffer the fate that befell Mexico when the peso became overvalued. Rather, he fears that Brazil may muddle through for an extended period when it could instead be fostering rapid growth. Such growth would follow from policies that encouraged more saving and investment and less consumption; a lower real exchange rate, even if this invited somewhat more inflation than at present; and continued free market reforms to enhance competitiveness and encourage productivity growth.

GEORGE J. BORJAS
Harvard University

RICHARD B. FREEMAN
Harvard University

LAWRENCE F. KATZ
Harvard University

How Much Do Immigration and Trade Affect Labor Market Outcomes?

IMMIGRATION AND TRADE—particularly with less developed countries (LDCs)—have become more significant to the U.S. economy since the 1960s than they were earlier in the postwar period. The number of immigrants relative to native-born workers has risen; an increasing proportion of immigrants come from less developed countries; and a disproportionate number of immigrants have relatively little schooling. The ratio of exports and imports to GDP has risen as well, and an increasing proportion of imports have come from less developed countries. Immigration and trade have thus increased the effective labor supply of less skilled workers in the United States, with potential consequences for relative wages and employment.

To what extent might the economic woes of less skilled and low-paid American workers be attributed to changes in trade or immigration? To what extent have immigration and trade benefited other Americans?

These questions have spurred considerable debate in recent years. Some analysts stress the potentially adverse distributional effects of immigration and trade on low-income Americans. Others stress their potentially positive effects on the economy. Standard models suggest

We are grateful to John Abowd, John DiNardo, Robert Lawrence, and Matthew Slaughter for helpful suggestions; to Marianne Bertrand, Alida Castillo-Freeman, and Gabriel Hanz for excellent research assistance; to Howard Shatz and Kenneth Troske for providing some of the data used in the paper; and to the National Science Foundation for research support.

1

that both immigration and trade alter national output *and* the distribution of income through the same mechanism—by increasing the nation's implicit supply of relatively scarce factors of production—so that their benefits and distributional costs are intrinsically related. While there is empirical evidence that trade may have more far-reaching benefits on economic performance, and one could argue that immigration may have positive or negative effects on the aggregate economy through economies or diseconomies of scale, trade and immigration are still likely to affect *relative* economic outcomes.[1] Factors for which immigration and trade are good substitutes will lose relative to factors that are complementary.[2]

This paper provides new estimates of the impact of immigration and trade on the U.S. labor market, taking account of the extensive debate that has developed since our earlier work.[3] We first review the dimensions of immigration and trade flows to the United States since the 1960s. Then we examine the relation between economic outcomes for native workers and immigrant flows to regional labor markets. We next use the aggregate "factor proportions approach" to simulate the impact of immigration and trade on national supplies of labor by skill under different counterfactuals. We also consider Adrian Wood's controversial claim that using input coefficients for the appropriate import-competing activities leads to much larger trade effects than we, or others, have estimated.[4] We then use the factor proportions approach to examine the contributions of immigration and trade to recent changes in U.S. educational wage differentials and attempt to provide a broader assessment of the impact of immigration on the incomes of U.S. natives. Finally, we offer some concluding thoughts.

Our major findings are as follows:

—Immigration does not have a consistent, discernible effect on area

1. On the beneficial effects of openness to trade on national economic performance, see Frankel and Romer (1996) and Sachs and Warner (1995).
2. This will be true unless essentially no unskilled American works in import-competing activities (because U.S. firms have shifted production to utterly different products) or competes with immigrants in the labor market (because all immigrants have skills that complement those of natives). With a fixed linear homogeneous production function, if trade or immigration raises GDP a lot, there will necessarily be large effects on the distribution of income (and small effects if GDP is raised slightly).
3. Borjas, Freeman, and Katz (1992).
4. Wood (1994, 1995).

economic outcomes; other regional factors dominate the ups and downs of area economies.

—The location decisions of the native population respond to immigration; the native flow to the primary immigrant-receiving state, California, has been greatly reduced by the influx of immigrants since 1970.

—Immigration has had a marked adverse impact on the economic status of the least skilled U.S. workers (high school dropouts and those in the bottom 20 percent of the wage distribution).

—Trade has had small effects on the overall implicit labor supply of the less skilled. However, the trade effect is larger if one assumes that economic activities displaced by imports employ technologies comparable to the least skilled plants in U.S. manufacturing industries.

These are not the final words on the effects of immigration and trade on the job market. We do not explore all of the possible avenues by which these flows influence labor market outcomes. For instance, we do not estimate the extent to which immigrants may take jobs that no native would take and so may overstate the effect of immigration on the less skilled.[5] Nor do we explore the potential effects of trade on native outcomes that occur entirely through prices (with no observed change in trade quantities), and thus we may understate the distributional effects of trade on outcomes.

The Two Shocks

The starting point for our analysis is the significant increase in immigration and trade that has occurred in the United States since the 1960s. While neither immigration nor trade flows are entirely exogenous shocks to the U.S. job market, the huge changes in recent years have come primarily from developments that are unrelated to contemporaneous labor market conditions in the United States. On the immigration side, the major impetus for the increased flow of legal immigration from less developed countries were the 1965 Amendments to

5. Hamermesh (1997) contrasts the quality of jobs held by immigrants and by natives and finds little support for this claim, so we doubt that this is a major consideration in assessing the effect of immigration.

Table 1. The Foreign-Born Population of the United States and Its National Origins, 1960–96

Units as indicated

Item	Foreign-born population				
	1960	*1970*	*1980*	*1990*	*1996*
In millions	9.7	9.7	14.1	19.8	24.6
As percentage of entire population	5.4	4.8	6.2	7.9	9.3
Distribution by origin[a]					
Canada and Europe	84	68	43	26	. . .
Caribbean and Latin America	9	19	31	43	. . .
Asia	5	9	18	25	. . .
Other	2	4	8	6	. . .

Source: Authors' calculations. Data for 1960 are from U.S. Bureau of the Census, *Historical Statistics of the United States, Colonial Times to 1870*, vol. 1 (Department of Commerce, 1975). Data for 1970–90 are from *Statistical Abstract of the United States* (various years). Data for 1996 are from the Census Bureau and are available on the bureau's worldwide web page.

a. Percent.

the Immigration and Nationality Act.[6] Illegal immigration has also responded to policy developments (such as the ending of the *bracero*, or guest worker, program in 1964), but probably depends more on the huge wage differential between Mexico and the United States than on U.S. labor market developments.[7] On the trade side, the worldwide movement toward more open trade, the increased productivity of workers in LDCs, the entry of China into the world economy, and changes in exchange rates have altered trade flows, irrespective of changes in the U.S. labor market.

Immigration

Immigration began to surge not long after the enactment of the 1965 amendments, reversing a long downward trend in the foreign-born share of the U.S. population. Table 1 quantifies these patterns. In 1960, 5.4 percent of the population was foreign-born; in 1970, the foreign-born share bottomed out at 4.8 percent. Between 1970 and 1996, the number of foreign-born persons increased by 15 million, raising the foreign-

6. Borjas (1990, chap. 2) provides a brief summary of the policy changes initiated by the 1965 legislation.

7. In particular, the illegal flow has certainly not been motivated by rising real wages for less skilled workers in the United States. Those wages have fallen in recent years. Hanson and Spilimbergo (1997) show that illegal immigration from Mexico (as proxied by border apprehensions) is particularly sensitive to labor market conditions in Mexico.

Figure 1. Percentage of Adult Population that Was Foreign Born, 1950–90[a]

Percent

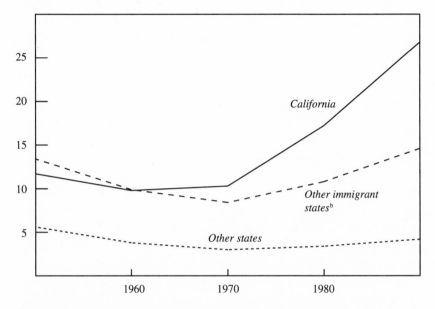

Source: Authors' calculations based on data from the census Public Use Microdata Sample (PUMS) (various years); see table 2 below for details.
a. Adults are aged eighteen to sixty-four.
b. New York, New Jersey, Illinois, Florida, and Texas.

born share of the U.S. population to 7.9 percent in 1990 and 9.3 percent in 1996. During this period, the proportion of immigrants from LDCs was rising.

Historically, immigrants have clustered in a small number of geographic areas, and this concentration has increased over time. In 1960, 60 percent of immigrants lived in one of the six main immigrant-receiving states: California, New York, Texas, Florida, New Jersey, and Illinois. By 1990, 75 percent of immigrants lived in these states, and over 33 percent lived in California alone. This geographic concentration reflects the propensity of immigrants to enter the United States through a limited number of gateway cities or states and spread out slowly to other areas of the country in subsequent years.[8] Figure 1 illustrates the impact of the immigrant supply shock on the percent of

8. Bartel (1989).

the adult population (aged eighteen to sixty-four) that was foreign-born in California, in other immigrant-receiving states, and in the rest of the country over the period 1950–90. Before 1970, the foreign-born share was stable or declining in each region. Between 1970 and 1990, this share almost tripled in California (rising from 10.3 percent to 26.8 percent), almost doubled in the other immigrant-receiving states (from 8.4 to 14.6 percent), and rose slightly in the rest of the country (from 3.0 to 4.2 percent).

The effect of immigration on native labor depends critically on the distribution of skills between immigrants and natives. If the skill distribution of immigrants matches that of natives, immigration will not affect the relative supply of skills and thus will not change the structure of wages. By contrast, if immigrants are less skilled than natives, immigration will shift the distribution of income toward the more skilled, and conversely if immigrants are more skilled than natives.

Table 2 compares the distributions of years of schooling for immigrants and natives in the United States and in California for 1990 and 1995, and also reports the immigrant contribution to the labor supply of workers with different years of schooling. The distribution of immigrants by educational attainment is more dispersed than that of natives. A disproportionately high number of immigrants have fewer than nine years of schooling, but also, a disproportionately high number have more than sixteen years of schooling. On average, however, immigrants have fewer years of schooling than natives—a difference that has grown over the past two decades, as the mean years of schooling in the immigrant population increased less rapidly than the mean years of schooling of natives. As a result, the immigrant contribution to the supply of skills has become increasingly concentrated in the lower educational categories. By 1995, one-half of workers with fewer than nine years of schooling and one-third of workers with fewer than twelve years of schooling were immigrants.

In 1995, over 30 percent of the working-age population in California was foreign-born; consequently, one can learn much by comparing California's experience with that of other states. California has an exceptionally large less educated immigrant population that stands in contrast to the high number of well-educated natives. The lower panel of table 2 shows that by 1995, 90 percent of Californians with fewer

Table 2. Distribution of Natives and Immigrants by Educational Attainment, United States and California, 1990 and 1995
Percent

Region and years of schooling	1990 census data			1995 CPS data		
	Natives	Immigrants	Immigrant share in skill group	Natives	Immigrants	Immigrant share in skill group
United States						
Fewer than 9	4.2	22.4	36.9	2.8	22.6	49.6
9 to 11	14.0	16.0	11.1	9.9	12.3	13.1
12	32.0	20.1	6.4	34.6	24.8	8.0
13 to 15	29.5	21.1	7.2	30.0	19.0	7.1
16	13.8	12.0	8.6	15.7	13.5	9.4
More than 16	6.6	8.4	12.1	7.1	7.8	11.7
California						
Fewer than 9	2.2	28.6	82.6	1.5	30.3	90.1
9 to 11	11.9	17.4	34.8	7.7	14.3	44.6
12	24.0	16.7	20.3	26.8	21.7	26.1
13 to 15	37.5	20.5	16.7	37.9	17.6	16.8
16	16.4	11.0	19.7	17.7	11.2	21.7
More than 16	7.9	5.8	21.2	8.5	5.0	20.3

Source: Authors' calculations. Data for 1990 are from the Census Bureau's Public Use Microdata Sample. Data for 1995 are from the Merged Outgoing Rotation Group (MORG) files from the Census Bureau's Current Population Survey (CPS). Throughout the paper, the authors use census and CPS data released in electronic form by the Census Bureau.
a. First two columns under each data set give, for the United States and California, the percentage of native-born persons or immigrants, aged eighteen to sixty-four, who have the given number of years of schooling. Third column under each data set gives the percentage of persons with the given educational attainment who are immigrants. Immigrants are those born abroad who are noncitizens or naturalized citizens. All others are natives.

than nine years of schooling and 68 percent of those with fewer than twelve years of schooling were foreign-born.[9]

Table 3 examines the distribution of immigrants and natives by occupation and industry. The first two columns of data report the percent distribution of native and immigrant workers among occupations and industries nationwide. If immigrants were randomly distributed by occupation and industry, the figures in these two columns would be

9. It is worth emphasizing that the U.S. labor market does not value natives and immigrants with the same educational attainment identically. In fact, the 1990 census indicates that there is roughly a 0.10 log point gap between the earnings of natives and immigrants with the same number of years of schooling. As a result, simple head counts of immigrants will exaggerate their contribution to labor supply. A more accurate picture is obtained by counting immigrants and natives in terms of efficiency units. Below, we calculate the contributions that "equivalent" immigrants make to labor supply.

Table 3. Representation of Immigrants, by Occupation and Industry, 1995ᵃ

Percent, except as indicated

Occupation or industry	U.S. distribution by occupation or industry			Percentage of workers who are immigrants	
	Immigrants	Natives	Ratio of immigrant to native distributionᵇ	United States	California
Occupation					
Managerial and professional specialty	21.2	28.2	0.75	7.6	16.5
Technical and related support	2.5	3.2	0.78	7.7	20.2
Sales	9.4	12.1	0.76	7.9	19.8
Administrative support, including clerical	9.7	15.4	0.63	6.4	18.2
Precision, production, craft, repair	11.7	11.0	1.06	10.5	29.5
Operators, fabricators	14.9	10.5	1.42	13.5	49.5
Handlers, equipment cleaners, helpers, laborers	5.7	4.2	1.36	12.9	40.3
Private household	2.1	0.5	4.20	31.5	63.7
Service, excluding private household	17.4	12.5	1.39	13.3	35.3
Farming, forestry, fishing	5.4	2.5	2.16	19.4	70.7
Industry					
Agriculture	5.0	2.3	2.17	19.0	68.3
Mining	0.3	0.6	0.50	5.1	19.4
Construction	6.4	6.6	0.97	9.7	24.4
Manufacturing	20.2	16.2	1.24	12.0	41.3
Transport, communication, utilities	5.3	7.2	0.74	7.5	19.0
Wholesale trade	4.4	3.9	1.13	11.0	30.4
Retail trade	17.7	16.5	1.07	10.5	29.4
Finance, insurance, real estate	5.0	6.3	0.81	7.9	19.3
Services	33.4	35.1	0.95	9.5	22.7
Government	2.3	5.2	0.44	4.5	11.4

Source: Authors' calculations based on data from the 1995 CPS, MORG file.
a. See table 2, note a for definition of immigrants.
b. Fist column divided by second column.

roughly the same. They are not. As the ratios of the immigrant share to the native share in the third column show, immigrants are more concentrated in lower skill occupations than natives and work in a different set of industries. There are relatively more immigrants working in farming occupations, in service jobs, as private household workers, and as operators and fabricators. There are relatively more immigrants in agriculture, in manufacturing, and in wholesale and retail trade. Immigrants are less likely than natives to work in white collar jobs—such as managerial and professional specialties, administrative support, sales and technical support—and are especially underrepresented in government jobs. In part these differences are due to lower educational attainment, but some of them cannot be so easily explained.

The last two columns of table 3 record the proportion of immigrants in different occupations and industries, for the United States and for California. The figures for the entire country provide another way of showing the concentration of immigrants in low-skill occupations and selected industries. The figures for California emphasize the importance of immigration in that state's economy. In some occupations, such as farming, private household, and operators and fabricators, about half or more of California's work force consists of immigrants. In 1995, immigrants made up 68.3 percent of its agricultural work force and 41.3 percent of its manufacturing work force. These numbers suggest that immigration may have affected the industrial structure of California. Between 1970 and 1990, the proportion of workers employed in immigrant-intensive industries fell by only 4.1 percentage points (8 percent) in California, as compared with an 8.6 percentage point (16 percent) decline in nonimmigrant states, and a 9.4 percentage point (20 percent) decline in the other immigrant-receiving states.[10] The fraction of California's workers employed in the private household industry fell less than in other states, and the fraction employed in apparel and accessories rose in California but declined elsewhere. To the extent that the industries spurred by immigration compete with similar industries located elsewhere in the country (as might be the case for manufacturing and, possibly, agriculture), the observed change in industry mix pro-

10. We define immigrant-intensive industries as those with a larger share of immigrants than the national average immigrant share of total employment; these comprise personal services (including private household services), agriculture, business and repair services, retail trade, and manufacturing.

vides yet another potential means by which the effects of immigration are diffused across the country.

Finally, while many immigrants work in manufacturing, many also work in nontraded sectors. The significant immigrant representation in services and retail trade highlights a critical difference between the potential effects of trade and of immigration on native workers. Less skilled natives can escape trade competition with low-paid workers overseas by specializing in the production of nontraded goods; the local sales clerk must live in the United States to deal with customers. Indeed, when no American competes with the Chinese in producing low-cost children's toys, increased imports of those toys benefit even less skilled Americans. But there is no such "cone of diversification" escape that allows native workers to avoid competition from immigrants. Immigrants can just as easily work in nontraded goods and services as in the traded goods sector.

Trade

The upper panel of figure 2 shows that the most widely used measure of trade, the ratio of exports plus imports to GDP, increased markedly from 1970 to 1980, stabilized in the 1980s, and has risen since 1990.[11] While much of the growth in the 1970s was trade between the United States and other advanced countries, the share of imports from LDCs (defined in this figure as all nonindustrial countries, exclusive of the petroleum producing countries) has increased continuously since the 1970s, accelerating in the 1990s.[12] The bottom panel of figure 2 shows that the ratio of imports from LDCs to U.S. GDP rose from 0.023 in 1980 to 0.028 in 1990 and to 0.041 in 1996. Nearly 40 percent of U.S.

11. The ratio $(EX + IM)$/GDP exaggerates the relative magnitude of trade, because EX (exports) and IM (imports) are measured in terms of sales, while GDP is a value-added concept. Sales are roughly twice GDP, so that a consistent indicator of the magnitude of trade in terms of the traded proportion of sales would be about half of $(EX + IM)$/GDP. Since the ratio of sales to GDP has not changed much over time, the growth of $(EX + IM)$/GDP roughly tracks the growth of $(EX + IM)$/sales.

12. We classify countries on the basis of their level of economic development when the implicit supply shock began, in the 1970s or 1980s. As a result, Japan is classified as an industrial nation, but the four "tigers" (Korea, Singapore, Hong Kong, and Taiwan) are classified as LDCs. On the questions of whether to treat Japan in the 1960s as advanced and whether to treat some of the tigers as advanced economies today, see Sachs and Shatz (1994).

Figure 2. Growing Openness and LDC Trade, 1970–96[a]

Ratio

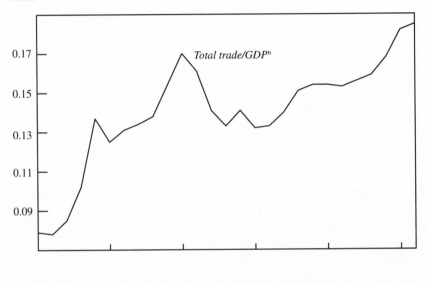

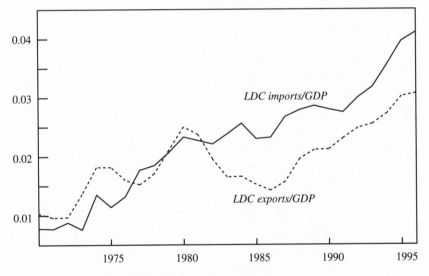

Source: Authors' calculations based on data from the *Economic Report of the President, 1997*.
a. LDC trade flows include those with trading partners other than Canada, Japan, Australia, New Zealand, South Africa, members of the Organization of Petroleum Exporting Countries, and the countries of western Europe.
b. Exports plus imports divided by GDP.

imports came from LDCs in 1996, and the largest trade deficit was with China, whose goods made up 6 percent of imports.

The effect of imports and exports on workers depends on the characteristics of workers in those industries affected by trade. If import-intensive industries disproportionately use less skilled workers and export-intensive industries disproportionately use more skilled workers, trade will shift the distribution of income from the less skilled to the more skilled.[13] Table 4 shows how the average characteristics of workers in American manufacturing industries in 1990 differed along trade lines calculated in two different ways. The lines listed as import- or export-weighted averages weight the characteristics of workers in each industry by the ratio of imports (or exports) to sales times the employment in the industry. The lines listed as high export or import intensity are obtained by ranking manufacturing industries by the ratio of exports or imports to sales, and then selecting off the top of the list until 10 percent of the manufacturing labor force is represented. The figures given for LDC import or export intensity are calculated in a similar manner, using LDC imports and exports to weight or categorize industries. For the rest of the economy, we differentiate between agriculture, which is a major exporter, and "all other" industries: services, trade, and government. Despite the growing international trade in services, the "all other" category can be roughly viewed as the nontraded sector for the purpose of comparison with manufacturing.

The table shows that in the manufacturing sector, the workers most affected by imports are disproportionately immigrants, women, blacks, and the less educated; whereas those most affected by exports are disproportionately native-born, nonblack, and educated men. Moreover, the wages of workers in the top 10 percent of importing industries were 0.53 log point below the wages of those in the top 10 percent of export industries, and the wages of the "average" import worker were 0.15 log point less than those of the average export worker. Classified by imports and exports with LDCs alone, the skill (wage) composition of the import-affected workers and the skill composition of the export-affected workers differ even more.

Looking beyond the manufacturing sector, however, the picture is

---

13. Trefler (1993) discusses the difficulties involved in calculating relative factor proportions.

Table 4. Demographic Composition of the U.S. Work Force, by Industry, 1990

Percent, except as indicated

Industry[a]	Immigrants	Women	Blacks	High school dropouts	College graduates	Log wage index[b]
All industries	9.1	41.3	10.0	14.6	24.8	0.00
Manufacturing	10.1	31.7	10.1	20.6	16.6	0.08
High import intensity	19.7	55.8	10.9	28.8	15.6	-0.14
Import-weighted average	12.5	38.1	10.0	22.5	15.9	0.04
High export intensity	8.8	25.7	6.8	9.7	30.7	0.39
Export-weighted average	9.8	29.5	8.8	17.0	20.5	0.19
High LDC import intensity	19.9	58.2	11.2	29.7	15.1	-0.17
LDC import-weighted average	15.7	48.5	10.7	27.2	13.8	-0.09
High LDC export intensity	11.1	34.0	6.9	14.4	22.4	0.20
LDC export-weighted average	10.1	30.3	8.8	17.5	19.8	0.17
Agriculture	12.7	17.9	4.7	29.5	13.1	-0.49
All other[c]	8.7	44.7	10.1	12.7	27.1	-0.01

Source: Authors' calculations. Data on imports and exports by industry are compiled by Robert Feenstra and are available on the worldwide web page of the National Bureau of Economic Research (NBER). Data on LDC imports and exports are from Sachs and Shatz (1994). Data on industry shipments are from the NBER Productivity Database, also available on the NBER's worldwide web page. Industry data on immigrants, women, and educational attainments are from the 1990 census PUMS. Data on blacks and on wages are averages of 1989-91 data from CPS MORG files.

a. Aggregations based on data at the three-digit level. High import or export intensity industries are obtained by ranking industries by the ratio of imports or exports to total shipments and then selecting industries off the top of the list until 10 percent of the manufacturing labor force is represented. LDC imports and exports are, respectively, those from and to less developed countries. Weighted averages weight each industry by employment times the import or export intensity ratio.

b. Log of hourly wage index constructed so that U.S. average log wage = 0.

c. Nonmanufacturing, nonagricultural.

more complex. Agriculture uses low-wage male workers to a greater extent than even the top 10 percent of importing industries in manufacturing. In the heterogeneous "all other" category, the proportion of women exceeds that in the average import sector; and the proportion of college graduates exceeds that in the average export sector. The different composition of the labor force in exporting and importing industries has two implications for trade-based explanations of changes in the U.S. job market. First, the fact that women are disproportionately concentrated in industries that import from LDCs suggests that LDC trade should have affected women more adversely than men. But rates of pay and employment for women have risen since 1970. The evidence thus suggests that there is something wrong with models in which the traded goods sector determines wages for women throughout the economy. The expansion of the "all other" category, which disproportionately employs women, can explain this seeming paradox in a more general model of wage determination. Second, the large and increasing difference between the skill mix of the top and bottom importing and exporting industries raises the possibility that trade may have particular adverse effects on the economic position of some less skilled workers.[14]

The Impact of Immigration: Area Studies

Suppose (1) that immigrant flows are uncorrelated with economic conditions in an area; and (2) that natives do not alter decisions about location or capital investment in response to immigration. Then comparing native outcomes or changes in outcomes between areas of more immigration and areas of less would offer a good way to isolate the impact of immigration on natives.[15] Put differently, one knows that immigrants flock to California. Why not just compare labor market

14. While table 4 shows data for 1990, we have also calculated the equivalent data for 1980; we find that the differentiation between the top 10 percent of import and export sectors increased between 1980 and 1990. One reason for this finding is that LDCs were more dominant in the high–import intensity sectors in 1990 than in 1980. Another is that the automobile industry (a large high-wage industry) was a more significant importer in 1980 than in 1990.

15. Grossman (1982) represents the first application of this approach. Her finding of a near zero correlation between native wages and immigrant penetration in a local labor market has been confirmed by most studies in this literature.

outcomes in California to the outcomes observed in the rest of the country?

The problem with contrasting native outcomes between immigrant-intensive areas and nonimmigrant areas is that neither proposition 1 nor 2 appears to be valid for the United States. The cities or states where immigrants cluster have done well in some periods and poorly in others, producing a potentially spurious correlation between immigration and area outcomes. For reasons that are probably unrelated to immigration, California is a high-wage state. As a result, immigration will appear to improve native economic opportunities in a cross-section dominated by California. To avoid this spurious cross-sectional spatial correlation, most analysts relate the *change* in the economic position of natives in an area over time to the *change* in the number of immigrants.[16] But a state's economy also fluctuates over time for reasons that are independent of immigration, creating the possibility of spurious longitudinal correlations as well. When California's economy booms, there will be a positive correlation between immigration and the economic position of natives; in a recession, the correlation will be negative. Elsewhere, we report that the time-varying conditions of individual states lead to unstable estimates of immigrant effects on native outcomes.[17] If one had perfect measures of how economic conditions change within a state and affect relative wages across skill groups, one would be able to control for those conditions and isolate the effect of immigration. Such measures, however, are not available.

Another problem with area analysis is that natives may adjust to the immediate impact of immigration in an area by moving their labor or capital to other localities until native wages and returns to capital are equalized across areas. For example, a large immigrant flow arriving in Los Angeles might well result in fewer unskilled workers from Mississippi or Michigan moving to California and a reallocation of capital from those states to California. A comparison of the wage of less skilled natives between California and other states, therefore, might show little difference because the effects of immigration were diffused around the economy, not because immigration had no economic effects.

16. See, for example, Altonji and Card (1991); LaLonde and Topel (1991), and Schoeni (1996).
17. Borjas, Freeman, and Katz (1996).

Regional Differences in Native Wages and Employment

We examine the link between immigration and native outcomes across areas for the periods 1960–70, 1970–80, and 1980–90, using data extracts from the 1960, 1970, 1980, and 1990 Public Use Microdata Samples (PUMS) of the decennial census. The extracts include all persons aged eighteen to sixty-four (as of the census year) who do not live in group quarters. In the 1960 and 1970 censuses, the data extracts are a 1 percent random sample of the population. In 1980 and 1990, the immigrant extracts form a 5 percent random sample and the native extracts form a 1 percent random sample. We define a person as an immigrant if he or she was born abroad and is either a noncitizen or a naturalized citizen; all other persons are classified as natives. Because immigrants are concentrated in particular educational groups, we examine the impact of immigration on the labor market outcomes of natives in five educational categories, or "skill groups": fewer than nine years of schooling, nine to eleven years, twelve years, thirteen to fifteen years, and at least sixteen years.

The labor market is likely to respond to supply shocks with price and quantity adjustments. Our measures of labor market outcomes are log weekly earnings and log annual earnings from the previous calendar year and the probability of working during the census week. The analysis of the employment probability uses all the observations in our data, while the analysis of weekly or annual earnings uses the subsample of persons who worked for pay at some time in the year preceding the census, were not self-employed, and were working in the civilian sector.

The geographic scope of the labor market in question can affect estimates of the impact of immigration. Studies of a small geographic area are more likely to miss effects of immigration than studies of large areas because native migration and capital responses may diffuse those effects in small areas. We use three alternative definitions of the geographic area: metropolitan areas, states, and census regions. An advantage of using states or regions as the geographic unit is that data at these levels are available for the entire period 1960–90. We limit the analysis of metropolitan areas to the 1980 and 1990 censuses, across which 236 metropolitan areas can be matched. The 1970 census PUMS identifies far fewer metropolitan areas and the 1960 PUMS does not identify any.

We use age-adjusted measures of labor market outcomes, estimated separately for male and female U.S. natives. We purge our data of age effects in the following way. Let y_{ijkt} be the labor market outcome for person i, residing in area j, belonging to skill group k, in census year t; and let Z_{ijkt} be a vector of dummy variables indicating whether the worker is aged eighteen to twenty-four, twenty-five to thirty-four, thirty-five to forty-four, forty-five to fifty-four, or fifty-five to sixty-four. Finally, let r_{jkt} be a fixed effect giving the age-adjusted ''average'' labor market outcome experienced by a native who lives in area j and belongs to skill group k in year t. We then estimate the following regression separately for each native group based on sex and education in each census year:

(1) $$y_{ijkt} = Z_{ijkt}\beta_{kt} + r_{jkt} + u_{ijkt},$$

where u_{ijkt} is the error term, assumed uncorrelated with the independent variables in the model. The age-adjusted measures of outcomes are given by the fixed effects r, evaluated at the mean age distribution of the native sample from the pooled 1970, 1980, and 1990 censuses.

We use the estimated fixed effects r to calculate first difference estimates of changes in the labor market outcome for each sex-education group. We define the change in outcome for a particular sex-education group in a particular region as

(2) $$\Delta r_{jkt} = r_{jkt} - r_{j,k,t-10}.$$

Table 5 summarizes the key patterns in our data, in terms of regression coefficients linking changes in wages or immigration from one decade to the next. The first and third rows report the results of regressing the change in age-adjusted log weekly earnings in the 1980s for a state-education cell on the change in log weekly earnings in the 1970s for the same state-education cell.[18] The regression includes a vector of education fixed effects; by including these, we isolate the secular correlation in wage growth within an educational group. The results reveal a strong *negative* relation in wage growth by state between the two periods. The coefficient in the male regression is -1, implying a complete reversal in the ranking of states by wage growth between the 1970s

18. The wage growth regressions are weighted by $(n_x n_y)/(n_x + n_y)$, where n_t gives the sample size in year t, and x and y are the years spanned by the period defining the dependent variable.

Table 5. State Cross-Section Autoregressions Estimating Changes in Native Earnings Growth and Immigrant Flows between Census Decades[a]

Sample	Dependent variable	Independent variable	Coefficient	R^2
Males	Wage growth, 1980–90	Wage growth, 1970–80	−1.052 (0.068)	0.640
	Wage growth, 1970–80	Wage growth, 1960–70	0.002 (0.084)	0.149
Females	Wage growth, 1980–90	Wage growth, 1970–80	−0.591 (0.073)	0.438
	Wage growth, 1970–80	Wage growth, 1960–70	0.179 (0.058)	0.456
All persons	Immigrant supply change, 1980–90	Immigrant supply change, 1970–80	1.498 (0.054)	0.753
	Immigrant supply change, 1970–80	Immigrant supply change, 1960–70	1.251 (0.098)	0.500

Source: Authors' calculations based on data from the census PUMS (various years).

a. Wage growth is defined as the log change in age-adjusted weekly earnings: $r_{jkt} - r_{j,k,t-10}$, from equation 2 in the text, where j represents one of the fifty states or the District of Columbia and k represents one of the five skill groups described in the text. Change in the immigrant supply, from equation 3 in the text, is $(M_{jkt} - M_{j,k,t-10})/N_{j,k,t-10}$, where M_{jk} and N_{jk} are the number of immigrants and natives, respectively, in the given state and skill group. Regressions include fixed effects identifying each skill group. Standard errors are shown in parentheses. Each regression contains 255 observations.

and the 1980s. Figure 3, which compares rates of growth of wages by state in the census data, illustrates this striking pattern.[19]

When we obtained this result, we initially wondered if it might largely reflect measurement error; the log of the 1980 weekly wage enters each side of the regression equation with opposite sign. This is not the case. We estimate an analogous regression using 1970–80 wage growth as the dependent variable and 1960–70 wage growth as the independent variable. This regression, reported in the second and fourth rows of table 5 and illustrated in figure 3, shows no correlation in wage growth for men between the two decades and a positive correlation for women.[20] We next wondered whether the result was due to some pe-

19. The figure ''aggregates'' the data across skill groups in a state by weighting the wages of workers with different levels of schooling by the national proportion of workers in each educational group.

20. Although the regional structure of wage growth changed over the period, the correlation matrix in wage levels indicates that these are strongly and positively correlated over time. Every single element in the wage level correlation matrix, for both men and women, over the period 1960–90 exceeds 0.91, where the matrix of correlation coefficients is weighted by the sample size in the state-education cell in the 1990 census.

George J. Borjas, Richard B. Freeman, and Lawrence F. Katz   19

Figure 3. The Changing Regional Wage Structure[a]

Change in log earnings, 1980–90[b]

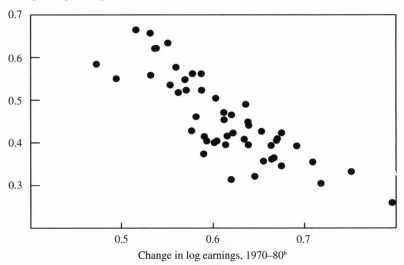

Change in log earnings, 1970–80[b]

Change in log earnings, 1970–80[b]

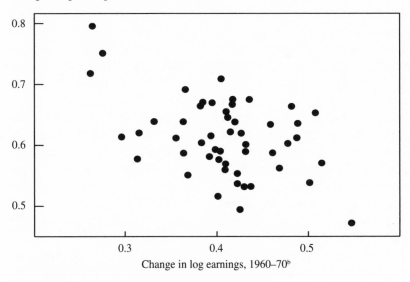

Change in log earnings, 1960–70[b]

Source: Authors' calculations based on data from the census PUMS (various years).
a. Each plotted point represents one of the fifty states or the District of Columbia.
b. Δln weekly earnings of natives aged eighteen to sixty-four.

culiarity in the census data. However, we reestimated these regressions using establishment data on average log weekly wages for workers covered by each state's unemployment insurance system and again found a strong negative correlation between wage growth by state in the 1970s and in the 1980s.

The fact that the high–wage growth states of the 1970s became low–wage growth states in the 1980s has a crucial implication for any analysis that exploits spatial differences to infer the effects of immigration on native outcomes. Since the states that received large numbers of immigrants in the 1970s also received large numbers of immigrants in the 1980s, the reversal of wage growth among states implies a reversal in the sign of the correlation between changes in wages and in immigration by state. As a result, one's inferences about the impact of immigration will almost certainly differ according to the period analyzed.

Formally, let M_{jkt} be the number of immigrants (both male and female) who live in region j and belong to skill group k in census year t, and let N_{jkt} be the number of (male and female) natives in that region and skill group. We define the change in labor supply due to immigration during the decade that ends in year t as

$$(3) \qquad\qquad \Delta m_{jkt} = \frac{M_{jkt} - M_{j,k,t-10}}{N_{j,k,t-10}}.$$

The fifth row of table 5 reports the results of regressing the change in the immigrant supply over 1980–90 on the change in the immigrant supply over 1970–80, including a vector of education fixed effects to isolate changes within educational groups. The regression shows a strong positive correlation between the growth of immigrants in a state in the 1970s and the growth of immigrants in that state in the 1980s. In the sixth row, we lag the regression by one decade; the correlation in supply shocks between the 1960s and the 1970s is also positive and is almost as strong.

The data thus indicate that immigration induced large supply shocks in the same states in the 1970s and in the 1980s. But they also show that the states that experienced high wage growth in the 1970s experienced low wage growth in the 1980s. The result is a reversal in the sign of the correlation between changes in immigration by state and changes in wages. The correlation between Δm and Δr by state switches from -0.19 in 1970–80 to 0.34 in 1980–90 for men, and from -0.18 to

0.44 for women. Studies that calculate spatial correlations between wage growth and immigrant supply shocks will not be able to obtain consistently negative or positive effects across different censuses unless they can control for the forces that caused the regional wage structure to change so dramatically over time. These unobserved structural forces are so strong that a consistent impact of immigration, if such exists, probably cannot be detected in an analysis of interarea differences.

In view of this observation, it is not surprising that our analysis of regional differences in wage trends show little systematic evidence that the immigrant supply shock had an impact on the weekly earnings of natives. For simplicity, we divide the country into three regions: California, the other five states that receive large numbers of immigrants (New York, Texas, Florida, New Jersey, and Illinois), and the remainder of the country.

Table 6 reports log weekly earnings in each of these regions for natives in each educational group relative to natives with exactly twelve years of education in the given region, from 1960 to 1990.[21] For almost every educational group, the pattern of wage differentials moves similarly in California, the other immigrant-receiving states, and the nonimmigrant states. Consider, for example, native men who have between nine and eleven years of schooling. In 1990, this group made up 14.0 percent of native adults. Native men in this educational group who lived in California earned 0.08 log point less than natives with a high school diploma in 1960 and 0.19 log point less in 1990. Their counterparts in the other immigrant-receiving states earned 0.12 log point less than natives with a high school diploma in 1960 and 0.24 log point less in 1990. The trend in the relative wage of this skill group was similar in the states that had few immigrants: -0.13 log point in 1960 and -0.24 log point in 1990. Thus from 1960 to 1990, the relative wage of this less skilled group of native men declined by about 0.11 log point in each of the regions, even though the immigrant shock to California was disproportionately less skilled. The natural "difference-in-difference" estimate of the immigrant wage effect—the wage growth of California's natives less the wage growth of natives in the nonimmigrant states—suggests that immigration did not affect native wage

21. The fixed effects for the aggregated regions are obtained by "adding up" r_{jkt} over the states in the region, with each state's observation weighted by the number of working natives in that state in the given census year.

Table 6. Relative Log Weekly Earnings of Natives by Skill Group, 1960–90
Log index[a]

Years of schooling	Year	Males			Females		
		California	Other immigrant states[b]	Other states	California	Other immigrant states[b]	Other states
Fewer than 9	1960	−0.215	−0.344	−0.383	−0.357	−0.395	−0.510
	1970	−0.193	−0.345	−0.359	−0.336	−0.331	−0.384
	1980	−0.194	−0.359	−0.361	−0.163	−0.271	−0.268
	1990	−0.331	−0.366	−0.343	−0.208	−0.374	−0.285
9 to 11	1960	−0.084	−0.120	−0.128	−0.196	−0.216	−0.247
	1970	−0.111	−0.175	−0.175	−0.208	−0.220	−0.220
	1980	−0.176	−0.212	−0.219	−0.207	−0.204	−0.186
	1990	−0.187	−0.235	−0.239	−0.215	−0.239	−0.218
13 to 15	1960	0.059	0.081	0.085	0.043	0.115	0.129
	1970	0.061	0.081	0.077	0.091	0.134	0.112
	1980	0.052	0.062	0.046	0.068	0.113	0.097
	1990	0.089	0.100	0.083	0.127	0.153	0.156
16 or more	1960	0.271	0.308	0.305	0.439	0.510	0.544
	1970	0.313	0.374	0.334	0.500	0.565	0.589
	1980	0.280	0.322	0.262	0.362	0.446	0.428
	1990	0.414	0.463	0.410	0.513	0.579	0.558

Source: Authors' calculations based on data from the census PUMS (various years).
a. Log of index constructed so that log earnings of natives with exactly twelve years of schooling = 0 in each sample year and region.
b. New York, New Jersey, Illinois, Florida, and Texas.

differentials. The one exception to this pattern is native men who have less than nine years of schooling, which is an extremely small group.

The raw data thus suggest that it is extremely difficult to obtain consistent estimates of the labor market effects of immigration from spatial correlations. Our efforts to find such effects support this inference. Consider the regression model

$$(4) \qquad \Delta r_{jkt} = \alpha_t + \beta_t \, \Delta m_{jkt} + v_j + \tau_k + u_{jkt},$$

where v_j is a fixed effect indicating the group's area of residence and τ_k is a fixed effect indicating the group's educational attainment. The education fixed effects net out any change occurring in the national market for workers with that level of education, while the area fixed effects net out the impact of the level of state economic activity on all natives residing in that state. They represent our best effort to control for factors unrelated to immigration that might affect outcomes across groups and states.

We measure the immigration supply shock as the change in the size of the immigrant population relative to the native population at the beginning of the decade (see equation 3). This measure differs from the first difference in the foreign-born share of the work force that is used in many area studies of immigration. It avoids the potential endogeneity of the immigration variable due to the possibility that the native population at the end of the decade depends on immigration, and also the potential endogeneity of labor force participation (of both immigrants and natives) to the immigrant supply shock.[22] Finally, we use the supply shock in the specific educational group as the measure of immigrant penetration. This variable helps us to better capture the ''own'' effects in the data.[23]

Table 7 presents our estimates of the coefficient β, from the 1960–90 census data. There is a great deal of variation in the estimated coefficients by scope of geographic area, sex, and time period, making it difficult to draw any robust generalization about the effects of immigration on labor market outcomes.[24] Consider, for example, the relationship between immigration and the employment probability for native men. The regression coefficients for the 1980s suggest that immigrant supply shocks lead to lower employment for native workers, and that this effect becomes more negative, the greater the scope of the geographic area. At the regional level, the regressions suggest that a 10 percentage point increase in the relative number of immigrants re-

22. We replicated the regression analysis using counts of workers, with little change in the underlying results.

23. Although it seems as if the specification in equation 4 ignores cross-effects between various types of immigrant workers and natives, the regressions do include area fixed effects. These fixed effects partly control for the supply shock attributable to the total immigrant flow into an area. We also experimented with alternative specifications of the regressions that allowed for an ''own effect'' as well as some cross-effects. However, the correlation between the own supply shock and the total supply shock is typically above 0.7, so that the data do not allow a reliable estimation of a more general model.

24. In Borjas, Freeman, and Katz (1996) we note that analysis of native wage growth in the 1980s shows that the spatial correlation became more negative as the geographic area under consideration was expanded. Table 7, however, indicates that the negative correlation between the regression coefficients and the scope of the geographic area disappears in earlier decades, in particular, in the 1960s.

Table 7. Estimating the Impact of Immigration on Native Earnings and Employment, First Difference Regressions[a]

Dependent variable and geographic scope	Coefficient on immigration variable					
	Males			Females		
	1980–90	1970–80	1960–70	1980–90	1970–80	1960–70
Log weekly earnings						
Regions	−0.126 (0.082)	0.008 (0.107)	0.813 (0.145)	0.015 (0.041)	0.377 (0.241)	1.130 (0.338)
States	−0.103 (0.057)	0.071 (0.075)	0.591 (0.107)	−0.022 (0.035)	0.373 (0.141)	0.203 (0.206)
Metropolitan areas	−0.061 (0.030)	...	...	0.014 (0.031)	...	...
Log annual earnings						
Regions	−0.174 (0.087)	−0.003 (0.139)	0.855 (0.177)	0.066 (0.068)	0.191 (0.299)	1.075 (0.425)
States	−0.110 (0.056)	0.066 (0.092)	0.674 (0.118)	0.006 (0.056)	0.303 (0.156)	0.829 (0.268)
Metropolitan areas	−0.054 (0.037)	...	...	0.024 (0.040)	...	...
Employment rate						
Regions	−0.045 (0.012)	0.127 (0.059)	−0.159 (0.044)	0.028 (0.013)	0.123 (0.119)	0.142 (0.059)
States	−0.025 (0.008)	0.079 (0.049)	−0.063 (0.031)	0.010 (0.011)	0.110 (0.094)	0.187 (0.054)
Metropolitan areas	−0.011 (0.013)	...	...	−0.003 (0.008)	...	...

Source: Authors' calculations based on data from the census PUMS (various years).
a. The dependent variable, for each specification, is the change (over the given decade) in the given labor market outcome (age-adjusted log earnings or employment rate) for natives in a given region, state, or metropolitan area j and given skill group k. The independent variable is the contemporaneous change in the relative immigrant supply, $(M_{jkt} − M_{j,k,t−10})/N_{j,k,t−10}$, where M_{jk} and N_{jk} are the number of immigrants and natives, respectively, in area j and skill group k. Regression equations, which are estimates of equation 4 in the text, include a constant term and fixed effects identifying each area and skill group. Standard errors are shown in parentheses.

duces the employment-to-population ratio of natives by about 0.45 percentage point. But this coefficient is implausibly large and positive in the 1970s and implausibly large and negative in the 1960s. The data also reveal little consistency in the results for weekly and annual earnings, or for men and women.

One way to interpret the inconsistent spatial correlations between changes in native outcomes and immigration over the period 1960–90 is that the economic impact of immigration on native labor market outcomes simply changes over time or differs by sex. That is, we have the "right" estimates, but they vary a great deal. We do not believe that this is so. If it were, the historical record would provide virtually no information about the future effects of immigration or of changes in immigration policy on native outcomes.

Our interpretation of the results in table 7 is that the spatial correlation between changes in native outcomes and immigration do not, in fact, measure what we want them to measure. The inconsistency in the signs of the correlations over time provides little information about the structural impact of immigration on the native labor market. Our finding that the pattern of regional wage changes has shifted dramatically over time—while the same regions keep receiving immigrants—suggests that unobserved factors are driving the evolution of the regional wage structure, that these factors have little to do with immigration, and that they dominate the data. The one valid inference from an analysis of spatial correlations is that immigration is not a major determinant of the regional structure of labor market outcomes for natives.

Immigration and Native Internal Migration

The fact that immigration is not consistently related to regional labor market outcomes for natives raises the question of why immigration effects are so weak at the regional level, despite the striking geographic clustering of immigrants. One hypothesis is that the immigration effect is diffused through the internal migration flows of native workers or capital. Previous research has focused on labor flows, without reaching a clear consensus of findings. Some studies find that metropolitan areas where immigrants cluster had lower rates of native in-migration and higher rates of native out-migration in the 1970s.[25] David Card reports

25. See, for example, Filer (1992) and White and Hunter (1993).

that the unexpected arrival of 120,000 *Marielitos* in Miami in 1980 did not raise the city's population growth over the next five years relative to demographic predictions made before the Mariel boatlift.[26] Consistent with these studies, William Frey and Kao-Lee Liaw find a strong negative correlation between immigration and the net migration rates of natives in the 1990 census.[27] By contrast, in a later study Card reports a slight positive correlation between the rate of growth in the number of native workers and the rate of growth in the number of immigrant workers by metropolitan area, over the period 1985–90.[28] Therefore it remains in question whether native internal migration is an important mechanism for diffusing the effects of immigration nationwide.

We address this issue by examining the population trends of natives and immigrants aged eighteen to sixty-four, by state, using decennial census data from 1950 to 1990.[29] We analyze data at the state level because the state of residence is the one measure of native location decisions that is available in each of these data sets. As with wage outcomes, it is instructive to compare population trends in California, other immigrant-receiving states, and nonimmigrant states. Table 8 reports the proportions of the total population, of natives, and of immigrants living in these areas from 1950 to 1990. As shown above, large-scale immigration to the United States resumed around 1970 and has continued since. Hence by contrasting changes in the residential location of the native population before and after 1970, one can assess the effects of immigration on native location decisions.[30] The period of analysis thus spans *both* the preimmigration pattern of internal migration (the "pretreatment period") and the postimmigration adjustments (the "treatment period").

The data reveal one important fact: up to 1970, the share of natives who lived in the major immigrant-receiving state, California, was rising rapidly; since 1970, the share of natives living in California has barely changed. Between 1950 and 1970 the fraction of natives who lived in California rose by 2.7 percentage points (39 percent): between 1950

26. Card (1990).
27. Frey (1995a, 1995b); Frey and Liaw (1996).
28. Card (1997).
29. We use the sample of persons who do not reside in group quarters.
30. The data clearly indicate that the migration patterns of the U.S. population (as opposed to cross-state differences in fertility and death rates) dominate shifts in population across states; see Blanchard and Katz (1992).

Table 8. Distribution of Native and Immigrant Populations, by Region, 1950–90[a]

Percent

Year	Entire population			Natives			Immigrants		
	California	Other immigrant states[b]	Other states	California	Other immigrant states[b]	Other states	California	Other immigrant states[b]	Other states
1950	7.2	26.9	65.9	6.9	25.4	67.7	10.4	44.4	45.2
1960	8.9	27.3	63.7	8.6	26.2	65.2	14.6	44.9	40.6
1970	10.2	27.1	62.7	9.6	26.2	64.2	20.1	43.8	36.0
1980	10.9	26.7	62.4	9.7	25.6	64.8	27.2	41.9	30.9
1990	12.4	27.0	60.7	10.0	25.5	64.4	33.8	40.0	26.1

Source: Authors' calculations based on data from the census PUMS (various years).
a. Sample includes individuals aged eighteen to sixty-four and not living in group quarters.
b. New York, New Jersey, Illinois, Florida, and Texas.

and 1960 it increased from 6.9 to 8.6 percent and between 1960 and 1970 it increased from 8.6 to 9.6 percent. In contrast, the fraction of natives living in California rose by only 0.1 percentage point from 1970 to 1980 and by just 0.3 point from 1980 to 1990, a cumulative increase of 0.4 point (4.2 percent).

If California's share of the total U.S. population had also stabilized between 1970 and 1990, one would perhaps conclude that the state had reached some equilibrium steady-state share of the population. But California's share rose from 10.2 percent in 1970 to 12.4 percent in 1990: a 2.2 percentage point (22 percent) increase. In fact, California shifted from growth based on native migration to growth based on immigrants. If the share of the native population in California had increased in the 1970s and 1980s at the same rate as in the 1950s and 1960s, 12.3 percent of natives would have lived in California in 1990.[31] An extrapolation of the pre-1970 demographic trends—that is, before the immigrant supply shock—accurately predicts the state's share of the entire U.S. population in 1990.[32] Figure 4 shows that the data point for California (like the points for each of the other immigrant-receiving states) lies close to the regression line linking the population growth rate in 1970–90 to that in 1950–70. This finding suggests that the increasing number of immigrants who chose to settle in California displaced the native net migration that would otherwise have occurred and thus diffused the economic effects of immigration from California to the rest of the country.

We formalize this insight with a simple regression model. We define the simple annualized population growth rate contributions for natives, $\Delta n_j(t, t')$, and immigrants, $\Delta m_j(t, t')$, as

$$(5) \qquad \Delta n_j(t, t') = \frac{N_{jt'} - N_{jt}}{L_{jt}} \div (t' - t)$$

and

---

31. Extrapolating the trend over 1950–70 to this later period implies that the native share would have grown by 2.7 percentage points between 1970 and 1990. Admittedly, this simple exercise assumes away the nonlinearities that may exist in the rate of change in California's population share.

32. Evidence provided by Blanchard and Katz (1992) presages this finding: their figure 1 shows that California lies on the regression line linking the rate of employment growth in 1970–90 to that in 1950–70.

Figure 4. Actual versus Predicted State Population Growth Rates, 1970–90[a]

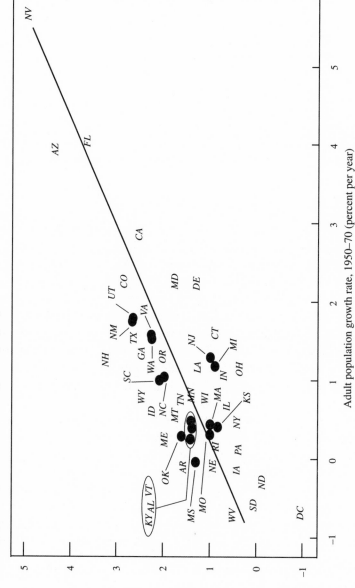

Adult population growth rate, 1970–90 (percent per year)

Adult population growth rate, 1950–70 (percent per year)

Source: Authors' calculations based on data from the census PUMS (various years).
a. Observations for the fifty states plus the District of Columbia are labeled by postal codes. The least squares line shown is given by $y = 0.75x + 0.86$, $R^2 = 0.68$.

Table 9. Estimating the Response of State Native Population Flows to State Immigrant Population Flows[a]

	Double differences	
First differences,	*1970–90*	*1970–90*
	minus	*minus*
1970–90	*1960–70*	*1950–70*
0.777	−0.756	−1.673
(0.311)	(0.278)	(0.285)

Source: Authors' calculations based on data from the census PUMS (various years).

a. For first differences specification, dependent variable is the average annual contribution of native population growth to overall population growth in each state; independent variable is the contribution of immigrant population growth. For double difference specifications, the changes in these average annual contributions (between periods given) are used as variables. For details, see equations 7 (first differences) and 8 (double differences) in the text. Sample comprises the fifty states plus the District of Columbia, except for the final column, which excludes Alaska and Hawaii. Standard errors are shown in parentheses.

$$(6) \qquad \Delta m_j(t, t') = \frac{M_{jt'} - M_{jt}}{L_{jt}} \div (t' - t),$$

where N_{jt} gives the number of natives living in state j in year t, M_{jt} gives the respective number of immigrants, and $L_{jt} = N_{jt} + M_{jt}$. We then estimate the following first difference regression model:

$$(7) \qquad \Delta n_j(70, 90) = a + b \, \Delta m_j(70, 90) + e_j,$$

where "70" and "90" indicate the census years 1970 and 1990, respectively, and e_j is the stochastic error. This regression links the annual growth rate of natives in a state to the growth rate of immigrants in that state, both relative to the state's total population in the base year, 1970. Because the dependent and independent variables are scaled by the same factor, the coefficient b measures the impact of an additional immigrant arriving in the state between 1970 and 1990 on the change in the number of natives living in that state during that period.

The sample contains fifty-one observations (for each state plus the District of Columbia). The first column in table 9 reports the estimated coefficient b.[33] The data reveal a positive and significant relation between immigration by state and change in the size of the native population. Does this positive coefficient imply that natives do not respond to immigration in their location decisions, or perhaps even respond by

33. All the first difference models estimated in this section are weighted by the factor $(n_x \, n_y)/(n_x + n_y)$, where n_t gives the sample size in year t, and x and y are the years spanned by the period defining the dependent variable. We also estimated the models separately for men and women, with little change in the results.

moving *to* areas penetrated by immigrants? How can one reconcile these results with the fact that native migration to the major immigrant-receiving state, California, effectively ended around 1970?

The key difference between the regression model in equation 7 and our earlier tabulations is that the first difference regression compares population growth among states with different levels of immigration in 1970–90, rather than native migration in a given state before and after the immigrant supply shock. The regression estimated in the first column of table 9 implicitly assumes that each state would have had the same rate of native population growth in the absence of immigration, so that California and Vermont were on the same population growth path. But if each state had its own growth path prior to immigration, and that growth path would have continued absent immigration, the regression gives a misleading inference about the effects of immigration. To isolate the impact of immigration on the net migration of native workers, one needs a difference-in-difference comparison of how a given state's population grows before and after the immigrant supply shock. The following double difference model provides such a comparison:

$$(8) \quad \Delta n_j(70, 90) - \Delta n_j(60, 70)$$

$$= \alpha + \beta \left[\Delta m_j(70, 90) - \Delta m_j(60, 70) \right] + v_j,$$

where the coefficient β measures the impact of an increase in the number of immigrants on the number of natives, relative to the "preexisting conditions" in the state. A useful interpretation of the double difference in equation 8 is that it imposes a particular structure on the state's fixed effect—the rate of population growth that the state was experiencing before the immigrant supply shock.

The second column of table 9 reports the coefficient from the double difference model, using the state's population growth from 1960 to 1970 as the counterfactual control.[34] Controlling for the state's pre-1970 population growth path changes the sign of the effect of immigration on native net migration from positive to negative. In fact, the estimated β suggests considerable displacement (the coefficient is not significantly different from -1).

---

34. The double difference models are weighted by $(n_x n_y n_z)/(n_y n_z + 4n_x n_z + n_x n_y)$, where n_t gives the sample size in year t, x and z are the years that span the period defining the dependent variable (with $z > y > x$).

The regression coefficient presented in the second column essentially reiterates the descriptive results presented in table 8. The negative coefficient reflects the facts that California experienced the largest immigrant supply shock and that its native population share stopped growing when the supply shock began. The third column of the table reestimates the double difference model using the annualized population growth rate over 1950–70 to control for conditions in the state before the immigrant supply shock. This regression yields an even more negative coefficient—indeed, it seems too negative, because it is larger than one in absolute value. This "excess sensitivity" is probably a functional form issue. It is unclear whether, in the absence of an immigration shock, California's share of the native population would have grown at the rapid rate of 1.4 percentage points per decade that prevailed over 1950–70. The only term in the regression that would capture this possible nonlinearity is the change in the rate of growth of the immigrant population.

Table 9 demonstrates that the sign of the impact of immigration on the growth of the native population depends critically on the counterfactual implicit or explicit in a particular regression model. While the data support the inclusion of a lagged native population growth rate in the model linking native net migration to immigration, this is not the reason why we prefer this model.[35] Selection of a model depends not simply on statistical results, but on the economic relevance of the counterfactual that it poses. We contrast native growth rates before and after the immigrant supply shock because this comparison may provide a plausible answer to the question of what would have happened to the native population if immigration had remained at pre-1970 levels; that is, the growth path that would have been observed if the immigrant supply shock had never occurred.

---

35. The double difference regression in equation 8 imposes two restrictions on the coefficients. In particular, the coefficient on the 1960–70 native growth rate is unity and the coefficient of the 1960–70 immigrant growth rate is equal, but of opposite sign, to the coefficient on the 1970–90 immigrant growth rate. The unrestricted regression is

$$\Delta n_j(70, 90) = 0.988 \, \Delta n_j(60, 70) - 1.218 \, \Delta m_j(70, 90) + 3.310 \, \Delta m_j(60, 70),$$
$$\quad\quad\quad\quad (0.167) \quad\quad\quad\quad (0.333) \quad\quad\quad\quad (0.925)$$

where the regression includes a constant term and standard errors are in parentheses. The restriction on the native coefficient is satisfied by the data, whereas the restriction on the immigrant coefficients is rejected (with a t statistic of 2.68).

Table 10. Distribution of Regional Adult Populations by Educational Attainment, 1950–90[a]

Percent

Region and year	Fewer than 9	9 to 11	12	13 to 15	16 or more
California					
1950	26.8	20.5	31.8	13.2	7.7
1960	20.9	21.8	32.6	15.0	9.7
1970	12.5	17.8	36.6	19.9	13.2
1980	9.6	13.2	34.2	24.8	18.3
1990	9.3	13.4	22.0	33.0	22.3
Other immigrant states[b]					
1950	39.8	20.6	25.1	7.8	6.7
1960	30.5	22.8	28.3	9.9	8.4
1970	19.1	21.2	35.1	12.9	11.6
1980	11.0	16.1	37.7	18.4	16.8
1990	6.6	14.2	29.2	28.1	21.8
Other states					
1950	42.6	20.0	24.0	7.9	5.4
1960	32.6	21.4	29.6	9.2	7.2
1970	19.7	20.8	37.2	12.1	10.2
1980	10.5	16.4	40.8	17.3	15.0
1990	5.0	14.3	33.3	28.0	19.4
United States					
1950	40.7	20.2	24.9	8.2	5.9
1960	31.0	21.8	29.5	9.9	7.7
1970	18.8	20.6	36.6	13.1	10.9
1980	10.5	16.0	39.2	18.4	15.9
1990	6.0	14.2	30.8	28.6	20.4

Source: Authors' calculations based on data from the census PUMS (various years).
a. Sample includes individuals aged eighteen to sixty-four and not living in group quarters.
b. New York, New Jersey, Illinois, Florida, and Texas.

Does Immigration Change Factor Proportions within a State?

The migration response of natives would completely diffuse the adverse effect of the immigrant supply shock on local labor markets if the native flows of particular skill groups counterbalanced the immigrant shock and left the relative factor proportions within a state unchanged. We now investigate whether this was, in fact, the case.

We begin by classifying workers according to the five educational groups defined above. Table 10 reports the trends in the factor shares of these skill groups in each of our three areas and in the United States as a whole. It therefore summarizes what happens to the relative supply of the skill groups in these regions as a result of both immigration and the internal migration flows of natives. There has been substantial convergence in the regional distribution of skills over 1950–90. At the beginning of the period, California had relatively few persons who lacked a high school diploma; in 1950, 47.3 percent of California's adult population had less than twelve years of schooling, as compared with 62.6 percent in the states without a strong immigrant presence. By 1990, 22.7 percent of California's population was in this educational group, as compared with 19.3 percent for the nonimmigrant states. California's share of less educated workers declined less rapidly than shares in the rest of the nation, both before and after the immigration shock. From being much more educated than the rest of the nation before 1970, the population of California has changed to a bimodal distribution, with a modestly larger share of both those with less than a high school degree and those with at least a college degree. Table 10 raises the question of whether the educational distribution of the populations of immigrant-receiving states moved closer to that of the rest of the country because of increased unskilled immigration or because of preexisting forces leading toward convergence in educational distributions across regions.

We formalize the analysis by estimating regression models designed to measure how the factor proportion of the various skill groups changed within a state over the period 1950–90. We define the change in factor proportions for skill group k in state j as

$$(9) \qquad \Delta p_{jk}(t, t') = \frac{L_{jkt'}}{L_{jt'}} - \frac{L_{jkt}}{L_{jt}},$$

where L_{jkt} gives the number of persons in state j belonging to skill group k at time t, and L_{jt} gives the total number of persons living in the state. We define the immigrant contribution to the change in factor proportions over the period as

$$(10) \qquad \Delta \widetilde{m}_{jk}(t, t') = \frac{M_{jkt'}}{L_{jt'}} - \frac{M_{jkt}}{L_{jt}}.$$

Consider the regression model

$$(11) \qquad \Delta p_{jk}(70, 90) = c + d\, \Delta \widetilde{m}_{jk}(70, 90) + v_j + \tau_k + e_{jk},$$

where v_j is a fixed effect indicating the state of residence and τ_k is a fixed effect indicating educational attainment. The empirical evidence presented in the previous section indicates that the growth rate of the total population in the state is essentially unrelated to immigration. This implies that one can treat the variable $\Delta\tilde{m}_{jk}(70, 90)$ as exogenous, despite the fact that the right-hand side includes a measure of $L_{j,90}$. The state fixed effect helps to define the immigrant supply shock in terms of within-state deviations, so that the coefficient d measures how factor proportions change within a state when a particular skill group experiences a supply shock.[36] The coefficient d has the interpretation

$$(12) \qquad d = \frac{L_{j,k,90} - \gamma L_{j,k,70}}{M_{j,k,90} - \gamma M_{j,k,70}},$$

where γ equals $L_{j,90}/L_{j,70}$, the state's population growth between 1970 and 1990.[37] If the state's population had not changed over the period (γ equal to one), the coefficient d would simply measure the change in the size of the population associated with the entry of an additional immigrant in that educational group ($\Delta L_{jk}/\Delta M_{jk}$). If there were no migration response in the native population, the coefficient d would then be one, while if native migration completely offset the immigrant supply shock, the coefficient would be zero. In fact, the state's population did increase over the period, for reasons independent of immigration. Consequently the coefficient d measures the impact of an additional immigrant on the total population relative to what would be expected if all groups had experienced neutral growth (at the rate γ) over the period 1970–90.

Table 11 reports the estimated coefficient d for a variety of regression specifications. The first row estimates the first difference model given by equation 11. The coefficient reported in the first column of data

---

36. If there were only two skill groups in the population, u and s, the fixed effect model of equation 11 would be numerically equivalent to the regression

$$\Delta p_{ju}(70, 90) - \Delta p_{js}(70, 90) = (\tau_u - \tau_s) + d\,[\Delta\tilde{m}_{ju}(70, 90)$$
$$- \Delta\tilde{m}_{js}(70, 90)] + (e_{ju} - e_{js}),$$

so that the regression would simply estimate how the difference in immigrant supply shocks between the two groups affects the factor proportions within the state.

37. In particular, note that $\Delta p_{jk}(t, t') = (L_{jkt'} - \gamma L_{jkt})/L_{jt'}$ and that $\Delta\tilde{m}_{jk}(t, t') = (M_{jkt'} - \gamma M_{jkt})/L_{jt'}$.

Table 11. Estimating the Impact of Immigration on State Factor Proportions, 1970–90[a]

Skill grouping and specification	Actual population counts		Efficiency unit counts	
	No initial conditions control	With initial conditions control	No initial conditions control	With initial conditions control
Five skill groups[b]				
First differences[c]	2.772	2.654	2.172	1.956
	(1.247)	(0.767)	(1.129)	(0.458)
Double differences[d]	0.721	−0.093	0.626	−0.254
	(0.284)	(0.285)	(0.271)	(0.261)
High school dropouts and all others				
First differences[e]	1.004	1.256	0.904	1.002
	(1.649)	(0.655)	(1.673)	(0.463)
Double differences[f]	1.224	−0.320	0.496	−0.336
	(0.703)	(0.469)	(0.330)	(0.298)

Source: Authors' calculations based on data from the census PUMS (various years).

a. For first difference equations, dependent variable is the change over the period 1970–90 in the proportion of people in state j who fall in skill group k [$\Delta p_{jk}(70,90)$]; independent variable is the immigrant contribution to this change in factor proportions [$\Delta \widetilde{m}_{jk}(70,90)$]. Double difference equations take the changes in these variables between the periods 1950–70 and 1970–90. Equations are estimated both by using actual populations counts and by using efficiency unit counts, which weigh each person by the typical wage of a person with the same characteristics in 1980. Where indicated, equations control for initial own-group factor proportions as measured in 1950. All equations include fixed effects identifying each region and skill group. Standard errors are shown in parentheses.

b. Fewer than nine years of schooling, ten to eleven years, twelve years, thirteen to fifteen years, and sixteen or more years.

c. $N = 255$.

d. $N = 245$.

e. $N = 102$.

f. $N = 98$.

suggests that d is strongly positive. An additional immigrant in a given skill group raises the total number of persons in that skill group by 2.8.[38] But we have argued that a more useful counterfactual exercise is to compare the growth rate of a particular skill group before and after the immigrant supply shock. This suggests the alternative double difference regression specification

(13) $\Delta p_{jk}(70, 90) - \Delta p_{jk}(50, 70)$

$$= \alpha + \delta \, [\Delta \widetilde{m}_{jk}(70, 90) - \Delta \widetilde{m}_{jk}(50, 70)] + v_j + \tau_k + e_{jk}.$$

The second row of table 11 shows that the estimated δ is 0.72. This implies, at most, a moderate native response to immigration within a skill group, indicating that immigration does alter factor proportions within a state.

Our discussion of the raw data describing trends in the differences of skill distributions between geographic regions, as shown in table 10, suggests that the regression models of equations 11 and 13 ignore a factor that played a key role over the period 1950–90: the convergence of skill distributions across states. This process was in operation before the immigrant supply shock began. To control for the convergence, we add to the regression model a variable giving the fraction of the state's adult population that belonged to educational group k in 1950: $L_{j,k,50}/L_{j,50}$. The resulting coefficients from the expanded specification are reported in the second column of table 11.[39] The inclusion of this ''initial conditions'' variable does not affect the estimated migration effect in the single difference model, but does reduce the impact of immigration on the total supply of workers in a given skill group to zero in the double difference model. In other words, when one controls for the state's preexisting conditions (both in terms of the initial skill distribution and the rate at which this distribution was changing before 1970), the evidence suggests that immigration does not alter the factor proportions of skill groups within a state.

---

38. Card (1997) also reports a positive correlation between the number of immigrants in a particular skill group who entered a local labor market and the number of similarly skilled natives who chose to reside in that labor market in the period 1985–90.

39. The coefficient of the 1950 factor proportion has a strong negative effect in all the models estimated in this section, suggesting the importance of convergence in educational levels across states.

The last two rows of table 11 report the regression results when we redefine skill groups by aggregating to the two groups whose factor proportions are most sensitive to immigration: workers with less than a high school education and workers with at least a high school education. The single difference models consistently yield a strong positive correlation between immigration and changes in factor proportions within these aggregated skill groups, but this positive effect vanishes when we control for the pre-1970 growth rates of the skill groups in the state and for the convergence process.

Finally, we convert the population counts into efficiency units by weighting each person by the relative wage of a person who has similar observed characteristics (that is, sex, age, education, and nationality) in the base period 1980.[40] Calculating supply shifts in terms of efficiency units yields a better measure of changes in the supplies of particular skill groups than the simple population counts used throughout our analysis. We use these efficiency unit counts to reestimate the various specifications; the last two columns of table 11 show that our regression results are not affected.

In sum, the answer to whether immigration affects factor proportions within a state appears to depend on how one specifies the counterfactual of what would have happened absent immigration. Under our preferred specification—which controls for the initial level and past change in state skill distributions—the evidence shows that much of the adverse impact of immigration on the economic opportunities of workers in areas directly affected by the immigrant supply shock was diffused across the country, as native migration flows responded to local influxes of immigrants.[41]

40. We divide the labor force aged eighteen to sixty-four into 280 distinct groups based on sex-age-education-nationality cells (2 sex groups × 5 age groups × 4 education groups × 7 nationality groups = 280 cells). The age groups are eighteen to twenty-four, twenty-five to thirty-four, thirty-five to forty-four, forty-five to fifty-four, and fifty-five to sixty-four; the educational groups are fewer than twelve years of schooling, twelve years, thirteen to fifteen years, and sixteen plus years; and the nationality groups are black U.S. natives, nonblack U.S. natives, Mexican immigrants, other Latin American immigrants, European immigrants, Asian immigrants, and other immigrants. We then calculate the average hourly wage for full-time workers in each cell using the 1980 census PUMS and weight individuals by the estimated average wage for their sex-age-education-nationality cell in 1980.

41. An alternative way to examine the effects of immigration would be to look at

The Aggregate Factor Proportions Approach

Trade theorists have long recognized that trade and immigration (and international capital flows) are potentially substitute ways for a country to make use of factors that are scarce within its borders.[42] Nevertheless, empirical studies of trade and immigration have proceeded independently. To the extent that trade and immigration are substitute means of altering effective national factor proportions, it is incorrect to analyze them separately. Examining how changes in trade affect U.S. workers without recognizing that in the absence of trade there will be increased economic incentives for greater immigration (or capital flows) will likely overstate the effects of trade. Examining how immigration affects U.S. workers without recognizing that reduced levels of immigration will create incentives for greater trade (and capital flows) will likely overstate the economic effects of immigration.

In earlier work, we tried to remedy this problem by analyzing how trade and immigration *together* alter the nation's endowments of labor skills.[43] The basic idea of our aggregate factor proportions approach is to compare the nation's actual supplies of skilled and unskilled labor to those it would have had at different levels of immigration or trade; and then to assess the relative wage consequences of these immigration- or trade-induced changes in factor supplies, where the effective factor endowment of a given skill group is the sum of the number of native workers, the number of immigrants, and the number of workers "em-

wages or employment on an occupational basis. Complaints by groups of mathematicians and software engineers about immigrant competition and the American Medical Association's proposal to restrict foreign supply of medical personnel show that native workers in these areas perceive considerable competition from foreign-born workers. There is, however, a major problem in using occupations as a unit of observation over the period covered by the immigration shock: the Census Bureau implemented a major reclassification of occupations between the 1970 and 1980 censuses (U.S. Bureau of the Census, 1989). Our own exploratory work relating occupational earnings to immigrant intensities suggests that empirical results are sensitive to the concordance among the occupations over the period. In our view, an occupations-based approach merits further study as an alternative to the spatial correlations approach, bearing in mind this basic problem. For an insightful study using occupations as the unit of analysis, see Friedberg (1996), who uses data on the occupational distribution of recent Russian immigrants to Israel before and after immigration to examine effects of immigration on Israeli natives.

42. See Mundell (1957) for this view of trade and immigration.

43. Borjas, Freeman, and Katz (1992, 1996).

bodied'' in net imports. We estimate the latter using fixed coefficient factor content calculations.

In its simplest form, our analysis uses a constant elasticity of substitution (CES) aggregate production function with two inputs: skilled labor (s) and unskilled labor (u). We postulate that relative wages are determined by the intersection of an inelastic (predetermined) short-run relative labor supply function and a downward-sloping relative labor demand function derived from the CES. In this framework, skilled wages relative to unskilled wages in year t, w_{st}/w_{ut}, will depend on the relative labor supplies in year t, x_{st}/x_{ut}, and the level of relative labor demand, so that

$$(14) \qquad \ln \frac{w_{st}}{w_{ut}} = \frac{1}{\sigma} \left(D_t - \ln \frac{x_{st}}{x_{ut}} \right),$$

where σ is the aggregate elasticity of substitution between skilled and unskilled workers and D_t indexes log relative demand shifts for skilled workers.[44] The impact of a given change in relative skill supplies depends inversely on the magnitude of σ.

As noted, the national (implicit) supply of skill group k at time t has three components: native workers (N_{kt}), immigrant workers (M_{kt}), and the effective supply of workers of type k contained in net trade flows (T_{kt}):

$$(15) \qquad x_{kt} = N_{kt} + M_{kt} + T_{kt} = N_{kt} \left(1 + \frac{M_{kt} + T_{kt}}{N_{kt}} \right).$$

The log relative supply of skilled workers is affected by the skill composition of the native work force and the relative contributions of immigration and trade to the supplies of skilled and unskilled workers:

$$(16) \qquad \ln \frac{x_{st}}{x_{ut}} = \ln \frac{N_{st}}{N_{ut}} + \ln \left(1 + \frac{M_{st} + T_{st}}{N_{st}} \right) - \ln \left(1 + \frac{M_{ut} + T_{ut}}{N_{ut}} \right).$$

---

44. The aggregate elasticity of substitution (σ) reflects not only technical substitution possibilities in production at the firm or industry level, but also consumer substitution possibilities across goods and services. The appropriate value of σ for assessing how aggregate changes in relative skill supplies affect relative wages is likely to be substantially larger than the elasticity of substitution in production of skilled and unskilled workers for a representative firm or industry.

We assume that the stock of immigrants at time t is predetermined relative to trade flows. Thus the separate contributions of immigration and trade to the log relative supply of skilled workers, $\ln(x_{st}/x_{ut})$, are given by

$$(17) \quad \text{immigration contribution} = \ln\left(1 + \frac{M_{st}}{N_{st}}\right) - \ln\left(1 + \frac{M_{ut}}{N_{ut}}\right)$$

and

$$(18) \quad \text{trade contribution} = \ln\left(1 + \frac{T_{st}}{L_{st}}\right) - \ln\left(1 + \frac{T_{ut}}{L_{ut}}\right),$$

where $L_{kt} = N_{kt} + M_{kt}$ is the direct labor supply of group k (both native- and foreign-born).

To use equations 14, 17, and 18 to assess how immigration and trade affect the wages of more skilled natives relative to those of less skilled natives, we need the following information: the change in the number of immigrants relative to natives with different levels of skill; the implicit change in skill supplies embodied in trade; and an estimate of the responsiveness of relative wages to relative skill supplies $(1/\sigma)$. We also need to aggregate heterogeneous workers into our aggregates of skilled and of unskilled labor. Since the aggregate factor proportions approach simulates what might have happened to the labor market under different immigration and trade scenarios, we must also carefully specify the counterfactual under consideration.

When Are Factor Contents Useful?

Under what conditions will this framework provide useful insight into the effects of immigration and trade on the labor market? The first condition is that changes in national relative skill supplies affect national relative wages. If the world economy were sufficiently integrated to create factor price equalization among countries, then relative labor supply conditions in the world would enter the wage determination equation.[45] Neither national demand nor national supply conditions

---

45. For this argument in relation to the world economy, see Leamer (1996a); and in relation to the Organisation for Economic Co-operation and Development, see Davis (1996) and Krugman (1995a).

would affect relative wages, except to the extent they changed relative demand and supply within the world economy. But a large body of empirical evidence shows that national economic conditions *do* affect relative wages by skill and education. Many time-series studies of the United States find that increases in the (detrended) relative supply of more educated workers are negatively related to changes in the relative wages of more educated workers.[46] Similar correlations have been found for many other countries, including Britain, Canada, South Korea, and Sweden.[47] Canada and the United States have sufficiently separate labor markets that differences in the rates of growth of the relative supply of college-educated workers from the 1970s to the 1980s help to explain the much larger growth in the college–high school wage differential in the United States during the 1980s.[48] More generally, research indicates that levels and changes in relative pay by skill across countries depend substantially on national wage-setting institutions and relative skill supplies.[49]

The second condition is that one can define skill categories to distinguish which groups of immigrants and natives are substitutes or complements. The standard assumption is that persons with the same number of years of schooling are perfect substitutes and those with different levels of schooling are imperfect substitutes (possibly, complements). But immigrants earn less than natives with the same schooling, so perhaps they should be viewed as substitutes for natives with modestly lower education. A sizable number of immigrants have less than nine years of schooling, which could make them complements even for native high school dropouts with nine to eleven years of schooling. And some immigrants work in specialized areas where they may complement natives with similar skills—for example, as language teachers or owners of specialty restaurants.

Determining which groups of immigrants compete with which groups of natives is not a trivial issue. If one uses years of schooling to define skill categories, one obtains different pictures of immigrant effects on factor proportions depending on where one cuts the schooling distri-

46. Freeman (1975); Katz and Murphy (1992); Murphy and Welch (1992).
47. On these countries respectively, see Schmitt (1995), Freeman and Needels (1993), Kim and Topel (1995), and Edin and Holmlund (1995).
48. Freeman and Needels (1993).
49. See, for example, Blau and Kahn (1996) and Freeman and Katz (1994).

bution. We deal with this problem by specifying competing native groups based both on alternative educational groupings and on the position of immigrants in the native earnings distribution.

The third condition is that the estimate of the effect of trade on national skill proportions captures the full impact of trade on wages. This is a contentious and difficult issue, on which trade economists have divergent views. Some believe that factor content analyses are essentially meaningless; others regard them as a valid measure of potential trade effects on the labor market for modest trade shocks relative to a well-defined baseline scenario. Some argue that all the information needed to assess the effects of trade on the labor market is contained in the prices of traded goods, which have magnified effects on wages, and that actual trade flows are irrelevant. Little did we realize when we wrote our 1992 paper using factor content analysis that the field would become such a battle zone.[50]

There are circumstances under which factor content analyses are justifiable in standard trade models. If one begins with autarky and then allows for trade, and trade is a modest proportion of the national economy, the change in national factor endowments due to the factor content of trade measures the pressure of trade for changes in relative wages.[51] In this scenario, as in our model, the fall of trade barriers creates a flow of tradables whose factor content times the reciprocal of the appropriate elasticity of substitution produces the implied effect of the opening of trade on relative wages.

But there are also circumstances under which the flows of traded goods may bear little or no relation to the pressure from trade on wages. As an extreme case, suppose that an LDC firm begins producing souvenirs of the Empire State building and informs souvenir stands that it can provide products at lower prices than U.S. producers. The souvenir stands will then inform American manufacturers that they have to meet the new price to keep their business. The U.S. firms, in turn, will tell their workers that the firms can stay in business only if the workers take a pay cut. If the workers accept the cut, the U.S. firms will maintain

50. On the problems with factor content analyses, see Leamer (1996b) and Deardorff and Hakura (1994); on their validity, see Deardorff and Staiger (1988), Krugman (1995b), Sachs and Shatz (1994), and Wood (1994, 1995); and on the irrelevance of actual trade flows, see Bhagwati and Dehejia (1994).
51. Deardorff and Staiger (1988); Krugman (1995b).

their hold on the souvenir market, with no new trade flows. But the threat of trade (like the threat of entry in a contestable market) will have reduced wages in the United States. In this example, the only "footprint" of trade is the change in the relative price of souvenirs. This is, in stark form, the argument that trade flows do not accurately reflect trade pressures on the labor market.

This model is difficult to assess empirically, and there have been only limited efforts to do so.[52] The analyst must show, first, that the domestic relative price of goods produced by the less skilled has fallen; and second, that this price change is due to the "unobservable" threat of trade rather than some other factor (for example, differences in sectoral rates of technological change or, as in the 1980s, a fall in the real value of the minimum wage). If foreign goods are imperfect substitutes for U.S.–made goods in the same sector, the analyst must assess the degree of substitutability. In a world in which product and labor demand curves in traded goods are not perfectly elastic at the "going world price" and in which native workers in the traded goods sector may earn some economic rents, trade may also alter the wage structure by making demand curves more elastic and squeezing those rents.[53] Moreover, the model implies that labor skill ratios fall within sectors, as firms substitute toward the low-skill workers displaced from import-competing industries—which is contrary to the observed rise in those ratios.[54] While the price-side model may be hard to estimate, it does suggest that factor content analyses that infer the effect of trade on implicit national factor endowments from observed trade flows are likely to understate the impact of trade on relative wages.[55]

There is yet another area of controversy in factor content analysis. The standard analysis estimates the labor supply embodied in traded goods using current average unit labor coefficients for different skill categories from import-competing and export-producing sectors in the

52. See, for example, Sachs and Shatz (1994), Krueger (1997), and Baldwin and Cain (1997).
53. On the elasticity of demand curves, see Rodrik (1997); on the squeezing of rents, see Borjas and Ramey (1995).
54. See Lawrence and Slaughter (1993), Berman, Bound, and Griliches (1994), and Autor, Katz, and Krueger (1997).
55. Baldwin and Cain (1997) provide a useful examination of the evidence on price effects and find similar modest impacts of trade on U.S. relative wages using both the price and factor content approaches.

home economy.[56] But Adrian Wood argues that one should not use unit labor coefficients from current advanced country production relations when assessing the factor content of imports from LDCs to advanced industrial nations.[57] One reason is that within every sector there is a wide distribution of labor input coefficients, reflecting differences in skill intensities of employment, differences in labor productivity, and differentiated products. If LDC trade has driven out the most unskilled labor–intensive modes of production from an import-competing industry, current average labor input coefficients will understate the effect of LDC trade in augmenting the effective supply of less skilled workers in advanced nations. The appropriate labor input coefficients are those for the marginal technologies and products that would expand in import-competing sectors absent this trade. Wood also argues that firms may alter their technologies or input coefficients in response to trade pressures.

We are sympathetic to Wood's argument. As he emphasizes, there is substantial heterogeneity in the relative utilization of less skilled workers (that is, high school dropouts) across plants. Tabulations from the Worker-Establishment Characteristic Database (WECD), an employer-employee matched database for U.S. manufacturing in 1990 compiled by the U.S. Bureau of the Census, show substantial differences in the educational composition of the work force within detailed manufacturing industries.[58] Within the typical three-digit industry, the employment share of high school dropouts in the bottom quarter of plants, ranked by average worker education, is 2.4 times the industry average (0.40 versus 0.17).[59] Mark Doms, Timothy Dunne, and Kenneth Troske find that establishments with less educated workers are much less likely to use new technologies than those with more skilled workers in the same industry. J. Bradford Jensen and Troske find that in most four-digit manufacturing industries in 1992, the ninetieth percentile plant (ranked by labor productivity) had labor productivity that was over three times that of the tenth percentile plant.[60] If LDC imports

56. See, for example, Sachs and Shatz (1994).
57. Wood (1994, 1995).
58. We are grateful to Kenneth Troske for these tabulations. The WECD is documented and described in Troske (1995) and Doms, Dunne, and Troske (1997).
59. The bottom quarter of plants, in terms of average worker education, employ 15 percent of all workers in the typical industry.
60. Doms, Dunne, and Troske (1997); Jensen and Troske (1997).

affect the less skilled and lower productivity segment of a three-digit industry, then the actual increment to the implicit supply of low-skilled workers from such trade flows could easily be three times larger than the estimates based on current average industry skill shares and labor productivity levels.

To address this issue, Wood takes input coefficients from LDCs and adjusts them for relative wages in the United States or western Europe to approximate marginal input coefficients and assumes that, absent trade, technologies would not improve in the traded goods sector. Elsewhere, we use input coefficients averaged over an earlier period (1967–87), but do not examine the sensitivity of results to alternative assumptions.[61] In the present study, we use U.S. input coefficients (skill shares) from past years (1970, 1980, 1990) and carefully specify our assumptions about the technology for producing import-competing and other goods and product demand responses.

The Facts to Be Explained

It is well documented that educational wage differentials and overall wage inequality have greatly increased in the United States since the late 1970s. Most estimates of changes in educational wage differentials are based on samples containing both U.S. natives and immigrants.[62] Since recent immigrants typically earn less than U.S. natives with the same level of education, the disproportionately growing share of immigrants among less educated workers in the United States means that the usual estimates may overstate changes in relative wages by education for U.S. natives. To assess the contributions of immigration- and trade-induced changes in relative labor supplies on the relative wages of U.S. natives requires estimates of changes in educational wage differentials for U.S. natives alone.

Table 12 presents estimates for three measures of educational wage differentials for natives between 1960 and 1995. The differentials are derived from cross-section regressions of log hourly earnings on five education dummies (zero to eight years of schooling, nine to eleven years, thirteen to fifteen years, sixteen years, and seventeen plus years,

61. Borjas, Freeman, and Katz (1992).
62. See, for example, Bound and Johnson (1992) and Mishel, Bernstein, and Schmitt (1997).

George J. Borjas, Richard B. Freeman, and Lawrence F. Katz 47

Table 12. Native Log Wage Differentials, by Educational Attainment, 1960–95[a]
Log point difference

Year	College graduate relative to high school graduate[b]	College or more relative to high school graduate[c]	High school or more relative to high school dropout[d]
1960	0.319	0.317	0.280
1970	0.362	0.374	0.312
1980	0.279	0.304	0.301
1990	0.412	0.458	0.374
1995	0.420	0.495	0.410

Source: Authors' calculations. Wage data for 1960–90 actually refer to 1959, 1969, 1979, and 1989 and are from the census PUMS. Wages for 1995 are extrapolated from the 1990 census PUMS, using observed changes between the February 1990 CPS and the 1995 CPS, MORG file.
a. Wages are hourly earnings of full-time native wage and salary workers aged eighteen to sixty-four, adjusted for age, sex, race, and region, as described in the text.
b. Log wage of natives with exactly sixteen years of schooling less that of natives with exactly twelve years.
c. Log wage of natives with sixteen or more years of schooling less that of natives with exactly twelve years.
d. Log wage of natives with twelve or more years of schooling less that of natives with fewer than twelve years.

with twelve years as the base group), a quartic in age, a female dummy, a nonwhite dummy, and three region dummies. Our samples comprise native full-time workers aged eighteen to sixty-four, from the 1960, 1970, 1980, and 1990 census PUMSs and the Merged Outgoing Rotation Group (MORG) file of the 1995 Current Population Survey (CPS) from the Bureau of Labor Statistics. The first column of table 12 displays the log wage gap between workers with exactly sixteen years of schooling (college graduates) and those with exactly twelve years of schooling (high school graduates). The second column expands the college group to include those with advanced degrees. Both measures of the college–high school wage differential expand modestly in the 1960s, contract in the 1970s, and increase substantially in the 1980s. The growth rate in the college–high school wage gap slows down from 1990 to 1995, but the increase over this period remains sizable when those with advanced degrees are included in the college group. The time pattern of changes in the college–high school wage gap for natives is quite similar to estimates for the overall U.S. work force, using samples that include both immigrants and natives.[63]

The last column of table 12 examines the wage of native high school dropouts relative to that of natives with at least twelve years of schooling. High school dropouts are the group most likely to be adversely

63. See, for example, Autor, Katz, and Krueger (1997).

affected by the recent growth of less skilled immigration and trade with LDCs. The relative earnings of native high school dropouts declined by 0.073 log point from 1980 to 1990 and continued to decline at the same rate in the early 1990s.

Note that there has been a decline in the relative wages of less educated workers since 1980, even though the relative supply (of both natives and immigrants) has continued to decline. Table 13 documents changes in the educational composition of direct U.S. labor input (natives plus immigrants), measured in full-time equivalents (or total hours worked), from 1960 to 1995.[64] Although the share of high school dropouts has declined consistently and the share of college equivalents has grown throughout the past thirty-five years, the rate of growth of the relative supply of more educated workers accelerated in the 1970s and decelerated in the 1980s. The slower growth of the relative supply of skills may help to explain the quite different outcomes for relative wages by education in the 1970s and in the 1980s and 1990s illustrated in table 12.

To examine the impact of the supply shifts induced by trade and immigration on native relative wages, we aggregate workers into skill groups in two ways. First, following David Autor, Katz, and Alan Krueger and also George Johnson, we aggregate the labor force into high school equivalents (all workers with twelve or fewer years of schooling and one-half of those with some college education) and college equivalents (all workers with at least a college degree and one-half of those with some college education).[65] Katz and Kevin Murphy show

64. Changes introduced in the 1990 census to the educational attainment question make it difficult to assess accurately changes in relative education supplies over the 1980s using the public use samples of the 1980 and 1990 censuses. The CPS continued to use the old question ("highest grade attended and completed") through 1991. Thus the 1980 and 1990 CPS, MORG files have consistent education coding and can be used to measure changes in relative supplies by educational group. The February 1990 CPS asked individuals about educational attainment with both the new and the old questions. We estimate changes from 1990 to 1995 using the February 1990 CPS and the 1995 CPS, MORG file. Changes from 1990 to 1995 should be interpreted with some caution, because the complete overhaul of the CPS in 1994, with the shift to computer-assisted interviewing, implies the possibility of unknown differences in responses to education questions. We use the coding scheme suggested by Jaeger (1997) for the new census and CPS education codes, classifying workers indicating twelve years of schooling but no degree as high school graduates. The data appendix of Autor, Katz, and Krueger (1997) provides additional information on these issues of data comparability.

65. Autor, Katz, and Krueger (1997); Johnson (1997a).

Table 13. Distribution of U.S. Workers by Educational Attainment, 1960–95

Percent

Year	Data source	Full-time equivalent emloyment shares[a]					
		High school dropouts[b]	High school graduates[c]	Some college[d]	College graduates[e,c]	College equivalents[f]	High school or more[g]
Levels							
1960	Census	49.5	27.7	12.2	10.6	16.7	...
1970	Census	35.9	34.7	15.6	13.8	21.6	...
1980	Census	20.7	36.1	22.8	20.4	31.8	...
1980	CPS, MORG	19.1	38.0	22.0	20.9	31.9	...
1990	CPS, MORG	12.7	36.2	25.1	26.1	38.6	...
1990	Census	11.4	33.0	30.2	25.4	40.6	...
1990	CPS, February	11.5	36.8	25.2	26.5	39.1	...
1995	CPS, MORG	9.0	33.7	29.4	27.9	42.6	...
Changes in log relative employment[h]							
1960–70	Census	...	...	...	...	3.19	5.62
1970–80	Census	...	...	...	...	5.26	7.61
1980–90	CPS, MORG	...	...	...	...	2.94	4.86
1990–95	CPS, February to MORG	...	...	...	...	2.94	5.41

Source: Autor, Katz, and Krueger (1997, table 1).
a. Hours worked by workers (natives and immigrants) in given skill group as proportion of all hours worked.
b. Fewer than twelve years of schooling.
c. Exactly twelve years of schooling.
d. Thirteen to fifteen years of schooling.
e. Sixteen or more years of schooling.
f. All those with sixteen or more years of schooling plus half of those with some college.
g. Twelve or more years of schooling.
h. Average annual log changes ($\times$ 100) in relative full-time equivalent employment shares.

50   *Brookings Papers on Economic Activity, 1:1997*

that detrended changes in the supplies of similar aggregates of college equivalents relative to high school equivalents do a reasonable job of explaining changes in a broad measure of the college–high school wage differentials such as that presented in the second column of table 12.[66] They estimate a version of equation 14 and find the elasticity of the relative wage of college graduates to changes in the relative supply of college equivalents is approximately -0.709 (implying an economy-wide estimate of the elasticity of substitution between college equivalents and high school equivalents, σ, of 1.41). Thus we calculate immigration- and trade-induced changes in the relative supplies of college and high school equivalents and examine the implied relative wage effects using the Katz-Murphy estimate of the wage elasticity.

Second, we divide the labor force into high school dropouts and all other workers and use an estimated wage elasticity for the response of the relative wage of dropouts to their relative supply of -0.322, from time-series estimates covering the period 1963–87 that we report in an earlier study.[67]

We address compositional changes within our broad educational groups by adjusting the changes in hours by skill group into efficiency units, by weighting each individual's hours by the average wage of an individual with similar observed characteristics (that is, sex, age, education, and nationality) in a base period (1980).[68]

The Effect of Immigration on Relative Labor Supplies

Table 14 shows our estimates of the contribution of immigration to labor supply in efficiency units by broad educational groups from 1960 to 1995. The first two columns display the immigrant-to-native effi-

66. Katz and Murphy (1992).
67. Borjas, Freeman, and Katz (1992).
68. Katz and Murphy (1992) provide a justification for this efficiency units approach to aggregation in measuring how relative supply and demand shifts affect relative wages by skill group. In the present study, we divide the labor force aged eighteen to sixty-four into 280 distinct groups based on sex-age-education-nationality cells (2 sex groups × 5 age groups × 4 education groups × 7 nationality groups = 280 cells). We calculate the average hourly wage for full-time workers in each cell using the 1 percent random sample from the 1980 census PUMS for natives and 5 percent random sample from the 1980 census PUMS for immigrants. Thus we weight each individual's annual hours of work by the estimated average wage for their sex-age-education-nationality cell in 1980. See note 40 for more details on the definition of the groups.

Table 14. Immigrant Contribution to Labor Supply, by Educational Attainment, 1960–95

Ratio

	Immigrant-to-native ratio[a]						
	High school dropouts versus graduates			High school versus college equivalents			
Sample and year	Dropouts[b]	Graduates[c]	Log gap[d]	High school[e]	College[f]	Log gap[d]
All immigrants						
1960	0.088	0.051	0.035	0.068	0.061	0.007
1970	0.069	0.046	0.022	0.051	0.059	−0.007
1980	0.109	0.058	0.047	0.063	0.073	−0.009
1990	0.242	0.079	0.141	0.094	0.090	0.004
1995	0.383	0.083	0.244	0.107	0.090	0.015
Post-1979 immigrants[g]						
1995	0.207	0.041	0.149	0.056	0.043	0.013

Source: Authors' calculations. Data for 1960–90 are from the census PUMS (various years); and for 1995, from the 1995 CPS, MORG file.
a. Ratios are in efficiency units, which weigh each worker by hours worked times the typical wage of a worker of the same age, sex, nationality, and education in 1980.
b. Fewer than twelve years of schooling.
c. At least twelve years of schooling.
d. $\ln(1 + M_{ut}/N_{ut}) - \ln(1 + M_{st}/N_{st})$, where M and N are, respectively, immigrant and native workers (in efficiency units), and u and s refer, respectively, to the lesser and greater of the two categories of educational attainment being compared.
e. All of those with twelve or fewer years of schooling plus half of those with some college.
f. All of those with sixteen or more years of schooling plus half of those with some college.
g. Immigrants who arrived before 1980 are treated as natives.

ciency unit ratios (M/N) for high school dropouts and those with at least twelve years of schooling. The third column follows equation 17 in presenting the immigration contribution to the log supply of dropouts relative to more educated workers. The estimates for all immigrants in table 14 show the growing contribution of immigration to the supply of high school dropouts, especially since 1980; the ratio of immigrants to natives among dropouts increased from 0.109 in 1980 to 0.383 in 1995.[69] These changes reflect both the rapid decline of the share of native labor force participants who are dropouts and the increased immigration since 1980, while there was little decline in the share of immigrant workers who have less than twelve years of schooling.

Some of the growth shown in table 14 in the immigrant contribution to the relative supply of dropouts since 1980 would have occurred even if immigration had been cut off in 1980. This is because of differences in the age structure of less educated immigrants and natives in 1980. To determine the effect on the labor supply by education of those immigrants who entered after 1979, in the last row of table 14 we treat all immigrants living in the United States before 1980 as natives. Post-1979 immigrants increased the relative supply of dropouts in 1995 by 0.149 log point, which is 0.048 log point smaller than the 0.197 log point increase from 1980 to 1995 shown in the upper panel of the table.

With our preferred relative wage elasticity for dropouts of -0.322, the estimates in the first three columns of table 14 imply that the immigrant contribution to the relative supply of dropouts can explain a change in the wage of dropouts relative to that of nondropouts of be-

69. The Census Bureau switched its approach to adjusting sampling weights by age, sex, race or Hispanic origin, and state starting with the implementation of the revised CPS survey in 1994. Barry Edmonston has pointed out to us, in personal communication, that demographers have raised concerns that the official sampling weights may underweight the Asian and American Indian populations by 30 percent or more in the 1995 CPS. Since Asians are disproportionately immigrants, and more educated than the typical immigrant, our tabulations of immigrant employment and efficiency unit shares from the 1995 CPS, MORG file may slightly overestimate the relative contribution of immigrants to less educated skill groups in comparison with more educated skill groups. We checked the sensitivity of all our findings from the 1995 CPS increasing the relative weights of Asians and American Indians in the sample by 30 percent. The effects of this adjustment are modest in every case and lead to no substantive changes in our conclusions. For example, the log relative supply contribution of immigrants to dropouts declines from 0.244 to 0.243 and the log relative supply contribution of immigrants to high school equivalents declines from 0.015 to 0.012, when the 1995 CPS sample is reweighted in this manner.

tween -0.048 and -0.063 log point from 1980 to 1995. Thus the factor proportions approach, treating immigrant and native efficiency units within the dropout and graduate skill categories as perfect substitutes, implies that immigration-induced changes in labor supply may account for 44 to 58 percent of the 0.109 log point decline in the relative earnings of dropouts over this period.

The last three columns of table 14 reveal only modest effects of immigration on the supply of high school equivalents relative to college equivalents. Since the education distribution of immigrants is bimodal—many have less than twelve years of schooling and many have college and advanced degrees—the effect of immigration on relative skill supplies is greatly diminished when one aggregates workers into high school and college equivalent workers. The estimate for all immigrants puts the immigration impact on the relative supply of high school equivalents at 0.024 log point from 1980 to 1995. The estimate for post-1979 immigrants indicates that these expanded the relative supply of high school equivalents by 0.013 log point in 1995. Using our preferred relative wage elasticity of -0.709, we estimate that the contribution of immigration to changes in the college–high school wage differential from 1980 to 1995 ranges from 0.009 to 0.017 log point; or 5 to 9 percent of the actual 0.191 log point increase in the college–high school wage differential for U.S. natives over this period.

We conclude that the immigrant-induced increases in relative labor supply are strongly concentrated on U.S. workers with fewer than twelve years of schooling and that the slowdown in the rate of decline of the relative supply of dropouts due to unskilled immigration may explain a sizable fraction of the decline in the earnings of dropouts relative to those with twelve or more years of schooling over the period 1980–95. In contrast, the immigrant supply contribution for a broader group of less educated workers is too small to account for even 10 percent of the sharp growth in the college–high school wage differential during this period.

In our assessment of the immigrant contribution to changes in skill supplies, we classify workers into skill groups by years of schooling. Under this approach, the impact of less skilled immigration on the relative supply of less educated natives is magnified by the rapidly declining share of high school dropouts in the native labor force. But low-wage and less skilled immigrants may compete with a broader group of low-wage natives than native high school dropouts. As an alternative way to measure immigrant-induced changes in labor market competition, we classify workers into skill groups based on their hourly wages rather than level of education. We sort workers by wages in each year (1980, 1990, and 1995) and define skill groups by percentile cut-off points in the native wage distribution.[70] We focus on two aggregation schemes: (a) workers with wages above and below the twentieth percentile of the native wage distribution (since the share of dropouts in the labor force in 1980, when the large immigration shock began, was approximately 20 percent); and (b) workers with wages above and below the sixtieth percentile of the native wage distribution (a group close in size to high school equivalents in 1980). Immigrant contributions to the relative supply of these two groups are determined by the difference in the ratio of immigrants to natives above and below the cut-off point in the native wage distribution defining the low- and high-skill aggregates. Thus we compare how the growth of immigration differentially affects fixed shares of low- and high-wage natives.

Table 15 presents our estimates of immigrant-induced supply shifts by skill groups defined by percentiles of the native wage distribution. It indicates that immigrants are increasingly concentrated in the lower parts of the native wage distribution. For all immigrants, the table shows that the log relative supply contribution of immigrants to the bottom 20 percent of natives relative to the upper 80 percent increased from 0.030 log point to 0.130 log point between 1980 and 1995. The lower panel shows that immigrants who arrived since 1980 expanded the relative supply of the bottom 20 percent of native workers in 1995 by a similar amount, 0.094 log point. Comparing these results with those in table 14, we conclude that the post-1979 immigration relative supply increment to less-skilled labor is modestly lower when measured relative to a fixed share of low-wage natives rather than relative to the declining share of high school dropouts. The contribution of recent immigrants to the relative supply of workers earning wages below the sixtieth native percentile is actually somewhat larger than the immigrant

70. Specifically, we adjust wages for differences in sex, age, and region. For each year, we run a regression of log hourly wages of U.S. natives on a quartic in age, a female dummy, an interaction of age and the female dummy, and three region dummies. We then sort both natives and immigrants by their adjusted log hourly wages (actual log hourly wage less the predicted wage from this native wage regression).

Table 15. Immigrant Contribution to the Labor Supply, by Wage Group, 1980–95

Ratio

	Immigrant-to-native ratio[a]								
	Twentieth percentile wage cut			Sixtieth percentile wage cut					
Sample and year	Bottom 20 percent	Top 80 percent	Log gap[b]	Bottom 60 percent	Top 40 percent	Log gap[b]
All immigrants						
1980	0.094	0.062	0.030	0.075	0.058	0.016
1990	0.149	0.085	0.057	0.110	0.079	0.028
1995	0.229	0.079	0.130	0.136	0.069	0.060
Post-1979 immigrants[c]						
1995	0.145	0.042	0.094	0.084	0.032	0.049

Source: Authors' calculations. Data for 1980–90 are from the census PUMS (various years); and for 1995, from the 1995 CPS, MORG file.

a. Ratio is hours worked by immigrants divided by hours worked by natives. Wage groups sort workers on the basis of whether their adjusted wages are above or below the wage received by natives in the given percentile of the adjusted wage distribution for natives. Wages are adjusted for age, sex, and region.

b. $\ln(1 + M_{sl}/N_{sl}) - \ln(1 + M_{ul}/N_{ul})$, where M and N are, respectively, the number of immigrant and native worker-hours, and u and s refer, respectively, to those in the lower and higher wage groups being compared.

c. Immigrants who arrived before 1980 are treated as natives.

effect on the relative supply of high school equivalents, since a disproportionate number of college-educated immigrants earn relatively low
wages.

Both the educational group and wage group approaches to measuring
the effects of immigrants on relative skill supplies may overstate the
effects of immigrant competition on low-skill natives. If immigrants
and natives with similar education, or wages, or both operate in partially
segmented labor markets, changes in immigrant supply may have little
impact on native wages. The growing share of immigrants in the lower
part of the native wage distribution may reflect declining labor market
conditions due to immigrant crowding into a segmented immigrant labor
market, rather than increased competition for low-wage natives. It is
difficult to assess this alternative hypothesis within our framework.
However, David Jaeger presents some aggregate and metropolitan area–
level data from the 1980 and 1990 censuses indicating that changes in
the relative supply of immigrants to natives within sex-education groups
have little effect on the immigrant-native wage gap for a given group.[71]
This evidence suggests that immigrants and natives may be nearly perfect substitutes in production within broad educational groups (as we
assume in our education-based approach).

The Effect of LDC Trade on Implicit Relative Labor Supplies

We next examine the extent to which increased trade between the
United States and less developed countries has implicitly augmented
the relative supply of less skilled workers in the U.S. labor market.
The growth of such trade has accelerated in the 1990s, with LDC
imports as a percentage of GDP rising from 2.3 percent in 1980 to 2.8
percent in 1990 and to 4.1 percent in 1996. Trade in manufactures with
less developed countries has the potential to affect less skilled U.S.
workers adversely, since, as illustrated in table 4, LDC imports are
concentrated in industries that disproportionately employ less educated
workers and exports to LDCs are found in industries that are much more
skill intensive. If the impact of LDC trade is concentrated on industries
disproportionately employing high school dropouts, and if the appropriate skill coefficients to assess the effects of such trade on the nation's
factor proportions differ greatly from the average skill coefficients used

71. Jaeger (1995).

in most factor content studies, LDC trade may have a significant effect on the least skilled workers, whose relative wages have been falling sharply.[72]

We examine the implications of eliminating trade with LDCs in manufactures, using equation 18 under different assumptions concerning the skill-intensity and productivity of U.S. production that would replace LDC imports. We first follow the standard practice of estimating the labor supply embodied in both LDC and developed country trade flows in a given year, using that year's average unit labor coefficients for different skill groups of U.S. production in the three-digit manufacturing industries in which the imports and exports arise. More precisely, we estimate the implicit labor supply (in efficiency units) of skill group k embodied in trade in manufactures in year t as

$$(20) \qquad T_{kt} = \sum_l e_{klt} L_{lt} \frac{TR_{lt}}{S_{lt}},$$

where e_{klt} is the proportion of group k (in labor efficiency units) in industry l in year t; L_{lt} is the total labor efficiency units used in industry l in year t; and TR_{lt}/S_{lt} is the ratio of imports less exports to shipments for industry l in year t. The proportional impact of trade on the labor supply of skill group k in year t is then given by T_{kt}/L_{kt} where L_{kt} is the total efficiency units of group k (both natives and immigrants) employed in the aggregate U.S. labor market in year t.[73]

We examine imports by source country and exports by receiving country for manufactures measured at the three-digit industry level. We classify western European countries (except Greece and Portugal), Australia, New Zealand, Japan, and Canada as developed countries and we include U.S. trade flows with all other countries in the LDC trade flow aggregate.

Table 16 shows the effect of LDC and developed country trade on

---

72. Thus analyses that aggregate workers into categories such as high school and college equivalents or production and nonproduction workers and assume that LDC imports displace domestic production at average current sectoral factor ratios (for example, Sachs and Shatz, 1994; Krugman, 1995a; and Lawrence, 1996) may understate the impact of LDC trade on the smaller but highly exposed group of least skilled workers (that is, high school dropouts).

73. Since overall U.S. trade and trade with LDCs in manufactures are not balanced, we implicitly assume that any scale (aggregate demand) effects of trade deficits have skill-neutral effects on labor demand.

Table 16. Implicit Contribution of Trade to Labor Supply, by Skill Group, 1980–90[a]

Ratio

Year and trading partners[c]	Ratio of trade-embodied labor to total labor[b]					
	High school dropouts versus graduates			High school versus college equivalents		
	Dropouts[d]	Graduates[c]	Log gap[f]	High school[e]	College[h]	Log gap[f]
1980						
LDCs	0.0012	−0.0026	0.0038	−0.0014	−0.0027	0.0013
Developed countries	0.0043	0.0012	0.0031	0.0029	−0.0003	0.0032
1990						
LDCs	0.0135	0.0031	0.0103	0.0068	0.0016	0.0052
Developed countries	0.0054	0.0023	0.0031	0.0044	0.0007	0.0037

Source: Authors' calculations. Data on skill group shares and industry employment are from the census PUMS (various years); and on industry shipments, from the NBER Productivity Database. Also (see note a) Sachs and Shatz (1994) and Autor, Krueger, and Katz (1997).

a. Imports (by country of origin) and exports (by receiving country) in manufactures are allocated to a consistent set of set of three-digit Census of Population industries, using trade flow data from Sachs and Shatz and industry code concordances from Autor, Katz, and Krueger. 1980 trade flows by country and industry are proxied by 1978 trade flows.

b. Estimated as T_{kt}/L_{kt}, where T_{kt}, trade-embodied labor, is $T_{kt} = \sum_j e_{jkt} L_{jt} (TR_{jt}/S_{jt})$; e_{jkt} is the fraction of all workers in industry j at time t who fall in skill group k; L represents total labor; and

TR/S is the ratio of imports less exports to shipments. Labor is measured in efficiency units, which weight each worker by hours worked times the typical wage of a worker of the same age, sex, nationality, and education in 1980.

c. Developed country trade includes trade with western Europe (except Greece and Portugal), Australia, New Zealand, Japan, and Canada. LDC trade includes all other trade flows.

d. Fewer than twelve years of schooling.

e. At least twelve years of schooling.

f. $\ln(1 + T_{ut}/L_{ut}) - \ln(1 + T_{st}/L_{st})$, where u and s refer, respectively, to the lesser and the greater of the two categories of educational attainment being compared.

g. All of those with twelve or fewer years of schooling plus half of those with some college.

h. All of those with sixteen or more years of schooling plus half of those with some college.

labor supply by education in 1980 and 1990, using the contemporary average unit labor coefficients and following the approach of equation 18. The implicit relative labor supply effects of trade are quite small in 1980 and increase only modestly (0.007 log point) from 1980 to 1990. There is no noticeable change in the impact of trade with developed countries on relative labor supplies in this period. We therefore conclude that it is likely that any possible "action" in trade's impacts on different skill groups in the United States will be found in the growing trade with LDCs—specifically, in the surge of 1990–95—and will only be substantial if LDC trade displaces activities that use less skilled labor much more intensively than is reflected in contemporary industry average labor skill coefficients.

Table 17 presents estimates of the implicit effect of LDC trade on labor supply by skill in 1980, 1990, and 1995, under three alternative counterfactuals: "low," "middle," and "high". In all three counterfactuals, we assume that the reduction in domestic production from the elimination of exports to LDCs would occur at contemporary industry average skill shares and labor productivity. Andrew Bernard and Jensen document that exporting plants are more productive and employ a substantially larger share of more skilled (nonproduction) workers, on average, than other plants within the same four-digit industry.[74] The marginal production affected by reductions in exports is likely to be that of plants in the lower part of the skill and labor productivity distribution of exporting plants. The average skill shares and productivity in the industry may be a reasonable proxy for these marginal exporting plants. The low counterfactual follows table 16 in assuming that imports and exports both embody labor supply at contemporary industry average skill intensities and productivity. The middle counterfactual assumes that the implicit labor efficiency units from LDC imports in each three-digit industry are replaced by domestic production using production methods lagged by ten to fifteen years, which typically utilize a larger share of less educated labor than contemporary industry average skill shares. The high counterfactual assumes that domestic production replaces LDC imports by using average industry skill shares and labor productivity from 1970 (before the growth of LDC imports in manufactures), and that consumers have inelastic demand for the goods, so

---

74. Bernard and Jensen (1995).

Table 17. Implicit Contribution of LDC Trade to Labor Supply, Alternative Counterfactuals, 1980–95[a]

Ratio

| Year and counterfactual[k] | Ratio of LDC trade-embodied labor to total labor[b] | | | | | |
| | High school dropouts versus graduates | | | High school versus college equivalents | | |
	Dropouts[d]	Graduates[c]	Log gap[f]	High school[g]	College[h]	Log gap[f]
1980						
Low	0.0012	−0.0026	0.0038	−0.0014	−0.0027	0.0013
Middle	0.0060	−0.0036	0.0096	−0.0008	−0.0038	0.0030
High	0.0094	−0.0022	0.0116	0.0013	−0.0028	0.0041
1990						
Low	0.0135	0.0031	0.0103	0.0068	0.0016	0.0052
Middle	0.0235	0.0019	0.0213	0.0093	−0.0012	0.0105
High	0.0824	0.0199	0.0595	0.0395	0.0095	0.0293
1995						
Low	0.0253	0.0040	0.0210	0.0110	0.0014	0.0095
Middle	0.0416	0.0022	0.0386	0.0149	−0.0022	0.0169
High	0.1372	0.0273	0.1016	0.0609	0.0163	0.0429

Source: Authors' calculations for 1980 and 1990 are based on the data used for table 16. For 1995, imports-to-sales ratios by industry equal 1990 imports-to-sales ratios times 1.413 (the ratio of the LDC imports-to-GDP ratio in 1995 to the same ratio in 1990); and exports-to-sales ratios are 1990 ratios multiplied by 1.415, to adjust for growth in the LDC exports-to-GDP ratio from 1990 to 1995. Data on skill group shares and industry employment for 1995 are from the 1995 CPS. MORG file.

a. See table 16, note c for definition of LDC trade, and also note a.

b. Estimated as TX_{kt}/L_{kt}, where TX_{kt}, trade-embodied labor, is $TM_{kt} - TX_{kt}$. TM_{kt} is $\sum_l e_{klb} p_{lt} L_{lt} (IM_{lt}/S_{lt})$, where e_{klb} is the fraction of all workers in industry l in base year b who fall in skill group k; p_{lt} is the productivity adjustment taken as part of the counterfactual; L represents labor, in efficiency units; IM is imports; and S is shipments. TX_{kt} is $\sum_l e_{klb} L_{lt} (EX_{lt}/S_{lt})$, where EX is exports.

c. The "low" counterfactuals use contemporary skill shares and productivity for both imports and exports as in table 16 for 1990 and 1980, but assume 1990 factor ratios for imports in 1995. The "middle" counterfactuals allocate efficiency units in imports in industry l in year t, $L_{lt}(IM_{lt}/S_{lt})$, to skill groups using 1980 average skill shares in that industry ($b = 1980$) for 1990 and 1995. and 1970 average skill shares ($b = 1970$) for 1980. Thus $p_{lt} = 1$ in the middle counterfactuals. The "high" counterfactual allocates imports in industry l to skill groups using 1970 average skill shares in l ($b = 1970$) and adjusts upward the total efficiency units used to replace imports in order to keep output constant, assuming no productivity growth from the base year to t. Thus $p_{lt} = (L_{lt}Q_{bl}/L_{bl}Q_{lt})$ in the high counterfactuals. All counterfactuals assume that exports in l use contemporary average skill shares and productivity for industry l.

d. Fewer than twelve years of schooling.

e. At least twelve years of schooling.

f. $\ln(1 + T_{ut}/L_{ut}) - \ln(1 + T_{st}/L_{st})$, where u and s refer, respectively, to the lesser and the greater of the two categories of educational attainment being compared.

g. All of those with twelve or fewer years of schooling plus half of those with some college.

h. All of those with sixteen or more years of schooling plus half of those with some college.

that the increase in domestic output to replace imports equals the real output contained in imports. The assumptions of no technological progress since 1970 and inelastic consumer demand are extreme. We believe that the middle counterfactual is the most realistic of the three.

The estimates of the impact on relative labor supplies of LDC trade under the middle and high counterfactuals in table 17 suggest much greater effects of the growth of LDC trade on educational wage differentials than does the assumption that LDC trade displaces domestic output at current average unit labor input coefficients. The middle and high counterfactuals imply that LDC trade augmented the relative supply of dropouts by 0.04 to 0.10 log point in 1995.[75] Under these assumptions, the elimination of LDC trade in 1995 would have increased the relative wage of dropouts by 0.012 to 0.033 log point, given our assumed relative wage elasticity of -0.322. The effects are larger than in table 16, but still modest, for the supply of high school equivalents relative to college equivalents under our preferred middle counterfactual.

Summarizing the Contributions of Immigration and Trade

Table 18 summarizes our aggregate factor proportions estimates of the contributions of the post-1979 immigration and LDC trade shocks to changes in educational wage differentials from 1980 to 1995, under different assumptions about the responsiveness of relative wages to changes in relative skill supplies. We examine the counterfactual of cutting off all immigration and all growth in trade flows with LDCs in January 1, 1980. Thus we present the implied wage effects of 1995 changes in skill supplies of immigrants who arrived after 1979 and of the implicit labor supplies embodied in the change in LDC trade flows between 1980 and 1995.

75. Our estimates of the effects of LDC trade on the implicit relative supply of high school dropouts in 1990 under the high counterfactual are roughly similar to Wood's (1995) estimates of the impact of LDC trade on unskilled workers for the same year, using adjusted LDC–based labor input coefficients. Wood estimates that LDC trade reduced the demand for skilled relative to unskilled workers in manufactures by 21.5 percent (0.20 log point). If we normalize our implicit labor supply effects of LDC trade in 1990 by labor efficiency units by skill group in manufacturing, rather than in the entire economy, we obtain an relative labor supply increasing effect (and relative labor demand decreasing effect) for high school dropouts of 18 percent (0.165 log point).

Table 18. Estimated Contributions of Immigration and LDC Trade to Growth in Log Wage Differentials, 1980–95[a]

Log points, except as indicated

| | Wage comparison | | | | | |
| | High school graduates versus dropouts | | | College versus high school graduates | | |
Item						
Assumed wage elasticity	−0.2	−0.322	−0.4	−0.5	−0.709	−1
Actual change, 1980–95	0.109	0.109	0.109	0.191	0.191	0.191
Estimated contribution						
Post-1979 immigration	0.030	0.048	0.060	0.007	0.009	0.013
LDC trade	0.006	0.009	0.012	0.007	0.010	0.014
Immigration plus trade	0.036	0.057	0.072	0.014	0.019	0.027
Percent contribution[b]						
Post-1979 immigration	27	44	55	3	5	7
LDC trade	6	8	11	4	5	7
Immigration plus trade	33	52	66	7	10	14

Source: Authors' calculations based on model described in text. Actual changes in log wage differentials are from table 12. Contribution of post-1979 immigration to labor supply is from table 14. Contribution of LDC trade to labor supply is a difference over 1980–95, from table 17, using the middle counterfactual.

a. Wage differentials are measured as differences in adjusted log wages, as described in the text. Actual change in differentials is expressed in log points, as are individual contributions.

b. Log point contribution of item as percentage of actual log point change, 1980–95.

This table highlights the fact that immigration has a much larger impact on U.S. native high school dropouts than does LDC trade. The impact of post-1979 immigrants on relative skill supplies can explain a 0.030 to 0.060 log point decline (27 to 55 percent of the actual decline) in the relative wages of high school dropouts over 1980–95, depending on the wage elasticity chosen. Increased LDC trade, under our preferred middle counterfactual and the −0.322 wage elasticity, explains less than 10 percent of the declining relative wage of dropouts. The table also shows that immigration and LDC trade have similar, relatively modest effects on the college–high school wage differential. In combination, they probably account for no more than 10 percent of the large, 0.191 log point increase in this differential from 1980 to 1995.

This paper asks how much immigration and trade affect labor market outcomes. Our answer is that the impact of increased immigration and LDC trade on the labor market does not explain much of the increase in the college wage premium or overall wage inequality in the United States. Other factors—such as an acceleration of skill-biased technological change, a slowdown in the growth of the relative supply of college graduates, and institutional changes in the labor market—are probably more important than immigration and trade in explaining the widening of the U.S. wage structure since the late 1970s. But the concentration of immigration and trade at the lower end of the skill distribution does explain an important part of the decline in the relative wage of high school dropouts. The reason is that a disproportionate share of immigrants has less than a high school education, and a disproportionate and rising share of imports is from sectors that employ such workers. Moreover, as in our earlier work, we find that immigration has a larger impact on less educated workers than does trade.[76]

Toward a Full Accounting of the Effects of Immigration

In standard models of immigration and trade, the income losses of natives who compete with immigrants or with imports are more than matched by the income gains of natives whose skills or capital complement those of immigrants or of imports. How large might these effects be? Since capital is a likely beneficiary of immigration, we take a step toward a fuller accounting of the distributional effects of immigration by extending our two-input (skilled and unskilled labor) model to incorporate capital as a third factor. We use this extended model to simulate the distributional and efficiency impacts of the post-1979 immigration flow and to check whether the conclusion that immigration explains much of the declining relative wage of high school dropouts holds up in such a framework.[77]

Suppose that one can represent the U.S. economy by an aggregate production function $f[K, bN, (1 - b)N]$, where K is capital, N gives the number of workers, and b gives the fraction of workers who are skilled. We assume that the production function has constant returns to scale and that natives own the capital stock. Then in a preimmigration regime, the national income accruing to native workers is

(20) $Q_N = f_K K + f_S b N + f_U (1 - b) N,$

76. Borjas, Freeman, and Katz (1992).

77. We concentrate on immigration both because our analysis suggests that the distributional effects of immigration are larger than those of trade and because the persistent trade imbalances and large volume of intraindustry trade mean that a full accounting of trade's effects would take us far beyond the labor market focus of this paper.

where f_i is the marginal product of input i, and S and U represent skilled and unskilled labor, respectively. The total increase in national income accruing to natives when the United States admits M immigrants equals

$$(21) \qquad \Delta Q_N = \left(K \frac{\partial f_K}{\partial M} + bN \frac{\partial f_S}{\partial M} + (1 - b)N \frac{\partial f_U}{\partial M} \right) M.$$

Assume that a fraction β of immigrants are skilled. Suppose, initially, that capital is infinitely elastic, so that $\partial f_K/\partial M$ is zero. Then if β equals b, immigration does not alter the relative factor ratio in the United States and natives neither lose nor gain from immigration (ΔQ_N is zero because all the terms in equation 21 vanish). Because the price of capital is fixed, immigration can only affect native incomes when β does not equal b. The United States has been admitting immigrants who, on average, are less skilled than native workers. Thus β is less than b, and there are both gains and losses from immigration; the winners are the skilled workers and the losers are the unskilled workers. The net gain to natives, however, is positive.[78]

Some studies of immigration assume that the capital stock (rather than the price of capital) is fixed. In this case, there would be a net gain to the United States from immigration, even when β equaled b. The gains would accrue to native-owned capital. In terms of equation 21, $K \partial f_K/\partial M$ would be positive, and the gains to skilled and unskilled workers would depend on the own effects of shifts in supply, as well as on the cross-effects among the three inputs.

Equation 21 can be evaluated numerically if one makes assumptions about the responsiveness of factor prices to an increase in immigrant labor supply. We simulate the model in this equation by using the two polar assumptions about capital and a set of assumptions about the responsiveness of factor prices to immigration. In particular, let ϵ_{ij} be the factor price elasticity $\partial \ln f_i/\partial \ln X_j$, where X_j is the quantity of input j. Daniel Hamermesh surveys an extensive literature that attempts to estimate these elasticities.[79] We used a variety of assumptions about these elasticities from the range that he provides. The simulation pre-

---

78. Borjas (1995) discusses the economic benefits from immigration using this framework and presents a more detailed discussion of the algebra underlying the simulations presented below.

79. Hamermesh (1993).

Table 19. Simulated Costs and Benefits of Post-1979 Immigration[a]

Item	Holding price of capital fixed	Holding capital stock fixed
Percent change in earnings		
Capital	. . .	6.50
Skilled native workers	0.35	−2.49
Unskilled native workers	−4.64	−4.57
Percent change in skilled-to-unskilled earnings ratio	4.99	2.08
Percent change in total native earnings	0.05	0.13
Dollar GDP gain, assuming $7 trillion GDP	3.5 billion	9.1 billion

Source: Authors' calculations based on model described in text. Data on factor GDP shares are from Autor, Katz, and Krueger (1997, table A1).

a. Changes relative to counterfactual of no immigration after 1979.

sented below uses estimates from the upper end of this range. Simulations based on smaller estimates yield both miniscule benefits and miniscule costs of immigration. In particular, we assume that $\epsilon_{SS} = -1.5$, $\epsilon_{UU} = -0.8$, and $\epsilon_{SU} = 0.05$.[80] This assumption builds capital-skill complementarity into the calculations.

The simulation requires estimates of the parameters b and β, as well as of the share of income accruing to each of the factors. We estimate these parameters from the 1995 CPS, MORG files. We define skilled workers as those having at least a high school education and unskilled workers as high school dropouts. The 1995 CPS then implies that b is 0.91 and β is 0.68 for immigrants who entered after 1979. We make the standard assumption that the labor share of income (for all workers) is 0.7. Using data from the study by Autor, Katz, and Krueger, we estimate that the skilled worker share of GDP is 0.661 and that of unskilled workers is 0.039.[81] Finally, we need an estimate of the immigrant supply shock. The 1995 CPS implies that post-1979 immigrants increased labor supply, in terms of full-time equivalent workers, by 5.5 percent.

Table 19 reports the simulation results, using both polar assumptions about capital. The first column of data gives the results when we assume that the price of capital is fixed (so that capital adjusts completely to the entry of immigrants). In this case, unskilled workers suffer a 4.6

80. These assumptions determine all the other elasticities in the model, because of the mathematical property that the relevant weighted average of factor price elasticities is zero.

81. Autor, Katz, and Krueger (1997, table A1).

percent decline in earnings, whereas skilled workers gain about 0.4 percent. This produces a change in the relative wage of these two groups of 5.0 percent, the same magnitude as estimated in our middle case in table 18. This redistribution generates a net gain for the U.S. economy of 0.05 percent of GDP, or roughly $3.5 billion per year in a $7 trillion economy. The second column gives the results when we assume that the capital stock is fixed. In this case, the main beneficiary of immigration is native-owned capital. The capitalists experience a 6.5 percent increase in income, while both skilled and unskilled workers suffer losses: 2.5 percent and 4.6 percent, respectively. The wage of skilled relative to unskilled workers changes by 2.1 percent. The net gain to the economy is 0.13 percent, which roughly translates into $9.1 billion a year. The simulation therefore reveals that the economic gains from immigration are small in such a massive economy.[82]

It is worth emphasizing that this simulation assumes that all workers within a given skill group are perfect substitutes. A more general analysis would take into account complementarities that might exist between some immigrants (such as those with fewer than nine years of schooling or those with specialized training) and some native workers. Such complementarities would increase the gains to the U.S. economy from immigration. A more complete model would also allow for gains from increased product variety associated with immigration. But our estimates may also overstate the "true" gain because they ignore the possibility that trade would substitute for immigration if fewer immigrants had entered the country. The bottom line from our simulations is that the economic impact of immigration is mainly redistributional and primarily affects a small group of the least educated U.S. native workers.

Conclusions

In the past two or three decades there has been a substantial growth in immigration and trade between the United States and the less developed countries. The large flow of less educated immigrants from LDCs and the rapid growth in U.S. imports of LDC manufactured goods has

---

82. Johnson (1997b) concludes from a similar but more detailed analysis that the effects of immigration on the national economy are even smaller than our estimates.

increased the effective supply of less educated labor relative to more educated labor in the United States. This, in turn, has raised questions about the potential contribution of trade and immigration to the rise in the wage differential between more and less educated workers.

Determining the effects of immigration and trade on economic outcomes is difficult. It is difficult because immigration and trade may have an effect on national labor market outcomes without greatly affecting relative outcomes in the regions most immediately touched by trade flows or immigrant flows. It is also difficult because many other factors affect the U.S. job market; without adequate controls for those factors, the influence of immigration or trade can be hard to discern in a given body of data. And, most important, it is difficult because one must specify a realistic counterfactual of how the economy would have developed, how native labor would have acted, and how firms would have produced goods, in the absence of the relevant immigration or trade flows. These counterfactuals, in turn, require good estimates of the magnitudes of various economic parameters.

In this paper, we try to specify appropriate counterfactuals and to quantify the potential effects of immigration and trade with different estimated or postulated parameters. We conclude that the effects of immigration and trade flows on relative skill supplies have not been substantial enough to account for more than a small proportion of the overall widening of the wage structure over the past fifteen years and have played only a modest role in the expansion of the college–high school wage differential in the United States. Under various plausible specifications, the main adverse effect of immigration and trade on U.S. native outcomes falls on workers with less than a high school education: the combined effects of immigration and trade may explain half of the decline of the relative wages of high school dropouts since 1980. Immigration has a particularly large impact on the outcomes for these workers because the flow of less educated immigrants into the country has been substantial; immigration increased the relative supply of workers with less than a high school degree by 15 to 20 percent over the period 1980–95. Increased trade from LDCs appears to have been much less important than immigration for the relative earnings of low-wage U.S. workers.

Comments and
Discussion

John DiNardo: Trade and immigration policy are each small aspects of a broader issue: how do we, or the government, treat those who happen to have been born outside the geographic boundaries of the United States? Given the scope of the subject, it should not be surprising that economists can play a small role, at best, in informing the larger issues that the question implies.

Moreover, when one asks the more narrow question—what has been the impact of immigration and trade on the economic well-being of the native-born worker?—the implied ceteris paribus, holding other political and economic institutions constant, is quite important. One might well expect increased immigration or trade to have very different consequences under very different institutions. Even defining the issue narrowly in this way leaves many questions of interest to economists.

This contribution by George Borjas, Richard Freeman, and Lawrence Katz elaborates substantially on their previous work: they undertake to develop a conceptual model that seeks, inter alia, to explain the degree of wage inequality experienced by both the U.S. native-born and by immigrants to the United States. The paper paints with a broad brush. The period 1960–90 has seen a great deal of change that has made an impact on labor markets: the rise of civil rights and women's rights movements and the decline of unionism, to name a few. Borjas, Freeman, and Katz, among themselves, have documented the effect of many of these changes in other research; here they train their focus on the impact of trade and immigration on the structure of wages.

My focus is the authors' critique of other researchers' work on im-

68

migration. A substantial portion of the paper is a critique of what Borjas, Freeman, and Katz refer to as area studies; notably, work by Joseph Altonji and Card, Robert LaLonde and Robert Topel, and Robert Schoeni that provides evidence against the view that recent immigration has disadvantaged native-born workers.[1] The paper also reexamines issues analyzed in related work by Kristin Butcher, Card, Frey, and Liaw.[2] Because of the quality of the empirical work in the present paper and in the others cited, it is easier than usual to focus more on what the facts *mean* than on what the facts *are*. Indeed, this paper and those that it critiques have several "facts" in common! In particular, all agree that wage changes across states, cities, or other regions and over time have essentially been uncorrelated with the changes in the number or fraction of immigrants living in a particular place. Further adding to the muddle for a dispassionate outsider, although Borjas, Freeman, and Katz critique area analyses, they bolster their case with an area analysis of their own.

Where, then, is the disagreement? In this paper Borjas, Freeman, and Katz seem to differ from other researchers in answer to the following question: how much of the observed disparity in economic status can be parsimoniously described as the outcome of shifts in the relative demand and supply of workers of different "skills"—that is, years of work experience and formal education—in a competitive labor market? To answer this question, the authors' aggregate proportions approach and the area analyses it critiques focus on a relationship of the following sort:

(A1)
$$\Delta \ln \left(\frac{w_{st}}{w_{ut}} \right) = -B \Delta \ln \left(\frac{x_{st}}{x_{ut}} \right).$$

Here, B is a parameter, x denotes total employment of skill group s or u at time t, w denotes average wage, and Δ denotes that a time difference of the data has been taken. The aggregate proportions approach and area analysis differ somewhat from this simple framework. For example, on the one hand, the area analyses surveyed allow for a greater number of skill categories, and the variables are additionally indexed by standard metropolitan statistical area (SMSA) or city. On the other

---

1. Altonji and Card (1991); LaLonde and Topel (1991); Schoeni (1996).
2. Butcher and Card (1991); Card (1990, 1997); Frey (1995a); Frey and Liaw (1996).

hand, the aggregate proportions approach includes "trade-embodied" employment in x_{st} and x_{ut}, and there are also other differences. Nonetheless, the theoretical models being assumed or tested share the following property: when the number of workers—measured as the *proportion* of workers of a given type—rises, the wage of those workers *relative* to other workers falls (or is predicted to fall).

How does this relate to the economic impact of immigration (or trade) on labor market outcomes? In both area analysis and the aggregate proportions approach, immigration and trade affect relative wages by changing the term on the right-hand side, x_{st}/x_{ut}. For example, the simple model predicts that if the diversity of immigrant "types" matches the diversity of types among the native-born, immigration would have little or no effect.

The work that Borjas, Freeman, and Katz critique attempts to test this relationship by observing that immigrants do not settle uniformly across SMSAs or cities. The area analyses by Altonji, Card, and Schoeni compare the immigration-induced changes in the proportions of different skill types to changes in relative wages of these skill types across SMSAs.[3] They find estimates that are small in magnitude; although fairly precise, these estimates are rarely different from zero at conventional levels of significance.

Likewise, in table 7 of the present paper, those specifications that are most analogous to these area analyses show much the same pattern. At levels of aggregation much broader than those used by Card and Schoeni, however, the estimates vary widely and sign patterns are inconsistent, with the standard errors generally rising as the geographic area under consideration becomes larger. (Due to the limitations of the census data, only relatively broad levels of aggregation can be straightforwardly compared across the entire period 1950–90.)

Notwithstanding these differences, Borjas, Freeman, and Katz, like Card, conclude that "immigration is not a major determinant of the regional structure of labor market outcomes for natives." They argue, however, that this finding should not militate against the conclusion that the inflows of foreign-born workers to the United States have been an important cause of the fall in the wages of workers with less than a high school education. Furthermore, given "plausible" estimates of

---

3. Altonji and Card (1991); Card (1997); Schoeni (1996).

labor demand parameters, the simple supply and demand framework used in their simulations suggests that the wages of workers with less than a high school education may have been greatly affected.

Given the structure of the simplest supply and demand framework, one explanation for this finding is that immigration does not induce changes in the relative supplies of skill types across regions. That is, the small response observed on one margin (wages) might be the result of a big response on another (native migration). Indeed, if the elasticity of native outflow of skill type k with respect to immigrant inflow of skill type k is unity, and if the supply and demand model is a good description of the data, then zero measured wage effects across geographic areas is exactly what one would predict.

It would be quite surprising if this elasticity were large, as such "skating rink" migration is little noticed in the demographics or economics literature. Randall Filer observes that "there has been little previous work dealing with the relation between immigrant arrivals and native migratory patterns."[4] In my experience, a large elasticity is hard to find.

Moreover, if native-born migration "undoes" the effect of immigration, it creates two new puzzles. First, as Borjas puts it, an "unresolved puzzle facing those who interpret the lack of correlation between immigration and native wages in the local labor market in terms of an economy-wide equilibrium process is clear: Why should it be that many other regional variations persist over time, but that the impact of immigration on native workers is arbitraged away immediately?"[5] The empirical literature is replete with examples of regional shocks that appear to be persistent and resistant to migration arbitrage by the native-born. Evidence on the economic fortunes of displaced workers have consistently found enduring effects of labor market conditions at the time of displacement on wages, for example. Olivier Blanchard and Katz conclude that a one-time adverse shock reduces a state's real wage for up to ten years before internal migration reequilibrates wages.[6]

The second puzzle is the mechanism by which internal migration diffuses immigrant shocks. In the context of equation A1, internal migration mitigates the observed regional variation induced by immi-

4. Filer (1992, p. 245).
5. Borjas (1994, p. 1700).
6. Blanchard and Katz (1992).

gration only to the extent that it undoes changes in skill shares. Yet Card finds that when low-skilled immigrants, for example, arrive in an SMSA, the proportion of low-skilled workers (both immigrant and native-born) in that SMSA rises slightly more than by one for one.[7]

Borjas, Freeman, and Katz take up this part of the puzzle in table 11, by attempting to test directly whether immigration changes factor proportions within a state. Using state-level data, they find that their results are quite sensitive to the "appropriate" choice of counterfactual. As a practical matter, this amounts to whether they employ first differences (comparing changes across adjacent censuses), "double differences" (comparing 1950–70 differences to 1970–90 differences), or double differences with an initial conditions control (a value for the proportion of a particular skill group in 1950).

The key parameter that the authors estimate in equation 11, d, takes a value of one if native migration flow is unresponsive to immigration inflow, and zero if natives leave an area at a rate of one for one with an increase in the number of immigrants in that area. In this latter case, increased migration from abroad for a particular skill group is completely off-set by increased out-migration by natives, leaving skill ratios untouched. The authors' preferred specification (double differences with a control for 1950 skill levels) does include this latter case in conventional confidence intervals.

However, their estimates range from a high of 2.8 (with a standard error of 1.2) to a low of −0.34 (with a standard error of 0.30). Indeed, in more than half of their sixteen specifications, which they helpfully report, the coefficient is not significantly different from one. That is, an increased flow of foreign-born individuals has no migration effect on the native population. These can be contrasted with the results of Card, who, using finer geographic groupings, unrestricted city effects, and data from the period 1985–90, finds estimates of about 1.18 (with a standard error of 0.03) for a similar parameter, even after use of instrumental variables estimators.[8]

It is useful to recall the authors' statement regarding the attempt to find wage effects of immigration through area analysis: doing so is difficult "unless [one] can control for the forces that caused the regional

7. Card (1997).
8. See Card (1997).

Figure A1. Distribution of Wages, 1979 and 1991ᵃ

Density

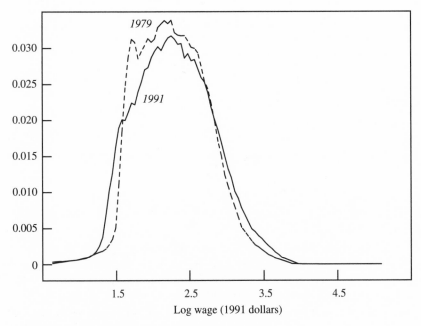

Log wage (1991 dollars)

Source: Author's calculations based on data from 1979 and 1991 CPS, MORG files.
a. Individual observations weighted by hours worked.

wage structure to change . . . over time.'' This argument would seem to apply with equal or more force in regard to migration across states over a forty-year time frame. Consider interstate migration during the period 1985–90. Florida, which Frey labels a high ''internal migration'' state, also received more foreign-born migrants than any state besides California and New York.[9] The reasons for the native and foreign-born migrations are likely quite different and seem hard to uncover by looking at state-level data. For example, within Florida, Miami is clearly dominated by immigration from abroad, whereas metropolitan areas such as Tampa–St. Petersburg, West Palm Beach, Fort Meyers, and Daytona Beach are dominated by internal migration. Within California, Los Angeles saw the biggest increase in foreign-born residents and

9. Frey (1995a).

Figure A2. Distribution of Wages, by Sex, 1979 and 1991[a]

1979 distribution

Density

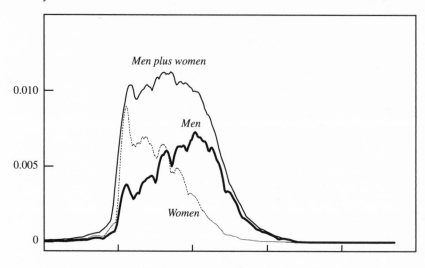

1991 distribution

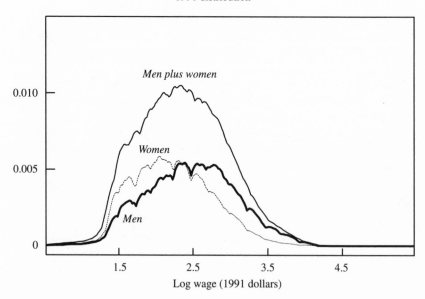

Log wage (1991 dollars)

Source: Author's calculations based on data from 1979 and 1991 CPS, MORG files.
a. Individual observations weighted by hours worked.

substantial out-migration by natives. San Diego, by contrast, saw high levels of immigration by both the foreign- and the native-born.

Borjas, Freeman, and Katz do not overstate their results, and I do not wish to overstate this criticism. While some conflicting results seem potentially reconcilable—Card and Frey differ in their treatment of city fixed effects, for example—Filer's analysis is not as easy to reconcile.[10] The evidence seems to suggest that a city or SMSA analysis with city fixed effects may be more appropriate than a state-level analysis with state fixed effects, but that is only one way of tying up disparate results. In short, although the authors' analysis of migration is helpful, I am not sure that it convincingly demonstrates that the United States is currently experiencing a "new white flight," as Frey describes it, nor that such a native-born migration is the reason why area analyses have not been able to find an effect of immigration on the wages of the native-born.[11]

Even if migration arbitrage is not occurring, other mechanisms for arbitrage do exist. Indeed, the trade literature may provide insight into immigration literature, as it is flush with possible mechanisms that may have implications that can be tested in state-level or SMSA analyses. Schoeni finds evidence suggesting that relative prices of goods across SMSAs are empirically important in analyzing regional wage differentials.[12] This seems a potentially fruitful area of inquiry.

As to the aggregate proportions approach, I am reluctant to conclude that it provides a more reliable way of predicting the impact of immigration on relative wages. The authors' simulations are based on the assumption that the principal mechanism by which immigration affects wages is shifting labor supply along a demand curve. Maybe this is correct; however, the approach provides no independent testable predictions. It can only be confirmed by the extent to which it is in accord with a priori beliefs about the size and directions of the effects. Sharp tests of the general-equilibrium approach taken in the paper are rare, perhaps largely because they are difficult or impossible.

I have one final concern, regarding the "macro" facts about wage inequality that need to be explained. This concern stems from important differences in the evolution of the distribution of wages for men and

10. Card (1997); Frey (1995a); Filer (1992).
11. Frey (1994).
12. Schoeni (1996).

women. In my own work with Kristin Butcher, we find that the patterns of wages changes for the native-born relative to those for immigrants since the late 1970s (the period in which changes in wages and immigration have been most dramatic) are quite different for men and women.[13] Several of the authors' findings are suggestive of this fact. Perhaps, as they suggest, the more comparable treatment of women and men since the popular upheavals that began in the 1960s have played a role.

Recent work by Nicole Fortin and Thomas Lemieux provides further indication of important differences in the evolution of men's and women's wages.[14] They find, for example, that when men's and women's wages are examined together, inequality in wages has changed very little since the late 1970s, apart from a minimum wage effect. Figure A1 presents estimates of the distribution of (hours-weighted) log wages in 1979 and 1991 (in 1991 dollars) for men and women together, based on CPS, MORG data. Figure A2, which displays wage distributions by sex, makes clear that the modest change depicted in figure A1 is the result of very different changes in the distributions of men's and women's wages.

In sum, the common thread of this paper and the research that it critiques appears to be that the increase in the foreign-born population can, at best, explain a small portion of the changes depicted in these figures and other changes in the wage structure over the period 1960–90. As the authors suggest, theirs are not the "final words." However, by carefully laying out so many new facts and reexamining some old ones, they have raised some new questions that deserve answers.

John M. Abowd: In contrast to DiNardo, I have something to say about the trade segment of this paper. Nevertheless I, too, focus my attention on the immigrant side of the paper.

One can think of this paper as the authors' attempt to resolve some of the questions that they raise in their 1996 paper for the *American Economic Review* and, earlier, in their 1992 paper; and, indeed, some of the questions that each of them raise in a variety of research on this subject.[1] What they are trying to do in the immigration section of this

13. Butcher and DiNardo (1997).
14. Fortin and Lemieux (1996).
1. Borjas, Freeman, and Katz (1992, 1996).

paper—and I wish that I could interpret the trade section the same way—is to press hard on the data to find an empirical or natural experiment that they can use to assess the labor market effects of immigration in the United States. In their own words, the object of their 1996 paper is to estimate the effect of immigration on native labor outcomes, which depends critically on the empirical experiment used to assess immigration. Thus one can think of the current paper as a serious assessment of a variety of ways of thinking about that natural experiment.

The conclusion that one's measure of the effects of immigration depends on the type of natural experiment used was a direct consequence of finding that cross-sectional analyses for native wage rates in the 1980 and 1990 census produce very different estimated effects for males. The authors' attempts to explain these differences, using the changes between the two censuses, also failed. The early tables of the present paper confirms these conclusions. The authors now claim that area-based studies of immigration effects, such as their earlier papers and a large number of papers that DiNardo mentions, miss the mark because there is consistent evidence that the effects of immigration to a specific geographic area are diffused to the rest of the economy.

In the present paper, the authors also attempt to refine their earlier estimates of the aggregate effects on implicit labor supply from net trade. In this regard, I think that their conclusions, although subjected to more sensitivity analyses than the conclusions of their early work, are not greatly modified. They do not address some of the criticisms that have been leveled at that technique, but they know this. If one accepts their view of the way in which international trade affects domestic factor markets—that is, factor price equalization does not occur in the labor market—their diagnostics are reasonably convincing.

My brief summary of the paper is as follows. First, the total gain to U.S. GDP from immigration is trivial. Specifically, the net gain to the economy is somewhere between $3.5 billion and $9.1 billion on a $7 trillion economy. But the redistributional effects, according to the authors' methods of assessment, fall almost entirely on unskilled workers and are responsible for about 40 percent of the real wage decline of high school dropouts compared with those with at least a high school diploma. That is a significant finding. The paper emphasizes that this is a good ballpark estimate for the redistributional effects of immigration on the right target group.

Although there is no attempt to estimate the total gain to U.S. GNP from trade, the estimated redistributional effects account for only about 8 percent of the real wage decline of high school dropouts compared with those with at least a high school diploma. So, the trade effects are considerably smaller than those of immigration; and that is not inconsistent with their earlier work on the subject, although it is inconsistent with some of the work that has been produced by some of the authors' competitors.

From the analysis of wage gains for those with a college degree or more, compared with those with a high school diploma, the effects of immigration and trade are found to be roughly comparable, with the same orders of magnitude, but very small—only about 5 percent in the authors' preferred estimate—and the variation in these effects is much smaller. I think it would be fair to say that they conclude that for the groups above the lowest skilled group, the effects of trade and immigration are relatively modest.

The section on immigration and the distribution of wages lies the heart of the new analyses that are presented in the paper. The starting point is the observation that area-based immigration studies find very different results, depending on their specification and time period. In postmodern terminology, this conundrum reflects the need to be precise about the counterfactual and the natural experiment—although, economists used to say just that the conclusion was sensitive to the dates or to the functional form of the regression analysis.

In the area studies, it is well documented that six states have received essentially all of the immigrants for decades: California, New York, New Jersey, Texas, Illinois, and Florida. The authors' wrinkle here is to document that one can form a natural experiment by comparing California to either the other immigrant-receiving states or all other (nonimmigrant) states. In their natural experiment, the authors apply a slightly different treatment to California, to all the other immigrant-receiving states, and to all the other states.

Consider table 8, which reports the regional distribution of native and immigrant populations since 1950. This table shows that the percent of all immigrants in the United States living in California rose from 10.4 percent in 1950 to 33.8 percent in 1990. Over the same period, this proportion fell slightly (from 44.4 percent to 40.0 percent) in the other immigrant-receiving states and dramatically (from 45.2 percent to 26.1 percent) in all other states. From 1950 to 1970 the percent of all U.S. natives living in California also rose (from 6.9 percent to 9.6 percent), whereas it was stable in the other immigrant-receiving states (25.4 percent to 26.2 percent) and fell slightly in the other states (from 67.7 percent to 64.2 percent). In the period 1970–90, the percentages of the native-born population in each of the three regions was essentially stable. That fact is critical for the way that the authors formulate the natural experiment at this aggregated level.

These facts motivate an analysis that asks what the labor markets in California, in the other immigrant-receiving states, and in the other states would have looked like if the 1970–90 immigration shock had not occurred and the native population growth rates over this period mirrored the growth rates in the 1960 to 1970 period. This restatement of the counterfactual is important for reasons documented in tables 6 and 7. These two tables show that immigrant flows into the different areas and education cells, which are the formalization of using California and the other immigrant-receiving states as the treatment groups for the natural experiment, do not have a consistent relation to the changes in native earnings. This is the authors' way of summarizing the fact that the shock—viewed as a shock to the area labor market or the area skilled labor market—has no consistent, predictable effect on the earnings of the shocked groups within those areas.

In particular, table 7, which reports the results of estimating equation 4, shows that the area-education shock in immigration has a measured association with the adjusted change in the area-education earnings and employment outcomes that shows no consistent pattern. Think of table 7 as the authors' best attempt to control for other factors in the change analysis. Here, one treats the shock to the area education-specific market as coming directly from the immigration of comparably skilled people into the labor market.

The authors correctly interpret the widely varying coefficients, which confirm the visual conclusion from the simple natural experiment in table 6, as implying that interpreting an area education increase in the immigrant population as a labor supply shock to an area education labor market is simply inconsistent with the data.

Table 8 restates the counterfactual. It is important to understand the full implications of table 8 and the associated regression analysis in table 9. In equations 5 and 6, the authors express the simple annual growth rate in an area's labor supply as the sum of the component due to natives, $\Delta n_j(t,t')$, and the part due to immigrants, $\Delta m_j(t,t')$, for area j between years t and t'. They then ask, in equation 8, whether the change in the annual native contribution to the population growth rate in area j between the periods 1960–70 and 1970–90 is related to the change in the immigrant contribution between the same periods. The regression analysis in table 9 confirms that there is a strong negative relation between these two changes in growth rates, which the authors interpret as implying that declines in native population growth in the different area markets exactly off-set the immigration shock in those markets. The offset is relative to the preexisting trend in native population growth in the market, rather than to a "no growth" counterfactual. So, this is their restatement of the critical natural experiment.

What does this imply for the simple natural experiment involving the three regional groups (California, other immigrant-receiving states, and all others)? Based on data in tables 1 and 8 and some population totals for the United States, one can compute that the population of the state of California grew at a simple rate of 3.4 percent over the period 1960–70 and at exactly the same rate over the period 1970–90. The native contribution over the period 1960–70, $\Delta n_{CA}(60,70)$, is 2.9 percent, and the immigrant contribution, $\Delta m_{CA}(60,70)$, is 0.5 percent. The other immigrant-receiving states grew at a simple rate of 1.7 percent over this period, purely as a result of growth in the native-born population. And the other states grew at 1.5 percent (1.6 percent from natives and −0.1 percent from immigrants). Over the period 1970–90, California continued to grow at the simple annual rate of 3.4 percent, now comprising 1.7 percent natives and 1.7 percent immigrants. Hence the difference in the native contribution to the population growth rate, $\Delta n_{CA}(70,90) - \Delta n_{CA}(60,70)$, is −1.2 percent, and the associated difference in the immigrant contribution shocks, $\Delta m_{CA}(70,90) - \Delta m_{CA}(60,70)$, is 1.2 percent. For the other immigrant-receiving states, the difference in the native growth rate contribution is −0.3 percent, and the difference in the immigrant contribution is 0.5 percent. Finally, for all other states, the difference in the native contribution to the growth rate is 0.0 percent and the difference in the immigrant contribution is 0.2 percent.

In greatly simplified form, this illustrates the authors' point: the native growth rate changed in an equal and off-setting manner. Hence there was no shock to the area labor markets. Rather, natives who would otherwise have been in the immigrant-receiving areas (especially California) diffused through the rest of the country. The authors' method implies that over the twenty-year period from 1970 to 1990, approximately 3.4 million native-born Americans stayed where they were rather than migrate to California, and an additional 2.0 million native-born Americans stayed where they were rather than migrate to the other immigrant-receiving states. I strongly suspect that the authors knew this before they conducted the rest of the analysis, and it strongly motivated the functional forms that are found in table 9.

Having estimated the effects of immigration, the authors turn to trade, continuing their earlier approach of trying to estimate the implicit increase in domestic labor supply from net trade flows. The main improvements over their 1996 paper are the attempt to estimate the flows by source (LDCs versus developed countries) and the use of microdata at the establishment level to distinguish the production technologies of plants within a given industry. These improvements permit them to calculate the implicit labor supply of net imports. Their most interesting findings are summarized in table 17, which considers the amount by which trade increases the (implicit) labor supply of different educational groups under three different technology assumptions. The "low" assumption means that the goods produced by LDCs use average current technology factor proportions. The "middle" assumption uses technologies that are ten to fifteen years old to estimate the factor proportions. And the "high" assumption assumes that the LDCs use technology from the 1970s. These proportions are based on the factor proportions in the relevant three-digit standard industrial classification from the appropriate period. There is no attempt to assess Robert Feenstra's argument that within-industry import-export behavior is more important than between-industry substitution in explaining the success of LDC penetration of U.S. product markets. If these estimates are to address the criticisms that have been leveled at the method, more data on LDC production processes and attention to within-industry import integration into the production process need to be included.

I think that the authors could make more progress. What is needed is some direct information on the age of the technology and on the processes used by the LDC producers. It is not clear that this evidence will support the high scenario. As Katz himself said at the Brookings

Panel meeting, if they had the technical data on how goods were made in LDCs, the authors would not necessarily have concluded that LDC producers were using older technologies that embodied a lot of lower skilled labor in their goods.

Let me finally talk a little bit about the authors' overall estimates. Table 19 summarizes the factor proportional analysis. It does so under the middle assumptions, so that the importing industries are using technologies that are ten to fifteen years old and thus are embodying relatively more less skilled labor than do the best producers currently. As described above, according to their analysis, most of the effect is focused on the lowest skilled group; that is, there is a fall in the wage of high school dropouts relative to all others. The percentage contributions show that post-1979 immigration is responsible for a fairly large proportion of this decline; using the middle elasticity estimate, about 40 percent of the decline in the real wage of high school dropouts relative to all others.

But regardless of which assumptions are used, the rest of the labor market is not very much affected. What the authors ought to conclude is that, yet again, they have presented a substantial amount of evidence to indicate that it is a very specific part of the domestic labor market— the less skilled group—that bears the brunt of the redistributional effect, both from immigration and from trade. The authors have marshaled a lot more evidence on the immigration side than was available before, but I do not think they have produced as much incremental evidence on the trade side. I would encourage them to obtain more direct evidence on the trade effects and to use less of the inferential evidence.

General discussion: William Branson described the paper as taking a closed economy view of trade effects because of its emphasis on quantities rather than relative prices. A model better reflecting the "trade view" would start with other countries having different factor endowment ratios, and so different factor price ratios, than the United States. As barriers to trade are lowered, the relative factor returns become more equal. In the United States, this results in a rise in the returns to skilled labor relative to unskilled labor. He noted that everything works off these relative price changes in this model, and quantities need not change much for trade to have these effects. Katz replied that in general-equilibrium models such as Paul Krugman's, the factor content of trade gives the same results as do the price changes. Since it is easier to work with quantities than prices in such a framework, he regarded the methodology in the paper as the right way to proceed. However, he acknowledged that the model could miss some trade effects operating only through prices, such as cases where workers receive rents that are eroded just by the threat of trade, when trade barriers fall. Robert Hall observed that by focusing on real GDP rather than consumption, the paper does not adequately measure the benefits of trade. If the terms of trade shift in favor of a country, GDP may not rise, although properly deflated real incomes will.

Branson also noted that Europe and the United States have had very different labor market outcomes in terms of wages and unemployment over the past decade, which suggests two different ways of reacting to the same shock. Katz saw this as evidence that institutions matter in determining wage outcomes. He also noted that countries with faster growth in the relative supply of educated workers had smaller increases in inequality, which conflicts with the "trade view" that only world factor proportions matter. He knew of no theoretical model that could integrate globalization and domestic institutions. Freeman pointed out another broad outcome not predicted by trade models: as the percentage of goods from LDCs increases, predominantly in industries such as apparel that disproportionately employ women, women's wages should fall. Yet they have risen in the United States and elsewhere, indicating that other factors have dominated women's relative wages.

William Nordhaus questioned some of the paper's other assumptions. He was curious about the evidence underlying the assumption of complementarity between skilled workers and capital. He had serious reservations about the returns to scale of the production function, which effectively assumes that immigrants can spread out without any congestion effects. Adding land, or any fixed factor, would make a large change to the calculated benefits of immigration. For example, putting land and other fixed factors into a Cobb-Douglas production function with a conservative coefficient of 0.05 and adding 5 percent to the labor force results in an $18 billion penalty for the labor increase, enough to reverse the sign of net benefits. And this does not even account for environmental effects, such as fixed national quotas on greenhouse gas emissions or sulfur dioxide, or congestion effects, which are likely to be important since the immigrants are going to some of the most congested parts of the country. He suggested that a measure of sustainable consumption by natives would better capture these effects. Robert Hall responded that there are positive externalities that could reverse these conclusions. Their existence is revealed by immigrants' own choices of where to live: they choose high-density areas because that is where the wages are highest, exactly because of these externalities. Even the notion that the United States is being overwhelmed by congestion is inaccurate, since studies have found, for example, that commuting times in Los Angeles have actually declined since 1950. Nordhaus clarified that he was not addressing the level of congestion today, but rather that the cost of adding to it through immigration was not being measured.

Several panelists discussed the use of educational attainment in the analysis of relative wages. Jonathan Gruber questioned whether years of schooling should have the same effect if they were received in the United States or abroad. James Duesenberry remarked that comparing years of schooling across time periods is hazardous, noting that in 1960, 49.5 percent of workers were high school dropouts, while in 1995 only 9 percent were. In addition, the personal characteristics of dropouts has changed dramatically over this period, as entirely different social forces have influenced whether people finished high school. Robert Shiller suggested that education is basically signaling, and the signal from any level of educational attainment changes over time. People in the category of dropout have changed over time; currently there are so few, and they tend to have specific ability differences, such as executive dysfunctions (where they are unreliable), attention deficit disorders, reading disabilities, or mental illnesses. He suggested using characteristics such as these, rather than educational attainment.

Katz noted that the paper is not assuming that high school dropouts were the same now as in 1960, but rather that the gap between the people in adjoining educational attainment cells is comparable. The evidence from the distribution of income, comparing the wages of the top twentieth percentile with the bottom eightieth, for example, indicates that the gap has been relatively steady. Regarding the type of data that Shiller suggested, Katz believed that panels classifying such disorders would not indicate whether the people were immigrants and so are not applicable to the paper's purpose. Freeman added that while Shiller raised the possibility that the rise in inequality reflected a drop in the abilities of people in the bottom groups, results from following cohorts of the same people revealed that wage trends are found within cohorts. Looking at high school dropouts from twenty-five years ago, wages were stable at first but have fallen sharply in the last twenty years.

Nordhaus suggested giving more attention to ethnicity, in addition to skills and education. According to assimilationists, immigrants face a wage penalty, but after a few generations their descendants regress toward the national average. Historically, Mexican immigrants have been the exception, suffering a wage penalty that has worsened over generations. Now native-born Hispanics might experience a similar effect with recent immigration depressing their earnings.

Nordhaus also observed that the paper's finding that immigration rather than trade accounted for the relative wage declines of the poorest workers is not reflected in the political discussion, which stresses trade protection over immigration reform. He recognized that attacks on immigration have always sounded a little Philistine and surely not politically correct. Yet in light of the effects of immigration on the bottom fifth of the income distribution, it was hard to avoid the conclusion that present immigration policies are badly flawed.

References

Altonji, Joseph G., and David E. Card. 1991. "The Effects of Immigration on the Labor Market Outcomes of Less-Skilled Natives." In *Immigration, Trade, and the Labor Market*, edited by John M. Abowd and Richard B. Freeman. University of Chicago Press.

Autor, David H., Lawrence F. Katz, and Alan B. Krueger. 1997. "Computing Inequality: Have Computers Changed the Labor Market?" Working Paper 5956. Cambridge, Mass.: National Bureau of Economic Research (March).

Baldwin, Robert E., and Glen G. Cain. 1997. "Shifts in U.S. Relative Wages: The Role of Trade, Technology, and Factor Endowments." Working Paper 5934. Cambridge, Mass.: National Bureau of Economic Research (February).

Bartel, Ann P. 1989. "Where Do the New U.S. Immigrants Live?" *Journal of Labor Economics* 7(4): 371–91.

Berman, Eli, John Bound, and Zvi Griliches. 1994. "Changes in the Demand for Skilled Labor within U.S. Manufacturing: Evidence from the Annual Survey of Manufactures." *Quarterly Journal of Economics* 109(2): 367–97.

Bernard, Andrew B., and J. Bradford Jensen. 1995. "Exporters, Jobs, and Wages in U.S. Manufacturing: 1976–1987." *BPEA, Microeconomics, 1995*, 67–119.

Bhagwati, Jagdish, and Vivek H. Dehejia. 1994. "Freer Trade and Wages of the Unskilled—Is Marx Striking Again?" In *Trade and Wages: Leveling Wages Down?*, edited by Jagdish Bhagwati and Marvin H. Kosters. Washington: American Enterprise Institute.

Blanchard, Olivier Jean, and Lawrence F. Katz. 1992. "Regional Evolutions." *BPEA*, 1:1992, 1–75.

Blau, Francine D., and Lawrence M. Kahn. 1996. "International Differences in Male Wage Inequality: Institutions versus Market Forces." *Journal of Political Economy* 104(4): 791–836.

Borjas, George J. 1990. *Friends or Strangers: The Impact of Immigrants on the U.S. Economy*. Basic Books.

———. 1994. "The Economics of Immigration." *Journal of Economic Literature* 32(4): 1667–717.

———. 1995. "The Economic Benefits from Immigration." *Journal of Economic Perspectives* 9(2): 3–22.

Borjas, George J., Richard B. Freeman, and Lawrence F. Katz. 1992. "On the Labor Market Effects of Immigration and Trade." In *Immigration and the Work Force: Economic Consequences for the United States and Source Areas*, edited by George J. Borjas and Richard B. Freeman. University of Chicago Press.

————. 1996. "Searching for the Effect of Immigration on the Labor Market." *American Economic Review, Papers and Proceedings* 86(2): 246–51.

Borjas, George J., and Valerie A. Ramey. 1995. "Foreign Competition, Market Power, and Wage Inequality." *Quarterly Journal of Economics* 110(4): 1075–110.

Bound, John, and George Johnson. 1992. "Changes in the Structure of Wages in the 1980's: An Evaluation of Alternative Explanations." *American Economic Review* 82(3): 371–92.

Butcher, Kristin F., and David E. Card. 1991. "Immigration and Wages: Evidence from the 1980's." *American Economic Review, Papers and Proceedings* 81(2): 292–96.

Butcher, Kristin F., and John DiNardo. 1997. "The Immigrant and Native-Born Wage Distributions: Evidence from United States Censuses." Unpublished paper. Boston University and University of California, Irvine (June).

Card, David E. 1990. "The Impact of the Mariel Boatlift on the Miami Labor Market." *Industrial and Labor Relations Review* 43(2): 245–57.

————. 1997. "Immigrant Inflows, Native Outflows, and the Local Labor Market Impacts of Higher Immigration," Working Paper 5927. Cambridge, Mass.: National Bureau of Economic Research (February).

Davis, Donald R. 1996. "Does European Unemployment Prop Up American Wages?" Working Paper 5620. Cambridge, Mass.: National Bureau of Economic Research (June).

Deardorff, Alan V, and Dalia S. Hakura. 1994. "Trade and Wages—What are the Questions?" In *Trade and Wages: Leveling Wages Down?*, edited by Jagdish Bhagwati and Marvin H. Kosters. Washington: American Enterprise Institute.

Deardorff, Alan V., and Robert W. Staiger. 1988. "An Interpretation of the Factor Content of Trade." *Journal of International Economics* 24(1–2): 93–107.

Doms, Mark, Timothy Dunne, and Kenneth R. Troske. 1997. "Workers, Wages, and Technology." *Quarterly Journal of Economics* 112(1): 253–90.

Edin, Per-Anders, and Bertil Holmlund. 1995. "The Swedish Wage Structure: The Rise and Fall of Solidarity Wage Policy?" In *Differences and Changes in Wage Structures*, edited by Richard B. Freeman and Lawrence F. Katz. University of Chicago Press.

Filer, Randall K. 1992. "The Effect of Immigrant Arrivals on Migratory Patterns of Native Workers." In *Immigration and the Work Force: Economic Consequences for the United States and Source Areas*, edited by George J. Borjas and Richard B. Freeman. University of Chicago Press.

Fortin, Nicole, and Thomas Lemieux. 1996. "Rank Regression, Wage Distributions, and the Gender Gap." CRDE Working Paper 1096. University of Montreal (April).

Frankel, Jeffrey A., and David Romer. 1996. "Trade and Growth: An Empirical Investigation." Working Paper 5476. Cambridge, Mass.: National Bureau of Economic Research (March).

Freeman, Richard B. 1975. "Overinvestment in College Training?" *Journal of Human Resources* 10(3): 287–311.

Freeman, Richard B., and Lawrence F. Katz. 1994. "Rising Wage Inequality: The United States vs. Other Advanced Countries." In *Working Under Different Rules*, edited by Richard B. Freeman. Russell Sage Foundation.

Freeman, Richard B., and Karen Needels. 1993. "Skill Differentials in Canada in an Era of Rising Labor Market Inequality." In *Small Differences That Matter: Labor Markets and Income Maintenance in Canada and the United States*, edited by David E. Card and Richard B. Freeman. University of Chicago Press.

Frey, William H. 1994. "The New White Flight." *American Demographics* 16(4): 40–48.

———. 1995a. "Immigration and Internal Migration 'Flight' from U.S. Metropolitan Areas: Toward a New Demographic Balkanisation." *Urban Studies* 32(4–5): 733–57.

———. 1995b. "Immigration Impacts on Internal Migration of the Poor: 1990 Census Evidence for U.S. States." *International Journal of Population Geography* 1: 51–67.

Frey, William H., and Kao-Lee Liaw. 1996. "The Impact of Recent Immigration on Population Redistribution within the United States." Research Report 96-376. University of Michigan, Population Studies Center (December).

Friedberg, Rachel M. 1996. "The Impact of Mass Migration on the Israeli Labor Market." Unpublished paper. Brown University (November).

Grossman, Jean Baldwin. 1982. "The Substitutability of Natives and Immigrants in Production." *Review of Economics and Statistics* 64(4): 596–603.

Hamermesh, Daniel S. 1993. *Labor Demand*. Princeton University Press.

———. 1997. "Immigration and the Quality of Jobs." Unpublished paper. University of Texas (February).

Hanson, Gordon H., and Antonio Spilimbergo. 1997. "Illegal Immigration, Border Enforcement, and Relative Wages: Evidence from Apprehensions at the U.S.–Mexico Border." Unpublished paper. University of Texas (March).

Jaeger, David A. 1995. "Skill Differences and the Effect of Immigrants on the Wages of Natives." Unpublished paper. U.S. Bureau of Labor Statistics (November).

———. 1997. "Reconciling the Old and New Census Bureau Education Questions: Recommendations for Researchers." *Journal of Business and Economic Statistics* 15(3): 300–09.

Jensen, J. Bradford, and Kenneth R. Troske. 1997. "Increasing Wage Dispersion in U.S. Manufacturing: Plant-Level Evidence on the Role of Trade and Technology.'' Paper prepared for the Council on Foreign Relations Study Group on Global Trade and Wages (March).

Johnson, George E. 1997a. ''Changes in Earnings Inequality: The Role of Demand Shifts.'' *Journal of Economic Perspectives* 11(2): 41–54.

———. 1997b. ''Estimation of the Impact of Immigration on the Distribution of Income Among Minorities and Others.'' Unpublished paper. University of Michigan (February).

Katz, Lawrence F., and Kevin M. Murphy. 1992. ''Changes in Relative Wages, 1963–1987: Supply and Demand Factors.'' *Quarterly Journal of Economics* 107(1): 35–78.

Kim, Dae-Il, and Robert H. Topel. 1995. ''Labor Markets and Economic Growth: Lessons from Korea's Industrialization, 1970–1990.'' In *Differences and Changes in Wage Structures*, edited by Richard B. Freeman and Lawrence F. Katz. University of Chicago Press.

Krueger, Alan B. 1997. ''Labor Market Shifts and the Price Puzzle Revisited.'' Working Paper 5924. Cambridge, Mass.: National Bureau of Economic Research (February).

Krugman, Paul R. 1995a. ''Growing World Trade: Causes and Consequences.'' *BPEA, 1:1995*, 327–77.

———. 1995b. ''Technology, Trade, and Factor Prices.'' Working Paper 5355. Cambridge, Mass.: National Bureau of Economic Research (November).

LaLonde, Robert J., and Robert H. Topel. 1991. ''Labor Market Adjustments to Increased Immigration.'' In *Immigration, Trade, and the Labor Market*, edited by John M. Abowd and Richard B. Freeman. University of Chicago Press.

Lawrence, Robert Z. 1996. *Single World, Divided Nations? International Trade and OECD Labor Markets*. Paris: Brookings and Organisation for Economic Co-operation and Development.

Lawrence, Robert Z., and Matthew J. Slaughter. 1993. ''International Trade and American Wages in the 1980s: Giant Sucking Sound or Small Hiccup?'' *BPEA, Microeconomics 2:1993*, 161–226.

Leamer, Edward E. 1996a. ''In Search of Stolper-Samuelson Effects on U.S. Wages.'' Working Paper 5427. Cambridge, Mass.: National Bureau of Economic Research (January).

———. 1996b. ''What's the Use of Factor Contents?'' Working Paper 5448. Cambridge, Mass.: National Bureau of Economic Research (February).

Mishel, Lawrence, Jared Bernstein, and John Schmitt. 1997. *The State of Working America, 1996–97*. Armonk, N.Y.: M. E. Sharpe.

Mundell, Robert A. 1957. ''International Trade and Factor Mobility.'' *American Economic Review* 47(3): 321–35.

Murphy, Kevin M., and Finis Welch. 1992. "The Structure of Wages." *Quarterly Journal of Economics* 107(1): 285–326.

Rodrik, Dani. 1997. *Has Globalization Gone Too Far?* Washington: Institute for International Economics.

Sachs, Jeffrey D., and Howard J. Shatz. 1994. "Trade and Jobs in U.S. Manufacturing." *BPEA, 1:1994,* 1–84.

Sachs, Jeffrey D., and Andrew Warner. 1995. "Economic Reform and the Process of Global Integration." *BPEA, 1:1995,* 1–118.

Schmitt, John. 1995. "The Changing Structure of Male Earnings in Britain, 1974–1988." In *Differences and Changes in Wage Structures,* edited by Richard B. Freeman and Lawrence F. Katz. University of Chicago Press.

Schoeni, Robert F. 1996. "The Effect of Immigrants on the Employment and Wages of Native Workers: Evidence from the 1970s and 1980s." Unpublished paper. RAND (February).

Trefler, Daniel. 1993. "International Factor Price Differences: Leontief Was Right!" *Journal of Political Economy* 101(6): 961–87.

Troske, Kenneth R. 1995. "The Worker Establishment Characteristics Database." Research Paper 95-10. U.S. Bureau of the Census, Center for Economic Studies (June).

U.S. Bureau of the Census. 1989. "The Relationship between the 1970 and 1980 Industry and Occupation Classification Systems" Technical Paper 59. Department of Commerce (February).

White, Michael J., and Lori M. Hunter. 1993. "The Migratory Response of Native-Born Workers to the Presence of Immigrants in the Labor Market." Working Paper 93-08. Brown University, Population Studies and Training Center (July).

Wood, Adrian. 1994. *North-South Trade, Employment, and Inequality: Changing Fortunes in a Skill-Driven World.* Oxford: Clarendon Press.

———. 1995. "How Trade Hurt Unskilled Workers." *Journal of Economic Perspectives* 9(3): 57–80.

BEN S. BERNANKE
Princeton University

MARK GERTLER
New York University

MARK WATSON
Princeton University

Systematic Monetary Policy and the Effects of Oil Price Shocks

THE PRINCIPAL OBJECTIVE of this paper is to increase our understanding of the role of monetary policy in postwar U.S. business cycles. We take as our starting point two common findings in the recent monetary policy literature based on vector autoregressions (VARs).[1] First, identified shocks to monetary policy explain relatively little of the overall variation in output (typically, less than 20 percent). Second, most of the observed movement in the instruments of monetary policy, such as the federal funds rate or nonborrowed reserves, is endogenous; that is, changes in Federal Reserve policy are largely explained by macroeconomic conditions, as one might expect, given the Fed's commitment to macroeconomic stabilization. These two findings obviously do not support the view that erratic and unpredictable fluctuations in Federal Reserve policies are a primary cause of postwar U.S. business cycles; but neither do they rule out the possibility that systematic and predictable monetary policies—the Fed's policy rule—affect the course of the economy in an important way. Put more positively, if one takes the VAR evidence on monetary policy seriously (as we do), then any case for an important role of monetary policy in the business cycle rests on

Thanks to Benjamin Friedman, Christopher Sims, and the Brookings Panel for helpful comments. Expert research assistance was provided by Don Redl and Peter Simon. The financial support of the National Science Foundation is gratefully acknowledged.
    1. See, for example, Leeper, Sims, and Zha (1996).

the argument that the choice of the monetary policy rule (the "reaction function") has significant macroeconomic effects.

Using time-series evidence to uncover the effects of monetary policy rules on the economy is, however, a daunting task. It is not possible to infer the effects of changes in policy rules from a standard identified VAR system, since this approach typically provides little or no structural interpretation of the coefficients that make up the lag structure of the model. Large-scale econometric models, such as the MIT–Penn–SSRC model, are designed for analyzing alternative policies; but criticisms of the identifying assumptions of these models have been the subject of a number of important papers, notably, by Robert Lucas and Christopher Sims.[2] Particularly relevant to the present paper is Sims's point that the many overidentifying restrictions of large-scale models may be both theoretically and empirically suspect, often implying specifications that do not match the basic time-series properties of the data particularly well. Recent progress in the development of dynamic stochastic general equilibrium models overcomes much of Lucas's objection to the traditional approach, but the ability of these models to fit the time-series data—in particular, the relationships among money, interest rates, output, and prices—seems, if anything, worse than that of traditional large-scale models.

In this paper we take some modest (but, we hope, informative) first steps toward sorting out the effects of systematic monetary policy on the economy, within a framework designed to accommodate the time-series facts about the U.S. economy in a flexible manner. Our strategy involves adding a little bit of structure to an identified VAR. Specifically, we assume that monetary policy works its effects on the economy through the medium of the term structure of open-market interest rates; and that, given the term structure, the policy instrument (in our application, the federal funds rate) has no independent effect on the economy. In combination with the expectations theory of the term structure, this assumption allows one to summarize the effects of alternative expected future monetary policies in terms of their effects on the current short and long interest rates, which, in turn, help to determine the evolution of the economy. By comparing, for example, the historical behavior of the economy with its behavior under an hypothesized alter-

2. Lucas (1976); Sims (1980).

native policy reaction function, we obtain a rough measure of the importance of the systematic component of monetary policy. Our approach is similar in spirit to a methodology due to Sims and Tao Zha; however, these authors do not attempt to sort out the effects of anticipated and partially unanticipated policy changes.[3] While our proposed methodology is crude, and certainly is not invulnerable to the Lucas critique, we believe that it represents a commonsense approach to the problem of measuring the effects of anticipated policy, given currently available tools.

To be able to compare historical and alternative hypothesized responses of monetary policy to economic disturbances, one needs to select some interesting set of macroeconomic shocks to which policy is likely to respond. We focus primarily on oil price shocks, for two reasons.[4] First, periods dominated by oil price shocks are reasonably easy to identify empirically, and the case for exogeneity of at least the major oil price shocks is strong (although, there is also substantial controversy about how these shocks and their economic effects should be modeled). Second, in the view of many economists, oil price shocks are perhaps the leading alternative to monetary policy as the key factor in postwar U.S. recessions: increases in oil prices preceded the recessions of 1973–75, 1980–82, and 1990–91, and James Hamilton presents evidence that increases in oil prices led declines in output before 1972 as well.[5] Further, one of the strongest criticisms of the neomonetarist claim that monetary policy has been a major cause of economic downturns is that it may confound the effects of monetary tightening and previous increases in oil prices.

The rest of the paper is organized as follows. We first document that essentially all the U.S. recessions of the past thirty years have been preceded by both oil price increases and a tightening of monetary policy, which raises the question to what extent the ensuing economic declines can be attributed to each factor. Discussion of this identification problem requires a digression into the parallel VAR-based literature

3. Sims and Zha (1995).
4. Hooker (1996a) also studies the effects of oil price shocks and their interaction with monetary policy in a VAR framework. However, he does not explicitly attempt to decompose the effect of oil price shocks on the economy into a part due to the change in oil prices and a part due to the policy reaction.
5. Hamilton (1983).

on the effects of oil price shocks; one main conclusion is that it is surprisingly difficult to find an indicator of oil price shocks that produces the expected responses of macroeconomic and policy variables in a VAR setting. After comparing alternative indicators, we choose as our principal measure of oil price shocks the "net oil price increase" variable proposed by Hamilton.[6]

We next introduce our identification strategy, which summarizes the effects of an anticipated change in monetary policy in terms of its impact on the current term structure of interest rates (specifically, the three-month and ten-year government rates). We show that this approach provides reasonable results for the analysis of shocks to monetary policy and to oil prices; and, in particular, we find that the endogenous monetary policy response can account for a very substantial portion (in some cases, nearly all) of the depressing effects of oil price shocks on the real economy. This result is reinforced by a more disaggregated analysis, which compares the effects of oil price and monetary policy shocks on components of GDP. Looking more specifically at individual recessionary episodes associated with oil price shocks, we find that both monetary policy and other nonmoney, nonoil disturbances played important roles, but that oil shocks, per se, were not a major cause of these downturns. Overall, these findings help to resolve the long-standing puzzle of the apparently disproportionate effect of oil price increases on the economy. We also show that our method produces reasonable results when applied to the analysis of monetary policy reactions to other types of shocks, such as shocks to output and to commodity prices.

After presenting the basic results, we look in more detail at their robustness and stability. Regarding robustness, we find that the broad conclusion that endogenous monetary policy is an important component of the aggregate impact of oil price shocks holds across a variety of specifications, although the exact proportion of the effect due to monetary policy is sometimes hard to determine statistically. We also find evidence of subsample instability in our estimated system. To some extent, however, this instability helps to strengthen our main conclusions about the role of endogenous monetary policy, in that the total effect of oil price shocks on the economy on output is found to be

6. Hamilton (1996a, 1996b).

strongest during the Volcker era—when the monetary response to inflationary shocks was also the strongest.

Our analysis uses interpolated monthly data on GDP and its components. Appendix A documents the construction of these data, and appendix B describes all of the data that we use.

Is It Monetary Policy or Is It Oil? The Basic Identification Problem

The idea that monetary policy is a major source of real fluctuations in the economy is an old one; much of its lasting appeal reflects the ongoing influence of the seminal work of Milton Friedman and Anna Schwartz.[7] Obtaining credible measurements of monetary policy's contribution to business cycles has proved difficult, however. As discussed above, in recent years numerous authors have addressed the measurement of the effects of monetary policy by means of the VAR methodology, introduced into economics by Sims.[8] Roughly speaking, this approach identifies unanticipated innovations to monetary policy with an unforecasted shock to some policy indicator, such as the federal funds rate or the rate of growth of nonborrowed reserves. Using the estimated VAR system, one can trace out the dynamic responses of output, prices, and other macroeconomic variables to this innovation, thereby obtaining quantitative estimates of how monetary policy innovations affect the economy. As John Cochrane notes, "this literature has at last produced impulse-response functions that capture common views about monetery policy''; for example, in finding that a positive innovation to monetary policy is followed by increases in output, prices, and money, and by a decline in the short-term nominal interest rate.[9] In addition, despite ongoing debates about precisely how the policy innovation should be identified, the estimated responses of key macroeconomic variables to a policy shock are reasonably similar across a

7. Friedman and Schwartz (1963).
8. Sims (1980); more recently, see Bernanke and Blinder (1992), Christiano and Eichenbaum (1992), Sims (1992), Strongin (1995), Bernanke and Mihov (1995), Sims and Zha (1995), and Leeper, Sims, and Zha (1996).
9. Cochrane (1996, p. 1).

variety of studies and suggest that monetary policy shocks can have significant and persistent real effects.

The VAR literature has focused on unanticipated policy shocks not because they are quantitatively very important—indeed, the conclusion of this literature is that policy shocks are too small to account for much of the overall variation in output and other variables—but because it is argued that cause and effect can be cleanly disentangled only in the case of exogenous, or random, changes in policy. However, looking only at unanticipated policy changes begs the question of how systematic, or endogenous, monetary policy changes affect the economy.[10]

Earlier work on the effects of monetary policy often does not make the distinction between anticipated and unanticipated policy changes.[11] These studies frequently find a very large role for monetary policy in cyclical fluctuations. An important recent example of this genre is an article by Christina Romer and David Romer.[12] Following the narrative approach of Friedman and Schwartz, Romer and Romer use Federal Reserve records to identify a series of dates at which, in response to high inflation, the Fed changed policy in a sharply contractionary direction. Their dates presumably correspond to policy changes with both an unanticipated component (because they were large, or decisive) and an anticipated component (because they were explicit responses to inflation); indeed, Matthew Shapiro shows that these dates are largely forecastable.[13] Romer and Romer find that their dates were typically followed by large declines in real activity and conclude that monetary policy plays an important role in fluctuations.

But as several critiques of Romer and Romer's article and the earlier work on anticipated monetary policy point out, studies that blur the

10. Cochrane (1996) has emphasized that even identification of the effects of unanticipated policy changes may hinge on distinguishing between anticipated and unanticipated changes, since an innovation in policy typically also changes the anticipated future path of policy. The analyst thus faces the conundrum of determining how much of the economy's response to a policy shock is due to the shock, per se, and how much is due to the change in policy anticipations engendered by the shock. The focus of this paper is different from that of Cochrane, in that we emphasize the effects of nonpolicy shocks, such as oil shocks, on anticipated monetary policy; but our methods could also be used to address the specific issue he raises.

11. Nor, for that matter, between changes in the money stock induced by policy and those induced by other factors. See, for example, Andersen and Jordan (1968).

12. Romer and Romer (1989).

13. Shapiro (1994).

distinction between anticipated and unanticipated policies suffer from precisely the identification problem that the VAR literature has attempted to avoid; namely, that it is not obvious how to distinguish the effects of anticipated policies from the effects of the shocks to which the policies are responding. This is not merely methodological carping, but is potentially of great practical importance in the postwar U.S. context, since a number of the most significant tightenings of U.S. monetary policy have followed on the heels of major increases in the price of imported oil.[14]

This point is illustrated in figure 1, which shows the historical behavior of the federal funds rate (here, taken to be an indicator of monetary policy) in the upper panel and the log-level of the nominal price of oil in the lower panel. Recessions, as dated by the National Bureau of Economic Research, are shaded. The upper panel also indicates the five dates identified by Romer and Romer that fall within our sample period. The lower panel shows, in analogy to the Romer dates, seven dates at which there were major disruptions to the oil market, as determined in part by Kevin Hoover and Stephen Perez.[15]

The upper panel of figure 1, taken alone, appears to support the neomonetarist case that tight money is the cause of recessions: each of the first four recessions in the figure was immediately preceded by a sharp increase in the federal funds rate, and the 1990 recession followed a monetary tightening that ended in late 1989. Peaks in the federal funds rate also tend to coincide with the Romer dates. However, the lower panel of figure 1 shows why it would be premature to lay the blame for postwar recessions at the door of the Federal Reserve: as was first emphasized by Hamilton, nearly all of the postwar U.S. recessions have also followed increases in the nominal price of oil, which, in turn, have been associated with monetary tightenings.[16] Further, many of these oil price shocks were arguably exogenous, reflecting a variety of developments both in the Middle East and in the domestic industry, as indicated by the Hoover-Perez dates. Thus the general identification problem is here cast in a specific form: what portion of the last five

14. See Dotsey and Reid (1992) and Hoover and Perez (1994).
15. Hoover and Perez (1994), in their critique of the Romer and Romer approach, introduce six dates, which are, in turn, based on a chronology due to Hamilton (1983). We have added August 1990, the month when Iraq invaded Kuwait.
16. Hamilton (1983).

Figure 1. Federal Funds Rate, Oil Prices, and NBER Recessions, 1965–95[a]

Federal funds rate (percent)

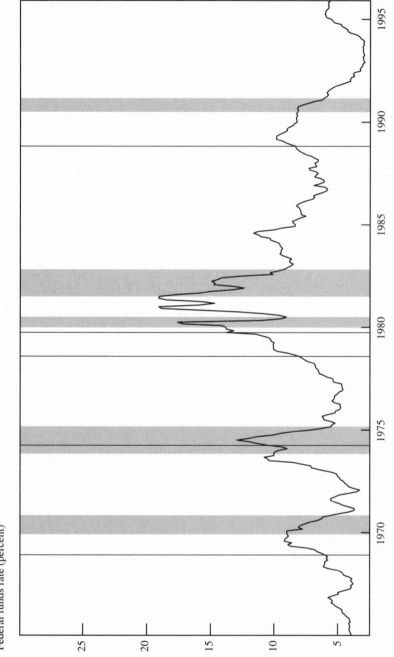

Log crude oil price index[b]

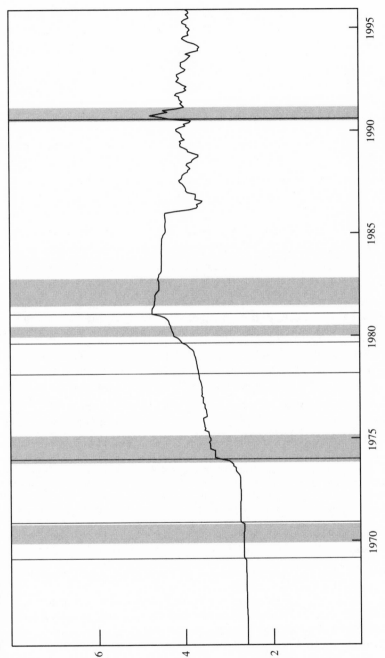

Source: CITIBASE, series FYFF (federal funds rate) and PW561 (crude oil prices); see appendix B for details of all variables. Also (see note a) Romer and Romer (1989) and Hoover and Perez (1994).
a. Data are monthly; tic marks correspond to January. Shaded bands correspond to recessions as dated by the National Bureau of Economic Research. In the upper panel, vertical lines mark contractionary policy changes by the Federal Reserve, as dated by Romer and Romer. In the lower panel, vertical lines mark oil market disruptions, as dated by Hoover and Perez, plus the month of August 1990,
when Iraq invaded Kuwait.
b. Log of index that is constructed so that 1982 = 100.

U.S. recessions, and of aggregate output and price fluctuations in general, was due to oil price shocks, per se, and what portion was due to the Federal Reserve's response to those shocks? To answer this question requires a means of measuring the effects of anticipated or systematic monetary policies.[17]

Measuring Oil Price Shocks and their Effects

We propose to identify the importance of the monetary policy feedback rule in a modified VAR framework. In order to do that, however, one needs to find an appropriate indicator of oil price shocks to incorporate into the VAR systems. This is a more difficult task than it may appear at first. The most natural indicator would seem to be changes in the nominal oil price; and indeed, in an article which helped to initiate the literature on the effects of oil price shocks, Hamilton shows that increases in the nominal price of oil Granger-cause downturns in economic activity.[18] However, the arrival of new data has shown this simple measure to have a rather unstable relationship with macroeconomic outcomes, leading subsequent researchers to employ increasingly complicated specifications of the "true" relationship between oil and the economy.[19] In particular, Hamilton argues in his more recent work that the correct measure of oil shocks depends very much upon the precise mechanism by which changes in the price of oil are supposed to affect the economy, a question for which many answers have been proposed but on which there is little agreement.[20] For our purposes, the exact channels through which oil affects the economy are not crucial.

17. In this paper, we take as given that anticipated as well as unanticipated monetary policies influence the real economy, owing to the existence of various nominal rigidities. Our objective is to provide an estimate of the real impact of the systematic component of monetary policy, as opposed to testing the null hypothesis that this component is neutral.

18. Hamilton (1983), to the surprise of many, also demonstrates that there appears to have been a close relationship between oil price increases and recessions even before the major OPEC shocks of the 1970s.

19. See, for example, Mork (1989), Lee, Ni, and Ratti (1995), Hamilton (1996a), and Hooker (1996a, 1996b).

20. Possibilities discussed by Hamilton (1996a) include aggregate supply effects operating through costs of production and the indirect effects of wage rigidity; aggregate demand effects; effects arising from the interaction of uncertainty about future energy prices and the irreversibility of investment; and asymmetric sectoral impacts that force costly reallocations of resources.

What matters is that one can identify an exogenous movement in the price of oil that has a significant and a priori plausible reduced-form impact on the economy.

Figure 2 illustrates the effects of some alternative measures of oil price shocks on selected variables, as indicated by estimated impulse response functions (IRFs). Each IRF is based on a five-variable VAR that includes, in this order: (1) the log of real GDP; (2) the log of the GDP deflator; (3) the log of an index of spot commodity prices; (4) an indicator of the state of the oil market; and (5) the level of the federal funds rate. Data are monthly; the VAR is estimated using a constant and seven lags, as determined by the Akaike information criterion (AIC); and the sample period is 1965–95.[21] Only the impulse responses of real GDP, the GDP deflator, and the federal funds rate are shown, in each case over a forty-eight-month horizon and for an oil price shock normalized to correspond to a 1 percent increase in the current nominal oil price. Dashed lines correspond to one standard error bands. As is standard in the VAR literature on the effects of monetary policy, the index of commodity prices is added to the VAR to control for information that the Fed may have about future inflation which is not captured by the other variables in the system.[22] The federal funds rate is included as an indicator of monetary policy.[23] The ordering of the oil indicator after the macroeconomic variables imposes the reasonable

21. Appendix A describes the construction of monthly data for GDP and the GDP deflator. The logarithm of real GDP is detrended with a cubic spline with three equally spaced knot points imposing equality of the levels and first two derivatives at the knot points. The resulting estimated trend component is essentially piecewise linear, with a break in the early 1970s reflecting the productivity slowdown. Other data are from the CITIBASE electronic database, available from Citicorp Database Services (see appendix B). The CITIBASE labels for the series are: FYFF (federal funds rate), PSCCOM (commodity price index), and PW561 (nominal oil price index, Producer Price Index for crude oil and products). We focus here on full sample results; we discuss possible subsample instabilities below.

22. The inclusion of the commodity price index is suggested by Sims (1992) as a way of eliminating the so-called price puzzle in monetary policy VARs. In the present context, it is important to note that, for most of its history, the commodity price index appears to have excluded oil and other energy prices (a little uncertainty remains because of the poor documentation of the series). Since 1987, an oil price has been included in the index. As we report below, however, there is little evidence that its inclusion has any substantive effect on our results.

23. Results from Bernanke and Blinder (1992), Bernanke and Mihov (1995), and Friedman and Kuttner (1996) suggest that it is reasonable to use the funds rate as a policy indicator, except possibly during the 1979–82 reserves-targeting period.

Figure 2. Responses to a 1 Percent Oil Price Shock, Four Specifications[a]

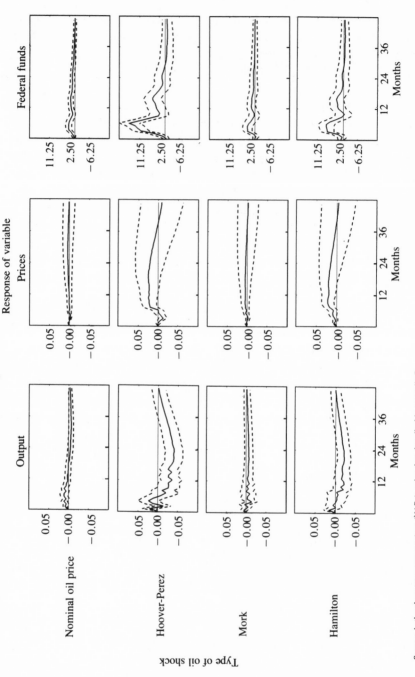

Source: Authors' vector autoregressions (VARs), using data described in appendix B.

a. Graphs show forty-eight month response of variables to each of four oil shock specifications. Vertical axis scales represent percent deviations of variables (basis point deviations for the federal funds rate). Dashed lines represent one-standard-error bands. Sample period is 1965–95.

assumption that oil price shocks do not significantly affect the economy within the month. Similarly, ordering the funds rate last follows the conventional assumption that monetary policy operates with at least a one-month lag. The results are not sensitive to these ordering assumptions, as we document below in the context of a larger system.

In figure 2 we report results for four alternative indicators of the state of the oil market; one is a slight variation of the original Hamilton indicator, the other three are more exotic indicators that have been developed in ongoing attempts to identify a stable relationship between oil price shocks and the economy:

—Log of the nominal Producer Price Index (PPI) for crude oil and products; the nominal oil price, for short. Hamilton employs the log-difference of the nominal oil price, which, given the presence of freely estimated lag parameters, is nearly equivalent to using the log-level. Given the other variables included in the VAR, this indicator is also essentially the same as that used by Julio Rotemberg and Michael Woodford.[24]

—Hoover-Perez. These are the oil shock dates identified by Hoover and Perez plus August 1990, as discussed in regard to figure 1.[25] To scale these dates by relative importance, for each month we multiply the Hoover-Perez dummy variables by the log change in the nominal price of oil over the three months centered on the given month.

—Mork. After the sharp oil price declines of 1985–86 failed to lead to an economic boom, Knut Mork argued that the effects of positive and negative oil price shocks on the economy need not be symmetric.[26] Empirically, he provided evidence that only positive changes in the relative price of oil have important effects on output. Accordingly, in our VARs we employ an indicator that equals the log-difference of the relative price of oil when that change is positive and otherwise is zero.[27]

24. Hamilton (1983); Rotemberg and Woodford (1996).
25. Hoover and Perez (1994).
26. Mork (1989).
27. We measure the relative price of oil as the PPI for crude oil divided by the GDP deflator. Mork (1989) argues that the PPI for crude oil is a distorted measure of the marginal cost of oil during certain periods marked by domestic price controls; he therefore measures oil prices by refiner acquisition cost instead, for the period for which those data are available. We choose to stick with the crude oil PPI for simplicity, and because we feel that there are also problems with the refiner acquisition cost as a measure of the marginal cost of crude.

—Hamilton. In response to the breakdown of the relationship between output and simpler measures of oil price shocks, Hamilton has
proposed a more complicated measure of oil price changes: the "net
oil price increase."[28] This measure distinguishes between oil price increases that establish new highs relative to recent experience and increases that simply reverse recent decreases. Specifically, in the context
of monthly data, Hamilton's measure equals the maximum of (a) zero
and (b) the difference between the log-level of the crude oil price for
the current month and the maximum value of the logged crude oil price
achieved in the previous twelve months. Hamilton provides some evidence for the usefulness of this variable, using semiparametric methods,
and Hooker also finds it to perform well, in the sense of having a
relatively stable relationship with macroeconomic variables.[29]

The deficiencies of the simplest measure of the state of the oil market,
the nominal price of crude oil, are apparent from figure 2. In particular,
for our 1965–95 sample period, a shock to the nominal price of oil is
followed by a *rise* in output for the first year or so and by a slight short-
run *decline* in the price level. Both of these results (which have been
verified in the recent literature on oil price shocks) are anomalous,
relative to the conventional wisdom about the effects of oil price shocks
on the economy. As indicated in note 29, other simple measures, such
as the relative price of oil, give similarly unsatisfactory results.

The three more complex indicators (Hoover-Perez, Mork, and Hamilton) produce "better looking" IRFs, in that output falls and prices
rise following an oil price shock, although generally neither response
is statistically significant. The point estimates of the effect of an oil
price shock on output suggest a modest impact from an economic perspective. For example, in the case of the Hamilton indicator, the sum

28. Hamilton (1996a, 1996b).
29. Hamilton (1996b); Hooker (1996a). We also experimented with VARs including
the log-difference of the nominal price of oil (the indicator used by Hamilton, 1983);
the log of the real price of oil (the nominal oil price divided by the GDP deflator); the
log-difference of the real price of oil; and the log of the nominal price of oil weighted
by the share of energy costs in GDP (as suggested by William Nordhaus at the Brookings
Panel meeting). As the results obtained were very similar to those using the log nominal
price of oil, we do not report them here. The literature provides yet additional indicators
of oil price shocks. Those proposed by Ferderer (1996) and Lee, Ni, and Ratti (1995),
for example, focus on the volatility of oil prices rather than the level. For simplicity,
we ignore these second-moment-based measures and concentrate on measures that are
functions of the level of oil prices.

of the impulse response coefficients for output over the first forty-eight months is -0.538, implying that a 1 percent (transitory) shock to oil prices leads to a cumulative loss of about 0.5 percent of a month's real GDP, or 0.045 percent of a year's real GDP, over four years. As is touched on below, more economically and statistically significant effects of oil price shocks are estimated (a) when the latter part of the sample, which contains the somewhat anomalous 1990 episode, is omitted; and (b) when the VAR system is augmented with short-term and long-term market interest rates.

Figure 2 also shows that for all four indicators of the oil market, a positive innovation to oil prices is followed by a rise in the funds rate (tighter monetary policy), as expected, and the response is generally statistically significant. This funds rate response illustrates the generic identification problem: without further structure, it is not possible to determine how much of the decline in output is the direct result of the increase in oil prices, as opposed to the ensuing tightening of monetary policy.

This brief exercise demonstrates a main result of the recent literature on the macroeconomic effects of oil prices, that finding a measure of oil price shocks that "works" in a VAR context is not straightforward. It is also true that the estimated impacts of these measures on output and prices can be quite unstable over different samples, as discussed below. For present purposes, however, based on the evidence of the literature and our own analysis (including figure 2), we choose the Hamilton net oil price increase measure of oil price shocks for our basic analyses.[30] As we discuss further below, we have checked the robustness of our exercises to the use of alternative oil market indicators; in general, we find that when a given oil-market indicator yields reasonable results in exercises like those shown in figure 2, our alternative simulations also perform reasonably.

Measuring the Effects of Endogenous Monetary Policy

Figure 2 shows that, at least for some more complex—some might argue, data-mined—indicators of oil prices, an exogenous increase in the price of oil has the expected effects on the economy: output falls,

---

30. In particular, Hooker (1996a) finds that the Hamilton measure is the most stable across subsamples.

prices rise, and monetary policy tightens (presumably in response to the inflationary pressures from the oil shock). Since James Tobin's Brookings paper, however, it has been argued that oil and energy costs are too small relative to total production costs to account for the entire decline in output that, at least in some episodes, has followed increases in the price of oil.[31] A natural hypothesis, therefore, is that part of the recessionary impact of oil price increases arises from the subsequent monetary contraction.

Sims and Zha attempt to provide rough estimates of the contribution of endogenous monetary policy changes in a VAR context.[32] Their approach is to "shut down" the policy response that would otherwise be implied by the VAR estimates; for example, by setting the federal funds rate (the monetary policy indicator) at its baseline level (the value that it would have taken in the absence of the exogenous nonpolicy shock). The difference between the total effect of the exogenous non-policy shock on the system variables and the estimated effect when the policy response is shut down is then interpreted as a measure of the contribution of the endogenous policy response.

As Sims and Zha correctly point out, this procedure is equivalent to combining the initial nonpolicy shock with a series of policy innovations just sufficient to off-set the endogenous policy response. Implicitly, then, in the Sims-Zha exercise, people in the economy are repeatedly "surprised" by the failure of policy to respond to the nonpolicy shock in its accustomed way. The authors argue, not unreasonably, that it would take some time for people to learn that policy was not going to respond in its usual way; so that, for deviations of policy from its historical pattern that are neither too large nor too protracted, their estimates of the policy effects may be acceptable approximations. This justification is similar to the one that Sims uses in earlier articles for conducting policy analyses in a VAR setting, despite the issues raised by the Lucas critique.[33]

31. Tobin (1980). See also Darby (1982), Kim and Loungani (1992), and Rotemberg and Woodford (1996). Rotemberg and Woodford argue that a monopolistically competitive market structure, which leads to changing markups over the business cycle, in principle can explain the strong effect of oil price shocks.
32. Sims and Zha (1995). Counterfactual simulations in a VAR context have also been performed by West (1993) and Kim (1995); neither paper distinguishes anticipated from unanticipated movements in policy.
33. See, for example, Sims (1986).

Rather than ignoring Lucas's argument altogether, however, one might try to accommodate it partially in the VAR context, by acknowledging that it may be more important for some markets than for others. In particular, the evidence for the relevance of the Lucas critique seems much stronger for financial markets—for example, in the determination of the term structure of interest rates—than in labor and product markets, which has led some economic forecasters and policy analysts to propose and estimate models with rational expectations in the financial market only.[34] In that spirit, we modify the Sims-Zha procedure for measuring the effects of endogenous policy by assuming that interest rate expectations are formed rationally (and in particular, that financial markets anticipate alternative policy paths), but that the other equations of the VAR system are invariant to the contemplated policy change. The latter assumption can be rationalized by assuming either that expectations of monetary policy enter the true structural equations for output, prices, and so forth only through the term structure of interest rates; or, if other policy-related expectations enter into those structural equations, that (for policy changes that are not too large) these respond more sluggishly than financial market expectations, as proposed by Sims.[35] Although our method is obviously neither fully structural nor immune to the Lucas critique, it provides an interesting alternative to the Sims-Zha approach.

More specifically, we consider small VAR systems that include standard macroeconomic variables, short-term and long-term interest rates, and the federal funds rate (as an indicator of monetary policy). We make the following assumptions:

—First, that the federal funds rate does not *directly* affect macroeconomic variables such as output and prices; a reasonable assumption, since the funds rate applies to a very limited set of transactions (overnight borrowings of commercial bank reserves). Hence the funds rate is excluded from the equations in the system determining those variables. However, the funds rate is allowed to affect macroeconomic variables indirectly, through its effect on short-term and long-term interest rates, which, in turn, are allowed to enter every equation that deter-

---

34. See Blanchard (1984) on the comparative relevance of the Lucas critique. See Taylor (1993) for an example of a model with rational expectations limited to the financial market.

35. Sims (1986).

mines a macroeconomic variable. Note that the assumption that monetary policy works strictly through interest rates is conservative, as it ignores other possible channels, such as the exchange rate and the "credit channel." In this sense, our estimates should represent a lower bound on the contribution of endogenous monetary policy.

—Second, following many previous authors, that the macroeconomic variables in the system are Wold-causally prior to all interest rates. That is, in our monthly data, we assume that interest rates respond to contemporaneous developments in the economy, but that changes in interest rates do not affect "slow-moving" variables such as output and prices within the month. This is a plausible assumption, given planning and production lags.[36]

—Third, that the funds rate is Wold-causally prior to the other market interest rates. That is, the covariation between innovations in the funds rate and in other interest rates is caused by the influence of monetary policy changes on interest rates, rather than by the response of the policymakers to market rates within the month. This is a strong assumption, although it appears to give fairly reasonable results in the context of the expectations theory of the term structure. It may be justified if the term premium contains no information about the economy that is not also contained in the other variables seen by the Fed. Below, we briefly discuss an alternative ordering assumption that allows for considerable reaction by the Fed to current market interest rate movements.

Formally, let $\mathbf{Y}_t$ denote a set of macroeconomic variables, including the price of oil, at date t. Similarly, let $\mathbf{R}_t = (R_t^s, R_t^l)$ represent the set of market interest rates; specifically, the three-month Treasury bill rate (the "short rate," R_t^s) and the ten-year Treasury bond rate (the "long rate," R_t^l). Finally, the scalar FF_t is the federal funds rate. Under the assumptions above, the restricted VAR system is written

$$(1) \qquad \mathbf{Y}_t = \sum_{i=1}^{p} (\pi_{yy,i} \mathbf{Y}_{t-i} + \pi_{yr,i} \mathbf{R}_{t-i}) + G_{yy} \boldsymbol{\epsilon}_{y,t}$$

36. As Sims points out, however, the assumption is less plausible for the commodity price index, which is included in the nonpolicy block as an information variable; see Leeper, Sims, and Zha (1996).

$$(2) \quad FF_t = \sum_{i=1}^{p} (\boldsymbol{\pi}_{fy,i}\mathbf{Y}_{t-i} + \boldsymbol{\pi}_{fr,i}\mathbf{R}_{t-i} + \boldsymbol{\pi}_{ff,i}FF_{t-i})$$

$$+ \boldsymbol{\epsilon}_{ff,t} + \mathbf{G}_{fy}\boldsymbol{\epsilon}_{y,t} + \mathbf{G}_{fr}\boldsymbol{\epsilon}_{r,t}$$

$$(3) \quad \mathbf{R}_t = \sum_{i=1}^{p} (\boldsymbol{\pi}_{ry,i}\mathbf{Y}_{t-i} + \boldsymbol{\pi}_{rr,i}\mathbf{R}_{t-i} + \boldsymbol{\pi}_{rf,i}FF_{t-i})$$

$$+ \boldsymbol{\epsilon}_{r,t} + \mathbf{G}_{ry}\boldsymbol{\epsilon}_{y,t} + \mathbf{G}_{rf}\boldsymbol{\epsilon}_{ff,t},$$

where the π and G terms are matrices of coefficients of the appropriate dimensions, the ϵ terms are vectors of orthogonal error terms, and constant terms have been omitted for notational convenience. For equation 1, the exclusion of FF_{t-i} follows from the first assumption above, that the funds rate does not directly affect macroeconomic variables; and the exclusion of $\epsilon_{r,t}$ and $\epsilon_{ff,t}$ is implied by the second assumption, that innovations to interest rates do not affect the nonpolicy variables within the period.

In order to apply the expectations theory to identify a relationship between the funds rate and the market interest rates, and to implement our policy experiments, it is useful to decompose the market rates into two parts: a part reflecting expectations of future values of the nominal funds rate, and a term premium. We define the following variables:

$$(4) \qquad \bar{R}_t^s = E_t \left(\sum_{i=0}^{ns-1} \omega_{s,i} FF_{t+i} \right)$$

$$(5) \qquad \bar{R}_t^l = E_t \left(\sum_{i=0}^{nl-1} \omega_{l,i} FF_{t+i} \right)$$

$$(6) \qquad S_t^s = R_t^s - \bar{R}_t^s$$

$$(7) \qquad S_t^l = R_t^l - \bar{R}_t^l,$$

where $ns = 3$ months and $nl = 120$ months are the terms of the short-term and long-term rates, respectively; the weights, ω, are defined by

$$\omega_{s,i} = \beta^i \bigg/ \sum_{j=0}^{ns-1} \beta^j \text{ and } \omega_{l,i} = \beta^i \bigg/ \sum_{j=0}^{nl-1} \beta^j; \text{ and } E \text{ is the expectations}$$

operator. We set the monthly discount factor, β equal to 0.997, so that β^{12} is equal to 0.96^{37}. The $\overline{\mathbf{R}}$ variables defined in equations 4 and 5 are the "expectations components" of the short and long market interest rates, and the residual $\mathbf{S}$ terms in equations 6 and 7 are time-varying term-cum-risk premiums associated with rates at the two maturities. Note that the time series of the two components of short and long interest rates are easily calculated from current and lagged values of $\mathbf{Y}$, FF, and $\mathbf{R}$, using the estimated π parameters in equations 1–3. In particular, finding the estimated expectations components of short and long rates is purely a forecasting exercise and does not require structural identifying assumptions.

With these definitions, it is useful to rewrite the model of equations 1–3 as

$$(8) \qquad \mathbf{Y}_t = \sum_{i=1}^{p} [\pi_{yy,i}\mathbf{Y}_{t-i} + \pi_{yr,i}(\overline{\mathbf{R}}_{t-i} + \mathbf{S}_{t-i})] + G_{yy}\boldsymbol{\epsilon}_{y,t}$$

$$(9) \quad FF_t = \sum_{i=1}^{p} (\pi_{fy,i}\mathbf{Y}_{t-i} + \pi_{fr,i}\mathbf{R}_{t-i} + \pi_{ff,i}FF_{t-i})$$

$$+ \ \epsilon_{ff,t} + G_{fy}\boldsymbol{\epsilon}_{y,t} + G_{fs}\boldsymbol{\epsilon}_{s,t}$$

$$(10) \quad \mathbf{S}_t = \sum_{i=1}^{p} (\lambda_{sy,i}\mathbf{Y}_{t-i} + \lambda_{sr,i}\mathbf{R}_{t-i} + \lambda_{sf,i}FF_{t-i})$$

$$+ \ \epsilon_{s,t} + G_{sy}\boldsymbol{\epsilon}_{y,t} + G_{sf}\epsilon_{ff,t}.$$

Equation 8 is identical to equation 1, except that the two market interest rates have been broken up into their expectations and term premium components. Equations 9 and 10 correspond to equations 2 and 3, with the interest rates, $\mathbf{R}$, replaced by the corresponding term premiums, $\mathbf{S}$. Since the difference between $\mathbf{R}$ and $\mathbf{S}$ is the expectations component of interest rates, which is constructed as a projection on current and lagged values of observable variables, equation 10 are equivalent to equations 2 and 3. In particular, the coefficients in equations 9 and 10 are simply combinations of the coefficients in equation 3 and the projection coefficients of the federal funds rate on current and lagged variables.

---

37. This weighting function and the value of β are suggested by Shiller, Campbell, and Schoenholz (1983).

We work with the system of equations 8–10 because it simplifies the imposition of some alternative identifying restrictions. Our main identifying assumption, discussed above, is that the federal funds rate is Wold-causally prior to the other interest rates in the model; this corresponds to the assumption that $G_{fs} = 0$ in equation 9. However, an alternative assumption, which allows for two-way causality between the funds rate and market rates, is that shocks to the federal funds rate affect other interest rates contemporaneously only through their impact on expectations of the future funds rate (that is, funds rate shocks do not affect term premiums contemporaneously); this corresponds to the restriction that $G_{sf} = 0$ in equation 10. Note that this alternative assumption allows the funds rate to respond to innovations in term premiums. In both cases, we assume that G_{yy} is lower-triangular (with ones on the diagonal), as in conventional VAR analyses employing the Choleski decomposition. In most of our applications, the "macro block" consists of real GDP, the GDP deflator, the commodity price index, and Hamilton's net oil price increase variable, in that order; as we show below, our results are robust to the placement of the oil market indicator.

To illustrate how we carry out policy experiments, consider the scenario of greatest interest in this paper: a shock to the oil price variable. The base case, which incorporates the effects of the endogenous policy response, is calculated in the conventional way, by simulating the effects of an innovation to the oil price variable using the system of equations 8 to 10. Among the results of this exercise are the standard impulse response functions, showing the dynamic impact of an oil price shock on the variables of the system, including the policy variables.

To simulate the effects of an oil price shock under a counterfactual policy regime, we first specify an alternative path for the federal funds rate—more specifically, deviations from the baseline impulse response of the funds rate—in a manner analogous to the approach of Sims and Zha.[38] However, we assume that financial markets understand and anticipate this alternative policy response; by assuming "maximum credibility" of the Fed's announced future policy, we stand in direct contrast to Sims and Zha, who assume that market participants are purely

38. Sims and Zha (1995).

backward-looking. To incorporate this assumption into the simulation, we calculate the expectations component of interest rates, $\overline{\mathbf{R}}_{t+i}$, $i = 0$, 1, ..., that is consistent with the proposed future path for the federal funds rate. We then resimulate the effects of the oil shock in the system of equations 8–10, imposing values of $\overline{\mathbf{R}}_t$ consistent with the assumed path of the funds rate, and also choosing values of $\epsilon_{ff,t}$ such that the assumed future path of the funds rate is realized. Note that this method can be used to construct alternative impulse response functions based on full-sample or subsample estimates and to simulate counterfactual economic behavior for specific episodes, such as the major oil price shocks. We use it in both ways below.

Some Policy Experiments

With the methodology described above, we are able to perform a variety of policy experiments, using estimates from our sample period, January 1965 through December 1995. The VAR is estimated using a constant and seven lags, as determined by AIC.

A Monetary Policy Shock

To check on the reasonableness of the basic estimated system, we begin with the conventional analysis of a monetary policy shock, modeled here as a 25 basis point innovation to the federal funds rate. The effects of an innovation to the federal funds rate are traced out in a seven-variable system that includes output, the price level, the commodity price index, the Hamilton oil measure, the funds rate, and the short and long term premiums. Figure 3 presents the resulting impulse response functions. As described above, the values of the short and long term premiums at each date are calculated by subtracting the expectations component of short and long rates (based on forecasts of future values of the funds rate) from the short and long rates themselves. In this base case analysis, equivalent results are obtained by directly including the short and long rates in the VAR (ordered after the funds rate), and the implied responses for short and long rates are included in figure 3. In the data, there are large low-frequency movements in the term premium of the long rate, with trend increases of about 1 per-

Figure 3. Responses to a Monetary Policy Shock, Seven-Variable System[a]

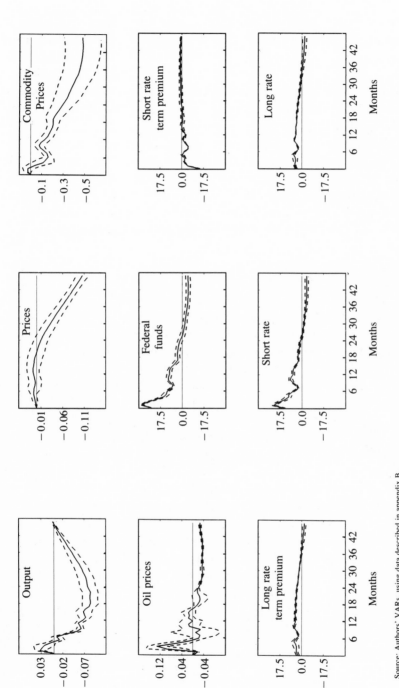

Source: Authors' VARs, using data described in appendix B.
a. Graphs show forty-eight month response of variables to a 25 basis point innovation in the federal funds rate. Vertical axis scales represent percent deviations of variables (basis point deviations of interest rate variables). Dashed lines represent one-standard-error bands. Sample period is 1965–95.

centage point in both the 1970s and the 1980s. We remove this trend variation with a cubic spline (specified as described in note 21). As we report in the section on robustness below, leaving the long premium undetrended does not significantly affect the results.[39] Impulse response functions to the funds rate innovation in figure 3 are shown with one-standard-error bands.

The results of this exercise will look quite familiar to those who know the recent VAR literature on the effects of monetary policy. The innovation to the funds rate (initially 25 basis points, peaking at about 35 basis points) is largely transitory, mostly dying away in the first nine months. Output declines relatively quickly, reaching a trough at about eighteen to twenty-four months and then gradually recovering. The price level responds sluggishly, but eventually declines, nearly two years after the policy innovation. Commodity prices also decline, and do so much more quickly than does the general price level.

The model's only exclusion restriction, that the funds rate does not belong in the "upper block" (which includes the oil indicator, output, prices, and commodity prices), conditional on the presence of short-term and long-term interest rates in that block, is marginally rejected: the p values for the exclusion of the funds rate from the upper block are, respectively, 0.01 for the output equation, 0.06 for the price level equation, 0.23 for the commodity price equation, and 0.18 for the oil equation. However, the effects of this exclusion do not seem to be economically very significant. For example, if we compare the effects of a funds rate shock on output in the restricted, seven-variable system with the analogous effects in the conventional, unrestricted, five-variable system (excluding the market interest rates), we obtain virtually identical results.

An interesting new feature of the seven-variable system is that it allows one to examine the responses of market interest rates to monetary policy innovations, and in particular, to compare these responses to the predictions of the pure expectations hypothesis. Looking first at short-

---

39. Fuhrer (1996) shows that the large movements in the long rate can be explained in a way consistent with the expectations hypothesis if the market was making rate forecasts at each date based on a particular set of beliefs about how the Federal Reserve's objective function has varied over time. However, there is nothing in Fuhrer's analysis that connects these hypothesized beliefs with the actual time-series behavior of the funds rate.

term (three-month) rates, a 25 basis point innovation to the funds rate implies about a 15 basis point increase in the short rate, and the two rates then decline synchronously. This seems quantitatively reasonable. To check the consistency of this response with the expectations hypothesis, one can look at the behavior of the short rate term premium, which, by construction, is the difference between the actual short term rate and the short term rate implied by the pure expectations hypothesis. The short rate term premium is significantly negative immediately following a funds rate innovation, implying that in the first month or two after an innovation to the funds rate, the short-term interest rate is estimated to respond less than would be predicted by the expectations hypothesis. However, the short rate term premium quickly becomes statistically and economically insignificant, suggesting that the expectations hypothesis is a reasonable description of the link between the funds rate and the short-term interest rate after the first month.

The long-term interest rate is a different story. As shown in figure 3, the long rate responds by about 5 basis points to the impact of a 25 basis point innovation in the funds rate, and the response remains above zero for some three years, which again does not seem unreasonable. However, comparison of the responses of the long-term interest rate and the long rate term premium reveals that they are very close, the latter being slightly less than the former. The implication is that the expectations theory explains relatively little of the relationship between the funds rate and the ten-year government bond rate. This finding is not so surprising, given the transitory nature of funds rate shocks compared with the duration of these bonds. The estimated behavior of the long term premium thus constitutes some evidence that long rates "overreact" to short rates, a phenomenon that has frequently been documented in the term structure literature (although, we appear to find less overreaction than is typically reported in the literature).[40]

Simulations of the Effects of an Oil Price Shock

Since our expanded model seems to perform reasonably in the case of an innovation to monetary policy, we now turn to the exercise of

40. An alternative explanation for the overreaction of the long rate is that the policy shock is imperfectly identified. Note, for example, the slight "output puzzle"—output increases in the first few months after the policy shock. Possibly a better identification scheme would eliminate the overreaction.

greatest interest, which is to use the model to decompose the effects of an oil price shock into direct and indirect (that is, through endogenous monetary policy) components. Figure 4 shows impulse responses following a shock to Hamilton's net oil price increase measure under three scenarios.

The first scenario, which we label "base," shows the impulse responses of the variables to a 1 percent innovation in the nominal price of oil in the seven-variable system. This is a normal VAR simulation, except that the funds rate does not enter directly into the equations for output, prices, commodity prices, or the oil indicator. This case is intended to show the effects on the economy of an oil price shock, *including* the endogenous response of monetary policy, in contrast with the next two simulations, which involve alternative methods of shutting off the policy response.

The second scenario we label "Sims-Zha" (with some abuse of terminology). In this case we simply fix the funds rate at its base values throughout the simulation, in the manner of Sims and Zha.[41] However, recall that in contrast to the original Sims-Zha exercise, in our system the funds rate does not enter directly into the block of macroeconomic variables. Rather, the funds rate exerts its macroeconomic effects only indirectly, through the short-term and long-term interest rates included in the system. Thus in this exercise, we are effectively allowing the change in the funds rate to act through its unconstrained, reduced-form impact on market interest rates (which are ordered after the funds rate).

The third scenario, which we label "anticipated policy," applies our own methodology, described above. We again set the funds rate equal to its baseline values; that is, we shut off the response of monetary policy to the oil shock and the changes induced by the oil shock in output, prices, and so forth. But in this case, we let the two components of short-term and long-term interest rates be determined separately. The expectations component of both interest rates is set to be consistent with the future path of the funds rate, as assumed in the scenario. The short and long term premiums are allowed to respond as estimated in the base model. (Below, we also consider a case where the term premiums are kept at their baseline values.) For the simple, constant funds rate case being examined here, the Sims-Zha and anticipated policy approaches

41. Sims and Zha (1995).

Figure 4. Responses to a Hamilton Oil Price Shock, Seven-Variable System[a]

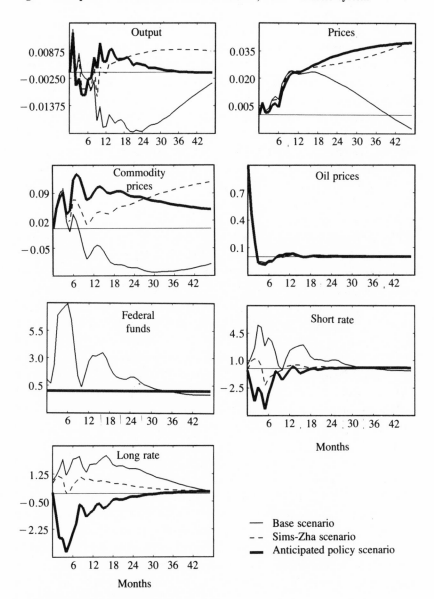

Source: Authors' VARs, using data described in appendix B.

a. Graphs show forty-eight month response of variables to a 1 percent Hamilton oil price shock. Sims-Zha and anticipated policy scenarios eliminate the normal response of monetary policy. Vertical axis scales represent percent deviations of variables (basis point deviations of interest rate variables). Sample period is 1965-95.

show roughly similar departures from baseline. Note, however, that the former cannot distinguish between policies that differ only in the expected future values of the funds rate, whereas, in principle, the latter approach can make that distinction.

The results of figure 4 are reasonable, with all variables exhibiting their expected qualitative behaviors. In particular, the absence of an endogenously restrictive monetary policy results in higher output and prices, as one would anticipate. Quantitatively, the effects are large, in that a nonresponsive monetary policy suffices to eliminate most of the output effect of an oil price shock, particularly after the first eight to ten months. The conclusion that a substantial part of the real effects of oil price shocks is due to the monetary policy response helps to explain why the effects of these shocks seems larger than can easily be explained in neoclassical (flexible price) models.[42]

The anticipated policy simulation results in modestly higher output and price responses than the Sims-Zha simulation in figure 4. The differences in results occur largely because the anticipated policy simulation involves a negative short-run response in both the short and long term premiums, and thus lower interest rates in the short run. Figure 5 repeats the anticipated policy simulation of figure 4, but with the response of the term premiums shut off; that is, the funds rate is allowed to affect the macroeconomic variables only through its effects on the expectations component of market rates. This alternative simulation attributes somewhat less of the recession that follows an oil shock to the monetary policy response, but endogenous monetary policy still accounts for two-thirds to three-fourths of the total effect of the oil price shock on output.

As another exercise in counterfactual policy simulation, we examine the three major oil price shocks followed by recessions: OPEC 1, OPEC 2, and the Iraqi invasion of Kuwait. Figure 6 shows the results, focusing on the behavior of three key variables (output, the price level, and the funds rate) for the five-year periods surrounding each of these episodes (respectively, 1972–76, 1979–83, and 1988–92). Each panel shows three paths of the given variable. One line depicts the actual historical path of the variable. The line marked ''federal funds endog-

---

42. It should be emphasized that we are not arguing that the policies actually followed by the Fed in the face of oil shocks were necessarily suboptimal; the usual output-inflation trade-off is present in our simulations, and we do not attempt a welfare analysis.

Figure 5. Responses to a Hamilton Oil Price Shock, No Premium Term Response[a]

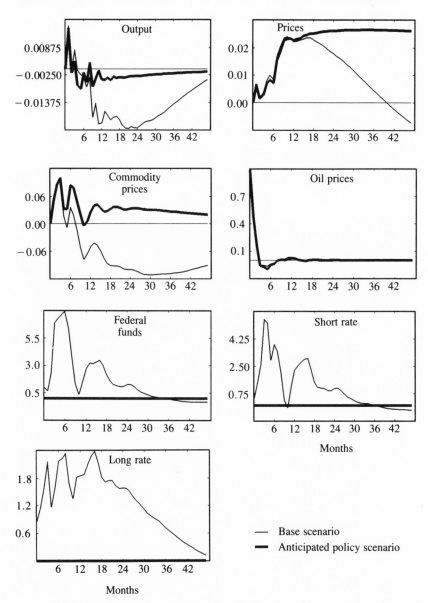

Source: Authors' VARs, using data described in appendix B.
a. Graphs show forty-eight-month response of variables to a 1 percent Hamilton oil price shock. Scenarios are as those shown in figure 4, except that the responses of term premiums are shut off. Vertical axis scales represent percent deviations of variables (basis point deviations of interest rate variables). Sample period is 1965–95.

Figure 6. Simulating Three Historical Oil Price Shocks[a]

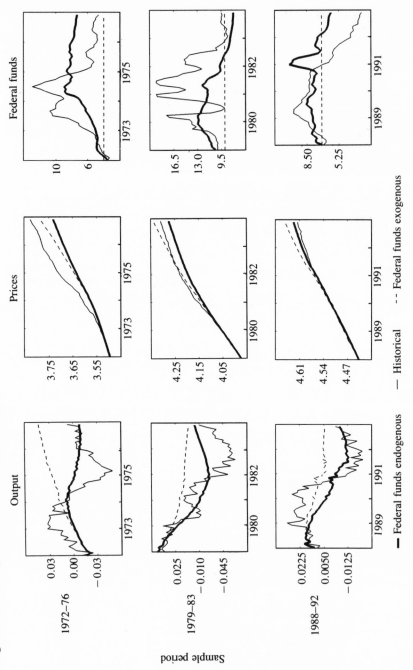

Source: Authors' VARs, using data described in appendix B.
a. For each of three historical episodes, graphs compare actual behavior of variables with their predicted responses under two alternative scenarios, described in the text. Vertical axis scales show log level of (detrended) output, log level of prices, and the federal funds rate in percent.

enous'' shows the behavior of the system when the oil variable is repeatedly shocked, so that it traces out its actual historical path; all other shocks in the system are set to zero; and the funds rate is allowed to respond endogenously to changes in the oil variable and the induced changes in output, prices, and other variables. This scenario is intended to isolate the portion of each recession that results solely from the oil price shocks and the associated monetary policy response. Finally, the line marked ''federal funds exogenous'' describes the results of an exercise in which oil prices equal their historical values, all other shocks are shut off, and the nominal funds rate is arbitrarily fixed at a value close to its initial value in the period. (Term premiums are allowed to respond to the oil price shock.) This last scenario eliminates the policy component of the effect of the oil price shock, leaving only the direct effect of the change in oil prices on the economy.

Several observations can be made from figure 6. First, the 1974–75 decline in output is generally not well explained by the oil price shock. The pattern of shocks reveals, instead, that the major culprit was (non-oil) commodity prices. Commodity prices (not shown) rose very sharply before this recession and stimulated a sharp monetary policy response of their own, as can be seen by comparing the historical path of the funds rate with its path in the federal funds endogenous scenario, in which the commodity price shocks are set to zero. The federal funds exogenous scenario, in which the funds rate responds to neither commodity price nor oil price shocks, exhibits no recession at all, suggesting that endogenous monetary policy (responding to both oil price and commodity price shocks) did, indeed, play an important role in this episode.

The results for 1979–83 generally conform to the conventional wisdom. The decline in output through 1981 is well explained by the 1979 oil price shock and the subsequent response of monetary policy. After the beginning of 1982, the main source of output declines (according to this analysis) was the lagged effect of the autonomous tightening of monetary policy in late 1980 and 1981. Note that if one excludes both the monetary policy reaction to the oil price shocks and the autonomous tightening of monetary policy by Federal Reserve Chairman Paul Volcker (as in the federal funds exogenous scenario), the 1979–83 period exhibits only a modest slowdown, not a serious recession.

The experiment for 1988–92 similarly shows that shutting off the policy response to oil price shocks produces a higher path of output and prices than otherwise; again, compare the paths of the endogenous monetary policy and exogenous monetary policy scenarios. One puzzle that emerges is why the substantial easing of actual policy from late 1990 did not move the actual path of output closer to the alternative policy scenario. It is possible that special factors, such as credit problems, may have been at work.

Oil, Money, and the Components of GDP

The application of our method for separating the direct effects of oil price shocks and the indirect effects operating through the monetary policy response leads to a rather strong conclusion: the majority of the impact of an oil price shock on the real economy is attributable to the central bank's response to the inflationary pressures engendered by the shock.

A check on the plausibility of this result, using a different identifying assumption and more disaggregated data, is provided by figure 7. This figure is based on the seven-variable VAR system employed above (real GDP, the GDP deflator, commodity prices, the Hamilton oil market indicator, the funds rate, and short-term and long-term interest rates), with the funds rate excluded from the first four equations. To this system we add, one at a time and without feedback into the main system, eight components of GDP: consumption, producer durables expenditure, structures investment, inventory investment, residential investment, government purchases, exports, and imports.[43] With these systems we conduct two experiments. First, we examine the impulse responses obtained when the Hamilton oil price variable is shocked by 1 percent and the federal funds rate is allowed to respond endogenously (these responses are shown by dashed lines in figure 7). Second, we examine the impulse responses to an exogenous federal funds rate shock of equal maximum value to the endogenous response of the funds rate in the first scenario (shown by solid lines). We think of this exercise as a comparison of the total effect of an oil price shock, including the

---

43. Except for consumption, which is available at the monthly frequency, monthly data for the GDP components are interpolated by state space methods; see appendix A. Components are measured relative to the exponential of the trend for the logarithm of real GDP, as calculated from the spline regression described in note 21.

Figure 7. Sectoral Responses to Oil Price and Monetary Policy Shocks[a]

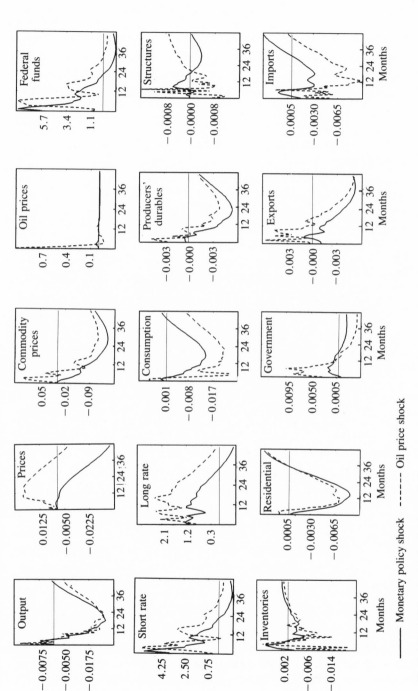

——— Monetary policy shock   – – – – – Oil price shock

Source: Authors' VARs, using data described in appendix B.
a. Graphs show forty-eight month response of variables to a 1 percent Hamilton oil price shock and to a federal funds rate innovation comparable to that resulting from the oil price shock. Vertical axis scales represent percent deviations of variables (basis point deviations of interest rate variables). Sample period is 1965–95.

endogenous monetary response, with the effect of a monetary tightening of similar magnitude but not associated with an oil price shock. To the extent that the two responses are quantitatively similar, it seems reasonable to attribute most of the total effect of the oil price shock to the monetary policy response. Note, however, that we are using a different identification assumption here than above; that is, we implicitly assume that the economy responds in the same way to endogenous and exogenous tighenings of monetary policy.

The results of shown in figure 7 provide substantial support for the view that the monetary policy response is the dominant source of the real effects of an oil price shock. In particular, the response of output is virtually identical in the two scenarios, implying that it matters little for real economic outcomes whether a change in monetary policy of a given magnitude is preceded by an oil price shock or not. Very similar responses across the two experiments are also found at the disaggregated level, especially in equipment investment (producers' durable equipment), inventory investment, and residential investment. Slightly greater effects for the scenario including the oil price shock are found for consumption and structures (although the latter difference is quantitatively small and statistically insignificant). Government purchases responds more strongly in the scenario that includes the oil price shock, for reasons that are not obvious.

The differences between the two scenarios are also instructive. The experiment that includes the initial oil price shock does show a substantial inflationary impact in the short run, which gives some indication as to why the Fed responds so vigorously to such shocks. On the margin, the oil price shock also raises commodity prices and the long-term interest rate (presumably, reflecting an increased risk premium) and it leads to increased real exports and decreased real imports (net of terms-of-trade effects). These responses are as expected.

Some Alternative Experiments

Although we have focused on the role of systematic monetary policy in propagating oil price shocks, our methodology applies equally well to other sorts of driving shocks. As a further check on the plausibility of our method, we briefly consider two alternative cases: a shock to commodity prices and a shock to output.

A COMMODITY PRICE SHOCK. Figure 8 looks at the effects of a shock to the commodity price index in our original seven-variable system. As with the oil price shock studied in figures 4 and 5, we consider three scenarios. First, in the base scenario we calculate the impulse responses resulting from a 1 percent innovation in commodity prices, allowing monetary policy (as represented by the federal funds rate) to respond in its normal way. Second, we examine the effects of shutting off the policy response, using the Sims-Zha methodology described above. Finally, we shut off the monetary policy response by means of our anticipated policy approach. For simplicity, in the anticipated policy simulation we set the responses of the term premiums to zero (as in figure 5), so that both short-term and long-term nominal interest rates are effectively assumed not to respond to the shock to commodity prices.

Figure 8 shows that a 1 percent innovation in commodity prices has an ambiguous effect on output: real GDP rises for the first year but declines thereafter. Prices rise unambiguously. One explanation for these results is that what we are labeling a positive shock to commodity prices is, in fact, a mixture of an adverse shock to aggregate supply and an expansionary shock to aggregate demand. The federal funds rate rises sharply in response to an increase in commodity prices, which we interpret as the Fed's response to the inflationary surge; other interest rates also rise. The oil price indicator responds very little in the short run to a commodity price innovation, which is reassuring, in the sense that it confirms that the commodity and oil price variables are not excessively collinear.

Shutting down the monetary policy response to the commodity price shock, by either the Sims-Zha or the anticipated policy method, leads to the expected response. Analogous to the case of oil price shocks, the recessionary impact of a commodity price shock is eliminated and the inflationary impact is magnified. Although it may well be the case that the innovation in commodity prices is not a cleanly identified supply shock, there is no evidence that an increase in commodity prices depresses real activity in the absence of a monetary policy response.

AN OUTPUT SHOCK. Figure 9 shows analogous results when the driving shock is a shock to output. As with the commodity shock, we compute

Figure 8. Responses to a Commodity Price Shock, No Term Premium Response[a]

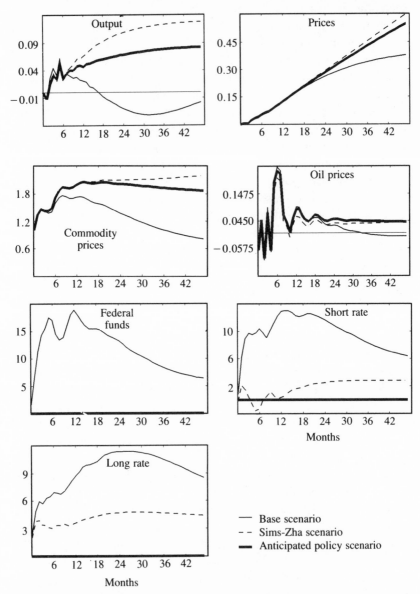

Figure 9. Responses to an Output Shock, No Term Premium Response[a]

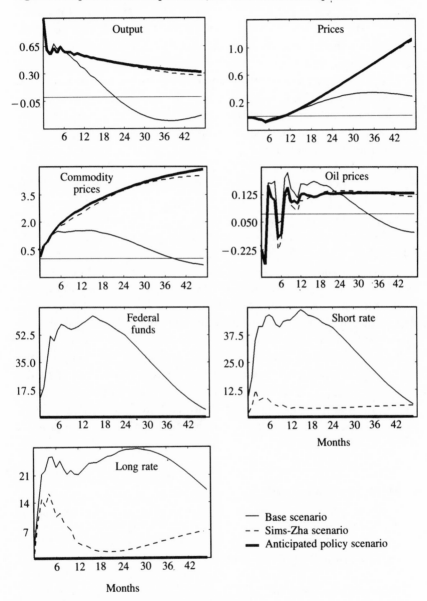

Source: Authors' VARs, using data described in appendix B.
a. Graphs show forty-eight month response of variables to a 1 percent output shock when the responses of term premiums are shut off. Sims-Zha and anticipated policy scenarios eliminate the normal response of monetary policy. Vertical axis scales represent percent deviations of variables (basis point deviations of interest rate variables). Sample period is 1965–95.

the impulse response functions for three cases: a base case in which monetary policy is allowed to respond in its normal way to the output shock, and cases corresponding to the Sims-Zha and anitcipated policy methods for shutting down the policy response. As before, we assume no response of the term premiums.

Admittedly, like a shock to commodity prices, an output shock does not have a clear a priori economic interpretation; it is an amalgam of various random factors affecting output, holding constant the other variables included in the system. However, based on figure 9 it seems reasonable to interpret output shocks in this system as being dominated by aggregate demand fluctuations: a positive output shock is followed by increases in oil prices, commodity prices, and the general price level, as well as in all three interest rates. Because the historical tendency of monetary policy is to ''lean against the wind,'' when the normal policy response is shut off, the effects of the aggregate demand shock (as we interpret the output shock) are all the greater. Figure 9 shows that in the Sims-Zha and anticipated policy scenarios, the output effect of the shock is much more persistent and prices rise by more than in the base case. Interest rates are lower, reflecting easier monetary policy. Note that in this analysis, the Sims-Zha and anticipated policy approaches give almost identical results.

These experiments demonstrate that our methods for shutting down the response of monetary policy are applicable to, and give reasonable results for, shocks other than oil price shocks. It would be interesting to combine our methodology with identified VAR techniques that could give a sharper structural interpretation to innovations estimated in the macro block of the model.

Robustness and Stability

We return to our main theme, the role of systematic monetary policy in amplifying the real effects of oil price shocks, to consider the robustness and stability of our results.

Robustness of the Results

We perform a variety of checks for robustness, some of which (such as shutting down the term premium response) are alluded to above. To provide more systematic information, table 1 reports some summary statistics from alternative specifications of our VAR system. We consider (a) three alternative oil-market indicators; (b) three alternative orderings of variables within the VAR; and (c) two alternative detrending assumptions. We also calculated results for alternative measures of output (for example, industrial production), alternative measures of the price level (for example, the personal consumption expenditure deflator and the consumer price index), and alternative interest rate maturities; but since none of these variable substitutions have important effects on our findings, they are omitted from the table.

The first row of table 1 reports results for the Hamilton oil indicator (our base specification), whereas the second and third rows substitute the Mork and Hoover-Perez indicators, respectively (see figure 2). The fourth row corresponds to ordering the federal funds rate after, rather than before, the two open market interest rates. The fifth row orders the Hamilton oil market indicator first in the system, and the sixth row orders the oil market indicator third—after output and prices, but before the commodity price index. The seventh row is for a specification in which output and the long rate term premium are not detrended, and the eighth row reports results when all variables in the system are detrended by a cubic spline (as described in note 21).

For each of the eight alternative specifications, table 1 reports the effects on output and prices of a 1 percent oil price shock, under (a) a standard simulation, allowing for the endogenous response of policy to the oil price shock; (b) the Sims-Zha simulation, in which the federal funds rate is fixed at its baseline value; and (c) the anticipated policy simulation. Under the heading "output," we report the sum of the impulse response coefficients for output for the first twenty-four months after the oil price shock, which we employ as a measure of the output loss associated with the shock. Under the heading "prices," we report the twenty-fourth impulse response coefficient for prices, divided by two, which can be interpreted as the increment in the annual average inflation rate over the first two years following the shock. Standard errors, calculated by Monte Carlo methods employing 500 draws per specification, are shown in parentheses. The table also shows the differences between the baseline (endogenous policy) specification and the results obtained under the Sims-Zha and anticipated policy assumptions, again with the associated standard errors.

Table 1. Robustness of Results to Alternative Specifications[a]

Specification	Baseline scenario		Sims-Zha scenario		Anticipated policy scenario	
	Output	Prices	Output	Prices	Output	Prices
Oil market indicator						
Hamilton	−0.308	0.009	0.133	0.013	0.179	0.016
	(0.334)	(0.014)	(0.361)	(0.015)	(0.565)	(0.022)
Difference from baseline	⋯	⋯	0.440	0.004	0.486	0.007
			(0.156)	(0.006)	(0.460)	(0.018)
Mork	−0.146	0.002	0.047	0.004	0.048	0.006
	(0.237)	(0.010)	(0.245)	(0.010)	(0.507)	(0.027)
Difference from baseline	⋯	⋯	0.193	0.002	0.194	0.004
			(0.065)	(0.003)	(0.449)	(0.026)
Hoover-Perez	−0.590	0.013	0.312	0.025	0.103	0.038
	(0.444)	(0.017)	(0.540)	(0.010)	(1.030)	(0.047)
Difference from baseline	⋯	⋯	0.901	0.012	0.693	0.025
			(0.355)	(0.013)	(0.920)	(0.045)
Ordering						
Federal funds last	−0.304	0.007	−0.079	0.009	0.237	0.015
	(0.356)	(0.015)	(0.371)	(0.015)	(0.682)	(0.024)
Difference from baseline	⋯	⋯	0.225	0.001	0.541	0.008
			(0.116)	(0.004)	(0.560)	(0.020)

Oil price first	−0.430 (0.391)	0.006 (0.015)	−0.111 (0.407)	0.009 (0.015)	0.012 (0.463)	0.011 (0.017)
Difference from baseline	· · ·	· · ·	0.319 (0.111)	0.003 (0.004)	0.441 (0.249)	0.006 (0.008)
Oil price third	−0.335 (0.331)	0.006 (0.014)	0.037 (0.360)	0.010 (0.015)	0.180 (0.525)	0.012 (0.017)
Difference from baseline	· · ·	· · ·	0.373 (0.145)	0.004 (0.006)	0.515 (0.404)	0.006 (0.011)
Detrending						
None	−0.065 (0.360)	0.006 (0.015)	0.195 (0.368)	0.008 (0.015)	0.349 (0.571)	0.008 (0.023)
Difference from baseline	· · ·	· · ·	0.260 (0.076)	0.001 (0.003)	0.414 (0.439)	0.002 (0.018)
All variables	−0.334 (0.323)	0.009 (0.007)	−0.034 (0.323)	0.000 (0.006)	0.330 (0.499)	−0.009 (0.015)
Difference from baseline	· · ·	· · ·	0.300 (0.099)	−0.009 (0.002)	0.664 (0.458)	−0.018 (0.014)

Source: Authors' calculations using data described in appendix B.

a. For eight different specifications (see text) and for the baseline, Sims-Zha, and anticipated policy assumptions regarding the response of monetary policy to an oil shock, the table shows the sum of impulse response coefficients over twenty-four months for output and the annualized inflation rate (the impulse response coefficient on month 24 divided by 2) resulting from a 1 percent shock to oil prices. Also shown are the differences in output and inflation effects from the Sims-Zha and anticipated policy simulations, relative to the baseline simulation. Standard errors are in parentheses. Estimates and standard errors are constructed by Monte Carlo methods, using 500 draws for each simulation.

The point estimates reported in table 1 are consistent with the findings discussed above (in figures 4 and 5, for example). In particular, the baseline simulations show that an oil price shock depresses output and increases inflation, by magnitudes that are reasonably comparable across all specifications. The Sims-Zha method of shutting off the monetary policy response tends to eliminate all or most of the negative effect of the oil price shock and, in almost all cases, increases the inflationary impact, as expected. The anticipated policy method of eliminating the policy response has even larger effects, fully eliminating the recessionary impact of the oil price shock in all cases. The standard errors for most entries in table 1 are quite high, reflecting the fact that the standard error bands on the impulse response functions spread out rather quickly.[44] However, the differences in the output responses between the baseline and alternative simulations are statistically significant in a number of cases, in particular, when the policy response is shut down by the Sims-Zha method.[45]

In general, our results appear to be qualitatively robust, although they are not always precisely estimated. In particular, a view that ascribes most or even all of the real effects of an oil price shock to the endogenous monetary response does not seem inconsistent with the data.

Stability of the Results: The Role of a Changing Policy Response

We take up the issue of subsample stability not only as a qualification of our results, but also because it appears that at least some of the observed instabilities of our system can be given an interesting economic interpretation. Indeed, we show that variations in the Federal Reserve's reaction function have something of the flavor of a natural

44. The standard errors are particularly high for the anticipated policy simulations, apparently reflecting, in part, the uncertainty associated with the long-term interest rate forecasts required by this method.

45. We also considered alternative models estimated with twelve lags, rather than the seven chosen by AIC. In this case, the finding that shutting off the monetary policy response eliminates the effect of the oil shock obtains at short horizons but not at the twenty-four-month horizon. The reason is that with twelve lags, the funds rate is estimated to rise in response to an oil price shock, but then to fall quickly below trend. Our alternative policy, which assumes no response throughout, is thus not effectively easier than the baseline policy over the twenty-four-month horizon.

experiment, which may help to improve the identification of the endogenous policy effect.

Some tests of the stability of the coefficients in our seven-variable base VAR, with lag lengths chosen by the Bayes information criterion, are reported in table 2. For simplicity, the funds rate is allowed to enter all equations. The upper panel, labeled "Quandt tests," gives asymptotic p values for the hypothesis that the coefficients of the variable listed in the column heading, together with the regression constant term, are stable over the sample period in the equation given by the row heading. Thus, for example, the Quandt tests show that the hypothesis that the coefficients on the price level in the oil equation are stable over the entire sample can be rejected at the 0.016 confidence level. In a similar format, the Chow split-sample tests reported in the lower panel of table 2 tests each set of coefficients for stability across the two halves of the sample. These tests are included because, unlike the Quandt tests, they are robust to heteroskedasticity.

There is substantial evidence of instability in the VAR system. The equation for the price level is clearly quite unstable, with p values near zero for most blocks of coefficients. The Quandt tests also suggest that there is instability in the coefficients relating the funds rate and the short-term and long-term interest rates. Nevertheless, stability of the output equation cannot be rejected.

It appears, however, that at least some of the instability in the link between oil and the macroeconomy may be due to a shift in the policy response. Figure 10 illustrates this point. The figure shows the output, price level, and federal funds rate responses to an oil price shock, as implied by systems estimated over the whole sample and over each of the three decades of the sample (1966–75, 1976–85, and 1986–95).

The full sample estimates of the effects of an oil price shock are as seen above. Note, though, how the responses vary over subsamples (keeping in mind that ten-year subsamples are short for this purpose). The output response across different periods is inversely correlated with the funds rate response. The sharpest decline in output occurs in the period 1976–85, which also exhibits the most aggressive rise in the funds rate. The strong response of monetary policy during this period presumably reflects the Federal Reserve's substantially increased concern with inflation during the Volcker regime. The output response is weakest in the 1986–95 subsample. In this case, there is virtually no

Table 2. Tests for Stability of Coefficients in the VAR[a]

Asymptotic p value

Equation	Regressor						
	Oil prices	Output	Prices	Commodity prices	Federal funds	Short rate	Long rate
Quandt tests							
Oil prices	0.000	0.004	0.016	0.004	0.188	0.267	0.461
Output	0.439	0.926	0.699	0.362	0.338	0.607	0.187
Prices	0.000	0.003	0.000	0.000	0.005	0.014	0.002
Commodity prices	0.002	0.177	0.129	0.000	0.001	0.170	0.045
Federal funds	0.012	0.042	0.041	0.483	0.000	0.001	0.000
Short rate	0.152	0.132	0.017	0.092	0.128	0.072	0.000
Long rate	0.644	0.116	0.782	0.459	0.004	0.001	0.609
Chow split-sample tests							
Oil prices	0.882	0.651	0.233	0.422	0.259	0.181	0.667
Output	0.757	0.633	0.591	0.303	0.115	0.919	0.839
Prices	0.000	0.000	0.000	0.000	0.000	0.001	0.000
Commodity prices	0.004	0.131	0.080	0.127	0.109	0.018	0.007
Federal funds	0.814	0.159	0.125	0.123	0.048	0.099	0.030
Short rate	0.809	0.359	0.187	0.335	0.557	0.152	0.031
Long rate	0.254	0.215	0.388	0.658	0.507	0.002	0.581

Source: Authors' calculations using data described in appendix B.

a. The table shows asymptotic p values for tests of the stability of the coefficients of the regressors shown in the column heading, together with the regression constant term, in the equation given by the row heading. The funds rate is allowed to enter all equations. Lag lengths are chosen by the Bayes information criterion. First differences are used for all variables except the oil price indicator, which, by construction, is the difference of various oil prices. The upper panel is based on Wald versions of the Quandt (1960) test over the middle 70 percent of the sample. The lower panel is based on heteroskedasticity-robust Wald tests for breaks at the sample midpoint. The p values are computed using the approximation due to Hansen (1997).

Figure 10. Responses to a 1 Percent Oil Price Shock, Alternative Sample Periods[a]

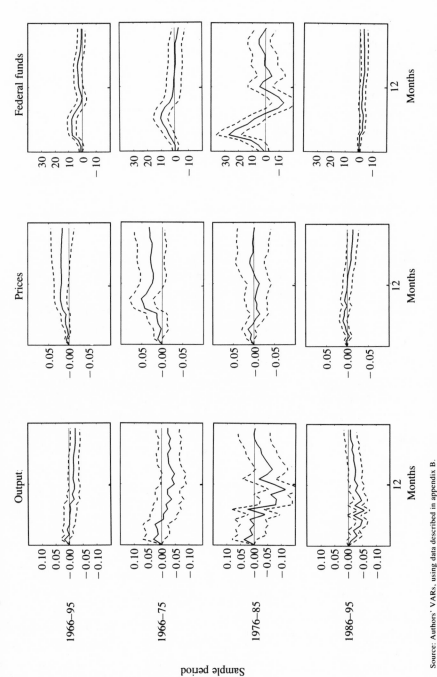

Source: Authors' VARs, using data described in appendix B.
a. Graphs show twenty-four-month response of variables to a 1 percent shock to the Hamilton oil price measure, estimated over four alternative sample periods. Vertical axis scales represent percent deviations of variables (basis point deviations for the federal funds rate). Dashed lines represent one-standard-error bands.

response in the funds rate. The atypical behavior of the funds rate during this period may reflect the presence of confounding factors, such as the weakness of financial sector balance sheets and the decline in consumer confidence that depressed the economy at the time of the one major oil shock of that subsample, the 1990 increase in prices. In any event, the subsample evidence is highly consistent with the view that the reduced-form impact of oil on the economy depends significantly on the monetary policy reaction function.

Conclusion

This paper offers both methodological and substantive contributions. Methodologically, we show how to modify standard VAR systems to permit simulations of the economy under alternative endogenous policies. Since our focus is on quantifying the economic impact of historical feedback policies, the alternative policy that we consider is very simple; a virtue of our approach is that it would not be difficult to extend the analysis to consider more interesting alternatives, for example, "Taylor rules." It would also be interesting to compare our results with those obtained from alternative (possibly, more structural) methodologies.

Substantively, our results suggest that an important part of the effect of oil price shocks on the economy results not from the change in oil prices, per se, but from the resulting tightening of monetary policy. This finding may help to explain the apparently large effects of oil price changes found by Hamilton and many others.

APPENDIX A

Interpolation of Monthly NIPA Variables

IN THIS PAPER we use interpolated monthly values of GDP, the components of GDP, and the GDP deflator. This appendix describes the interpolation process. The data and additional detailed estimation results are available on a distribution diskette from the authors, upon request.

We designate quarterly series by capital letters and monthly series by lower-case letters. Quarters are indexed by $T = 1, 2, \ldots, N$, and months by $t = 1, 2, \ldots, n$. Let Q_T be an (observed) quarterly variable that is to be interpolated—for example, real GDP—and let S_T be a scaling variable such that $Y_T \equiv Q_T/S_T$ is nontrending. Similarly, let q_t be the (unobserved) monthly series corresponding to Q_T—for example, montly real GDP—and let s_t be a scaling variable such that $y_t \equiv q_t/s_t$ is nontrending. Q_T and q_t are related by the identity

$$Q_T = \frac{1}{3} \sum_{i=0}^{2} q_{3T-i},$$

and hence Y_T and y_t are related by the identity

$$Y_T = \frac{1}{3} \sum_{i=0}^{2} y_{3T-i}(s_{3T-i}/S_T).$$

Interpolation is by state space methods. Suppose that there is a vector of (observable) interpolator variables at the monthly level, $\mathbf{x}_t$; industrial production, for example, is a monthly variable that provides information about within-quarter movements of real GDP. We assume that the unobserved monthly variable y_t is related to the interpolator variables according to the "causal," or "transition," equation

$$y_t = \mathbf{x}_t'\boldsymbol{\beta} + u_t,$$

where

$$u_t = \rho u_{t-1} + \epsilon_t, \qquad \epsilon_t \sim N(0,\sigma^2).$$

In our application, all transition equations include a constant term. When one or more of the interpolators becomes available midsample, all interpolators (including the constant term) are interacted with dummy variables and the possibility of a shift in the value of σ^2 is allowed for.

Let z_t be a monthly "indicator" variable that equals $Y_{t/3}$ in the third month of each quarter and is zero otherwise. Then the indicator, or "measurement," equations are given by

$$z_t = \frac{1}{3} \sum_{i=0}^{2} y_{t-i}(s_{t-i}/S_{3t}), \quad t = 3, 6, 9, 12, \ldots, n$$

and

$$z_t = 0 \times y_t, \text{ for all other values of } t.$$

The parameters β, ρ, and σ^2 are estimated by maximum likelihood, assuming Gaussian errors. Conditional on the estimated parameters, let $y_{t/\tau} = E_\tau y_t$, where E is the expectations operator. The interpolated values, given the full information set, are thus given by

$$q_{t/n} = y_{t/n} s_t.$$

This method is similar to that proposed by Chow and Lin (1971), although it allows for a more general treatment of the serial correlation in u_t.

To estimate the accuracy of the interpolation, one can use R^2 measures of fit. In levels, the measure of fit is

$$R^2_{levels} = \text{var}(y^2_{t/n})/\text{var}(y^2_t),$$

and in differences it is

$$R^2_{diffs} = \text{var}(\Delta y^2_{t/n})/\text{var}(\Delta y^2_t).$$

Table A1 lists the quarterly series that we interpolate, the corresponding monthly interpolators, and the measures of fit (corresponding to the scaled values of the variables). Variables are listed by their CITIBASE mnemonics, which are defined in appendix B. The scale variables used for real flow variables are personal consumption expenditures (GMCQ), at both the quarterly and monthly levels. The personal consumption expenditure deflator (GMDC), monthly and quarterly, is used as the scale variable in the interpolation of the GDP deflator.

Consumption data (disaggregated to durables, nondurables, and services) exist at a monthly frequency and thus do not have to be interpolated. Monthly GDP is calculated as the sum of the monthly GDP components (we ignore the slight deviations from that relationship caused by chain weighting).

The R^2 values suggest that the interpolators explain nearly all of the variability in the levels of the scaled series. With the exceptions of government consumption and the GDP deflator, they also explain nearly all of the implied month-to-month variation in the series.

Table A1. Interpolators and Goodness of Fit

Quarterly series interpolated[a]	Monthly interpolators[a]	R^2, by specification	
		Levels	Differences
GDPD	PWFSA PWFPSA PWIMSA PWCMSA	0.997	0.489
GIPDQ	IPE MSNDF[b] MSMAE[b]	0.999	0.775
GIRQ	IPIC MMCON CONFRC HSF	0.999	0.894
GISQ	IPIC MMCON CONIC CONCC	0.999	0.807
GVQ	Δ IVMFGQ Δ IVRRQ Δ IVWRQ	0.970	0.929
GGEQ	CONQC IPH FBO[b]	0.999	0.633
GEXQ	FSE602 FTE71 FTEF	0.999	0.919
GIMQ	FSM612 FTM333 FTM732	0.998	0.861

Source: Authors' calculations based on data described in appendix B.
a. Series identified by CITIBASE mnemonics; see appendix B.
b. Available beginning in January 1968.

APPENDIX B

Data

THIS APPENDIX describes the data series used in the paper. All data are from the CITIBASE electronic database, available from Citicorp Database Services. Series are identified by their CITIBASE mnemonic codes.

Quarterly series

GDPD   GDP deflator, index, 1992 = 100.

GEXQ   Exports of goods and services, chained 1992 dollars.

GGEQ   Government consumption expenditures and gross investment, chained 1992 dollars.

GIMQ   Imports of goods and services, chained 1992 dollars.

GIPDQ   Investment, producers' durables, chained 1992 dollars.

GIRQ   Investment, residential, chained 1992 dollars.

GISQ   Investment, nonresidential structures, chained 1992 dollars.

GVQ   Change in business inventories, total, chained 1992 dollars.

Monthly series

CONCC   Construction put in place, commercial, seasonally adjusted, 1987 dollars.

CONFRC Construction put in place, private residential building, seasonally adjusted, 1987 dollars.

CONIC   Construction put in place, industrial building, seasonally adjusted, 1987 dollars.

CONQC   Construction put in place, public, seasonally adjusted, 1987 dollars.

FBO   Federal budget, net outlay, not seasonally adjusted; deflated by interpolated government purchases deflator (GDFGEC), seasonally adjusted by the authors by means of a regression on monthly dummies.

FSE602 Exports, excluding military aid shipments, seasonally adjusted; deflated by the PPI for finished goods (PWF).

FSM612 General imports, seasonally adjusted; deflated by the PPI for finished goods (PWF).

FTE71   U.S. merchandise exports, nonelectrical machinery, seasonally adjusted; deflated by the PPI for machinery and equipment (PWME).

FTEF U.S. merchandise exports, agricultural products, seasonally adjusted; deflated by the PPI for farm products, processed foods, and feeds (PWFPF).

FTM333 U.S. merchandise imports, petroleum, and petroleum products, seasonally adjusted; deflated by the PPI for crude petroleum (PW561).

FTM732 U.S. merchandise imports, automobiles and parts, seasonally adjusted; deflated by the PPI for motor vehicles and equipment (PWAUTO).

FYFF Federal funds rate, percent.

FYGM3 Interest rate, three-month Treasury bills from the secondary market, percent.

FYGT5 Interest rate, five-year Treasury bonds, constant maturity, from the secondary market, percent.

FYGT10 Interest rate, ten-year Treasury bonds, constant maturity, from the secondary market, percent.

GMCQ Personal consumption expenditures, seasonally adjusted, chained 1992 dollars.

GMCDQ Personal consumption expenditures, durables, seasonally adjusted, chained 1992 dollars.

GMCNQ Personal consumption expenditures, nondurables, seasonally adjusted, chained 1992 dollars.

GMCSQ Personal consumption expenditures, services, seasonally adjusted, chained 1992 dollars.

GMDC Implicit price deflator, personal consumption expenditures, index, 1987 = 100.

HSF Housing starts, new private housing units, seasonally adjusted.

IP Industrial production index, total, seasonally adjusted, 1987 = 100.

IPE Industrial production index, business equipment, seasonally adjusted, 1987 = 100.

IPH   Industrial production index, defense and space equipment, sea-
         sonally adjusted, 1987 = 100.

IPIC   Industrial production index, construction supplies, seasonally
         adjusted, 1987 = 100.

IVMFGQ   Inventories, manufacturing, seasonally adjusted, chained 1992
         dollars.

IVRRQ   Manufacturing and trade inventories, retail trade, seasonally
         adjusted, chained 1992 dollars.

IVWRQ   Manufacturing and trade inventories, merchant wholesalers,
         seasonally adjusted, chained 1992 dollars.

MMCON   Manufacturing shipments, construction materials and supplies,
         seasonally adjusted; deflated by the PPI for materials and com-
         ponents for manufacturing (PWIMSM).

MSMAE   Manufacturing shipments, machinery and equipment, season-
         ally adjusted; deflated by the PPI for machinery and equipment
         (PWME).

MSNDF   Manufacturing shipments, nondefense capital goods indus-
         tries, seasonally adjusted; deflated by the PPI for capital equip-
         ment (PWFP).

PSCCOM   Spot market price index, all commodities, from Commodity
         Research Bureau, not seasonally adjusted, 1967 = 100.

PUNEW   CPI-U, all items, seasonally adjusted, 1982–84 = 100.

PW561   PPI, crude petroleum, not seasonally adjusted, 1982 = 100.

PWFPSA   PPI, capital equipment, seasonally adjusted, 1982 = 100.

PWFSA   PPI, finished goods, seasonally adjusted, 1982 = 100.

PWIMSA   PPI, intermediate materials, supplies, and components, sea-
         sonally adjusted, 1982 = 100.

PWCMSA   PPI, crude materials, seasonally adjusted, 1982 = 100.

Comments and Discussion

Christopher A. Sims: The broad aim of this paper is to go beyond the result, now widely confirmed in the empirical time-series literature on monetary policy, that surprise changes in monetary policy are a minor source of economic fluctuations. The nature of systematic reactions of monetary policy to the state of the economy could be a major determinant of the character of fluctuations, even though erratic disturbances to monetary policy are not. The paper concludes that the evidence is consistent with a major role for monetary policy; so large that, for example, most of the observed output effects of oil price shocks would disappear with a different monetary policy.

I agree with the main conclusion of the paper, but only because the authors have been so careful in stating it. I would emphasize more than they do how much uncertainty remains about the size of the real effects of monetary policy. It remains possible for a skeptic to maintain the view that the effects of both systematic and random shifts in monetary policy are negligibly small. My comments therefore emphasize the reasons to doubt that the effects of systematic monetary policy are large, despite the paper's evidence to the contrary.

The authors pursue their aim by focusing attention primarily on the reaction of the economy to surprise changes in oil prices. On the face of it, this focus is appealing, because most economists believe that they know roughly when large surprise changes in oil prices have occurred and have little doubt that these changes were distinct from surprise changes in monetary policy. Identification—separation of the interpretable disturbance from other sources of variation in the data—there-

143

fore promises to be easier than it would be with other types of private sector disturbances. This idea, it seems to me, has not turned out as well as one might have hoped.

In the first place, the intuition that historical oil price "shocks" are well understood and easily identified is incorrect. Although Hamilton's original work did not require elaborate filtering of the data, it appears that to extend it to the current time does require such filtering. In the present paper, four different measures of oil price shocks are shown in figure 2 to deliver four quite distinct estimated effects on the economy. The authors choose to proceed with Hamilton's filtration of the oil price data to generate their oil price shocks.

As the paper notes, the estimated effects of the oil price shock are small: a 1 percent oil price shock—which, by the definition of the variable, is expected to lead to a fairly persistent change in the actual level of oil prices—leads, in figure 4, only to a 0.02 percent response of the price level and a 0.025 percent output response at the peak of the responses. This is the size of the pure supply-side effect on GDP that one would expect if oil-related energy inputs had a 2 percent factor share, and most economists would expect estimated reduced-form effects of oil price increases to be larger than that. (This assumes that domestic oil is treated correctly as a primary input and that imports of foreign oil are treated correctly as intermediate inputs in GDP accounting, a perhaps dubious assumption.) It would be useful in assessing these results to know both the response of the oil price level, as opposed to the filtered variable, to this shock and the size of a one standard deviation shock to the filtered oil price measure.

Furthermore, though taken from different models, both the first row of table 1 and the error bands in the bottom row of figure 2 show that the responses of the variables to an oil shock could easily be zero and yet still consistent with the data; one-standard-error bands about the responses barely clear zero. It is true that table 1 shows that the *difference* in the response of the economy in the case where monetary policy responds according to historical norms and the case where it pegs the interest rate is fairly sharply defined by the data and is in the direction expected by the authors. But since the oil shock itself has turned out to be something of a will-o'-the-wisp, the idea that economists' intuitive knowledge of the size and nature of oil shocks would help with identification ends up not having contributed much.

The paper also shows some results for "output" and "commodity price" shocks. These are derived from the statistical model and are harder to interpret than oil shocks. The model gives them no interpretation, except that they are different from and independent of monetary policy shocks. But while these model-based shocks probably mix conceptually distinct non–monetary policy influences on the economy, they do have the advantage of having large effects and accounting for much of the observed variance in the data. It is encouraging to see in figures 8 and 9 that the effects of systematic monetary policy as measured with the oil shocks seem to be confirmed with the output and price shocks, but it is disappointing that all of the careful analysis of robustness and statistical strength centers on the less sharply defined oil price shocks.

The authors point out that previous experiments with analyzing the effects of systematic changes in monetary policy in identified VAR models have stuck to replacing the estimated policy rule in the model with something else. This kind of exercise implicitly assumes that in forming expectations of future policy actions, private agents treat all deviations of policy variables from their historical patterns of behavior as unsystematic deviations from the historical policy rule. The Lucas critique warns that this can lead to error.

My own view of the Lucas critique is that it explains that it is always a mistake to imagine that one can implement changes in policy that have probability zero according to the model of policy underlying private sector behavior. The implication is that if one can contemplate changing the coefficients of the "rule," or "reaction function," those coefficients should have been modeled as stochastic in the first place. There is an internal contradiction in pretending that one can change the coefficients, even though the public is modeled as absolutely certain that they can never change.

While this point is correct in principle, it is difficult to implement in practice. Especially for policy changes quite different from any that have been observed historically, estimation of an appropriate stochastic model that allows for such changes will be difficult and may need to rely heavily on guesswork and a priori knowledge. It is therefore a good idea, where possible, to focus attention on policy changes that are not too dramatic, which can reasonably be modeled as sequences of random disturbances to the policy behavior that is explicit in the model. This applies even when one is generating variations in policy by changing coefficients that in the model are treated as nonstochastic. The changes in coefficients are best chosen so as to correspond to not too dramatic sequences of shocks to the model's original policy rule.

The type of rule change studied in this paper—a shift to an exogenously fixed funds rate from a historical policy that, by contrast, made the funds rate react very sharply to inflationary disturbances—is dramatic. As is made clear in the recent literature on the interaction of monetary and fiscal policy, in particular, the seminal paper by Eric Leeper, a fixed interest rate as policy rule (contrary to some discussions elsewhere in the literature) is consistent with a uniquely determined price level.[1] However, this is true only if the fixed interest rate rule is accompanied by an appropriate fiscal policy, and the appropriate fiscal policy in this case is quite different from that consistent with a determinate price level in the context of an "anti-inflationary" monetary policy. Since in this authors' model fiscal policy has to be thought of as wrapped into the "non–monetary policy" sector, one would expect to find that changing the monetary policy rule alone to a fixed interest rate form would imply unsustainably explosive behavior of prices; and indeed, figures 4, 5, 8, and 9 show that this is exactly what emerges. Private agents are likely to recognize that such a shift in the monetary policy rule is unsustainable and therefore to expect it to end, or to be followed by a shift in fiscal policy. This makes interpreting the effects of the authors' exercise rather difficult. Their paper in places reads as if a different monetary policy might actually have eliminated the output effects of oil price or even output shocks. But since the alternate monetary policy considered is not sustainable, this interpretation does not seem to me correct. The simulations suggest instead only that by delaying or dampening an interest rate response to inflationary pressures, the monetary authority can trade delay or dampening of the output effects for increased inflationary effects. It would also have been interesting to see an analysis of effects of less extreme shifts in the policy rule that would have been sustainable; for example, smaller or slower, rather than zero, interest rate responses.

The authors attempt to respond to the Lucas critique by building into the model one particular form of endogenous adjustment of private sector expectations to the change in policy rule. They impose the the-

1. Leeper (1991).

oretical term structure relationships between the federal funds rate, another short rate, and a long rate. Then they attribute to those private agents doing interest rate arbitrage perfect foresight of the new policy fixing the federal funds rate. It is apparent from the figures that this modification of the model does nothing to correct the fundamental problem that the change in policy rule is unsustainable. Indeed, one might think that the sector most likely to realize that fixing the federal funds rate is not a sustainable policy, in the absence of a change in fiscal policy, is the bond market. Requiring that the bond market, but no one else, treat the policy as firmly in place forever therefore seems exactly backward from what might be plausible. Furthermore, this adjustment to the model is not in fact very large, as is made clear by the closeness of the simulation paths for many variables in cases where this adjustment is imposed and in those where it is not. The estimated statistical model already captures the strong tendency of the federal funds rate and other short rates to move together—a relation not very different from the theoretical term structure relationship. And the connection of long rates to short rates, although it differs more between simulations, appears not to be of great importance for predicting the effects of shocks on prices and output.

Thus the exercise undertaken here is a step toward modeling private sector learning behavior that might, in principle, be useful. But because the term structure relationships are simple and well approximated in the original estimated model, it does not seem to me likely that this particular aspect of private sector expectations is of central importance in this endeavor.

The entire identified VAR literature on the effects of monetary policy runs the risk of overestimating the real effects of monetary policy. It is not hard to construct a stochastic equilibrium model in which monetary policy is neutral and certain types of technology shocks raise real interest rates and, later, lower real output. The essential ingredients are conventional Solow-residual technology shocks and increasing costs in the investment goods industry (or within-firm adjustment costs to investment). If the monetary authority did not react to such shocks, they would be a source of movements of interest rates and output in opposite directions that was not related to price behavior or to money stock behavior. One might think of the identified VAR literature on the effects of monetary policy as a search for restrictions on a macroeconomic time-series model in which some shock, labeled "monetary policy" and orthogonal to other shocks, moves interest rates up, money down, output down, and prices down, with possible delays in all these effects except the interest rate movement. If the data are generated by a model in which there are real shocks connecting real rates and future output movements, as I suggest, this identified VAR research strategy can easily end up confounding the real shocks with monetary policy. The variety of real effects found in this literature, and the tendency of real effects to be smaller in models estimated for countries other than the United States, gives me genuine concern that this may have happened.

Let me conclude by saying again that, despite the skeptical tone of my comments, I find this paper useful evidence on the effects of systematic changes in monetary policy that, on the whole, does weigh in favor of those effects being substantial. It is quite unlikely that monetary policy could come close to eliminating the output effects of oil, "commodity price," or "output" shocks, despite the authors' apparent evidence to the contrary. This strong conclusion rests on the their use of an unsustainable policy as the counterfactual alternative. But very substantial delay or smoothing of the output effects via monetary policy, at the expense of more inflation, probably would be possible.

Benjamin M. Friedman: This paper by Bernanke, Gertler, and Watson is a highly useful contribution to the empirical literature of monetary policy, both for its methodological approach and for some of its specific findings. I suspect that it, like the earlier paper by Sims and Zha on which it draws, will fruitfully spur further research following this kind of empirical strategy. Indeed, as I suggest below, this way of thinking about how monetary policy affects the economy has at least one potential application that may help to inform an issue of very great importance for the practical conduct of monetary policy, both in the United States and elsewhere.

The best way to place in context the empirical strategy taken by this paper is to recall the parallel distinctions, between what is systematic and what is unsystematic and between what is anticipated and what is unanticipated, that have stood behind much of the literature of monetary policy from the past two decades. At the theoretical level, the argument made by Robert Lucas, Thomas Sargent and Neil Wallace, and others was that the only monetary policy actions that have real effects are those that are *unanticipated*. As is now well understood, this proposition rests on a variety of assumptions—for example, perfect competition and perfectly flexible wages and prices—that few actual economies of practical interest satisfy. Nevertheless, because achieving analytical precision about the failure of those assumptions and about the macroeconomic consequences of that failure is highly problematic (it is difficult to spell out precisely how competition is imperfect and why wages and prices are sticky), the presumption that only unanticipated monetary policy actions have real effects has continued to underlie—sometimes explicitly but nowadays more often implicitly—much of modern research in the field. Further, as the standard assumption of rational expectations is usually applied, any part of the conduct of monetary policy that is systematic (for example, the central bank's always raising interest rates following a decline in unemployment or a surge in inflation) is assumed to be anticipated, and so in this line of thinking it is also assumed to be without real effects.

At the empirical level, the parallel argument has been that even if such systematic monetary policy actions did affect real economic activity, it would be impossible to distinguish those effects from the independent consequences of the events to which monetary policy was reacting. (For example, to the extent that the central bank simply moves interest rates in response to prior observed inflation, any subsequent effect on real output could just as well be attributed to the inflation itself as to the consequent movement in interest rates.) Hence the appeal of the vector autoregression approach in this context is that it focuses only on those monetary policy actions determined to be *unsystematic,* in the sense that the VAR cannot explain them in terms of prior movements in other variables. One danger of this approach is that a VAR that includes too much information may overexplain the movement of monetary policy in terms of prior movements in other variables. Such a VAR will erroneously shrink the remaining component, which is taken to be unsystematic and therefore also unanticipated, to the point that it then appears to have only trivial economic consequences. But the main point is that the empirical rationale for assessing the effects of monetary policy by looking only at its unsystematic variation, which continues to be in widespread use, resonates closely with the now outdated theoretical presumption that, at least for purposes of effects on real variables, only unanticipated policy actions matter. There is an inherent congruence between the two lines of thinking.

The principal thrust of the approach taken by Bernanke, Gertler, and Watson is to sever that connection by designing a way to use the empirical VAR methodology to investigate specific aspects of *systematic* monetary policy. To be sure, the paper simply presumes, rather than shows, that systematic and therefore anticipated monetary policy actions can have real effects. But for readers who accept that there are reasons why this may be so and who do not require that the empirical model used to investigate these effects be explicitly tied to a theoretical model detailing how they come about, the resulting advance is clear. And indeed, the authors find that the specific aspect of systematic monetary policy on which they choose to focus—the central bank's response to oil price shocks and to the consequences of those shocks for prices and output—does have sizable real effects. This finding is both interesting and important. (To be clear, the *within month* response of monetary policy to an oil price shock would be unanticipated and therefore presumed to have real effects, even in a Lucas-style model. Although the paper is not specific on this distinction, I assume that the bulk of the real effects that the authors attribute to the monetary policy response to oil price shocks results from movement in the policy variable occurring after the month in which the oil price moves.)

As indicated at the outset, I suspect that this methodology has an immediate application of potentially great importance. A question that has rightly attracted widespread attention, among industrial as well as developing countries, is how price inflation affects a country's ability to maintain real economic growth. Evidence shows that above some modest level (the high single-digit range), inflation does reduce the average pace of real growth over time. A familiar view, however, is that inflation negatively affects real growth not because inflation, per se, matters in this context, but because the central bank acts to resist inflation; and in a world in which the Lucas-Sargent-Wallace assumptions do not obtain, it can only do so by slowing (''sacrificing'') real output. The methodology used in this paper seems potentially able to address this question too. If so, the findings would be very valuable.

Although both the methodology and the findings of Bernanke, Gertler, and Watson's paper are highly useful, three specific aspects give cause for reservation. First, as they are at some pains to emphasize, there is substantial evidence of instability in their results across the three decades of their sample. In particular, as figure 10 clearly shows, the ''systematic'' response of monetary policy to oil price shocks in the Volcker period was far greater than either earlier or later.

A question that this instability immediately raises is whether it is reasonable to view the more energetic anti-inflationary monetary policy of the Volcker era exclusively as a response to an oil price shock. I believe that the Federal Reserve System under Paul Volcker adopted a policy broadly aimed at reducing the U.S. inflation rate, and that the rise in oil prices in 1979 and 1980 was only one element in the inflation process against which it directed its policy. The results plotted in the middle right-hand panel in figure 6, showing that the simulated response to the historical oil shock accounts for only a small part of the increase in the federal funds rate during 1981–82, are certainly consistent with this view. Because of the *post hoc ergo propter hoc* character of VAR analysis, the Bernanke-Gertler-Watson paper may attribute to the specific response (here and in other subperiods) of monetary policy to oil price shocks what was actually the more general conduct of monetary policy, based on other considerations.

The findings of subsample instability also highlight the difficulty of identifying what ''systematic'' policy means in the first place. For purely empirical purposes of extracting impulse responses and variance decomparisons from past data, systematic simply means whatever happened on average across the arbitrarily chosen sample under study. But as is the case in this paper, researchers often seek to connect this purely empirical notion of systematic behavior with the concept of policy ''rules,'' so as to go on to draw inferences about the consequences of the central bank following one rule rather than another. As a number of people (Sims, John Taylor, and I, among many others) have argued in one context or another, it is not clear that in practical settings the central bank is ever following a rule, in the crucial dual sense that its actions are not only systematic but also perceived to be so and therefore properly anticipated by the relevant public. The fact that estimating the authors' VAR over the 1976–85 sample delivers the federal funds rate response shown in the right-hand panel of the third row in figure 10 does not necessarily make this response a characterization of systematic monetary policy in any substantive sense.

A second set of reservations stems from the authors' use of oil price shocks as the principal empirical vehicle for their study of systematic monetary policy. To put it bluntly, does the Hamilton idea really make sense? For example, should one really think of the 1957–58 recession in the United States as a ripple from the 1956 Suez affair? To take Hamilton's idea seriously would require a major rethinking of most of post–World War II U.S. business cycle history—which clearly has not happened in the decade and a half since Hamilton's intriguing paper appeared. The authors of the present paper are perhaps more secure in that the role of oil prices is more plausible in at least two, possibly three, of the five recessions covered in their sample, which mostly postdates Hamilton's. Even so, I suspect that their difficulty in finding a measure of oil price shocks that satisfactorily fits the oil facts to the macroeconomic data is a warning of just this problem.

Finally, several aspects of the authors' treatment of interest rates also bear closer attention. The assumption that interest rate movements are a sufficient statistic for the channels by which monetary policy affects macroeconomic activity is, by itself, not unusual. Indeed, the authors may well overemphasize its limitations. Costs of financing (including opportunity costs) are an important factor in many kinds of spending decisions, and for this purpose interest rate fluctuations may also plausibly stand in for at least part of the relevant movement in either exchange rates or broader asset prices. While the strong rejection of the restriction excluding the federal funds rate from the output equation is somewhat surprising, the authors are presumably correct that the practical effects of imposing this restriction are small. Further, it is my conjecture that if a stock price index were included in the VAR, the data would accept this restriction. (Because the analysis in this paper depends so crucially on the role of short- and long-term interest rates, however, there is probably much to be learned from examining the coefficients of these interest rates in the output equation, as well as the impulse responses relating output to the independent components of the two interest rates. It would therefore be useful to show explicitly these key elements of the analysis.)

The potential problem, however, is the strong implied rejection of the expectations hypothesis of the term structure of interest rates, which the authors use as the organizing principle for this part of their model. Normally, within this framework, the "term premium" included in any specific interest rate is a substantive reflection of borrowers' and lenders' attitudes toward such features as the risk and liquidity of the underlying debt instrument. But in this paper, the term premium simply serves to undo the behavior that the built-in expectations hypothesis implies that interest rates should be following (see, for example, figure 3). Moreover, the results plotted in figure 4 for prices and the long-term rate are dramatically at variance with standard notions of how inflation expectations affect nominal interest rates. In this experiment, not surprisingly, moving from the base simulation to either the Sims-Zha simulation or the anticipated policy simulation results in far higher prices and hence much greater inflation. But in the Sims-Zha simulation the long-term interest rate is uniformly below its level in the base simulation, and in the anticipated policy simulation it even declines absolutely. So much for the notion that investors rationally anticipate the consequences of monetary policy for future inflation and incorporate the resulting inflation expectations into current bond prices!

These three sets of reservations notwithstanding, I applaud the broader methodological direction taken by Bernanke, Gertler, and Watson and retain my sense that their finding of quantitatively significant effects from systematic monetary policy is both correct and important.

General discussion: Participants generally accepted the authors' conclusion that the output declines following oil price shocks had come mainly from the responses of monetary policy to the shocks. Several also discussed the plausible magnitude of oil shock effects themselves. One issue was how much an oil price increase, or a decrease in oil supply, should affect potential output; a second was whether oil price increases reduce demand and lead to lower levels of utilization of productive capacity. Robert Hall observed that, for infinitesimal changes in oil prices, the ability of the United States to produce should not be impaired by a rise in the price of imported oil, even if it reduces oil use; the derivative of real GDP with respect to the price of oil is zero no matter how large the adjustment, with Division GDP. However, he and William Nordhaus agreed there could be effects on potential GDP as the equilibrium supply of domestic factors adjusted to the change in oil prices. George Perry added that some estimates from earlier studies, such as a reduction of several percentage points of GDP from OPEC 1, were too large to be viewed as a supply-side effect. However, taking into account the effect of an oil price increase on aggregate demand, where the price increase could be analyzed approximately like an increase in excise taxes with high-saving foreigners getting the revenue, a large short-run impact on GDP was believable. He added that the allocation of such an impact between a "fiscal" and a monetary effect would depend, somewhat arbitrarily, on how baseline monetary policy was defined.

Nordhaus raised several issues about the appropriateness of the various measures of oil shocks used by the authors. He suggested that almost any theory, whether Perry's that the short-run impact of increases could be regarded as a tax paid to foreigners or Sims's that it should be treated simply as an increase in input prices, should lead to some measure involving oil purchases relative to the size of the economy. This scaling makes an enormous difference. For the last three oil shocks in the sample, he calculated the increased costs of imported oil, with quantities fixed, were 1.8 percent of GDP in 1973, 1.0 percent of GDP in 1979, and 0.2 percent of GDP in 1990. Using this measure would preserve the peaks of the Hamilton series, but the shocks would be progressively smaller. Nordhaus also noted that the paper ignores the negative oil shock of 1986, when the price decline corresponded to a negative shock of 0.5 percent of GDP. He reasoned that the failure to scale the shocks, along with the fact that the positive shocks of 1986 and 1990 were quickly reversed, may explain why the responses in the two subperiods look so different in the authors' analysis. William Brainard agreed with Nordhaus's argument for scaling the shocks and added that it might be useful to construct a similar measure indicating the magnitude of the redistribution between domestic producers and consumers.

Robert Shiller observed that the stochastic properties of the oil price series seemed to have changed after the Organization of Petroleum Exporting Countries broke up in 1986. Before that, the oil price was a series of plateaus separated by sudden jumps, so that changes seem to have a lot of information. But afterward, the oil price looks like a mean-reverting process, so the movements have less information. He reasoned that the public may realize this difference, which would explain why oil price changes are no longer big news. Reflecting on the widespread concerns about oil in the 1970s and 1980s, Shiller suggested that the long view is important in economics and the best way to deal with an anomaly is to wait it out until it disappears. He suggested that may have happened with oil.

References

Andersen, Leonall C., and Jerry L. Jordan. 1968. "Monetary and Fiscal Actions: A Test of Their Relative Importance in Economic Stabilization." Federal Reserve Bank of St. Louis *Review* (November): 11–24.

Bernanke, Ben S., and Alan S. Blinder. 1992. "The Federal Funds Rate and the Channels of Monetary Transmission." *American Economic Review* 82(4): 901–21.

Bernanke, Ben S., and Ilian Mihov. 1995. "Measuring Monetary Policy." Working Paper 5145. Cambridge, Mass.: National Bureau of Economic Research (June).

Blanchard, Olivier J. 1984. "The Lucas Critique and the Volcker Deflation." *American Economic Review, Papers and Proceedings* 74(2): 211–15.

Chow, Gregory, and An-loh Lin. 1971. "Best Linear Unbiased Interpolation, Distribution, and Extrapolation of Time Series by Related Series." *Review of Economics and Statistics* 53(4): 372–5.

Christiano, Lawrence J., and Martin Eichenbaum. 1992. "Identification and the Liquidity Effect of a Monetary Policy Shock." In *Political Economy, Growth, and Business Cycles,* edited by Alex Cukierman, Zvi Hercovitz, and Leonardo Leiderman. MIT Press.

Cochrane, John H. 1996. "What Do the VARs Mean? Measuring the Output Effects of Monetary Policy" Unpublished paper, University of Chicago (August).

Darby, Michael R. 1982. "The Price of Oil and World Inflation and Recession." *American Economic Review* 72(4): 738–51.

Dotsey, Michael, and Max Reid. 1992. "Oil Shocks, Monetary Policy, and Economic Activity." *Federal Reserve Bank of Richmond Economic Review* 78(4): 14–27.

Ferderer, J. Peter. 1996. "Oil Price Volatility and the Macroeconomy." *Journal of Macroeconomics* 18(1): 1–26.

Friedman, Benjamin M., and Kenneth N. Kuttner. 1996. "A Price Target for U.S. Monetary Policy? Lessons from the Experience with Money Growth Targets." *BPEA, 1:1996,* 77–125.

Friedman, Milton, and Anna Jacobson Schwartz. 1963. *A Monetary History of the United States, 1867–1960.* Princeton University Press.

Fuhrer, Jeffrey C. 1996. "Monetary Policy Shifts and Long-Term Interest Rates." *Quarterly Journal of Economics* 111(4): 1183–209.

Hamilton, James D. 1983. "Oil and the Macroeconomy Since World War II." *Journal of Political Economy* 91(2): 228–48.

———. 1996a. "Analysis of the Transmission of Oil Price Shocks Through the Macroeconomy." Unpublished paper. University of California, San Diego (August).

156   *Brookings Papers on Economic Activity, 1:1997*

——. 1996b. "This is What Happened to the Oil Price-Macroeconomy Relationship." *Journal of Monetary Economics* 38(2): 215–20.

Hansen, Bruce E. 1997. "Approximate Asymptotic *P* Values for Structural-Change Tests." *Journal of Business and Economic Statistics* 15(1): 60–67.

Hooker, Mark A. 1996a. "Exploring the Robustness of the Oil Price-Macroeconomy Relationship: Empirical Specifications and the Role of Monetary Policy." Unpublished paper. Wellesley College (September).

——. 1996b. "What Happened to the Oil Price-Macroeconomy Relationship?" *Journal of Monetary Economics* 38(2): 195–213.

Hoover, Kevin D., and Stephen J. Perez. 1994. "Post Hoc Ergo Propter Hoc Once More: An Evaluation of 'Does Monetary Policy Matter?' in the Spirit of James Tobin." *Journal of Monetary Economics* 34(1): 47–73.

Kim, In-Moo, and Prakash Loungani. 1992. "The Role of Energy in Real Business Cycle Models." *Journal of Monetary Economics* 29(2): 173–89.

Kim, Soyoung. 1995. "Does Monetary Policy Matter in the G-6 Countries? Using Common Identifying Assumptions About Monetary Policy Across Countries." Unpublished paper. Yale University (January).

Lee, Kiseok, Shawn Ni, and Ronald A. Ratti. 1995. "Oil Shocks and the Macroeconomy: The Role of Price Variability." *Energy Journal* 16(4): 39–56.

Leeper, Eric M. 1991. "Equilibria Under 'Active' and 'Passive' Monetary and Fiscal Policies." *Journal of Monetary Economics* 27(February): 129–47.

Leeper, Eric M., Christopher A. Sims, and Tao Zha. 1996. "What Does Monetary Policy Do?" *BPEA, 2:1996*, 1–63.

Lucas, Robert E. Jr. 1976. "Econometric Policy Evaluation: A Critique." *Carnegie-Rochester Conference Series on Public Policy* 1: 19–46.

Mork, Knut Anton. 1989. "Oil and the Macroeconomy When Prices Go Up and Down: An Extension of Hamilton's Results." *Journal of Political Economy* 97(3): 740–44.

Quandt, Richard E. 1960. "Tests of the Hypothesis that a Linear Regression System Obeys Two Separate Regimes." *Journal of the American Statistical Association* 55(290): 324–30.

Romer, Christina D., and David H. Romer. 1989. "Does Monetary Policy Matter? A New Test in the Spirit of Friedman and Schwartz." In *NBER Macroeconomics Annual 1989*, edited by Olivier Jean Blanchard and Stanley Fischer. MIT Press.

Rotemberg, Julio J., and Michael Woodford. 1996. "Imperfect Competition and the Effects of Energy Price Increases on Economic Activity." *Journal of Money, Credit, and Banking* 28(4, part 1): 549–77.

Shapiro, Matthew D. 1994. "Federal Reserve Policy: Cause and Effect." In *Monetary Policy*, edited by N. Gregory Mankiw. University of Chicago Press.

Ben S. Bernanke, Mark Gertler, and Mark Watson   157

Shiller, Robert J., John Y. Campbell, and Kermit L. Schoenholtz. 1983. "Forward Rates and Future Policy: Interpreting The Term Structure of Interest Rates." *BPEA, 1:1983*, 173–223.

Sims, Christopher A. 1980. "Macroeconomics and Reality." *Econometrica* 48(1): 1–48.

———. 1986. "Are Forecasting Models Usable for Policy Analysis?" *Federal Reserve Bank of Minneapolis Quarterly Review* 10(1): 2–16.

———. 1992. "Interpreting the Macroeconomic Time Series Facts: The Effects of Monetary Policy." *European Economic Review* 36(5): 975–1011.

Sims, Christopher A., and Tao Zha. 1995. "Does Monetary Policy Generate Recessions?" Unpublished paper. Yale University and Federal Reserve Bank of Atlanta (December).

Strongin, Steven. 1995. "The Identification of Monetary Policy Disturbances: Explaining the Liquidity Puzzle." *Journal of Monetary Economics* 35(3): 463–97.

Taylor, John B. 1993. *Macroeconomic Policy in a World Economy: From Econometric Design to Practical Operation.* W.W. Norton.

Tobin, James. 1980. "Stabilization Policy Ten Years After." *BPEA, 1:1980*, 19–71.

West, Kenneth D. 1993. "An Aggregate Demand-Aggregate Supply Analysis of Japanese Monetary Policy, 1973–1990." In *Japanese Monetary Policy*, edited by Kenneth J. Singleton. University of Chicago Press.

ROBERT J. SHILLER
Yale University

Public Resistance to Indexation: A Puzzle

THE INDEXATION OF payments makes excellent sense for all sorts of long-term contracts. Future payments should not be expressed in currency units, but instead tied to an index of consumer prices or an index of wholesale prices, of wages, of incomes, or of components of income. History shows that the real value of currency units has been so unstable that it is better to use practically any one of these indexes to specify future payments in contracts than to specify payments in terms of fixed currency.

And yet there has been relatively little use of indexation, except in situations of extremely variable inflation. People seem to have a preference for specifying their obligations and opportunities, long-term as well as short-term, in local currency units. That the public should generally want to denominate contracts in currency units—despite all the evidence that it is not wise to do so and despite the obvious examples from nominal contracts of redistributions caused by unexpected inflation—should be regarded as one of the great economic puzzles of all

I thank Emre Deliveli for conducting personal and questionnaire surveys in Turkey. I also thank my other research assistants, Aslak Aunstrup, David Bilas, Texas Hemmaplardh, Taimur Khan, Chaeri Kim, Randolph Kim, Marc Lanoue, John Lippman, Bang Nguyen, Raymond Rivera, Leonidas Spiliopoulos, Jeffrey Talpins, David Trujillo, and Zaki Wahhaj. Ali Alpay, Bülent Gültekin, Eytan Halfon, William Nordhaus, Serkan Savaşoğlu, and Mark Warshawsky made helpful suggestions. I also wish to thank Perihan Üçer of the Turkish government; and participants of a workshop at the Russell Sage Foundation Summer Institute in Behavorial Economics at the University of California, Berkeley, July 24, 1996, for hammering out a number of helpful suggestions. This work was supported by a grant from the National Science Foundation, under the auspices of the National Bureau of Economic Research.

159

time. The success of the U.S. Treasury's first issuance of consumer price–indexed debt in January 1997 does virtually nothing to diminish the salience of this puzzle.

It is the premise of this paper that the answer to the puzzle must be sought in terms of human behavior that is complex and situation-specific, and that many factors impinge on people's thought processes. It requires serious work to try to gain an understanding of the indexation-resistant mind set that gives rise to irrational, partly rational, and sometimes even rational reasons for avoiding indexation. The final resolution of the puzzle may not be simple. The fact that resistance to inflation indexation is a worldwide phenomenon (at least, where inflation risk is not enormous) does not argue against the complexity of the answer. People are both very complex and at the same time very similar to one another. There is, moreover, a well-developed global culture, emphasized by sociologists, that encourages similar thinking on numerous issues.[1]

In this paper, I first outline the argument that indexation is advisable—in case there is any doubt—and indicate its historical precedents. Next, I describe the current extent of indexation in the United States and Turkey. Turkey is chosen for comparison with the United States because it continues to have very high and variable inflation (it has not reduced inflation in recent years, as have many other high-inflation countries), and yet the indexation of contracts is rare. I then present results of a survey conducted in these two countries, by means of interviews and questionnaires, designed to explain why people are resistant to indexation. Identical questions (except for translation) were asked in both countries.

I regard the results of this endeavor as only partially successful in illuminating the nature of public resistance to indexation. I conclude with some general thoughts about this issue and offer a partial resolution of the puzzle.

The Importance of Indexation

Through much of history, price levels have been notoriously unstable over long periods of time. Table 1 shows the standard deviations of

1. See, for example, Featherstone (1990).

Table 1. Statistics on Inflation and Real Per Capita Growth, Selected Countries[a]
Percentage points, except as indicated

Country	Standard deviation of inflation[b]		Standard deviation of growth[c]		Inflation-growth correlation[d]
	Ten-year intervals	Twenty-year intervals	Ten-year intervals	Twenty-year intervals	
Argentina	4.0×10^8	1.1×10^{12}	16.0	20.9	−0.48
Brazil	5.2×10^8	5.3×10^{10}	30.1	29.7	−0.31
Canada	39.5	74.5	11.8	12.8	0.26
Chile	3.1×10^5	4.7×10^6	14.1	15.3	−0.58
France	46.5	94.7	16.1	30.5	−0.71
Germany (West)	15.1	19.2	20.1	37.6	−0.47
India	43.5	108.5	14.9	19.1	−0.18
Indonesia	1.7×10^5	1.3×10^6	25.0	25.0	−0.73
Italy	125.1	346.2	17.8	35.6	−0.80
Japan	34.4	42.2	42.2	102.4	0.02
Korea	135.7	618.7	34.1	54.4	−0.19
Mexico	4,291.3	2.6×10^4	18.1	26.0	−0.83
Nigeria	213.7	692.6	66.1	51.2	−0.31
Turkey	1,926.2	3.6×10^4	14.1	15.8	−0.61
United Kingdom	83.4	174.4	4.7	6.5	−0.77
United States	32.3	60.5	7.8	8.6	−0.42

Source: Author's calculations based on data from the Penn World Tables, mark 5.6 (accessed on the worldwide web page of the National Bureau of Economic Research).

a. For a given country, the standard deviation of inflation or growth is the standard deviation of an annual series of overlapping ten- or twenty-year percentage changes (not annualized). For most countries, the overlapping intervals span the period 1950–92, so that the first ten-year interval is 1950–60 and the last is 1982–92; the exceptions are Argentina (1950–90), Indonesia (1960–92), and Korea (1953–91).

b. Inflation is measured as the percentage change in the implicit GDP deflator.

c. Growth is measured as the percentage change in real per capita GDP.

d. Correlation between series of overlapping ten-year inflation and growth intervals.

ten- and twenty-year percentage changes in price levels for sixteen countries. The standard deviations of long-term inflation rates can be interpreted as measures of uncertainty about inflation over long horizons. Almost no econometrician presumes to forecast inflation beyond a few years; the uncertainty is truly enormous. Even in the United States, where inflation uncertainty is very low by international standards, it has made long-term nominal debt very risky in real terms. Jeremy Siegel points out that in the United States, long-term government bonds have been even riskier than stocks in terms of real twenty-year returns.[2] Inflation has been very unstable for many advanced and

2. Siegel (1994, p. 34). His sample period is 1802–1992.

otherwise exemplary countries. One could, in fact, say that only in Germany has there been no substantial uncertainty about price levels. And there has not been any substantial change in constitutions or monetary technology since these data were collected to indicate that this historical experience is no longer relevant.

To put these numbers into perspective, one should recognize that it does not take large changes in annual inflation rates to achieve large changes in the price level over ten or twenty years. Suppose, for example, that for the next twenty years the inflation rate is equally likely to average 2 percent and 4 percent—or about plus or minus 1 percentage point from current levels, a range that is often seen between different professional forecasts of inflation for just one year ahead. Then prices are equally likely to rise by 49 percent and 119 percent in twenty years.

Table 1 also shows the standard deviations of ten- and twenty-year changes in real per capita gross domestic product for the sixteen countries. Comparison of the data in the table reveals that while both inflation and real income are unstable (and both risks should ideally be hedged), the inflation rate has been far more unstable. Because of the swings in real income, it can be argued that many payments (such as social security) should be indexed in terms of an aggregate income index rather than a price index.[3] The puzzle that this paper tries to understand is the public's lack of interest in either form of indexation.

In general, in a long-term contract neither side benefits from specifying payments in terms of units of currency, since neither side benefits from pure random shocks. When there is great uncertainty about the future direction of prices, both debtors and creditors benefit from indexation. When contracts are not indexed, if inflation turns out to be much higher than expected, creditors are wiped out. If inflation turns out to be much lower than expected, debtors go bankrupt. Both of these potential problems can be prevented simply by indexing the contract when it is first written.

Indexing payments is virtually costless; only a few words need to be added to a contract and the calculations necessary to implement indexation are trivial. Because the indexation calculations are so simple, there is little avenue for legal maneuvering to avoid compliance. Since

---

3. See Shiller and Schneider (1995), Shiller (1993), Brainard and Dolbear (1971), Fischer (1983b), and Merton (1983).

indexation is so nearly costless, one may regard not indexing (and so specifying future payments in units of currency) as equivalent to writing a contract that ties future payments to the outcome of a horse race or a coin toss. Why would anyone do it?

That payments in long-term contracts should be tied to some index, such as a consumer price index (CPI), has been been widely agreed on by economists for over a century and a half. According to Irving Fisher's history of thought on indexation, it was advocated in the nineteenth century by Joseph Lowe and G. Poulett Scrope.[4] In 1875 William Stanley Jevons recommended that the indexation of private contracts "might be made compulsory, in the sense that every money debt of, say, more than three months' standing, would be varied according to the tabular standard [index], in the absence of an express provision to the contrary."[5] Fisher's history documents an ever increasing number of economists who advocated indexation from 1875 onward, and the number continues to grow. Recent advocates of inflation indexation include James Tobin, Milton Friedman, Stanley Fischer, and Zvi Bodie.[6]

Thus the public's resistance to indexation is a great puzzle. To sum up, the effects of inflation on real payments are so enormous as to be obvious, dealing with these problems by writing indexed contracts entails almost no costs in terms of computation or legal complexity, and economists have been vocally advocating indexation. Some analysts refer to the existence of money illusion (identified by Fisher as a tendency to confuse real and nominal quantities) as a puzzle, but it is not really so.[7] It should not be surprising that people often make mistakes. What is really puzzling is that nearly everyone, including educated and highly informed people, resists taking elementary steps to heed the experts' commonsense advice to use indexation.

The Extent of the Puzzle

Efforts by U.S. economists and other opinion leaders to establish a standard for the indexation of contracts have achieved success only for

4. Fisher (1934); Lowe (1822).
5. Jevons (1875, p. 331).
6. Tobin (1971); Friedman (1974); Fischer (1986); Bodie (1990).
7. Fisher (1928).

a limited array of contracts and often only for short time intervals. The success of their Turkish counterparts has not, despite the high inflation in that country, been any more encouraging.

The United States

The issuance, on January 29, 1997, of the first inflation-indexed U.S. federal government bonds, the so-called TIPS (Treasury Inflation Protection Securities), ten-year bonds yielding 3.449 percent, is widely described in the media as a success.[8] Indeed, the experience with these bonds hints that indexed debt might someday be a success. This first issue has prompted a few issues of private indexed debt and has spurred the Chicago Board of Trade to file for permission to trade futures and options on TIPS. But if this indexed bond issue is now, in fact, a clear success, it is so only relative to pessimistic expectations. The $7 billion issued represents only about one-tenth of 1 percent of the U.S. federal debt. More will be issued (quarterly auctions are planned), but there is little evidence of a public clamor for indexed debt.[9] Treasury Secretary Robert Rubin described demand at the first auction as "predominantly institutional."[10] Media accounts confirm that, even though the Treasury kept the minimum denomination small ($1,000) to attract individual investors, retail brokers report little interest from individual investors. Part of the reason for the lack of immediate public interest can be found in the media coverage. In general, reports do not seem to be written to inspire enthusiasm in individual investors. For example, *Consumer Reports* writes: "As attractive as the inflation-indexed notes appear, it

8. Some people may consider as indexed the bonds with gold clauses (guaranteeing payment in gold rather than dollars) that became common in the late nineteenth century, when the free-silver movement threatened massive inflation in the United States. But these were tied to another form of money, not to a price index. Moreover, the buying power of gold was quite unstable. However, there is one very early instance of true indexed bonds in the United States. In 1780, the State of Massachusetts issued bonds tied to an index of four commodity prices; see Willard Fisher (1913). This issue was refinanced by conventional debt in 1786. Apparently, protecting indexed bond holders from inflation became politically difficult to sustain at a time of widespread discontent about wartime inflation, sentiments that in Massachusetts culminated in Shay's Rebellion.

9. The second auction of TIPS, on April 8, 1997, has been described as less successful than the first. This time $8 billion were sold, but at the higher yield of 3.65 percent.

10. "Treasury Auctions Inflation-Linked Debt," *Facts on File News Digest*, January 30, 1997.

may make sense to wait and watch instead of plunging right in.''[11]
These accounts have emphasized such issues as doubts about possible
revisions of the Consumer Price Index; the risk that because the inflation
component of TIPS is taxable, some bondholders may have to pay more
in taxes on them than they receive in interest income; and the possibility
that TIPS may be difficult to sell later, because the secondary market
is weak. They do not seem to acknowledge the superiority of indexed
bonds over nominal bonds in terms of inflation risk; the real riskiness
of nominal debt appears not to be an issue for them.

There have been almost no private initiatives to issue similar bonds,
nor indexed home mortgages or other kinds of indexed indebtedness.
Irving Fisher persuaded the Rand Kardex Company, a company that he
had helped to found, to issue indexed debt in 1925. But this first attempt
at creating private indexed debt in the United States did not spur imi-
tators. Ultimately, "after the Rand Kardex Co. was merged in a larger
organization (the Remington Rand Inc.) this issue was converted into
ordinary preferred stock and bonds to gain a wider market than was
possible for an infamiliar form of security.''[12] J. Huston McCulloch
points out that indexed debt appears to have been illegal between 1933
and 1977, but there have been no legal obstacles since.[13] When inflation
picked up after 1977, there was a small flurry of proposals and efforts
to establish markets for indexed mortgages (for example, by the Tim-
bers Corporation, the Utah State Retirement System, and the Fund for
an Open Society) and indexed bonds (for example, by the Real Dollar
Corporation and the Fund for an Open Society), but they soon disappeared with the decline in inflation rates after the recession of 1981–
82.[14] The issuance of the TIPS in January 1997 was followed, within
about a week, by some private issues of indexed debt. The Tennessee
Valley Authority issued $300 million on February 5, J. P. Morgan and
Co. issued $200 million and Toyota Motor Credit Corporation issued
$100 million on February 6, and Salomon Inc. issued $450 million in

11. "New Inflation-Proof Bonds: Should They Be in Your Portfolio?", *Consumer Reports* 62, April 1997, p. 89.
12. Fisher (1934, p. 112).
13. McCulloch (1980).
14. Fischer (1983a) finds no solid reasons for the absence of privately issued indexed debt in the United States and instead falls back on two possible hypotheses: that borrow-ers' expectations of inflation may have been larger than those of lenders, and that the uncertainty about inflation was not great.

CPI-linked debt on February 7. The Federal Home Loan Bank System also issued indexed debt in the wake of the TIPS.[15] Yet in the following month and a half, the media reported no further indexed issues. While these private issues of indexed debt are encouraging, and one can hope that a market for privately issued indexed debt is forming, there is not yet any firm evidence that there will be a substantial amount of indexed debt in the United States in the future.

Even though the United States has historically experienced relatively low levels of uncertainty about inflation by world standards, failure to index debt has involved tremendous redistributions between debtors and creditors. Such redistributions have occurred in every period of U.S. history characterized by unanticipated inflation or deflation. For example, the last couple of decades of the nineteenth century were deflationary times, and since people did not seem to anticipate the deflation properly, debts were magnified. Farmers and other debtors, borrowing at fixed rates, tended to go bankrupt. Their dissatisfaction gave rise to the Greenback party, the Populist party, and the National Silver party, and was a dominant political force in the national elections of 1892 and 1896. William Jennings Bryan's famous "Cross of Gold" speech in 1896, which won him the nomination for the presidency, was, in effect, a plea for inflation in order to spare debtors who had been ruined by deflation. But these political movements lost their force when prices started rising again after 1896.

At the end of World War II, the U.S. federal debt was exceptionally high (for the time) because the government had borrowed rapidly and extensively to pay for the war: in 1945 it stood at $260 billion, well over a year's gross national product. By 1951, just six years later, unanticipated postwar inflation had pushed the Consumer Price Index up by 44 percent, meaning that 30 percent of this debt had effectively been repudiated. Much of the economic cost of the war was thrown on unwitting debt holders. Likewise, whereas in 1971 a new home buyer faced a conventional fixed mortgage rate of 7.7 percent, by 1981 the price level, measured by the CPI, had risen by 124 percent. In effect, more than half of the real debt in a long-term mortgage had been forgiven—and mortgage rates reached 16.6 percent in 1981, reflecting

15. "CPI-Linked Corporate Debt Tops $1.0 Bln on Week," *Reuters Financial Service*, February 7, 1997.

the much higher expected inflation rates. These few examples show the magnitudes of the redistributions caused by nominal contracts.

In the United States, social security payments and military pension plans are indexed to inflation, but private pensions are not substantially indexed. The Teachers Insurance and Annuity Association and College Retirement Equities Fund (TIAA-CREF), the largest private pension fund in the country and the pension provider for U.S. colleges and universities, allows its TIAA annuitants to select between a standard and a graded annuity, of which the latter uses the Consumer Price Index to adjust payouts so that they remain more nearly constant in real terms. A standard TIAA annuitant lost almost 70 percent of the value of the annuity payment to inflation over the period 1970-95. The graded annuity was first offered in 1982, and yet by 1994 only 14 percent of TIAA annuitants were choosing this option.[16]

The TIAA graded annuity is not really indexed to inflation, it merely adjusts payouts so that they will be constant in real terms through time if inflation is as expected. The payout of the graded annuity depends on the returns to funds invested. Therefore when these funds are invested in fixed incomes, there will still be losses if there is unexpected inflation. In principle, the CREF offers better protection than the TIAA against inflation, but 61 percent of the TIAA and CREF life annuity and minimum distribution contracts issued in 1994 were in TIAA.[17]

Alimony and child support awards are other examples of very long-term contracts. Alimony often continues until one spouse dies or the spouse receiving the award remarries. Child support awards typically last through the minority of the children and through their postsecondary education. Since these contracts are often so long term and represent such a significant fraction of individual incomes, one would think that all of them would be indexed. In fact, they are only very rarely indexed to inflation. The legal literature on indexation and alimony in the United States—a literature apparently confined to the period before inflation fell in the mid-1980s—implies little use of indexation in alimony or

16. For both the loss on the standard TIAA annuity and the graded annuity, see Francis P. King, "The TIAA Graded Payment Method and the CPI," *TIAA-CREF Research Dialogues* 46, December 1995 (available on TIAA-CREF's worldwide web page).

17. This percentage is inferred from Francis P. King, "Trends in Selection of TIAA-CREF Life-Annuity Income Options, 1978–1994," *TIAA-CREF Research Dialogues* 48, July 1996, table 6 (available on TIAA-CREF's worldwide web page).

child support.[18] To confirm that indexation is still rare in this arena, my research assistant telephoned six divorce lawyers and asked, "What percent of alimony agreements are indexed to inflation?" Four of the six answered none. Two answered that they had seen such agreements, but not recently.

Child support payments are often partially indexed, to the extent that they specify that the noncustodial parent must pay for medical insurance, life insurance, and education. However, as noted by legal scholar Robert Wilson: "As judicial policy has developed, it has not required that similar protection be extended to the monthly cost of raising the children. . . . The court decree does not require that the noncustodial parent bear his or her fair share of the cost of future inflation. The court is cognizant of the impact of inflation; it has recognized the problem of increases in the cost of living for more than fifty years. . . . [Yet] it seems that the courts presently include a COLA [cost of living allowance] provision to protect the child support order from inflation only when the parties have so agreed in a stipulation."[19] Change in the real value of alimony payments can be overcome only by costly and difficult to obtain modifications made by divorce courts.

Long-term option or warrant strike prices are only rarely indexed. Futures contracts could be designed so that hedgers would be protecting the real value of their inventories, rather than the nominal value, but they never are.

The absence of indexation schemes may also be responsible for a relative dearth of fixed long-term contracts in the United States. If one is constrained to write contracts in nominal terms, then one might logically keep all contracts short or include various escape clauses (such as call provisions or refinancing options) that effectively shorten contracts. It is difficult to measure the extent of benefits that might accrue if long-term contracts defined in fixed real terms were widely accepted. Since indexation has never been widespread, the potential welfare improvements that such contracts might provide have never emerged.

The indexation of wages became widespread in the United States during World War I, but was dropped in the 1920s, a period of stable

18. See, for example, Cynthia C. George, "Combatting the Effects of Inflation on Alimony and Child Support Orders," *Connecticut Bar Journal* 57(3), 1983, pp. 223–35.
19. Wilson (1980, pp. 137–38).

prices.[20] It was revived in the inflation of the 1970s, but appears to have fallen sharply since the deep recession of 1981–82, when firms were unable to cut real wages, despite stagflation.[21] The aversion to wage indexation currently expressed by firms when negotiating with labor might be interpreted as a recognition of the importance of applying a little "grease" to the wheels of the labor market. Some obfuscation of the stark realities may help people to accept changes in real income more easily.

Indexation of wages and salaries really ought to be considered in a special category, not entirely parallel to indexation of the other kinds of contracts discussed above. Possibly, it appears problematical because of the emotions and comparisons with nominal standards that have entered the rhetoric and politics of wage bargaining. The indexation of wages and salaries has been blamed for the structural inflation seen in Latin American countries.[22] Moreover, people seem to have a pathological aversion to seeing wage cuts on paper, even though real wage cuts concealed by inflation are acceptable.[23]

With the possible exception of labor markets, where the use of indexation is clouded by other considerations, the history of the United States largely seems to be one of missed opportunities for indexation.

Turkey

Countries that have experienced high and variable inflation, such as Argentina, Brazil, and Chile, have often widely adopted indexation for long-term contracts. This is not surprising; under such circumstances, the defects of long-term nominal contracts ought to be extremely obvious. And yet there are still other countries with high and variable inflation, such as Turkey, that do not index to any substantial degree.[24]

In 1995, when the Turkish consumer price index showed an inflation rate of 88.1 percent, only three of the 104 countries for which data are

20. See Fisher (1934).

21. See Robert S. Gay, "Union Settlements and Aggregate Wage Behavior in the 1980s," *Daily Labor Report* 235, p. D-1, December 6, 1984.

22. See Cavallo (1983).

23. See Groshen and Schweitzer (1995), Akerlof, Dickens, and Perry (1996), and Card and Hyslop (1997).

24. Inflation in Turkey, although massive, has not quite reached the hyperinflationary proportions seen in Argentina or Brazil in the past couple of decades. Some observers believe that it is the lack of indexation that has enabled Turkey to avoid real hyperinflation.

given in the International Monetary Fund's *International Financial Statistics* had higher inflation rates: Zaire, Suriname, and Russia (which has since tamed the inflation). The problem one faces in studying high inflation in the 1990s is that most countries that experienced high inflation in the postwar period have reduced it dramatically; inflation is down throughout most of the world. In Turkey, however, inflation has not been below 20 percent per year since the late 1970s. It has also been extremely variable, as table 1 shows. All forms of indexed contracts have been legal in Turkey since January 1980, when Turgut Özal, undersecretary to Prime Minister Süleyman Demirel, liberalized the economy.

Certain prices in Turkey are now commonly quoted in U.S. dollars or deutsche marks. In the newspapers of major cities, house prices are almost always advertised in dollars. By contrast, in small towns house prices are mostly quoted in Turkish lira (TL). The same is true of apartment rents: large urban and wealthy areas favor dollars or deutsche marks and more rural areas, Turkish lira. The prices of commercial real estate and expensive electronic goods are often set in dollars. Overall, though, the great majority of prices are set in Turkish lira.

Currency exchanges are widespread in Istanbul, about as common as fast food restaurants. Many people carry U.S. dollars or deutsche marks, but instead of paying in these foreign currencies, they convert them into Turkish lira at the last possible minute, even for small expenditures. In some cases, a person may even exchange currency before going to the movies.

The Turkish government had never issued inflation-indexed debt before late February 1997, when the equivalent of U.S. $148.9 million was issued to the public.[25] Turkish news media have apparently shown little interest, and there was reportedly "low participation" in the issue.[26] In April 1994, as part of a stabilization program, the government

25. The Turkish government unsuccessfully attempted to market indexed bonds in 1996.

26. One explanation offered by the media for the poor showing of the Turkish indexed bonds runs as follows: "Inflation and political woes also hampered the treasury's sale of two-year inflation-indexed bonds. . . . 'The timing of the first inflation-indexed bond auction was not good. Political uneasiness, higher-than-expected inflation data, falling stocks, rising bond yields lowered demand for the auction,' said a private bank treasurer." (Tulin Aygunes, "Turkish Bond Yields Jump on Politics, Inflation," Reu-

advised banks to create one-year time deposits linked to the Turkish wholesale price index (''TEFE''). Turkish banks now advertise, alongside a variety of nominal interest rate accounts, these TEFE + savings accounts.

To gauge the status of indexation in Turkey, my research assistant Emre Deliveli interviewed a number of people in Istanbul, including ten lawyers who handle divorce cases, ten bond dealers, and three labor union officials. These interviews reveal that indexation is almost never used for alimony or child support payments, corporate bonds, or labor contracts. Instead, the problems caused in nominal contracts by inflation are dealt with by effectively keeping the contracts short. Alimony and child support payments are regularly modified by their courts, despite the costs and conflicts, just as in the United States. Debt and labor contracts are for the short term.

When asked about public resistance to indexation, Turkish interviewees were not often clear. Sometimes they cited mistrust of the price index and concerns that even if the index were correct, people might not be able to pay the higher payments resulting from indexation. None of them knew of any tax disadvantages to indexation. Some said that lack of understanding is not an issue; everyone understood indexation perfectly well.

Respondents judged that dollarization is used for about 10 percent of alimony and child support settlements, particularly for more wealthy clients, but that corporate bonds and labor contracts are not dollarized at all. One explanation offered as to why dollarization is not used more widely is that the exchange rate has been unstable. One respondent said that the Turkish lira fell from 9,000 to the dollar to 40,000 to the dollar in a matter of days. While this statement is an exaggeration (it took a couple of years, not days), the real buying power of the U.S. dollar has, in fact, been very variable in Turkey. For example, according to government CPI and exchange rate figures, it increased by 57 percent between 1993 and 1994. The resultant change in local real values in a dollarized contract would have been enormous.

ters Financial Service, March 4, 1997.) The government has issued small quantities of debt tied to foreign exchange in the past, starting with the Turkish Prime Ministry Public Participation Fund in 1987.

Addressing the Puzzle

It would seem to be easy to tell why nobody is interested in indexation: just ask your neighbor. The answers should be immediate. And yet the economics profession apparently does not have a good understanding of the issue. It is the thesis of this paper that the reasons for the lack of public interest in indexation are not so easily discerned. People do not initially remember how they have arrived at their opinions; one must work with them. What may, at first, seem to be gut-level prejudices or impulsive rejections ultimately derive from a constellation of views and assumptions, the full implications of which must be worked out before one can achieve real understanding.

Informal Interviews

The first step in addressing the puzzle of public resistance to indexation was to obtain an informal impression of public opinion through personal interviews. A dozen Yale University students selected people in the New Haven area at random to interview about inflation. The students called random listings in the telephone book and also interviewed passers-by in a shopping mall, students in a vending machine area at a Yale library, workers striking Yale University on the street, and the employees of a local restaurant, several of whom were Turkish. Some students also did some library research on views on indexation. I met with the students, individually and in groups, every week or so for a semester to discuss what we were learning and to hammer out questions for formal questionnaires. This informal interview stage of the project was very important, for we listened to the issues that people brought up and were able to pose follow-up questions; that is, to pursue their lines of argument. It also made for much improved questionnaires, since we got an advance look at people's reactions to the questions and whether they were misinterpreting them.

One of the most striking findings from the responses to the informal interviews is that many, though by no means all, people seem to have a visceral resistance to indexation: they trust dollars, not formulas. Several respondents said, ''I want to know how much money I will be getting.'' It was also commonly said that ''the indexed plan is too risky,'' as if people regard the prospect of getting fewer dollars as a bad outcome, even though this would occur only if prices were also low.[27] But much more than such impulse reactions must be at work to prevent any substantial public acceptance of indexation.

Questionnaire Design

The second step of the project was to design formal questionnaires. Many of the questions that I wanted to ask about indexation could not be asked without posing leading questions, which suggested concepts that might not otherwise be on people's minds. Therefore, in order to discern whether people were merely being very agreeable, two sets of questions were used in the United States, questionnaires A and B. Most questions appear on both, but with different, often opposite, wording. Only questionnaire A was used in Turkey, since this is sufficient for international comparison.

Some questions are included in both questionnaires A and B with identical wording. In these cases, the ordering of the multiple choice answers is always reversed in questionnaire B, except for the no opinion category, which is always last. In the discussion below, the ordering shown for these questions is that of questionnaire A. Some questions cannot be translated into Turkish literally because of the different conditions in Turkey, notably, the much higher inflation. Below, any substantial differences are indicated in square brackets. I discuss the questions in the order in which they appear on the questionnaires, not in order of importance.

Random samples from all over the United States, derived from telephone books, were purchased from Survey Sampling, Inc., and a random sample from the town of Marmaris, Mugla, Turkey, was extracted from the local telephone book. Marmaris lies on the west coast of Turkey, a region with somewhat higher levels of income and education than the national average.

For each of the three types of questionnaire—"USA-A," "Turkey," and "USA-B"—four hundred copies were initially mailed out with a letter explaining the social purpose of the survey and informing participants that their responses might help to formulate public policy toward indexation. A few weeks later, a second letter and replacement

27. Fisher (1928, 1934) makes similar observations about public reactions to proposals for indexation.

questionnaire was sent out to all who had not responded to the first. In the United States, a third letter and replacement questionnaire were sent out to those still failed to respond.

There were 140 responses (35 percent) to questionnaire A in the United States, 161 responses (40 percent) to questionnaire B in the United States, and 99 (25 percent) responses to questionnaire A in Turkey, giving a total of four hundred responses, or an overall response rate of one-third. There were fewer responses in Turkey because the questionnaire was only mailed twice. The response rate is not as high as one would like but, given the difficulty of the questionnaire and the subject matter, one might not be able to do better.

The characteristics of the respondents are shown in table 2. The level of education is high. It is possible that it would be difficult to survey the opinions of the uneducated, less sophisticated fraction of the population. Perhaps the opinions of the more educated and sophisticated people are most salient, since they tend to be the opinion leaders and to advise friends and relatives who are less informed about contracts and investments.

Money Illusion and the Framing of Questions

It should be noted at the outset that money illusion is one factor that reduces interest in indexation. Fisher finds that people show little awareness of the effects of aggregate price level changes on their lives and have a tendency to think in terms of quantities measured in local currencies as standards of value.[28] Eldar Shafir, Peter Diamond, and Amos Tversky confirm empirically that given calculations presented in dollars, people tend to choose stable dollar amounts, and given calculations presented in real goods and services, they tend to choose stable real amounts.[29] That answers to questionnaire items are affected by the wording of the questions and by associations that the wording suggests is well known to psychologists: "framing" affects responses.

Shafir, Diamond, and Tversky also show that people seem to have a preference for receiving nominal pay increases, even if they know that prices have gone up just as much. The authors base this finding on comparisons of choices made in scenario questions across groups of

28. Fisher (1928).
29. Shafir, Diamond, and Tversky (1997).

Table 2. Characteristics of Survey Respondents
Percent, except as indicated

	Questionnaire		
Characteristic	*USA-A*	*USA-B*	*Turkey*
Sex			
Male	75	75	80
Female	25	25	20
Birth year			
1970–79	5	3	21
1960–69	16	11	35
1950–59	23	21	21
1940–49	26	23	18
1930–39	12	15	3
1920–29	12	17	2
1910–19	7	8	0
Before 1910	1	1	0
Educational attainment			
Less than high school graduate	4	7	9
High school graduate	24	17	14
Some college	25	24	17
College graduate	30	28	44
Graduate or professional school	17	23	16
Annual income			
Less than $25,000[a]	11	21	29
$25,000–$70,000[b]	67	55	47
More than $70,000[c]	21	24	24
Number of respondents	140	161	99

Source: Author's survey.
a. In Turkey, less than 600 million Turkish lira (TL).
b. In Turkey, 600 million TL to 3 billion TL.
c. In Turkey, more than 3 billion TL.

respondents. I attempt, elsewhere, to replicate their findings in a much less subtle way, by asking directly about this tendency, and I compare the answers of randomly selected people with those of professional economists at major universities.[30] I ask:

> Do you agree with the following statement? "I think that if my pay went up I would feel more satisfaction in my job, more sense of fulfillment, even if prices went up just as much." [Please indicate how much you agree, on a scale from 1 to 5.]

30. Shiller (1997).

Response in percent

	1: fully agree	*2*	*3: undecided*	*4*	*5: completely disagree*	*Sample size*
US-All	28	21	11	14	27	112
Economists	0	8	3	13	77	79

While most of the "US-All" sample of noneconomists did not fully agree with the statement, about half of them chose answers 1 or 2. It is striking that so many would agree, since this question is essentially asking them to admit to irrational behavior. Some of the noneconomists wrote remarks on the questionnaire, saying that they knew that it was irrational to choose answers 1 or 2, but they wanted to do so anyway. In contrast, most of the economists completely disagreed with the statement.

It is difficult to say to what extent the anomalies of judgment that such money illusion produces are responsible for public apathy toward indexation. If the dependence of answers on framing is the result of casual errors made by respondents who are only marginally interested in answering correctly, then it is perhaps unlikely to be solely responsible for the widespread apathy to indexation. If there is satisfaction in receiving nominal pay increases, even if prices go up as much, it may still be that when people think seriously about major economic decisions, they set aside such feelings. Advocates of indexed contracts make an effort to frame the discussion in a way that encourages support, and presumably opinion leaders who take more time to think about the issues may prevent people from acting wrongly because of casual errors.

It is my hypothesis that more is at work in producing apathy toward indexation than simple money illusion. Money illusion just does not seem to be strong enough to prevent people from taking steps to protect their own welfare when they really understand the importance of the issue. In a sober and collected moment, people ought to be able to make correct decisions about indexation. To resolve the puzzle, it is necessary to characterize further the worldview that makes it difficult to convince people of the importance of indexation, even when their attention is focused on the subject and the framing issues are explained to them.

A Preliminary Exercise on Indexation

A fundamental problem of designing a questionnaire for this study is that inflation and indexation are complicated concepts, which people may think that they understand but, in fact, do not. As a researcher, one must decide whether one is interested in people's answers from their current state of mind or in the answers that they give after one has forced them to confront what these terms mean, thereby educating them about the basic definitions and issues. And how does one know if they understand them?

This study is primarily interested in the more informed judgments that people make after some thought. The questionnaires begin with a brief description of the issues and then quiz respondents on the mathematics of indexation. Making respondents work problems on indexation forces them to come to grips with the issues and also allows one to assess whether they do understand the issues. A disadvantage of this method is that it reduces response rates, by intimidating many who might otherwise respond.

All three versions of the questionnaire begin with the following explanation:

In this questionnaire we seek your opinions on the subject of *inflation* and *indexation*.

By *inflation*, we mean the rate of increase in the cost of living (of the average price of goods and services you buy, of the Consumer Price Index) as computed from data on actual prices.

By *indexation*, we mean agreeing now to tie the amounts of money you will receive or pay at future dates to the inflation rates the government announces in the future, so as to preserve real buying power. We say then that the payments are "indexed," or that there is an "Escalator Clause" or a "Cost of Living Allowance (COLA)."

Example of Indexation: Mr. Smith [Ahmet Bey] who is retiring right now chooses a pension that is fully indexed to inflation. He is promised $1,000 a month in today's dollars [20 million a month in today's Turkish lira], indexed to inflation. If inflation turns out to be 5 percent [50 percent] over the next year, he will be getting $1,050 [30 million TL] a month next year. If inflation turns out to be −5 percent [−50 percent] over the next year (prices are falling) he will be getting $950 [10 million TL] a month next year.

Immediately after this example, the following question is posed:

1(A, B). If *inflation* was 3 percent [75 percent] over the past year, then by definition this means that:

[Please circle one number]

1. If we look at prices of many different things, 3 percent [75 percent] of them are too high.
2. Prices are on average 3 percent [75 percent] higher than they were last year
3. Wages are on average 3 percent [75 percent] higher than they were last year
4. Prices are going up 3 percent [75 percent] more than wages are
5. Do not know

Response in percent

	1	*2*	*3*	*4*	*5*	*Sample size*
USA-A	3	84	1	12	1	138
USA-B	1	79	0	17	3	159
Turkey	6	72	5	15	1	97

From the answers to this question, it seems very clear that most people in both countries understood what inflation is after reading the introduction. The tendency of some to select answer 4 reveals that some might, in effect, define inflation as a decrease in real wages. Still, no more than one in six chose this answer.

Respondents are then asked to work mathematical problems in order to test their understanding of indexation:

2(A, B). Ms. Walter [Ayşe Hanım] is disabled, and is living off of *fully indexed* disability plan income. In 1996 she is receiving $500 [5 million TL] a month in disability payments. If inflation turns out to be 10 percent [50 percent] between 1996 and 1997, then in 1997 she will be receiving:

1. $450 [2.5 million TL]
2. $500 [5 million TL]
3. $550 [7.5 million TL]
4. Do not know

Response in percent

	1	*2*	*3*	*4*	*Sample size*
USA-A	4	2	94	1	139
USA-B	3	1	94	3	160
Turkey	2	4	91	3	98

3(A, B): If inflation turns out to be − 10 percent [− 50 percent] (prices falling) then in 1997 Ms. Walter [Ayşe Hanım], with her *fully indexed* plan, will be receiving:

1. $450 [2.5 million TL]
2. $500 [5 million TL]
3. $550 [7.5 million TL]
4. Do not know

Response in percent

	1	*2*	*3*	*4*	*Sample size*
USA-A	94	2	4	1	140
USA-B	85	7	2	6	161
Turkey	76	17	4	3	99

Respondents did remarkably well on both questions, giving correct answers most of the time. Some Turkish respondents seemed to have a little difficulty in dealing with a situation in which prices fall by 50 percent in a year and imagining that payments might be cut in half in nominal terms, but overall the responses support the notion that people understand indexation.

The following question is intended to confirm that, after working these problems, respondents understand that indexation does preserve real values:

4(A, B). In the above question, if all prices really fall 10 percent [50 percent] in 1997, what, in theory, ought to be the change between 1996 and 1997 in the real buying power of Ms. Walter's [Ayşe Hanım's] *indexed* disability income?

1. In 1997 she can buy more goods and services than in 1996
2. She can buy exactly the same amount in both years
3. In 1997 she can buy less goods and services than in 1996
4. Do not know

Response in percent

	1	*2*	*3*	*4*	*Sample size*
USA-A	15	76	9	1	139
USA-B	18	70	10	3	156
Turkey	39	49	11	0	99

Three-quarters of the United States respondents and half of the Turkish respondents chose the correct answer, 2. It is curious that among those who answered otherwise, there was a definite bias toward the belief that the indexed contract provides more goods and services (answer 1). This could be a sign of a powerful tendency to think in nominal terms, even after working the mathematical problems correctly. There is, however, another possible interpretation: people do not believe that the price index does what it is said to do. Moreover, although the survey does not sample economists, they would probably also show some tendency to pick answer 1, because of the substitution effect. Both of these issues are discussed below.

The overall interpretation of the results presented above is that respondents, by and large, had little trouble with the basic concepts of indexation, at least after they were explained to them. Most of them understood that indexation preserves real buying power rather than nominal quantities. This does not mean that people are always ready to give such enlightened answers. Media accounts of indexation schemes rarely, if ever, give as thorough an explanation of the essential quantitative concepts regarding indexation as the questionnaires used in this study.

Direct Questions

When asked directly whether they would choose an indexed contract, most respondents said that they would:

5(A). Imagine that you are in Ms. Walter's [Ayşe Hanım's] situation. Experts' best guess is that there will be 3 percent [25 percent] a year inflation indefinitely, but really they aren't sure. Which disability income plan would you prefer?

1. The *indexed* plan as with Ms. Walter [Ayşe Hanım] (tied to future inflation rates as computed from data on actual future prices by government statisticians)
2. An *unindexed* plan that increases payments 3 percent [25 percent] a year, regardless of inflation
3. I am indifferent between the two plans or don't know

Response in percent

	1	*2*	*3*	*Sample size*
USA-A	65	29	7	136
Turkey	85	9	6	86

The majority of respondents, after having answered the preceding questions, chose indexation. The substantial minority that did not can provide insights into public resistance to indexation. It is important to note that those in the USA-A sample who chose answer 2, the unindexed plan, were almost as likely to answer question 4 correctly as the overall sample: 67 percent of those who chose answer 2 for question 5 also chose answer 2 to question 4 (of the entire U.S. sample, 73 percent chose answer 2 for question 4).

When the inflation rate built into the unindexed plan was changed from 3 to 10 percent and the unindexed plan was placed first in the list of answers, more people still chose the indexed plan than the unindexed plan:

5(B). Imagine that you are in Ms. Walter's situation. Experts' best guess is that there will be 10 percent a year inflation indefinitely, but really they aren't sure. Which disability income plan would you prefer?

1. An *unindexed* plan that increases payments 10 percent a year, regardless of inflation
2. The *indexed* plan as with Ms. Walter (tied to future inflation rates as computed from data on actual future prices by government statisticians)
3. I am indifferent between the two plans or don't know

Response in percent

	1	*2*	*3*	*Sample size*
USA-B	44	47	9	153

This overall show of support for indexation seems to stand in contradiction to the apparent lack of public interest in indexation. Possibly, the flow of the preceding questions made it clear that the "correct" answer was the indexed plan, and most respondents did not want to appear foolish. Perhaps more interesting than the answers to question 5 are the explanations of these answers given in response to the following question:

6(A, B). Can you explain why you made the choice that you did in question 5?

On the one hand, among respondents who chose the indexed plan, the most common answer to question 6 was some restatement of the basic message of the early questions: indexed plans guarantee real buying power and are safer. On the other hand, there were 103 U.S.

respondents, but only nine Turkish respondents, who picked the un-indexed plan or said they were indifferent.

Reading the answers given by U.S. respondents who chose no in-dexation in question 5, I conclude that they fall into several major categories. The most common explanation by USA-B respondents who chose the unindexed plan was to refer to the 10 percent inflation fore-cast, either expressing doubt that inflation would be so high, or saying that they expected to receive more under the unindexed plan: 42 percent of the USA-B respondents who chose no indexation appeared to offer the latter as a reason to prefer unindexed contracts. Only 7 percent of the USA-A respondents who chose the unindexed plan seemed to expect to receive more under that plan. These contrasting results do highlight a tendency for people to be concerned with the expected return on assets, as well as their risk-reduction benefits—and it is rational to have such concerns. The results show that one should not ask whether people want an indexed plan without specifying its terms or expected returns. People are attentive to these details and their answers will be influenced by the assumptions that they make about these details if they are left unspecified in the question.

The most common explanation given by USA-A respondents who chose the unindexed plan (49 percent), and the second most common explanation given by USA-B respondents who did so (27 percent), was that nominal contracts are inherently desirable, or indexation is too risky. Their answers include:

> Bird in hand is worth two in bush!

> It's a safer choice.

> I would rather have a fixed increase, than take a chance of a decrease in inflation.

> I would rather receive a definite 3 percent increase each year than gamble whether or not the rates will increase or decrease each year.

> Yes the sure thing, better than a gamble.

> I would like to have a good idea of what I'll be getting, 10 percent will always be 10 percent. But the indexed plan appears to have many un-knowns and with that comes fear and apprehension.

Of these, several respondents said that they did not like the possibility that they might see their benefits shrink if inflation were lower than expected; any such decrease would seem unpleasant, unfair, or unwise:

I would prefer the unindexed plan because even though I would theoretically still be at the same standard of living, I think I would have trouble
adjusting to the idea of living on "less" money.

You may at times be lower than what inflation actually is [with the
unindexed plan], but it is never good to go backwards.

The next most common explanation, offered by 17 percent of the
USA-A respondents and 5 percent of the USA-B respondents who chose
the unindexed plan, was doubt that the government inflation numbers
were valid for their individual circumstances:

I think some of the government figures are wrong and buy [sic] smart
shopping you should be able to adjust.

Aging brings new cost-of-living expenses in goods and services (medical
could be disastrous).

If all things have equal choice I would be ok, but in my experience all
goods and services would not go down in a free enterprise situation.

The government knows no more about future inflation than I. I picked
[answer] 2 just to be safe.

Of these, several respondents thought that the government's national
inflation numbers could not be accurate in describing their geographical
region:

Figures on inflation are general (nationwide) while true inflation hits the
working family where they live (regional).

Index rates must be tied only to the actual location where the income is
to be received, i.e., KS inflation could be different than your CT
inflation.

There were also several respondents who raised the possibility that the
statisticians who compute the government inflation numbers are not to
be trusted:

Government statistics are manipulated.

3 percent a year is guaranteed! Government statisticians are stupid and
report what there [sic] were told to report.

A few respondents did not believe that the indexed plan would pay out
as promised:

I doubt indexed plan would continue to be backed if inflation ran away.

Index plan is a theory and the way inflation is going social security could not handle the index plan.

And a few seemed to associate indexation schemes with government interference:

It would seem that an unindexed approach leaves us with a little more of a free market.

The Turkish respondents who chose the indexed plan offered similar explanations to those of the Americans in question 6, noting that indexation preserves real buying power. However, there was also a prominent theme of disbelief that inflation in Turkey would be as low as 25 percent a year. One respondent pointed out that a 1996 labor contract by a well-known firm specified a 32.9 percent wage increase for the first six months and another 34 percent for the subsequent six months. Fewer Turkish respondents than Americans chose the unindexed plan or were uncertain, and there are only nine corresponding answers to question 6. These appear to follow the same general themes as those from the United States, showing a bias toward desiring fixed nominal returns or questioning the relevance of the index to respondents' own situations:

I don't want to be tied to an uncertain inflation rate.

Because the 25 percent increasing plan is more of a guarantee.

In today's Turkey, I wouldn't sign any contract indexed to something because there are always different and abnormal increases.

A couple of these respondents appeared to expect that inflation would be less than 25 percent a year in Turkey:

The experts are not certain. Because of this, instead of increasing, inflation will decrease. Then, it will not be of any use to me.

I believe it will be more profitable.

Four respondents mentioned lack of trust in the government:

Inflation rates prepared by the DIE [government department of statistics] are from time to time adjusted according to government politics. I mean it doesn't seem believable to me. Because of this, I'd choose [answer] 2 instead of the indexed plan.

Because DIE is not trustworthy.

I don't trust my country.

Nothing will happen in this country.

Some of the Turkish respondents who chose the indexed plan also mentioned concerns that the government cannot be trusted. The apparently higher proportion of Turkish respondents than Americans who lack trust in their government is not surprising. Widespread concern about government corruption in Turkey led to an unusually strong showing by the Islamic Welfare party (Refah) in the December 1995 elections. In July 1996, just before the questionnaire surveys were conducted, Welfare party leader Necmettin Erbakan became prime minister in a coalition government. This is the country's first Islamic government since Mustafa Kemal Atatürk created a modern, secular Turkey in 1923. Political observers interpret the change, in part, as reflecting a broad public perception of corruption or incompetence in the government and the hope that a new government might be different. It is perhaps not clear that concern about government corruption or incompetence would lead one to choose an unindexed contract; on the contrary, corrupt or incompetent officials might be more likely to inflate the currency than to doctor inflation numbers. In any case, this concern apparently has not biased the results of question 5 very far against indexation.

Some economists argue that people may prefer fixed nominal contracts because they have preexisting fixed nominal contracts. The potential significance of this argument is not as great as one might think at first because, as a result of the failure to index, most people avoid strict long-term nominal contracts; pension plans are the major exception. A long-term fixed rate home mortgage is another plausible candidate as a large nominal liability in the U.S. context. However, people can and do refinance their mortgages if inflation—and interest rates—declines. People paying or receiving fixed long-term alimony payments might worry about the price level changing, but in such an event their troubles would be limited, since they have the option of modifying their alimony contracts in court. Disabled people like Ms. Walter or retirees on defined benefit plans are rarely locked into any long-term nominal debt, so it is hard to find any evidence of long-term nominal contracts that could cause them not to want their pension or disability benefits indexed. Indeed, none of the answers to question 6, from either country, make any mention of indexation being problematic as a result of pre-existing nominal contracts.

Math Anxiety

Apparently, one reason why people do not respond well to indexation proposals is that these describe payments as determined by a mathematical formula. From the interviews in this survey, it seems that such formulas apparently touch deep anxieties or uncertainties in many people. Even though most questionnaire respondents chose indexation after working some indexation problems, it seems likely that some degree of math anxiety is inhibiting a strong public movement in favor of indexation. It is probably because of these anxieties that most news media avoid mathematics entirely: a newspaper writer will never include a mathematical formula in a story, even though it might enlighten a substantial number of readers.

If people feel that it is very difficult to understand indexation, they will be reticent to introduce it into contracts of any complexity, fearing it to be a distraction or obstacle that will prevent full appreciation of the benefits of the contract. Moreover, if people are never made to understand some of the basic quantitative concepts of indexation fully, they will have difficulty in judging whether a specific indexed contract serves their interests. For example, an ill-informed person might easily misinterpret the difference between the stated yield on a nominal bond and the stated yield on an indexed bond as an "insurance premium" against inflation-induced fluctuations in income, rather than understanding it simply as an expected inflation rate.[31] This confusion will make indexed bonds appear much less attractive.

To see why people would arrive at the conclusion that indexation is hard to understand, think of the kinds of news stories that they regularly encounter. Some present the level of the Consumer Price Index, a number like 253.2. Many people must feel that they do not know what

31. Some popular accounts of indexed bonds seem to encourage just such confusion. For example, syndicated columnist Stephen Higgins writes: "The obvious point is that these bonds will pay a slightly lower interest rate than conventional Treasury bonds. Analysts estimate the total return will be 3 to 4 percent a year. But conservative investors interested in protecting principal won't necessarily consider that an obstacle." ("A Few Things You Should Know about Inflation Indexed Bonds," *New Haven Register*, December 8, 1996, p. F1.)

this number means. Occasionally there are stories about the various price indexes, perhaps discussing the rebasing of indexes or alleged biases in them. It is easy to see how people might throw up their hands and start to think that it is asking too much to expect them to understand what it is all about.

The survey asks directly about math anxiety in the context of indexation:

7(A). Do you agree with the following statement? "I am not sure that I fully understand all the mathematics of indexation; if I had to sign a contract that had an indexation clause in it, I would feel the need to talk to someone more knowledgeable about indexation." [Please indicate how much you agree, on a scale from 1 to 5.]

1. Strongly agree
2. Agree somewhat
3. Neutral or no opinion
4. Disagree somewhat
5. Strongly disagree

Response in percent

	1	2	3	4	5	Sample size
USA-A	30	36	7	17	11	137
Turkey	25	49	4	10	12	92

7(B). "I feel confident that I understand the mathematics of indexation well; if I had to sign a contract that had an indexation clause in it, I wouldn't feel the need to talk to someone more knowledgeable about indexation."

1. Strongly agree
2. Agree somewhat
3. Neutral or no opinion
4. Disagree somewhat
5. Strongly disagree

Response in percent

	1	2	3	4	5	Sample size
USA-B	32	36	8	14	9	153

The results are not very enlightening. In questionnaire A and in the Turkish questionnaire, which suggest that there might be math anxiety, there is some tendency for respondents to agree that it is an issue. But in questionnaire B, where the question is reworded to suggest that the respondent might feel confident about such calculations, the answers were reversed. It should be noted that these responses were given by people who had just answered the math problems, and not by the people who threw the questionnaires away.

It seems likely, despite the lack of solid evidence here, that math anxiety is an issue. Various hints of an aversion to mathematical formulae and preference for nominal quantities seemed to come through in the informal interviews but are difficult to incorporate into a questionnaire. It seemed that, in contrast with an abstract mathematical indexation formula, the nominal quantities in unindexed contracts have more tangible value. Perhaps people associate nominal contract payments with stronger mental images of coins and notes—attractive, dignified, finely detailed art objects that have acquired deep, symbolic, cultural value. People seem to attach importance to having cash. Respondents noted, for example, that people all around the world want to hold dollars, or that there is a common consensus about the value of the dollar. Some seemed to be saying that the dollar never loses value, but the economy changes around it. By contrast, to put one's faith in an index number apparently requires trusting some mathematics that only a few, remote people understand. Still, these nuances tended to be fleeting and may disappear under further questioning, so it is hard to know how important they might be in explaining why indexation is not more widespread.

Doubts about the Accuracy of the Consumer Price Index

Another reason why enthusiasm for indexation is not stronger is that many people do not trust the price indexes. In the interviews, some people expressed mistrust in these numbers, but their remarks were often flippant and hard to interpret. One possibility, suggested by some of the interviewees as well as the answers to question 6 discussed above, is that people think that the numbers might be fraudulent:

8(A). "An important reason not to trust contracts indexed to inflation is that someone in the government might deliberately falsify the inflation numbers to take advantage of people like me."

1. Strongly agree
2. Agree somewhat

3. Neutral or no opinion
4. Disagree somewhat
5. Strongly disagree

Response in percent

	1	*2*	*3*	*4*	*5*	*Sample size*
USA-A	21	24	16	27	13	139
Turkey	18	43	4	21	13	91

8(B). "An important reason to trust contracts indexed to inflation is that those people in the government who are responsible for the inflation numbers are basically honest and trustworthy."

1. Strongly agree
2. Agree somewhat
3. Neutral or no opinion
4. Disagree somewhat
5. Strongly disagree

Response in percent

	1	*2*	*3*	*4*	*5*	*Sample size*
USA-B	6	29	20	28	18	158

The results give some suggestion that fraud might be important, especially in Turkey, where 64 percent agreed at least somewhat. The U.S. answers are not strongly biased toward this opinion, but perhaps it is significant that people are not more uniformly confident in government statistics.

It is also possible that people are skeptical about the inherent value of the numbers, whether or not those who produce them are deliberately fraudulent:

9(A). "The government inflation numbers are almost useless in describing my cost of living increases; the national inflation rate says little about inflation in the things that I tend to buy in the places where I buy them."

1. Strongly agree
2. Agree somewhat
3. Neutral or no opinion
4. Disagree somewhat
5. Strongly disagree

Response in percent

	1	*2*	*3*	*4*	*5*	*Sample size*
USA-A	24	32	18	18	8	140
Turkey	18	36	8	23	15	92

9(B). "I believe that the government inflation numbers are pretty accurate in describing my cost of living increases; the national inflation rate accurately describes the inflation in the things that I tend to buy in the places where I buy them."

1. Strongly agree
2. Agree somewhat
3. Neutral or no opinion
4. Disagree somewhat
5. Strongly disagree

Response in percent

	1	*2*	*3*	*4*	*5*	*Sample size*
USA-B	5	41	12	31	12	157

There was not a lot of agreement to question 9, and when the wording was reversed in questionnaire B, faith in the numbers improved. Indeed, in talking to people about the accuracy of inflation numbers, it appeared that many had a resigned faith, a sense that all prices inevitably march with these numbers.

And yet, despite these answers, there does seem to be widespread mistrust of some sort. The survey pursues the theory that the inflation numbers may be trustworthy now, but that they would become untrustworthy if inflation became very high:

10(A). "When inflation gets very high, prices of individual items jump around a lot more relative to each other, and so the inflation rate becomes a much worse measure of the increase in the cost of living."

1. Strongly agree
2. Agree somewhat
3. Neutral or no opinion
4. Disagree somewhat
5. Strongly disagree

Response in percent

	1	*2*	*3*	*4*	*5*	*Sample size*
USA-A	18	36	29	14	4	139
Turkey	23	51	4	15	8	93

10(B). "When inflation gets very high, prices of individual items tend to fall in line with the inflation rate, all marching up at the same rate, and so the inflation rate becomes a much better measure of the increase in the cost of living."

1. Strongly agree
2. Agree somewhat
3. Neutral or no opinion
4. Disagree somewhat
5. Strongly disagree

Response in percent

	1	*2*	*3*	*4*	*5*	*Sample size*
USA-B	11	25	11	37	16	157

The responses to both versions of question 10 are mildly supportive of the notion that people feel that the accuracy of inflation numbers would be questionable if inflation were high.

Overall, the evidence suggests some tendency to mistrust the inflation numbers, which may be a factor in public resistance to indexation, even if it is not important enough to explain the resistance by itself. If mistrust of published index numbers were the only obstacle, people could define their own indexes for the purposes of their contracts, as the State of Massachusetts did in the very first indexed bond issue, in 1780.[32]

Perceptions of Substitution Bias

Some of the respondents in the informal interviews suggested that they avoided most of the effects of inflation by "smart shopping"; that

32. The Massachusetts indexed bond issue of 1780 defined its own price index in terms of four commodities (see note 8). In modern times one could, for example, index long-term contract payments to an average of prices that regularly appear in newspaper advertisements. Thus the index would be given a formal definition without any reliance on government index numbers.

is, by switching from high-priced full-service stores to discount stores and by avoiding those items that show the greatest increases in prices. If cream cheese becomes expensive, they might switch to peanut butter and not suffer much from the price change. Such reasoning calls to mind the well-known substitution bias in Laspeyres price indexes, such as the U.S. Consumer Price Index.

Laspeyres price indexes are biased toward overestimating the increase in the cost of obtaining a fixed level of utility, so long as relative prices change during the process of inflation. The reason for this bias is that when relative prices change, people can substitute the items that become relatively less expensive for those that become more expensive. A contract that promises that a person will receive a fixed amount in real dollars as measured by the Consumer Price Index allows that person to consume the same market basket as before. Thus the person can be no worse off, and in fact will generally be better off, since relative price changes create opportunities for substitution.

Economists have concluded, however, that in recent U.S. experience the substitution bias has not amounted to much. The U.S. Senate Advisory Commission to Study the Consumer Price Index concludes that the commodity substitution bias is only 0.4 percent a year and the outlet substitution bias is only 0.1 percent a year, for a total bias of 0.5 percent a year.[33] Jack Triplett concludes that the substitution bias in the U.S. CPI is no greater than 0.1 percent per year. Steven Braithwait estimates this substitution bias at 0.1 percent per year, and Marilyn Manser and Richard McDonald give a range from 0.14 to 0.22 percent per year. Alastair Cunningham's rather lower estimate for the U.K. Retail Price Index, 0.05 percent per year, presumably results from the yearly reweighting of this Laspeyres price index.[34] Ultimately, the estimates of substitution bias are low because people do not, in fact, tend to shift much of their consumption away from items whose prices have increased more, and also because the variation in relative prices is not very large.

Assuming that people understand the substitution bias at some level, is it possible that they overestimate the extent of the bias?

33. U.S. Senate, Committee on Finance (1996).
34. Triplett (1975); Braithwait (1980); Manser and McDonald (1988); Cunningham (1996).

11(A). "Even when there is 3 or 4 percent [80 to 100 percent] inflation, there are still some prices that go down, or don't go up so much, and someone with fixed income might escape any real effects of inflation just by smart shopping, switching to those items that go up less."

1. Strongly agree
2. Agree somewhat
3. Neutral or no opinion
4. Disagree somewhat
5. Strongly disagree

Response in percent

	1	*2*	*3*	*4*	*5*	*Sample size*
USA-A	9	44	5	26	15	138
Turkey	4	17	4	25	49	95

11(B). "When there is 3 or 4 percent inflation, there is no escaping that one needs to have about 3 or 4 percent more income to live as well; there is no way that "smart shopping," trying to switch purchases towards items whose prices are going up less or going down, is going to save you from the ravages of inflation."

1. Strongly agree
2. Agree somewhat
3. Neutral or no opinion
4. Disagree somewhat
5. Strongly disagree

Response in percent

	1	*2*	*3*	*4*	*5*	*Sample size*
USA-B	23	34	8	28	6	158

12(A, B). If inflation is 10 percent [100 percent] a year, how much more income does a smart shopper who is a little flexible about what he or she buys need to be just as well off? Please give a number, even if it is only a guess.

	Median (percent)	*Sample size*
USA-A	10	136
Turkey	100	85
USA-B	10	154

These answers offer no support for the impression that people think that they can escape the effects of inflation by substituting for other goods.

Lack of Appreciation of Concavity of Utility Function

Understanding the welfare benefits of indexation is dependent on knowing the concavity of the utility function over the relevant range. The benefits from indexing to actual inflation, as opposed to grading payments in accordance with expected inflation, are entirely related to risk management, and hence to the concavity of utilities. One might ask whether this concavity is prominent in people's minds. Perhaps their appreciation of the concavity of their utility functions is not automatic; perhaps the concavity must be fairly extreme or vividly illustrated before they are aware of it. They may be accustomed to assessing risk in terms of linear utility unless the importance of concave utility functions is firmly impressed on them.

It is not easy to elicit whether people think about this concavity, but the survey tries a couple of questions. If people reliably make judgments in terms of utility theory, they should be able to recognize that theory when it is stated:

13(A). Which of the following two statements sounds better to you:

1. "Sure I might lose out on an unindexed plan if inflation is higher than expected, but offsetting this, I might win big if inflation is lower than expected. In my mind, it all averages out, so I don't care if I am indexed."
2. "With an unindexed plan, the possibility that I will be a lot poorer if inflation is higher than expected weighs more heavily in my mind than the possibility that I will be a lot richer if inflation is less than expected. Being poorer hurts more than being richer feels good, and thus indexation makes me feel better off on balance.
3. Neither or no opinion

Response in percent

	1	*2*	*3*	*Sample size*
USA-A	13	56	32	136
Turkey	18	68	13	92

13(B). "Sure I might lose out on an unindexed plan if inflation is higher than expected, but offsetting this, I might win big if inflation is lower than expected. In my mind, as long as indexed plans aren't biased to pay out more or less, I don't care if I am indexed."

1. Strongly agree
2. Agree somewhat

3. Neutral or no opinion
4. Disagree somewhat
5. Strongly disagree

Response in percent

	1	*2*	*3*	*4*	*5*	*Sample size*
USA-B	6	21	32	21	19	155

It must be admitted that respondents did pretty well in choosing the economist's answer to question 13(A); they do seem aware of the implications of concave utility functions.[35]

Prejudice against Indexed Instruments

Any presumed benefits from indexation that are due to risk reduction might be offset if people think that expected returns are lower on indexed than unindexed contracts. When presented with the possibility of purchasing U.S. government indexed bonds, respondents to the informal interviews often expressed prejudice against them, asserting that such bonds could not be expected to perform well as investments. This leads one to wonder if there might really be public prejudice against indexed bonds, per se. Hence the survey asks following question:

13'(B). How much more money would you expect indexed bonds to pay bond holders, on average, in the long run, when compared to conventional (unindexed) bonds? (This is a question about expected long-run historical average returns, averaging over many different historical periods and investor experiences, not a question about what will happen to any one investor.)

1. Indexed bonds will pay much more on average
2. Indexed bonds will pay somewhat more on average
3. Indexed bonds will pay about the same on average
4. Indexed bonds will pay somewhat less on average
5. Indexed bonds will pay much less on average
6. Do not know

35. A translation error in question 13(A) on the Turkish questionnaire was brought to my attention after the questionnaire was distributed: the word "richer" in the first sentence of answer 2 was rendered as "poorer." The second sentence of answer 2 was translated correctly. Perhaps respondents realized that the mistranslated sentence made no sense and responded instead to the intended meaning; at least, the similarity between the Turkish and U.S. responses suggests this.

Response in percent

	1	2	3	4	5	6	Sample size
USA-B	9	33	20	10	1	26	156

Surprisingly, there was, if anything, a prejudice in the other direction: more people seemed to think that the indexed bonds would pay out more. This result does not support the hypothesis that a prejudice against indexed bonds is a factor diminishing public support for indexation. Possibly, the prejudices voiced in the personal interviews are nothing more than typical investor prejudices about government bonds, rather than attitudes to indexation. It may still be the case that on seeing the lower initial yields that indexed bonds tend to offer, people start to think that they will do less well than unindexed bonds over time.

Lack of Uncertainty about Future Inflation

For any given concavity of the utility function, indexation is important as a risk management device only if people feel that inflation is fairly uncertain. However, there seems to be some lack of appreciation of the potential for unforecastable price level movements. It is hard to characterize the nature of people's uncertainty about future prices, but the survey tries a couple of questions to this end:

14(A). We want to know how accurately you think that financial experts in America [Turkey] can predict the price level in 2006, ten years from now. Can you tell us, if these experts think that a "market basket" of goods and services that the typical person buys will cost $1,000 [100 million TL] in 2006, then you think that it will probably actually cost: between $ ___ [TL] and $ ___ [TL].

	Median ratio (high/low)	Sample size
USA-A	4/3	121
Turkey	3/2	76

14(B). How accurately do you think that financial experts in America can predict the price level in 2006, ten years from now? By the price level, we mean the price of all items that people buy, the Consumer Price Index. (This may be a tough question, but we want to gauge how well you think that we really can predict future inflation, so please try to give an answer.)

Experts will probably be accurate within a range of plus or minus _____ percent.

	Median	*Sample size*
USA-B	10	148

Respondents report extremely low levels of uncertainty. The Turkish sample's median ratio of 1.5 between high and low estimates, suggesting a 50 percent confidence interval of plus or minus 20 percent, seems especially low. To get some sense of the potential for uncertainty about the price level in Turkey, note that the Turkish CPI increased two and a half-fold between 1964 and 1974, thirty-fold between 1974 and 1984, and 119-fold between 1984 and 1994. If one takes these decades as plausible scenarios for the next decade, one might rather suggest a high-to-low ratio of something like 119/2.5, or nearly 50.

The uncertainty that Americans report is fairly consistent across the two ways of asking the question. This uncertainty is low enough that one might well question whether indexation is a good idea. Suppose, for example, that people have log utility and think that without indexation they have an equal chance of getting an income of one unit and an income of 4/3 units in ten years. By standard expected utility theory, eliminating this risk (replacing the uncertain income in ten years with a certain income of 7/6 units) is worth only about 1 percent of their income in ten years, or of the order of 10 basis points per year for ten-year investments. Thus in deciding whether to invest in indexed bonds, the question whether these will pay more or less, on average, than unindexed instruments will swamp the issue of risk management. Essentially the same conclusion follows from the Turkish responses. With log utility, people would pay only about 2 percent of income in ten years to replace an equal chance of getting an income of 1.5 units and an income of 1 unit with a sure income of 1.25 units.

Perceived Relevance of Inflation Innovations

The variability in the CPI numbers does not necessarily represent uncertainty to individuals. The interview responses suggest that people sometimes feel that they already know the future path of that part of the CPI that is relevant to their own experience and that only the measurement error in the CPI is unforecastable. It is hard to write a question that pins down this idea, but the survey tries the following:

15(B). "People don't know today what the increase in their own cost of living will be next year and for understanding their own cost of living they would learn a lot from next year's inflation numbers if they could get them today."

1. Strongly agree
2. Agree somewhat
3. Neutral or no opinion
4. Disagree somewhat
5. Strongly disagree

Response in percent

	1	2	3	4	5	Sample size
USA-B	24	50	14	9	3	156

Respondents tended to agree with this statement, suggesting that information revealed by the Consumer Price Index is generally trusted and contradicting the hypothesis that people do not think that CPI information is relevant to themselves.

Perception That Inflation Harms Working People and Firms

In another paper on public perceptions of inflation, I conclude that most people think that the real income of working people is harmed by inflation.[36] Wages are perceived as responding only sluggishly to inflation. This is confirmed by the present survey:

16(A, B). If the government were to become irresponsible with money management and allow the inflation rate to go up so much that prices double [go up ten-fold] (increase by 100 percent [1,000 percent]) in the next five years, how much do you think that the income (measured in dollars) of the typical wage earner would go up in the same interval of time? [Note that if income goes up by 100 percent [1,000 percent], then in terms of real buying power the wage earner would be unaffected by the inflation, since income goes up just as much as prices.]

1. 200 percent [2,000 percent] or more (great increase in real buying power)
2. 150 to 199 percent [1,500 to 1,999 percent]
3. 120 percent to 149 percent [1,200 to 1,499 percent]
4. 80 percent to 119 percent [800 to 1,199 percent] (real buying power is about the same)

36. Shiller (1997).

5. 50 to 79 percent [500 to 799 percent]
6. 0 percent to 49 percent [0 to 499 percent]
7. Less than 0 percent (income in dollars would go down)

Response in percent

	1	*2*	*3*	*4*	*5*	*6*	*7*	*Sample size*
USA-A	2	1	3	29	36	26	3	131
USA-B	3	1	1	15	29	42	9	150
Turkey	1	5	5	22	45	12	11	85

These answers reveal that people have a striking tendency to doubt that incomes will keep up with inflation. This seems to explain a lot about the failure to index. Such a view appears also to explain why people do not index alimony payments. If the father's income is not expected to keep up with inflation, then he cannot be expected to be able to pay the increased alimony. The answers to question 16 do not so directly explain why people do not show more interest in buying government bonds, since in this scenario they are on the receiving side of the equation.

If people think that inflation hurts working people, then one might expect them to think that it helps companies. The survey asks:

16'(B). "If there is really a lot of inflation, then companies that promised complete wage indexation (full cost of living allowances) to their employees will probably be in trouble: the companies will have trouble paying all the increased wages out of the money the company is making."

1. Strongly agree
2. Agree somewhat
3. Neutral or no opinion
4. Disagree somewhat
5. Strongly disagree

Response in percent

	1	*2*	*3*	*4*	*5*	*Sample size*
USA-B	29	43	7	15	6	86

Surprisingly, the weight of the evidence shows that people think that inflation hurts companies too. If this is a valid interpretation, part of the reason that one does not see more COLA clauses in labor contracts might be that people think that these are too big a concession from business to expect.

This line of thought is perhaps not so surprising, given the tendency of people to think that inflation hurts everybody.[37] In fact, many people seem to have trouble with the economist's notion that inflation redistributes wealth among people:

17(A, B). Who gets hurt more by unexpectedly high inflation?

1. Creditors (those who lent money)
2. Debtors (those who borrowed money)
3. Don't know

Response in percent

	1	*2*	*3*	*Sample size*
USA-A	44	48	8	133
USA-B	44	48	9	151
Turkey	76	21	2	85

American respondents seemed very unsure about the answer to question 17; responses were almost equally divided between answers 1 and 2. When those who chose answer 2 were asked in interview to explain why they did so, some replied, essentially, that under a high inflation regime debtors would suffer a decline in real income, which would make it difficult for them to pay their debts. Creditors, people seem to think, are rich bankers, who have the means to ensure that they do not suffer from inflation.[38] The terms "debtor" and "creditor" are apparently interpreted by many respondents as "poor and middle class" and "rich," respectively. Indeed, respondents tend mainly to use the distinction between the poor and middle class and the rich and rarely talk in terms of debtors and creditors. In light of this, the survey asks:

18(B). Who gets hurt most by unexpectedly high inflation?

1. Poor people
2. The middle class
3. Rich people
4. Don't know

Response in percent

	1	*2*	*3*	*4*	*Sample size*
USA-B	46	47	3	4	153

37. See also Shiller (1997).
38. Lippman (1996).

These results show strong expectations that the rich will not suffer from inflation.

High Inflation Scenarios

When discussing the possibility of high inflation, interviewees tended to describe such a scenario as involving a great deal of economic chaos and social unrest. This tendency is manifest in the answers to the following question, whose wording was taken, in part, from the mouths of some of the interviewees:[39]

19(A). "If there is high inflation (over 10 percent [200 percent] a year) in the future, it is likely that the inflation will spark economic and social chaos (events such as widespread corporate bankruptcies, riots in the streets, hunger)."

1. Strongly agree
2. Agree somewhat
3. Neutral or no opinion
4. Disagree somewhat
5. Strongly disagree

Response in percent

	1	*2*	*3*	*4*	*5*	*Sample size*
USA-A	12	42	12	22	12	137
Turkey	49	37	7	4	2	89

Respondents show quite strong agreement with question 19. The effect of this belief is probably to reduce support for indexation: if extreme inflation results in such chaos, it is possible that something unforeseen will invalidate an indexed contract. That indexed contracts might be frustrated in such times is investigated below.

Expectations of Government Intervention

Some of the skepticism about indexed contracts expressed in the interviews seemed to involve doubts about likely future government actions. Although interviewees were not often articulate about this, it appears that people might believe that the government will often, to

39. This tendency is also documented in the tabulation of answers to open-ended questions in Shiller (1997).

some extent, frustrate the purpose of long-term contracts in attempting to equalize incomes after the fact.

It is well known that the government does frustrate some people's efforts to protect their real incomes, for example, through the progressive tax system and means testing for many government programs and services. Moreover, there is one historical example of the U.S. government effectively repudiating an analogue of indexed government debt: government bonds that promised payment in gold. This occurred in 1933, when the government annulled the gold clause after the price of gold had increased.[40] Very highly inflationary periods are often also periods of national crisis, and sociologists have noted that calamities tend to cause "sharp reallocation of wealth" and to release "powerful forces tending to rectify economic inequalities."[41] Possibly people feel that such potential government actions weaken the case for indexation. The survey asks:

20(A). "If there is a lot of inflation in the future, then the government won't really allow those people who bought long-term indexed bonds to get any real benefit from the indexation. All the other people who didn't buy the bonds can vote, and they won't tolerate the indexed bond holders making extra money while everyone else is suffering. Under pressure from voters, the government will figure out some tax rule or the like to take the gains from indexation away from indexed bond holders."

1. Strongly agree
2. Agree somewhat
3. Neutral or no opinion
4. Disagree somewhat
5. Strongly disagree

Response in percent

	1	*2*	*3*	*4*	*5*	*Sample size*
USA-A	11	37	20	21	10	137
Turkey	8	47	13	23	9	90

This leading question is turned into an affirmative statement for questionnaire B:

20(B). "If there is a lot of inflation in the future, then I trust that the U.S. government will really allow those people who bought long-term

40. See Cassel (1936) and Hawtrey (1939).
41. Sorokin (1942, pp. 150, 152).

indexed bonds to get full benefit from the indexation. The government would make sure that no tax law change or other government provision would ever compromise the real purpose of indexation."

1. Strongly agree
2. Agree somewhat
3. Neutral or no opinion
4. Disagree somewhat
5. Strongly disagree

Response in percent

	1	2	3	4	5	Sample size
USA-B	8	25	14	31	21	154

These results support the notion that people think it somewhat likely that the government will frustrate the purpose of indexation. Most people agree, at least somewhat, with question 20(A). In the questionnaire B version, most people disagree that the government can be trusted. Note that despite indications that Turkish people are very concerned about corruption in their government, their answers are virtually identical to those of the Americans. Perhaps question 20 is not seen to be about corruption but about powerful political or moral forces in society.

Collective Response Patterns

Individuals sometimes seem to lack interest in taking actions that might put them ahead of society as a whole, especially if these appear not to conform to customary standards or universally approved behavior. There is a sense of social cohesion in economic vicissitudes; that is, there appears to be a sense of sharing with others, sometimes even resentment of those who think they have outsmarted the others. Sociologists have noted, moreover, a strong tendency for collective response to disaster, and it has been shown above that the prospect of very high inflation appears to be widely perceived as a potential national disaster.[42]

That collective feelings affect market decisions is confirmed by survey work conducted by Maxim Boycko, Vladimir Korobov, and I in various countries.[43] In the context of such social cohesion, people will

42. On collective response to disaster, see Baker and Chapman (1962).
43. Shiller, Boycko, and Korobov (1991, 1992).

make economic choices that are commonly recognized as wise and customary, but they may not have an emotional commitment to studying and acting on unusual economic proposals that would set them apart from others. By contrast, an education in economics or business studies seems rather to encourage an attitude of self-congratulation about having made more sensible economic decisions than most people.

It is difficult to study such feelings of social cohesion among the general public in a paper of this scope. I make a weak effort to provide some evidence that noneconomists have such feelings as regards inflation:

21(A). "Somehow, the fact that inflation affects nearly everyone makes the threat of problems created by inflation seem of less concern to me personally; maybe it's shared feeling for other Americans, maybe it's the idea that if we are all in the same boat together none of us feels so bad about lowered buying power because of inflation. Thus I am just not that interested in being one of the few who are protected from the effects of inflation."

1. Strongly agree
2. Agree somewhat
3. Neutral or no opinion
4. Disagree somewhat
5. Strongly disagree

Response in percent

	1	*2*	*3*	*4*	*5*	*Sample size*
USA-A	2	12	18	28	40	137
Turkey	8	26	15	11	40	89

Respondents tend to disagree with this statement, contrary to my expectations. The question is reversed for questionnaire B, suggesting the opposite answer:

21(B). "Somehow, the fact that inflation affects nearly everyone makes the threat of problems created by inflation seem of more concern to me personally. If we are all in the same boat together, it hurts much more."

1. Strongly agree
2. Agree somewhat
3. Neutral or no opinion
4. Disagree somewhat
5. Strongly disagree

Response in percent

	1	*2*	*3*	*4*	*5*	*Sample size*
USA-B	12	31	24	23	9	154

Respondents did not tend to disagree with this statement, again, contrary to my expectations. These results of questions 21(A) and 21(B) are not really supportive of the notion that people are relatively uninterested in taking measures that would set them apart from their friends and neighbors in times of national stress. This issue could be studied with much more care. It is likely that further work would reveal that although such collective feelings do not provide a stand-alone explanation of public resistance to indexation, they do help to explain why there tends not to be action on indexation.

Conclusion

Economists have been perplexed for a very long time by the public's continuing reliance on long-term nominal contracts in the face of a potential for massive inflation. In the 1830s Scrope wrote: "And what a farce it surely is to talk of property being effectively protected in a country in which an unseen and secret cause may, within a few years, transfer property to the amount of 1,500 millions from one set of people to another, contrary to the intentions and understanding of the parties?"[44] Well over a century and a half have gone by, and the farce continues. Is there any hope that the public will one day see the error of their ways and start routinely indexing long-term contracts?

This survey finds that the idea of indexation is indeed not hard for many people to understand. Most respondents were able to articulate the theory of indexation, if asked to do so; most even seemed to embrace the idea of indexation, after having demonstrated their understanding of it. Yet their tendency to accept indexation on the questionnaires only heightens the puzzle, since the general public shows so little interest. The survey response mirrors the understanding of indexation that Irving Fisher seemingly successfully conveyed in business forums in the first

44. Quoted in Fisher (1934, p. 28).

part of this century, and highlights the frustration that he must have felt when he tried to get action on his proposals for indexation.

I argue that the explanation for the lack of enthusiasm for indexation cannot be monocausal. People have a lot of thoughts about inflation that together conspire to produce the belief that indexation plans are not a very good idea. Economists will continue to be puzzled until they try to appreciate the collective impact of several different aspects of people's world views.

Money illusion does, to some extent, seem to be an important factor in the puzzle. Many people do say, "I want to know how much money I will be getting." And these are often the very people who have just correctly explained how indexation preserves real buying power. Money illusion would be an insubstantial factor in public resistance to indexation if it were nothing more than an impulsive response or a tendency to make mistakes in answering simple questions. In fact, it is probably important because it supports other judgments about the value of indexation.

Notable among the popular notions that reduce the impact of proposals for indexation is a widespread lack of appreciation of the potential uncertainty of inflation. The risk that the price level will be very different than predicted ten years hence is not prominent in people's minds; people give low estimates of this uncertainty, even in a high-inflation country such as Turkey. This may be partly due to self-censorship by opinion leaders. It might be thought that describing high-inflation scenarios that are of low or moderate probability is not appropriate for normal public discourse. Perhaps opinion leaders fear that they will be seen as shouting fire in a crowded theatre and as promoting the very inflation that is feared. When experts are silent about the potential for bad inflationary outcomes, it is natural that people might forget about these possibilities.

People tend to think of inflation not as causing arbitrary redistributions from debtors to creditors, but as an insidious disease that harms virtually everyone. They tend to believe that individual real incomes are massively eroded by high inflation, harming debtors and creditors, firms and individuals. Thus another factor reducing public support for indexation is the expectation that indexed payments will be very hard to meet, should there be a lot of inflation. In the divorce court, it seems too much to ask that the noncustodial parent must automatically make greatly increased payments if inflation picks up a lot. In labor-management disputes, it seems too much to ask that companies increase wages by the full amount dictated by indexation if there is a lot of inflation. As regards private defined benefit pension plans, employees might think it reasonable that their real benefits should decline if inflation picks up and harms the company that they work for.

It is not clear that people are entirely in error to think of inflation in these terms. Historically, inflation has tended to pick up in decades when the real economy is growing less fast, as students of economic growth theory show.[45] Table 1 reports correlations between inflation rates and growth rates of real GDP. Fourteen of the sixteen estimated correlation coefficients are negative, partly due to the fact that the productivity slowdown that started in the 1970s coincided with a tendency toward higher inflation in many countries. Thus unusually inflationary times have tended also to be bad times for the real economy. Few economists seem to be so aware of this tendency as the general public. There is no clear theory to support such a strong correlation, and the past correlation may be due to particular circumstances that will not be replicated in the future. In a study comparing economists' views of inflation with those of the public, I find that the economists' answers tended to imply that they viewed inflation as merely redistributing income from creditors to debtors, much more than as causing major systemic problems.[46]

The lack of public enthusiasm for indexation is probably also largely due to the impression that indexation has never been a serious topic of discussion. Despite the survey's failure to find that math anxiety is an important issue, I still think that this has inhibited public discussion of indexation. One finds scant mention of inflation risk or indexation in popular books of financial advice, and one has the sense that the author who does mention the topic perceives difficulty in sustaining the reader's interest. Try bringing up personal risk management through indexation at a dinner party and the reaction is likely to be as if the topic were out of bounds, too obscure or technical. Indeed, such an idea is likely to provoke laughter. By contrast, imagine how different the reception would be of an apparently informed and forceful opinion about

45. See, for example, Bruno (1995).
46. Shiller (1997).

the future direction of the stock market. The public does not react with equal interest to all topics in economics and risk management through indexation must rank low on the list.

Another factor that does appear to contribute to public resistance to indexation is the notion that the government might not really allow the effects of the contract to unfold as planned. This is probably a source of public apathy toward many kinds of long-term planning.

Not all of the suggestions that emerged from the individual interviews as to why people are so indifferent to indexation are sustained by the results of the questionnaires. The written results do not seem to support the hypotheses that people do not understand the implications of concave utility functions, that they are prejudiced against indexed instruments as inherently paying a lower return, or that they have social feelings that reduce their urgency to deal with inflation. It is, probably premature, however, to rule out these ideas altogether.

People in both the United States and Turkey do seem to trust price indexes in one sense: many have a fatalistic belief that nothing can be done to escape the inflation that is measured. Some do express doubts that indexation will work correctly in their own cases, fearing that prices of the goods that they buy will not move with measured inflation. It is plausible that such doubts prey on the minds of more people than express them and may inhibit action, even though the survey finds that, by and large, people do believe the government's inflation numbers, at least in normal times.

The evidence presented here is not entirely negative about the potential for public acceptance of indexation schemes. It is important that questionnaire respondents seemed largely to accept indexation after having worked problems on it. If opinion leaders come across strongly for indexation, emphasizing that there is still substantial risk of high inflation in the future and that unexpected inflation causes unnecessary and arbitrary redistributions, one might expect to see stronger public support for such schemes.

One problem for advocates of indexation is that much of the advice that they give has to be rather complicated. Experts cannot endorse all indexed contracts; indeed, in a period of economic transition, when indexation becomes more prominent, many parties will try to use public confusion about indexation to their own advantage. Indexation is only beneficial when it is the outcome of all parties wrestling with the advantages and disadvantages offered by contracting in real terms.

The indexed government debt offered by the United States in January 1997 illustrates well the complexity of the message that must be given to the public. Certainly, experts should not recommend that everyone invest for their retirement in this debt without regard for its yield. The government might issue so few of these bonds that they are overpriced. Moreover, modern portfolio theory does not say that people should save only with indexed bonds, but argues that sophisticated investors should try to hold a market portfolio, using indexed bonds, as the risk-free rate, only to adjust the level of risk in their portfolio to their own preferences. Exclusive reliance on indexed bonds for retirement is simple advice that would only be appropriate for people who are not comfortable with portfolio investing. This is a complicated message, and I do not think that it has ever been conveyed effectively in the media.

Matters become even more complicated if one tries to advise people to take the optimal strategy to hedge their other economic risks. People who believe that the past negative correlation between inflation and real income growth can be extrapolated might try to use nominal contracts to hedge real income risk.[47] If people in one country wanted to exploit this correlation and use nominal debt as a vehicle for international risk sharing, they would not take on all sorts of nominal long-term contracts with others in their own countries, as seems to be the case at present. Rather, people in one country would short their own country's nominal debt and go long foreign countries' nominal debt—hardly a common practice today. This scenario suggests some moral hazard issues, since governments can create inflation whenever they want it. The optimal management of income risk is a very complex matter for which there are no obvious prescriptions.

But although it cannot simply be said that indexed contracts are always better than unindexed contracts for all parties, the message that a better deal can be struck between parties with indexed contracts than those with nominal contracts ought not to be too difficult to get across to the public, if it is done in a sufficiently cookbook fashion, spelling

---

47. Kim (1996) argues, based on a theory originated by Lucas (1982), that people should hold nominal debt of foreign countries to hedge risk in their own national income.

out what is commonly accepted as good procedure. Most people adopt contracts that they believe are standard, trusting to the wisdom of others, and if better provisions come to be accepted as the standard, these will be used.

A pessimistic view of the prospects for widespread indexation of contracts may be warranted, but one should not give up all hope that substantial indexation might somehow be promoted. It may be realistic to hope that in coming decades, current plans might result in a greater proportion of the U.S. national debt being indexed than the roughly 15 percent that is indexed in the United Kingdom.[48] The United States is a powerful force in international public opinion, and it is possible that the initial steps taken by the U.S. Treasury will motivate public discourse in a more effective way than have the prior steps taken by many foreign governments. One can hope that the example set by the United States may spill over to create a more widespread view around the world that indexation is a sound idea.

Rather than pinning one's hopes on such a possibility, however, one should think of some more radical steps that might be taken to promote indexation. Since government officials apparently cannot commit their successors not to inflate the currency in the future, it is important for governments to encourage the formulation of contracts that protect people against such contingencies. The evidence from this survey suggests that this is better done more transparently than indexation is usually described. The public could be encouraged to write contracts in terms of a "real dollar" or a "contract dollar," thereby cutting out the math anxiety issue induced by index numbers, reframing the discussion solidly in real terms, and perhaps making it seem less likely that contracts will be frustrated by future government actions. This is an old idea, anticipated in the "compensated dollar" proposed by Simon Newcomb and Irving Fisher.[49] It has been implemented in Chile, with a unit of account called the unidad de fomento (UF), which is tied to a consumer price index. Chilean prices are often quoted in UF. Such efforts to help the public with the concept of indexation might ultimately produce much wider acceptance.

The most important step that can be taken to encourage the public to

---

48. See Campbell and Shiller (1996).
49. Newcomb (1879); Irving Fisher (1913).

accept economists' advice and index various long-term contracts is to institutionalize the practice, write it into codes or standard procedures, as Jevons essentially argued in 1875. One could, indeed, follow Jevons's proposal—although it seems quite a radical step—and pass a law stating that all long-term contracts drawn up after a given date will automatically be indexed, unless they explicitly specify otherwise.

Governments have occasionally shown willingness to issue indexed debt, but they have not done more than offer it. A bolder step would be to eliminate long-term government nominal debt entirely, replacing it with indexed debt. The effect would be dramatic in encouraging public acceptance of indexed debt: this would become the standard. Congress could legislate penalties (such as the partial withdrawal of tax exemptions) for pension plans that offered fixed nominal retirement annuities, encouraging them to substitute indexed annuities. Courts could routinely index alimony, child support, and personal damages settlements. For most of these applications, it would be best to index to an income aggregate, such as national income, rather than the CPI, because of income's better risk-sharing properties.[50]

Other efforts to institutionalize indexation could include indexing wages and salaries, although the case for this idea is perhaps not very strong, since, as noted above, labor negotiations are complicated by strong emotions and rivalrous comparisons that make for downward rigidity in quoted wages. While I believe that it is very important to encourage indexation, the example of labor markets suggests that the methods should be chosen with care.

50. See Shiller and Schneider (1995). See also Brainard and Dolbear (1971), Fischer (1983b), Merton (1983), and Shiller (1993).

Comments
and Discussion

Charles L. Schultze: This paper reports and interprets the results of a survey carefully designed to dig out the reasons why people do not "see the error of their ways and start routinely indexing long-term contracts." Many of the questions in the survey are ingeniously constructed to test various hypotheses about why indexation is not more popular. The responses and Shiller's analysis provide useful insights into people's attitudes on indexation and inflation, and offer some thoughtful explanations of what lies behind them. In the end, Shiller is so pessimistic about the unwillingness of the private sector to adopt indexation for contracts, but so convinced of its welfare-improving consequences, that he proposes a series of fairly radical governmental mandates and incentives to pull the public, kicking and screaming, toward widespread indexation.

I concentrate on two issues arising from the paper. First, Shiller's survey actually demonstrates substantial support for indexation among those at the receiving end of payments—the demand side of the market for indexation. The resistance to indexation probably stems chiefly from the supply side—the potential issuers of indexed obligations. Their views are not represented in the survey. Second, I suggest some of the potential costs of indexation. The immediate impact of those costs falls on the suppliers of indexed obligations and may explain their resistance to indexation. The existence of such costs should also be seen as qualifications to Shiller's conclusions about the desirability of almost universal indexation.

212

The Demand for Indexed Obligations

It is my reading of the answers to Shiller's survey that those who are on the receiving side of long-term obligations are quite supportive of indexation. Of the twenty-one questions in the survey, only one directly asks how people feel about indexation. The USA-A group of respondents was asked to choose between a pension stream whose nominal annual value would grow at the inflation rate expected by experts—namely, 3 percent a year—and another stream starting at the same nominal value but indexed to the consumer price index. Sixty-five percent of the respondents chose the indexed stream, compared with only 29 percent who picked the fixed nominal stream (7 percent answered that they did not know or were indifferent)—a majority for indexation of 2¼ to 1.

The USA-B group was asked the same question, except that the inflation rate expected by experts is 10 percent a year. In this group, only 47 percent picked the indexed plan and 44 percent chose the steady nominal stream. But, as Shiller notes, the most common reason given by those in the USA-B group for rejecting the indexed scheme was that they thought the 10 percent expected inflation rate too high, given the current rate of less than 3 percent. Economists are trained to think in terms of unrealistic hypotheticals: assume an economy of perfect competition or a perfect capital market. But even well-educated lay people are much less accustomed to making trade-offs between unrealistic hypotheticals in an unfamiliar field. And so a number of respondents, quite naturally, found a guarantee of 10 percent annual increases in pension benefits a much better deal than an indexed stream. It is almost surely true that had the USA-B group been given the question with the 3 percent inflation forecast, a much bigger majority would have chosen indexation.

This interpretation is strengthened by the Turkish response. The Turkish alternative was posed as a choice between a pension growing at a forecasted inflation rate of 25 percent a year and an indexed system. Given the history of inflation over the past two decades in Turkey, 25 percent appears an unrealistically low inflation forecast. And so Turkish respondents favored the indexed system by an overwhelming 85 to 9 percent margin. It may be partly coincidental, but is nevertheless suggestive, that the USA-B group showed a majority in favor of indexation that was 18 percent lower than that of the USA-A group, while the Turkish group had a majority for indexation 20 percent *higher* than that of the USA-A group. When the question is posed in terms of what respondents believe to be a realistic expected rate of inflation, they consistently prefer indexation by a quite substantial majority, probably about two to one.

An analogous question could have been posed about indexed bonds, asking for a choice between indexed and nonindexed streams of income. It is most likely that respondents, in their role as bond buyers, would have shown a hefty majority for indexed bonds, as they did in the case of pensions.

There are several aspects of the paper that, at first reading, make it appear more pessimistic about demand-side attitudes toward indexation than may really be warranted. For example, substantial space is devoted to exploring the implications of three questions on which a majority or plurality expressed the beliefs that the official price indexes might be rigged by the government, would fail to mirror their own experience, or would become a worse measure of inflation when inflation was high.[1] And another question elicited the response that, confronted with high inflation, the government would somehow weasel out of its obligation. Given these suspicions, the choice of indexation by a two-to-one majority should be taken as a particularly strong endorsement of the concept.

The Supply of Indexed Obligations

The chief barrier to a more widespread use of indexation apparently does not lie with the potential recipients of indexed payments. Rather, it comes from the potential suppliers, whose views were not included in Shiller's survey. In the short and intermediate run, the issuers of indexed obligations incur risk-bearing costs. These costs will be reflected in the price of the obligations being issued. Had the costs been explicitly reflected in the comparisons presented to survey respondents, the vote for the indexed alternative would presumably have been lower—but then, the puzzle would have partially disappeared.

---

1. The USA-B group was evenly split on the issue of whether the official price index mirrored their cost of living.

INDEXED BONDS. Underlying the questions that Shiller poses in his survey and also his policy proposals is the view that except for wages, indexation has no costs. In a world where all surprises were nominal shocks of the immaculate conception type—that is, a monetary disturbance leads to a quick, simultaneous, and equal change in the level or rate of inflation in all prices—there would indeed be no costs to indexation for either party to long-term contracts, only risk-reducing welfare gains. But the literature has long recognized that in the case of supply shocks, indexation can increase the risks borne by issuers of inflation guarantees and can therefore be costly. The discussion has usually been carried on in the context of evaluating the indexation of wages, but it also applies, with differing degrees of importance, to other types of indexation.

Take the case of indexing a private bond issue. There are three reasons why indexation might increase the risks faced by a firm. First, some inflation surprises originate from supply shocks. In such cases, the increase in average product prices that gives rise to an additional nominal obligation under indexation will not be matched by an equivalent increase in a firm's ability to pay. Second, monetary shocks work their way through the economy by complex processes, which, in the transition period, may involve substantial changes in the relative prices and fortunes of individual firms. Moreover, during periods of moderate inflation, a large positive inflation surprise is more likely than a large negative one. For a while, an increase in nominal obligations need not be matched by an increase in ability to pay. Ultimately, with a purely monetary shock, the change in monetary obligations and resources should match, but the indexing firm could face a temporary cash squeeze.

Third, experience teaches that there is often a substantial negative covariance between large inflations and the fortunes of firms. In the medium run, equity prices seem to be negatively correlated with inflation.[2] This is partly because of the non-neutral effect of inflation on the effective tax rate on capital income (which could be fixed if the tax system were also fully indexed, although at the cost of some substantial complexities). But even without the tax effect, there would be a negative correlation between inflation and equity values, reflecting the fact

2. See, for example, Summers (1981).

that substantial inflation surprises—whether originating in nominal or
real shocks—eventually bring on Federal Reserve stringency accompanied by a period of unused capacity and depressed profits. It may be
a coincidence that the period of high inflation in the United States from
1968 to 1982 was accompanied by a fourteen-year bear market in stocks
and an almost steady decline in the before-tax return on corporate
capital—but I do not think so.

Indexation adds to the risks of firms issuing obligations that come
due over the short and medium run, and so has a cost to private issuers,
which must be expected to affect the real yield negatively. Buyers of
private bonds, in fact, face not a costless trade-off between indexed
and unindexed isues, but a choice between the risk reduction afforded
by indexed bonds and a higher expected real yield on the unindexed
bonds. Surely it is not correct to argue that indexing such long-term
contracts is costless and ought to be universally adopted.

This logic obviously does not imply that firms should issue no indexed bonds. As one element in a financial plan, indexing some fraction
of fixed liabilities might make sense for a firm, both to take advantage
of the dispersion of risk preferences and inflation forecasts among potential buyers and because, in the longer-run, the neutral money shock
components of inflation should dominate transitory and supply-side
phenomena.

The fact that there have been so few private indexed issues is a
puzzle. In a 1983 article, Lawrence Summers shows that during most
of the period from the Civil War to the inflation of the late 1960s,
nominal bond yields were far too stable to have incorporated a premium
systematically reflecting the fluctuations in expected inflation.[3] And in
the sustained inflation of the 1970s, supply-side shocks were prominent,
reducing the attractiveness of indexed bonds to potential issuers. I
suspect that these two phenomena may, in part, explain the rarity of
indexed private bonds.

Those who take on such long-term obligations as alimony face somewhat the same problem as bond issuers. To the extent that inflation
surprises are purely monetary in origin, so that all relative factor and
output prices stay unchanged, indexation would be welfare-improving
for both parties. But in the short and intermediate run, inflation is

3. Summers (1983).

sometimes far from neutral with respect to relative prices and inflation risks may not be symmetrical. While indexation that costs the recipient nothing may be unambiguously welfare-improving for that recipient, it can be risk-increasing for the payer.

PRIVATE PENSIONS. I confine my attention here to the question of indexing pensions during a worker's retirement years.[4] Few, if any, private pension plans provide a nominal annual benefit that increases each year by a fixed amount, according to the inflation rate expected when the pension begins. Rather, most pension plans simply provide a fixed nominal annual amount, whose magnitude is determined in a variety of ways (although during the high-inflation years 1977–82, about half of large and mid-sized firms did grant increases to cover at least a modest fraction of the inflation that had occured). But for simplicity, assume that one is comparing an indexed plan and an unindexed plan of equal nominal expected present value, when calculated at the expected rate of inflation.

Currently, a private firm could match its indexed pension obligations with an appropriate accumulation of indexed Treasury bonds and, to a first approximation, avoid any increased risk. But if, like most firms, it prefers to fund its pension plan with a mixed portfolio that includes private stocks and bonds, indexing the plan could put it in a worse position in terms of the trade-off between risk and returns. Even if private indexed bonds were available, for the reasons discussed above there would be some cost, by way of a lower real return. And stocks are not a good hedge for inflation in the short and intermediate term. The schedule of risk-return opportunities for funding the indexed obligations would pivot in an unfavorable direction. And to the extent the firm's pension plan is not fully funded, the risks associated with the residual obligation will tend to increase, for the three reasons listed above in the discussion of the costs of indexed bonds. The cost of providing the indexed plan would rise, and presumably this would eventually be reflected in the compensation package. On balance, the change might still be worthwhile from the pensioners' viewpoint, but it may not be costless.

---

4. Munnell (1979) spells out the significant difficulties faced by private firms in providing inflation protection in pension formulas during the working life of an individual, given the substantial number of job changes that the typical worker makes during his or her career.

The situation is yet more complicated. Inflation is only one of the portfolio risks that retirees face. As Summers has pointed out, retirees ought to be interested in optimizing the real risk-return characteristics of their overall portfolios in the light of their own preferences. If the inflation risk associated with their pensions is removed by indexation, they will wish to add risk elsewhere, so as to shift their portfolios back toward the old risk-return balance.[5] But for the many retirees with limited nonpension assets, that may be a very circumscribed option.

In sum, given the existence of a basic social security pension indexed to inflation, public policy ought not to be devising tax penalties to push private firms with defined benefit pension plans toward inflation indexing, as Shiller urges. Rather, it should encourage the continuation of the current shift toward defined contribution plans, under which retirees can optimize across a wide range of risk-return options, presumably with safeguards against hasty and uninformed actions. Their portfolios could certainly include indexed Treasury securities. As a side benefit, defined contribution pension plans would greatly simplify the task of making pensions portable for a mobile work force.

Some Final Thoughts

Shiller recognizes that indexing wages could cause some problems and excludes wages from his otherwise universal recommendations for indexation. But it is certainly possible that if public policy were successful in getting the public to think exclusively in terms of indexation, this habit of thought would affect the attitudes about wages that underlie the informal and implicit contracts governing longer-term employment relationships. The fact that in the American economy real wage cuts are accepted through inflation erosion, in circumstances where nominal cuts are strongly resisted, provides flexibility in relative real wages that keeps the nonaccelerating inflation rate of unemployment lower than that in Europe, where workers do think more explicitly in indexed terms and where resistance to wage cuts takes the form of real wage rigidity.

As an aside, Shiller suggests in his penultimate paragraph that it would be preferable to index many types of long-term obligations to national income rather than to prices. Indexing payment streams to national income would require issuers of indexed obligations to hedge

5. Summers (1982, pp. 1, 14).

them in a thick and well-developed worldwide market for income claims. I have neither the time nor the necessary familiarity with the recent literature on the creation of macromarkets, some of it produced by Shiller himself, to deal with this issue. But my cursory look at some of this literature suggests that if one waits until such markets develop, indexation will be a long time coming. On balance, Shiller successfully makes the case that the indexation of long-term obligations is too little practised. But he overstates the potential net benefits from the spread of indexation and his policy proposals go too far.

Robert E. Hall: In this paper, Robert Shiller bravely tackles an important piece of the puzzle of nominal contracting. He asks why contracts are so often stated in monetary terms when, over history, almost every monetary unit has been drastically unstable. Indexation of contracts to the cost of living provides a simple and inexpensive way around the perils of the nominal contract, yet surprisingly few contracts are indexed. Shiller brings a lot of new evidence to the discussion.

This issue divides the Woodward-Hall household. Susan Woodward has worked hard to build the infrastructure for indexation, especially in the key area of mortgages, whereas I have put my efforts into pushing schemes to make the dollar so stable that indexation would be unnecessary. One or the other should be out of this business within the next decade.

The most interesting findings of Shiller's paper are as follows:

—Over the horizon relevant for personal financial planning—ten, twenty, or more years—dispersion in the price level has historically been huge in both the United States and Turkey (see table 1). Nevertheless, people seem to believe that prospective dispersion will be tiny (see questions 14A, 14B).

—Indexation is close to costless. There are no significant legal barriers. People understand inflation and indexation. They do not see the mathematics as a serious obstacle. They strongly prefer indexation in an abstract hypothetical setting, when the choice is fair.

—People see graduation—adjustment for expected future inflation— as an important part of the benefit of indexation, as one would expect, given their understatement of uncertainty about inflation.

—Other than TIPS (the new indexed bonds sold by the U.S. Treasury) and some private debt, little debt is indexed in the United States or in Turkey. Indexation of wages is a familiar idea, but the practice is rare in the United States today. By far the biggest element of indexation in the U.S. economy is social security payments.

—The recently issued TIPS are held not by individuals but by institutions.

—In both the United States and Turkey, people use short-term contracts with frequent renegotiation in circumstances where long-run indexed contracts would serve their purposes better.

—People trust the dollar, and even the Turkish lira, and are skeptical that the cost of living will be properly measured or that the government would permit the large adjustments that would occur in highly inflationary times.

—As is apparent in Shiller's earlier work, the public holds a completely different view of inflation from a monetary economist. In the public's view, inflation occurs when the economy falls apart and all groups suffer lower real income. In particular, wages do not rise in parallel with prices.

Shiller's most important conclusion, by far, is that the public grossly understates the prospective dispersion of the price level. This misunderstanding is the biggest obstacle to indexation: the public seriously underestimates the prospective benefits of indexation. Another important conclusion is that indexed debt and other indexed contracts lack credibility. Shiller's analysis also emphasizes that the government and personal financial advisers do not push indexation as the solution to personal financial problems. The bottom line is that there should be much more aggressive federal sponsorship of widespread indexation to correct the public's ignorant lack of interest. The government should introduce an unidad de fomento, like that in Chile. All federal debt should be indexed.

Shiller's discussion of the unidad de fomento is commendable, but he should have given it more attention. The UF has delivered effortless indexation of all forward transactions in Chile. In brief, the UF is an abstract monetary unit without any corresponding medium of exchange. Transactions are carried out in pesos, which are provided by a standard central bank setup. The UF is defined as enough pesos to buy the cost of living bundle. Each day, a box in the lower right corner of the financial page of every Chilean newspaper reports the day's peso content of the UF. All forward contracts, without exception, are stated in

UF's—savings accounts, leases, employment contracts, mortgages, and so forth. When the time comes to make a payment on an obligation, the UF amount is multiplied by that day's peso content of the UF, and the payment is made in pesos. The Chilean public shifted quickly to the system in 1980 and has used it ever since. The UF's character as a monetary unit rather than an indexation scheme is apparently the secret of its success. Why does the public accept an alternative real monetary unit so easily when indexation is such a hard sell? It is equally difficult to say why the system has not been adopted in any other country. During recent monetary reforms in Argentina and Brazil, there was public debate on adopting a unidad de fomento, but I believe that Chile is still the only country enjoying the benefits of easy universal indexation.

Shiller concentrates on individual views about inflation and the potential safeguard from indexation. It is worth mentioning how different the situation is at the business level. Indexation is the rule, not the exception, in business-to-business contracts. CPI indexation is rare, but indexation to cost indexes for suppliers is close to universal in longer term contracts.

Shiller focuses on the general public and its devotion to nominal forward contracts. Other pockets of devotion also provide obstacles to indexation. Bankers have huge amounts of experience with nominal deals and none with real ones. And, as Shiller notes but does not pursue, the financial press is an absolutely consistent source of misinformation about indexation.

He is persuasive that public demand will not deliver beneficial indexation in the United States, nor even in Turkey. He gives too little attention to push from the suppliers of indexed financial arrangements. Here, the history of adjustable rate mortgages is instructive. Prospective homeowners did not go to banks and ask for mortgages indexed to interest rates. The public has always favored fixed-rate mortgages with the same determination that Shiller shows it favors nominal rather than real payments. Adjustable rate mortgages were pushed into the mortgage market by institutions that found it profitable to originate them and then package them for the secondary market. The same would happen with mortgages indexed to price levels.

Shiller downplays indexation issues in pensions. First, his statement that military pensions and social security payments alone are indexed is correct only in a narrow sense. Defined benefit plans generally tie retirement benefits to final-year earnings. Also, many firms make adjustments to benefits on the basis of subsequent inflation, even though there is no contractual requirement to do so. As a result, pension funds are the natural purchasers of indexed government debt, in order to hedge their real pension obligations.

As Shiller's work shows—both in this and earlier papers—Americans love the dollar. They use it excessively. Shiller's answer to the public's resistance to indexation is a huge national investment in creating indexed financial products and training people to use them as alternatives to the dollar. Surely an American unidad de fomento should be considered as an alternative. But there is also another answer: change the dollar so that it provides the benefits of indexation without altering the characteristics that are comfortable and familiar to the public. Alan Greenspan has made a lot of progress along these lines. Shiller quite properly stresses uncertainty about the purchasing power of the dollar over intervals of decades. There is no reason to doubt the Federal Reserve's ability to stabilize the dollar to the extent that the twenty-year-ahead conditional distribution of the CPI has a mean equal to the current value of the CPI and a standard deviation of less than 4 percent. In other words, it is easily within the Fed's grasp to validate the tight conditional distribution that people actually hold, despite its historical inaccuracy. It would be a mistake for the Fed to promise to keep the price level close to a prescribed target each year—because of occasional inflationary shocks—but it would be reasonable to ask the Fed to nudge the price level back toward target each year, so that the twenty-year-ahead conditional distribution has a mean equal to the target level and little dispersion. The Greenspan Fed is coming close to this ideal.

The real problem—as Shiller is obviously aware—is that there is no guarantee that the Fed will not fall back into the hands of the kind of people who permitted the extreme dispersion of the price level shown in table 1. The public's suspicion about the viability of indexation is supported by one important episode in U.S. history: in 1933 the government removed indexation provisions from private contracts; gold clauses, which effectively caused future payments to be made in gold, were invalidated in contracts already in effect and prohibited in new contracts. Note that the issue in this case is a little different from the main concern that Shiller considers: the shielding of debtors is common to both, but not the removal of cost of living indexation. Respondents to his survey doubt that the government would permit the increase in the burden on debtors that indexation would bring in the case of high inflation. In 1933 the government did not permit the increase in the burden on debtors that would have occurred as a result of an increase in the dollar price of gold. Had contracts been indexed to the cost of living rather than to gold, indexation would have protected debtors, and surely the government would not have stepped in.

Shiller's paper invites dabbling in explanations of the public's devotion to the national monetary unit, and I cannot resist. First, I reiterate the importance of his point that the public constantly hears that the dollar is the right way to think about future value and is hardly ever taught to think in real terms. One of the first steps in teaching intertemporal economics is to get students out of this mode, so grown-up economists cannot understand why the public thinks differently. Second, the public sees the monetary unit of value in just the same light as other publicly defined units of weight and measure. Even economists would have trouble switching to a world where the length of the mile, the weight of a pound, and the duration of an hour were determined as policy variables and had huge amounts of dispersion over ten- or twenty-year periods. If these units were unstable, the Shillers (and Woodwards) of the profession would advocate the indexation of contracts stated in miles, pounds, or hours. But surely our current approach is better. People write contracts in these units with no fear that they will change. And the public thinks that the dollar has the same property. So why not indulge this belief by adopting a monetary policy that keeps the purchasing power of the dollar in a band of a few percentage points around a prescribed constant?

General discussion: James Duesenberry suggested that one reason why people may not like indexation could be confusion about whether indexation would be full or partial; indexing alimony when wages are not indexed could increase, rather than decrease, an individual's risk. Shiller noted that the supposition that people dislike bond indexation because some of their other contracts are not indexed is not supported by the survey data: not a single person gave such an explanation. Robert Moffitt pointed out that the indexation of child support payments to inflation would be unnecessary if support payments were indexed to the wages of the parent making the payments. But Robert Hall thought that such a system was inferior to indexation because, like a tax, it would create adverse incentives. Benjamin Friedman suggested that the lack of markets in indexed securities might not reflect an absence of potential demand. The standard Wall Street line is that securities are not bought, they are sold. So the question "Why don't people want to buy indexed securities?" could be asked about any product. The more relevant question is, "Why aren't the issuers or the investment bankers pushing this product?" Sales will grow only when the financial industry devotes itself to making a sales pitch. He speculated that as the supply of indexed bonds rose, they would be appropriately priced and marketed.

Friedman also mentioned Zvi Bodie's argument that the inflation risk facing wealth owners with long horizons can be largely eliminated by investing in short-term debt investments and rolling over the portfolio. Although that investment strategy risks changes in the real rate of interest, that risk is relatively minor as compared with the risk due to inflation on long-term nominal bonds. Hence the value of indexation may be less than Shiller suggests. In a similar vein, Ben Bernanke noted that Shiller assumes that real bonds are strictly preferable to nominal bonds, which may or may not be true, depending on the individual's portfolio. So the puzzle to be solved is one of a broader set of portfolio puzzles, and, by his own logic, Shiller should advocate government intervention forcing people to optimize their portfolios in other ways, too!

Friedman suggested that some of the survey results about people's dislike of inflation could reflect the fact that to many people, "inflation" simply means "bad times"—falling incomes or profits or increased unemployment. If people are feeling more vulnerable these days, as some surveys suggest, they may be fearful of any number of possible "bads." Moffitt added that the hypothesis of workers' increased feeling of vulnerability is consistent with actual experience, such as the increase in the variance of transitory earnings in the United States in the 1980s.

Katherine Abraham was distressed by Shiller's findings of public distrust of government agencies. If 45 percent of the public does not trust government data, there is a major credibility problem. She noted that the BLS has instituted many procedures attempting to insulate its statistics from politics and hoped this would assure the public that its indexes are not subject to political manipulation. The Bureau of Labor

Statistics avoids capricious changes in methods—and indeed, has been criticized for moving too slowly—believing that moving with deliberate speed should help to ensure trust in the numbers produced. It should be possible to encourage critical and constructive discussion without undermining public confidence in the data. But she wondered whether some of the public's current mistrust was a spill-over from the CPI debate, which has grown from a scientific debate to national news, with headlines announcing deep problems with the CPI. Charles Schultze believed the mistrust of government responses related to government in general, and not to a particular agency. When asked whether they would agree or disagree that the government would make sure that no tax law change or other provision would ever compromise the real purpose of indexation, he did not find it surprising that almost all respondents disagreed. Jonathan Gruber questioned the assumption of Shiller's survey that people have sufficient mathematical ability to evaluate the results of inflation or indexing. He noted other surveys showing that around a third of the public cannot add up a restaurant check, and asked whether those who responded to the survey were better educated than average, and hence not representative? Shiller indicated that the respondents were quite well educated—even in Turkey, half the respondents had some college education. Bernanke cautioned that Islamic codes on the financial system may influence some of the Turkish answers.

Duesenberry urged careful thought about the effect of indexation on the aggregate behavior of the economy. If monetary and fiscal authorities are prone to mistakes, or the economy is subject to external supply shocks, indexation could amplify the problem, creating a less stable, and possibly more inflationary, economy. He noted that Brazil provides an example of indexation run amok. The Brazilian experience also raises the question of how indexation would affect a government's debt structure and interest payments. Gruber agreed that indexation might alter the dynamics of the economy. In his research he has found that the costs of many employer mandates from the government are fully passed on to real wages, not through nominal wage cuts but through price increases. If the economy were fully indexed, this method of passing on costs would be removed. The adjustment of real wages would have to take place by some other, possibly more costly, mechanism.

References

Akerlof, George A., William T. Dickens, and George L. Perry. 1996. "The Macroeconomics of Low Inflation." *BPEA, 1:1996*, pp. 1–77.

Baker, George W., and Dwight W. Chapman. 1962. *Man and Society in Disaster*. Basic Books.

Bodie, Zvi. 1990. "Inflation Insurance." *Journal of Risk and Insurance* 57(4):634–45.

Brainard, William, and F. T. Dolbear. 1971. "Social Risk and Financial Markets." *American Economic Review, Papers and Proceedings* 61(2): 360–70.

Braithwait, Steven D. 1980. "The Substitution Bias of the Laspeyres Price Index: An Analysis Using Estimated Cost-of-Living Indexes." *American Economic Review* 70(1): 64–77.

Bruno, Michael. 1995. "Does Inflation Really Lower Growth?" *Finance and Development* 32(3): 35–38.

Campbell, John Y., and Robert J. Shiller. 1996. "A Scorecard for Indexed Government Debt." In *NBER Macroeconomics Annual 1996*, edited by Ben S. Bernanke and Julio J. Rotemberg. MIT Press.

Card, David, and Dean Hyslop. 1997. "Does Inflation Grease the Wheels of the Labor Market?" In *Reducing Inflation: Motivation and Strategy*, edited by Christina D. Romer and David H. Romer. University of Chicago Press.

Cassel, Gustav. 1936. *The Downfall of the Gold Standard*. Oxford: Clarendon Press.

Cavallo, Domingo F. 1983. "Comments on Indexation and Stability from an Observer of the Argentinean Economy." In *Inflation, Debt, and Indexation*, edited by Rudiger Dornbusch and Mario Henrique Simonson. MIT Press.

Cunnningham, Alastair W. F. 1996. "Measurement Bias in Price Indices: An Application to the UK's RPI." Working Paper 47. London: Bank of England (March).

Featherstone, Mike. 1990. *Global Culture: Nationalism, Globalization, and Modernity*. London: Sage Publications.

Fischer, Stanley. 1983a. "On the Nonexistence of Privately Issued Index Bonds in the U.S. Capital Market." In *Inflation, Debt, and Indexation*, edited by Rudiger Dornbusch and Mario Henrique Simonsen. MIT Press.

———. 1983b. "Welfare Aspects of Government Issue of Indexed Bonds." In *Inflation, Debt, and Indexation*, edited by Rudiger Dornbusch and Mario Henrique Simonsen. MIT Press.

———. 1986. *Indexing, Inflation, and Economic Policy*. MIT Press.

Fisher, Irving. 1913. "A Compensated Dollar." *Quarterly Journal of Economics* 27(February): 213–35.

———. 1928. *The Money Illusion*. New York: Adelphi.

————. 1934. *Stable Money: A History of the Movement*. New York: Adelphi.

Fisher, Willard C. 1913. "The Tabular Standard in Massachusetts History." *Quarterly Journal of Economics* 27(May): 417–51.

Friedman, Milton. 1974. "Monetary Correction." In *Essays on Inflation and Indexation*. Washington: American Enterprise Institute.

Groshen, Erica, and Mark Schweitzer. 1995. "The Effects of Inflation on Wage Adjustments in Firm-Level Data: Grease or Sand?" Unpublished paper. Federal Reserve Bank of New York.

Hawtrey, R. G. 1939. *The Gold Standard in Theory and Practice*, 4th ed. London: Longman, Green, and Co.

Jevons, William Stanley. 1875. *Money and the Mechanism of Exchange*. New York: D. Appleton.

Kim, Soyoung. 1996. "Essays in Monetary Policy and Finance in Open Economies." Ph.D. dissertation. Yale University.

Lippman, John. 1996. "Public Understanding of Inflation and Indexation." Unpublished paper. Yale University (April).

Lowe, Joseph. 1822. *The Present State of England in Regard to Agriculture, Trade, and Finance*. Reprint. New York: Augustus M. Kelley, 1967.

Lucas, Robert E. Jr. 1982. "Interest Rates and Currency Prices in a Two-Country World." *Journal of Monetary Economics* 10(3): 335–59.

McCulloch, J. Huston. 1980. "The Ban on Indexed Bonds, 1933–77." *American Economic Review* 70(5): 1018–21.

Manser, Marilyn E., and Richard J. McDonald. 1988. "An Analysis of Substitution Bias in Measuring Inflation, 1959–85." *Econometrica* 56(4): 909–30.

Merton, Robert C. 1983. "On Consumption Indexed Public Pension Plans." In *Financial Aspects of the United States Pension System*, edited by Zvi Body and John B. Shoven. University of Chicago Press.

Munnell, Alicia H. 1979. "The Impact of Inflation on Private Pensions." *New England Economic Review* 79(March–April): 18–31.

Newcomb, Simon. 1879. "The Standard of Value." *North American Review* September: 223–37.

Shafir, Eldar, Peter Diamond, and Amos Tversky. 1997. "On Money Illusion." *Quarterly Journal of Economics* (forthcoming).

Shiller, Robert J. 1993. *Macro Markets: Creating Institutions for Managing Society's Largest Economic Risks*. Oxford University Press.

————. 1997. "Why Do People Dislike Inflation?" In *Reducing Inflation: Motivation and Strategy*, edited by Christina D. Romer and David H. Romer. University of Chicago Press.

Shiller, Robert J., Maxim Boycko, and Vladimir Korobov. 1991. "Popular Attitudes toward Free Markets: The Soviet Union and the United States Compared." *American Economic Review* 81(3): 385–400.

————. 1992. "Hunting for *Homo Sovieticus*: Situational versus Attitudinal Factors in Economic Behavior." *BPEA, 1:1992*, 127–94.

Shiller, Robert J., and Ryan Schneider. 1995. "Labor Income Indices Designed for Use in Contracts Promoting Income Risk Management." Working Paper 5254. Cambridge, Mass.: National Bureau of Economic Research (September).

Siegel, Jeremy J. 1994. *Stocks for the Long Run: A Guide to Selecting Markets for Long-Term Growth*. Burr Ridge, Ill.: Irwin Professional.

Sorokin, Pitirim A. 1942. *Man and Society in Calamity: The Effects of War, Revolution, Famine, Pestilence upon Human Mind, Behavior, Social Organization and Cultural Life*. E. P. Dutton.

Summers, Lawrence H. 1981. "Inflation and the Value of Corporate Equities." Working Paper 824. Cambridge, Mass.: National Bureau of Economic Research (December).

————. 1982. "Observations on the Indexation of Old Age Pensions." Working Paper 1023. Cambridge, Mass.: National Bureau of Economic Research (November).

————. 1983. "The Nonadjustment of Nominal Interest Rates: A Study of the Fisher Effect." In *Macroeconomics, Prices, and Quantities: Essays in Memory of Arthur M. Okun*, edited by James Tobin. Brookings.

Tobin, James. 1971. "An Essay on the Principles of Debt Management." In *Essays in Economics*, vol. 1, *Macroeconomics*, edited by James Tobin. Chicago, Ill.: Markham.

Triplett, Jack E. 1975. "The Measurement of Inflation: A Survey of Research on the Accuracy of Price Indexes." In *Analysis of Inflation*, edited by Paul H. Earl. Lexington, Mass.: Lexington.

U.S. Senate. Committee on Finance. 1996. *Final Report of the Advisory Commission to Study the Consumer Price Index*. S. Prt. 104-72, 104 Cong., 2 sess. Government Printing Office.

Wilson, Robert D. 1980. "Inflation-Proof Child Support Decrees: Trajectory to a Polestar." *Iowa Law Review* 66(1): 131–52.

SUSAN DYNARSKI
Massachusetts Institute of Technology

JONATHAN GRUBER
Massachusetts Institute of Technology

Can Families Smooth
Variable Earnings?

THE LABOR MARKET in the United States is marked by considerable year-to-year variation in individual earnings.[1] In theory, variation in the earnings of family heads need not be a source of welfare loss to families. Families can rely on their own savings, the labor supply of other family members, and government tax and transfer programs to smooth this variation, so that family consumption remains unchanged. In practice, however, these sources of consumption smoothing may be far from adequate. This issue takes on particular salience in the United States today, because of a substantial increase in the instability of earnings over the past twenty years. As Peter Gottschalk and Robert Moffitt have shown, and as we confirm below, earnings variation has trended upward since the early 1970s. We estimate that over the period 1970–91, earnings variation has grown by a striking 76 percent.

The purpose of this paper is to assess the completeness and the sources of smoothing of idiosyncratic earnings variation. We use two survey data sets with information on income and consumption to estimate the relationship between variation in the earnings of household heads and variation in their families' consumption. In our analysis, we employ an instrumental variables (IV) strategy designed to deal with

We are grateful to Gary Burtless, Robert Moffitt, James Poterba, Steven Pischke, and seminar participants at the Massachusetts Institute of Technology and the Brookings Panel meeting for helpful comments, and to Weiyang Cheong and Farhan Zaidi for research assistance. Jonathan Gruber acknowledges financial support from the National Institute on Aging and the National Science Foundation.
    1. See, for example, Gottschalk and Moffitt (1994).

the important problem of measurement error in earnings changes calculated from these data.

We find that families are fairly well able to smooth consumption in the face of variation in the heads' earnings. Such variation has a relatively small effect on nondurables expenditure, with 10 cents or less of each dollar change in the head's earnings being reflected in consumption. There is a somewhat larger effect on durables expenditures, however, with each dollar of earnings change corresponding to a 17 cent change in durables purchases. We also find a larger consumption response to earnings changes induced by changes in wage rates than to those induced by changes in hours of work. And we find evidence of an asymmetric response to earnings changes, with earnings reductions producing a larger effect than earnings increases, particularly for durables expenditures.

These findings raise the question of how families are able to smooth their consumption. We consider two sources of smoothing: offsetting income flows, the most important of which come from the government tax and transfer system, and self-insurance through saving. We find that smoothing through these two channels is roughly equal, with each dollar of earnings change for the head resulting in a 35 to 50 cent offsetting change in other souces of family income and a 25 to 40 cent change in saving.

We then consider the particular effect of unemployment—a large, plausibly exogenous, source of earnings variation. Overall, the consumption effects of unemployment-induced earnings loss are fairly similar to those due to year-to-year earnings variation. But in the case of unemployment, the government plays a somewhat larger consumption smoothing role, with 50 to 55 cents of each dollar in earnings loss compensated by increased transfers and reduced taxes; only about one-quarter of the unemployment-induced earnings loss is smoothed through saving. We also document considerable heterogeneity in the ability of families to smooth earnings variation arising from unemployment, which is consistent with the skewed nature of wealth holding in the United States. For low-education (and low-wealth) households, loss of earnings through unemployment has a much stronger effect on consumption.

Finally, we turn to time-series evidence on the relationship between earnings instability and consumption instability. We find that earnings variation rises sharply during recessions, whereas consumption variation is much less cyclical. This finding is consistent with the substantial smoothing seen in the microdata. But we conclude with a puzzle: there have been parallel rises in the instability of consumption and of earnings. While the estimates are somewhat sensitive to the definition of consumption, these twin time-series trends are at odds with the microdata evidence of considerable consumption smoothing.

The paper proceeds as follows. We first motivate our analysis by revisiting the time-series evidence on earnings variation. Next, we situate our analysis in the context of the related literature. We then introduce the data and discuss the empirical issues involved in estimating the extent of consumption smoothing. We then present our estimates of the ability of families to smooth year-to-year variation in earnings and examine the sources of consumption smoothing. Next, we focus on the specific case of unemployment, modeling consumption smoothing, sources of insurance, and heterogeneity in the response to unemployment-induced earnings losses. Finally, we present time-series evidence on the relationship between earnings instability and consumption instability and discuss our overall conclusions.

Motivation: Rising Earnings Instability

The starting point for our analysis is the striking findings of two papers by Gottschalk and Moffitt.[2] Using data from the Michigan Panel Study of Income Dynamics (PSID), the authors document a rise in the transitory component of the earnings of household heads in the 1980s. They find that this transitory component rose by 42 percent from the 1970s to the 1980s. We begin our analysis by revisiting this question, extending their analysis in a number of ways.

The PSID is a longitudinal survey that has been carried out continuously since 1968, following the same sample of families and their "split-offs" over time. The original sample consisted of a nationally representative cross-section of families and a subsample of those in poverty; in the analysis below, we use both samples in order to increase the precision of the estimates. Throughout the analysis, we weight our

2. Moffitt and Gottschalk (1993); Gottschalk and Moffitt (1994).

tabulations and regressions by the PSID sample weights in order to reproduce a nationally representative sample. We obtain very similar findings when we use the nationally representative sample alone, with or without sample weights.

Our analysis of earnings instability differs from that of Gottschalk and Moffitt along several dimensions. First, our sample includes all male heads aged twenty to fifty-nine who are not full-time students; Gottschalk and Moffitt focus only on whites in this age range. Second, we examine total labor earnings, rather than just wages and salaries. Third, we add five years of data on labor income, extending the sample through the 1992 PSID, which includes earnings data for 1991. Fourth, we do not divide the period into two halves (Gottschalk and Moffitt use 1970–78 and 1979–87), but rather, consider the entire period in one regression framework.

Finally, we use a different framework for modeling transitory income. There are a number of options for modeling the transitory component, none of which is fully satisfactory. Gottschalk and Moffitt focus primarily on an individual fixed effects model, where transitory income is defined as the deviation from individual average earnings (after absorbing a general age-earnings profile). We use a differences model, measuring deviations from the previous year's earnings as transitory. These approaches are very similar; indeed, with two observations they are identical. However, both suffer from having low power in distinguishing permanent shifts in earnings prospects from transitory changes.

To attempt to discriminate better between permanent and transitory changes, we also estimate models that include individual fixed effects in the differences specification. In this way, we allow for a specific growth path for each individual and only label as transitory deviations from that growth path. With this fixed effect, we hope to absorb any change in earnings that results from permanent changes in the head's tastes for work or leisure. This method is related to another approach used by Gottschalk and Moffitt, who include person-specific age-earnings profiles in one of their models.

Our basic analysis proceeds as follows. We first estimate a differences model over the period 1970–91. The model controls for time (with year dummies) and a number of family characteristics: a quartic in age; education (our three categories are high school dropout, high

Figure 1. Variation of Earnings, 1970–91[a]

Variance

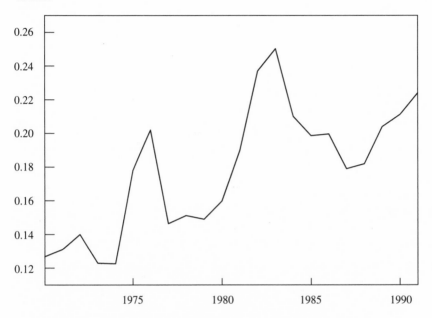

Source: Authors' calculations based on data from the Michigan Panel Study of Income Dynamics (PSID).
a. Figure plots, by year, the mean of the squared residuals produced in regressing changes in log earnings of the head on the family characteristic controls and year dummies described in the text and used throughout the paper.

school graduate, and college graduate); marital status and change in marital status; change in family size; change in the proportion of family size that is children; and change in family "food needs," a PSID measure that is a function of family size and the age of family members. These family composition controls are important for the consumption regressions reported below and are therefore included in each estimation. We include them in our earnings regressions in order to use consistent models across the different dependent variables.

We use the mean of the squared residuals for each year as the measure of aggregate transitory variation in that year. The results for labor earnings are shown in figure 1, which plots aggregate transitory variation against time. There are two findings of note. First, earnings variation has a strong countercyclical component; it peaks in the recessions of the mid–1970s, the early 1980s, and the early 1990s. Second, earnings variation has a strong upward trend: after the first two recessions,

Figure 2. Variation of Earnings, Individual Fixed Effects Included, 1970–91[a]

Variance

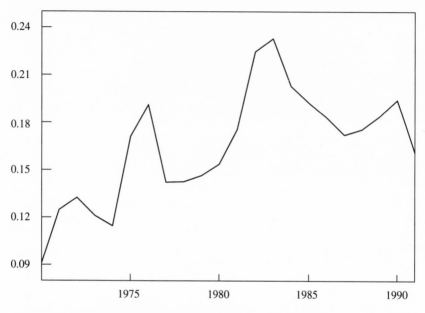

Source: Authors' calculations based on data from the PSID.
a. Produced by the same method as figure 1, except that this equation adds a person-specific fixed effect.

the variation returns to a level much higher than that before the recession. Over the entire period, the variation of earnings of heads rose by 76 percent.

In figure 2 we show the same labor earnings graph, but control for an individual fixed effect. The pattern is almost identical to that of figure 1, with the exception of a large drop in the last year that appears only in figure 2. Over the entire period, the rise in variation is almost identical in the two models. Thus, regardless of our specification, we confirm the conclusion of Gottschalk and Moffitt: transitory earnings variation has risen dramatically in the United States over the past twenty years.[3]

3. One potential problem with our fixed effects specification is that we posit that the individual effect is fixed over a very long period; some heads are in our sample for all twenty-three survey years. As a result, if individuals move to very different earnings trajectories later in their careers, the shifts will not be captured by this permanent

William Dickens, however, raises the key issue of the welfare implications of this finding.[4] If there is full consumption smoothing of variable earnings, there is potentially little welfare cost to this increased instability. But if individuals are not able to smooth their consumption over periods of high and low earnings, this increased variation may cause large welfare losses. Thus the bulk of our analysis is devoted to an assessment of the completeness of consumption smoothing of variable earnings. We first investigate this in a cross-sectional context; in the final section, we examine the time-series trend in consumption variation.

Background

The analysis of the following sections is closely related to two different strands of the literature on consumption behavior. The first tests the hypothesis of *full consumption insurance*. This benchmark is met when mechanisms for pooling risk, either within or across families, equalize the growth rate of the marginal utility of consumption across households. As demonstrated by John Cochrane, Angus Deaton, and Robert Townsend, the full consumption insurance hypothesis implies that the growth rate of consumption will depend only on the growth rate of aggregate resources and changes in household preferences (for example, as a result of aging or changes in family size).[5] Therefore this hypothesis implies that the growth in each household's consumption will not depend on changes in household resources that are uncorrelated with shifts in preferences, once time-series changes in endowments have been taken into account.

This theory has been tested by estimating a model of growth in consumption against growth in income, controlling for aggregate resources. If there is full consumption insurance, then idiosyncratic

component. We have replicated our findings using instead a rolling average model, whereby we estimate our fixed effects model over periods of six years (five differences) and take the average of the residuals for the individual over that period. This model allows the permanent component for each individual to evolve over time. The substantial upward trend remains under this approach, although one necessarily loses the cyclical variation.

4. Dickens (1994).
5. Cochrane (1991); Deaton (1992a); Townsend (1994).

variation in family resources should not be reflected in family consumption. Barbara Mace, using consumption data from the Consumer Expenditure Survey (CEX) of the Bureau of Labor Statistics, finds that one cannot reject the proposition of full consumption insurance. But Julie Nelson points out a host of problems with Mace's implementation and finds that once these issues are corrected, full consumption insurance is strongly rejected. Cochrane confirms this rejection in data from the PSID.[6]

Cochrane also notes, however, that this may not be a strong test, for two reasons. First, changes in income may be correlated with changes in preferences. For example, a desire for more leisure and fewer consumption goods could be manifested as correlated falls in income and consumption, biasing the analysis toward a rejection of the theory of full insurance. Second, there may be significant measurement error in income in survey data, which would bias toward finding consumption smoothing. To deal with these two sources of bias, Cochrane suggests replacing income with a series of measures of plausibly exogenous changes in the individual's environment: involuntary job loss, illness, strike days. He finds a strong rejection of full consumption insurance using these measures. Studies by Paul Burgess and others, Mark Dynarski and Steven Sheffrin, Martin Browning and Thomas Crossley, and Gruber find significant effects of unemployment on consumption as well. Gruber also shows that consumption responds to the generosity of unemployment insurance, using this exogenous source of income variation to further reject the full consumption insurance hypothesis.[7]

The present study is also closely related to microdata tests of Milton Friedman's *permanent income* hypothesis.[8] A key prediction of this

6. Mace (1991); Nelson (1994); Cochrane (1991). Additional tests of the benchmark of full consumption insurance are carried out by Altug and Miller (1990), who cannot reject this benchmark. Hayashi, Altonji, and Kotlikoff (1996) expand Altug and Miller's study to test for the presence of consumption insurance from others (as opposed to self-insurance) and strongly reject this proposition. In addition, there is a growing literature on consumption smoothing in developing countries; see, for example, Deaton (1992a), Paxson (1992), Townsend (1994, 1995), Morduch (1995), and Gertler and Gruber (1997).

7. Burgess and others (1981); Dynarski and Sheffrin (1987); Browning and Crossley (1996); Gruber (1997).

8. Friedman (1957). There is also a large literature on macrodata tests of the permanent income hypothesis, but testing for consumption insurance in a macro context is meaningless, since the key test is a comparison of consumption changes across persons.

hypothesis is that only permanent variation in income should be reflected in consumption, whereas transitory variation is absorbed through saving or dissaving. Robert Hall and Frederic Mishkin test this hypothesis by statistically decomposing income into its permanent and transitory components.[9] They find that transitory income changes do predict changes in consumption, which is consistent with the permanent income hypothesis only for very high interest rates. Further work in this framework considers the implications of measurement error, additional years of data, and the modeling of liquidity constraints.[10] The early literature does not produce very strong evidence against the permanent income hypothesis, on net; more recent articles find stronger rejections.[11]

There are two important distinctions between the full consumption insurance and the permanent income hypotheses.[12] First, the permanent income hypothesis draws a sharp distinction between transitory and permanent variation in income; the latter should be reflected in consumption decisions, while the former should not. But under the full consumption insurance hypothesis, neither transitory nor permanent idiosyncratic variation should be reflected in consumption; any change in resources, relative to aggregate shifts, should be smoothed through interpersonal transfers. The second key difference between these hypotheses is their treatment of self-insurance, as distinct from insurance by others. The permanent income hypothesis focuses on the use of self-insurance (through saving and dissaving) to smooth transitory income changes. But " 'self-insurance' through accumulation of assets is an *alternative* to consumption insurance, not a mechanism for implementing it."[13] Therfore the full consumption insurance hypothesis focuses on the role of interpersonal transfers.

This paper navigates a course between these two streams in the consumption behavior literature. First, we do not claim to achieve a

---

See Deaton (1992a) and Browning and Lusardi (1996) for superb reviews of the microdata and macrodata tests of the permanent income hypothesis.

9. Hall and Mishkin (1982).

10. See Altonji and Siow (1987) on measurement error, Mariger and Shaw (1993) on additional data, and Hayashi (1985) and Zeldes (1989) on liquidity constraints.

11. See Deaton (1992b) on the earlier literature and Browning and Lusardi (1996) on more recent articles.

12. See Cochrane (1991) and Hayashi, Altonji, and Kotlikoff (1996) for further discussion of these points.

13. Cochrane (1991, p. 960).

clean distinction between transitory and permanent variation in income. We follow the full consumption insurance hypothesis in specifying a simple model regressing change in consumption on change in earnings, rather than attempting a more formal decomposition into permanent and transitory earnings variation. We do condition on the set of covariates given above, which capture life-cycle changes in preferences (that is, due to age and family structure). And in the PSID sample, we are able to include an individual fixed effect in the differences specification, so that we are examining only deviations from a person-specific growth path. But even this relatively rich framework does not capture idiosyncratic permanent changes, such as a sudden promotion with a salary raise that causes a deviation from trend growth.

This is a problem in all previous analyses relating change in consumption to change in income. It is impossible to capture the theoretically appropriate measure of transitory income variation, so the analysis must rely on some empirical proxy. A number of studies take a reduced-form approach that is similar to ours. Another common approach to the problem is to model structurally the transitory component of the income process.[14] This solution consists of posing a particular autocorrelation structure for the transitory component of earnings and then using the covariance structure of earnings to fit this model. If the model that is fit is appropriate, then this structural approach is a more efficient means of identifying the transitory component of earnings; but it may yield a misleading inference if the model is inappropriate. In particular, this approach is very sensitive to the assumptions on the covariance structure of measurement error, relative to other transitory variance in earnings.

Rather than impose this set of structural assumptions, we follow the reduced-form specification adopted by the full consumption insurance literature. In a further attempt to separate permanent from transitory changes, we also consider the effect of earnings variation arising through change in hours of work (most likely transitory) and change in wages (most likely permanent). Regardless of the theoretical label that one attaches to it, the rising variation of earnings changes documented in the previous section merits examination. Has this earnings variation been reflected in consumption variation?

The second compromise between these two literatures is in our def-

---

14. See, for example, Abowd and Card (1989) and Moffitt and Gottschalk (1993).

inition of consumption insurance. We do not follow the strict interpretation of the full consumption insurance hypothesis in focusing only on the role of interpersonal transfers; rather, we focus on smoothing from any source, including self-insurance. Our tests are therefore more precisely an assessment of full consumption smoothing, rather than of interfamily insurance, per se. We do, however, extend our analysis to specify the sources of consumption smoothing: we measure the extent to which consumption smoothing is due to transfers from others (including the government) and to self-insurance, through saving and dissaving.

Relative to past work on tests of either the full consumption insurance or the permanent income hypotheses, our analysis offers four contributions. First, like Joseph Altonji and Aloysius Siow in the context of testing the permanent income hypothesis, but unlike the literature testing full consumption insurance, we introduce an instrumental variables strategy to deal with the potentially important problem of measurement error in earnings variation.[15] This is an important consideration in our context, since white noise measurement error in earnings changes would bias toward zero the earnings coefficient in our regressions.

Second, we do not simply test for deviations from the admittedly extreme benchmark of full consumption insurance, but actually quantify those deviations. How large is the effect of earnings variation on consumption variation? In the limit, with a large data set and a precise estimation strategy, one could reject full insurance with very small deviations. But with concave utility, the welfare loss from imperfect consumption smoothing rises nonlinearly with the deviation from full smoothing. Thus it is important to assess whether the deviations from full smoothing are empirically meaningful.[16]

Third, unlike all previous literature on these hypotheses, we focus not on variation in family income, but on variation in the earnings of the head alone. This has two advantages: by focusing on prime-age

15. Altonji and Siow (1987).
16. It is important to note that we approximate family living standards by consumption, thereby ignoring the benefits of leisure. Even if a family's consumption drops because of a reduction in the work hours of the head, its standard of living may in fact rise, due to the extra leisure that the head is enjoying. To the extent that leisure is negatively correlated with income, this lowers further the welfare cost of earnings variation. However, if one source of consumption smoothing is increased labor supply by the spouse, this will off-set the leisure gains of the head.

male heads, we are able to mitigate concerns about endogeneity through joint determination of consumption and hours of work; and we are able to assess how other forms of family income provide insurance against the earnings variation of the head. That is, we are able to go beyond an assessment of the completeness of consumption smoothing to investigate the sources of smoothing: to what extent does smoothing occur through transfers from others (primarily the government), and to what extent through self-insurance (primarily saving and dissaving)? Fourth, we explore the sensitivity of our findings to two different data sets, the PSID and the CEX.

There has been other recent work on changes in the distribution of income and consumption that is somewhat related to our analysis. Studies by Thesia Garner and by David Cutler and Lawrence Katz show that the widening of the income distribution in the United States since the early 1970s is reflected in a widening distribution of consumption.[17] Daniel Slesnick notes, however, that this finding is sensitive to the choice of equivalence scale and finds that consumption inequality has been falling over this period.[18] Cutler and Katz and also Orazio Attanasio and Steven Davis compare changes in mean consumption across groups (delineated by some combination of education, occupation, and age) with changes in mean income and find a strong relationship: groups whose wages suffered from the recent widening of the U.S. income distribution also suffered in terms of consumption.[19]

The finding that secular interpersonal increases in wage inequality are reflected in consumption, however, has little bearing on families' ability to smooth idiosyncratic intertemporal income variation. Indeed, Attanasio and Davis find that if they use higher frequency changes across groups, there is evidence of full consumption smoothing.

Data and Empirical Issues

The key constraint in carrying out an analysis that compares the variation of income and of consumption in the United States is the

17. Garner (1993); Cutler and Katz (1991).
18. Slesnick (1992). There is also related work on shifts in the distribution of family income, which has widened more quickly over the past twenty years than has the distribution of individual income; see, for example, Karoly and Burtless (1995).
19. Attanasio and Davis (1996).

quality of the available consumption data. Whereas high-quality income data are collected by a variety of sources, consumption data for a nationally representative sample are available from only two: the Panel Study of Income Dynamics and the Consumer Expenditure Survey.[20] This paucity of data, as well as the limitations of each of these surveys (noted below), have motivated studies at a higher level of aggregation, matching data from consumption in the CEX to higher quality data on income from other surveys, such as the PSID and the Current Population Survey (CPS) of the Bureau of Labor Statistics.[21] But such a strategy averages out the idiosyncratic variation in earnings that is of greatest interest, from our perspective.

The PSID collects a set of high-quality indicators of earnings and labor force attachment. In addition, in most years the survey has collected data on two subcomponents of consumption. The first is food: respondents are asked how much their family "usually" spends on food at home and away from home, as well as how much of their food is paid for by food stamps. The second is housing: families are asked for their expenditures on rent or mortgage payments in each year.[22] These two variables provide a very incomplete measure of consumption; using the more complete data of the CEX, we calculate that food and housing expenditures amount to only 34 percent of total consumption expenditures for the median family. Counterbalancing this key limitation of the PSID is the strong advantage that it is the only multiple year, nationally representative, longitudinal database on consumption expenditures available in the United States.

The CEX, by contrast, is the only survey in the United States that collects a complete inventory of consumption data. It has been collected on a regular basis since 1980.[23] This survey contains information on

20. Other longitudinal surveys focusing on particular population groups provide some consumption data; for example, Ohio State University's National Longitudinal Survey of Youth, for young adults, and for older persons, the Social Security Administration's Retirement History Longitudinal Survey and the National Institute on Aging's Health and Retirement Study.

21. See, for example, Cutler and Katz (1991), Attanasio and Davis (1996), Garcia, Lusardi, and Ng (1997), and Lusardi (1996).

22. In some years, data on utilities payments are also collected, but since these data are more frequently missing, we do not use them in this analysis.

23. There were periodic surveys before 1980, most recently in 1972–73. There are difficult issues of data comparability across these earlier surveys and the 1980s surveys; see Cutler and Katz (1991) for a discussion.

expenditure on several hundred separate categories of goods, collected for up to four consecutive quarters, and household demographic characteristics are collected at each interview as well. In addition, in the first and fourth interviews, information is gathered on labor force behavior and income.[24] Thus the CEX provides a short panel, with only two observations on both consumption and income. This is potentially an important disadvantage, in that it limits one to simple difference models in identifying the transitory component of earnings.

By using both of these data sources, we attempt to "triangulate" the estimates of interest. The CEX has data on food and housing consumption, which allow one to confirm estimates from the PSID. One can go beyond the PSID's consumption measures in the CEX. And one can move beyond simple differences models in the PSID.

Sample and Definitions of Variables

This section describes our samples from the Panel Study of Income Dynamics and the Consumer Expenditure Survey and discusses the construction of the earnings and consumption variables.

THE PANEL STUDY OF INCOME DYNAMICS SAMPLE. For the microdata analysis, we use PSID data only for 1976 onward, in order both to exploit the higher quality labor earnings data available in that period and to avoid the problem of missing data on consumption expenditure in the period 1973–75. Our sample consists of all male family heads who are between the ages of twenty and fifty-nine and are not full-time students. Our key dependent variable is consumption, for which we use three measures: food, housing, and the sum of food and housing. While the last is the broadest measure, it suffers from the fact that housing expenditures are missing in three years of our sample period (1982 and 1988–89), while food expenditures are only missing in two years (1988–89). Each of the components of food and housing is deflated by the item-specific annual consumer price index (CPI), and the real components are summed. Our key independent variable, earnings, is measured as the sum of wages and salaries, bonuses and overtime, and professional income.[25]

---

24. In theory, employment status and income are updated each quarter; in practice, for all but a very small share of observations these variables change only at the last interview.

25. This is not the same earnings variable as that used in the time-series analysis

One important issue with the PSID data is their timing. PSID interviews are carried out early in the year: 35 percent occur in February or March, another 40 percent in April, and another 20 percent in May. Earnings data collected at interview date t refer to the preceding year; that is, earnings data collected in April 1977 refer to calendar year 1976. The timing of the consumption question, which asks about "usual spending," is less obvious, and is the source of some disagreement among researchers who use the PSID. Hall and Mishkin argue that it refers to the previous year as well, while Stephen Zeldes argues that it refers to the time of the interview.[26] In either case, given that we are interested in the relationship between consumption and earnings over a calendar year, it seems most appropriate to match consumption from the April interview with labor earnings from the previous year (as collected at the same interview). If Hall and Mishkin are correct, this will be timed appropriately; if Zeldes is correct, it will be somewhat mistimed, but even so, consumption from shortly after the year has ended should be more tightly related to earnings last year than should consumption from the beginning of that year. Moreover, this most closely matches the only timing that one can use with the CEX, as described below.[27]

THE CONSUMER EXPENDITURE SURVEY SAMPLE. Our CEX data covers the period 1980–93, and our sample is once again male heads who are aged twenty to fifty-nine and are not full-time students.[28] The CEX provides data on expenditures on a variety of consumption items. We measure consumption by expenditure level; that is, we make no effort to amortize durables purchases, but rather, treat them as consumption in the year of purchase.[29] In addition, we provide results for a variety

---

above, since nonwage labor income is bracketed before 1976. In the time-series analysis, we relied on the PSID's constructed "labor income" variable, including imputed labor income from business activities, which is defined consistently throughout our sample period. The results of the aggregate analysis are very similar if we simply use wage income, which is also defined consistently throughout the period.

26. Hall and Mishkin (1982); Zeldes (1989).

27. Therefore the timing convention for our time-series analysis is to refer to data from interview date t as coming from year $t - 1$, which is the timing of the labor data.

28. In the PSID, married males are almost always automatically assigned to be the family head. In the CEX, the wife in a couple is sometimes assigned to be the head. In these cases, our observation is the male in the couple.

29. Rather than follow the CEX convention, which includes some tax payments in total expenditure, we redefine the concept to exclude taxes.

of subcomponents of consumption. Each subcomponent is deflated by the relevant (monthly) subcomponent of the CPI.

In the CEX, as in the PSID, timing is an important issue. The change in consumption is a difference across three quarters. As a result, one must control for seasonality. We do so by including the month of the interview as a control variable. The change in earnings is the change in annual earnings reported three quarters apart, so that the two reports overlap somewhat. In addition, the consumption data overlap somewhat with the income data: the first quarter's consumption data are from the year included in the last quarter's (annual) income report. Unfortunately, given the structure of the CEX, there is little that one can do to address these limitations.

CENSORING OUTLIERS. A potential source of concern in both of these data sets is outliers. To the extent that the large outliers in the consumption variables are real changes in consumption, it is important that they be included, as they may reflect instances of particularly poor consumption insurance. Yet to the extent that they are simply coding or reporting errors, it is inappropriate to include them. Also, there are changes over time in the top coding of the income variables, which affect the underlying measured variation.

We deal with both of these problems by censoring the top and bottom 1 percent of the distribution of our consumption and income changes in each year. These cutoffs are sufficient to ensure that the results are not affected by changes in top codes.[30] By censoring, we incorporate the information from these large changes, but do not allow them to have an undue influence on the regression estimates.

Table 1 presents the means of the key variables in our two data sets. The samples are very consistent. The PSID sample is slightly younger and less well educated, but earnings and consumption are very close to those of the CEX sample. The fact that the overlapping consumption data are so similar speaks to the reasonably high quality of the available PSID consumption information.

---

30. In addition, we impose a consistent top code of $100,000 on the nominal values of the head's wage income and his wife's labor income.

Table 1. Mean Characteristics of PSID and CEX Respondents[a]
Units as indicated

Characteristic	PSID data	CEX data
Distribution by educational attainment[b]		
High school dropout	0.20	0.16
High school graduate	0.55	0.55
College graduate	0.25	0.29
Age	38.9	40.5
	(10.5)	(9.9)
Married[b]	0.79	0.84
Family size	3.12	3.32
	(1.53)	(1.56)
Expenditures		
Food	4,367	3,891
	(2,370)	(2,534)
Housing	3,590	3,302
	(3,347)	(3,237)
Food plus housing	8,036	7,193
	(4,467)	(4,535)
Nondurables	. . .	18,894
		(13,902)
Total	. . .	23,481
		(19,616)
Income		
Head's earnings	23,288	23,330
	(19,005)	(16,577)
Wife's earnings	6,364	10,216
	(8,840)	(11,897)
Transfer payments		
Government	721	369
	(2,225)	(1,525)
Total	1,100	1,276
	(3,189)	(3,994)
Taxes paid	5,499	4,995
	(6,809)	(6,711)
Summary statistic		
N	59,323	48,368

Source: Authors' calculations based on data from the PSID and the Bureau of Labor Statistics's Consumer Expenditure Survey (CEX).

a. All entries except those for educational attainment are the mean values for the given characteristics, with standard deviations in parentheses. All mean values except for age, being married, and family size, are expressed in dollars.

b. Proportion of sample in each category.

Regression Framework

Our basic regression framework for estimating the ability of families to smooth variation in the earnings of the head is

(1) $\Delta C_i = \alpha + \beta \Delta Y_i + X_i' \delta + \epsilon_i$,

where C_i is consumption for family i, Y_i is the earnings of the head of family i, and X_i is a vector of the year dummies and family characteristic control variables described above. In the CEX, we replace the food needs variable with a more detailed set of controls for the age structure of the household: change in shares of family that are children under five years old, children over five, and adults over sixty-four.

We estimate this model in levels, rather than the log form traditionally used to test the full consumption insurance and permanent income hypotheses, because we are interested in estimating precisely how much consumption changes for each dollar change in earnings.[31] It is also of interest to examine this relationship in elasticity form, in order to compare the relative response of different types of consumption to earnings changes. Thus we also calculate elasticities, evaluated at the regression mean.

There are three important empirical concerns with interpreting β as a causal effect of earnings variation in equations such as (1). The first is measurement error. The PSID validation study finds that 15 to 30 percent of the cross-sectional variation in earnings is measurement error. Using matched data from the CPS and social security records, John Bound and Alan Krueger find that 20 to 25 percent of the variation in first differences is due to measurement error.[32]

A classic solution to the problem of measurement error is to employ an instrumental variables strategy. To be valid in this instance, the instrument must satisfy two conditions: it must be correlated with the change in earnings and uncorrelated with the error term in equation 1. An instrument that meets both of these requirements is an independent measure of change in earnings. We are able to construct such a measure by using information available in both the PSID and the CEX. Each

---

31. Although the first microdata test of the permanent income hypothesis (Hall and Mishkin, 1982) estimated the model in levels, most subsequent approaches have used logs, which is consistent with constant relative risk aversion utility functions.
32. See Duncan and Hill (1985) on the PSID, and Bound and Krueger (1991).

survey has variables that measure the number of hours worked in the previous year and the current wage rate.[33] The product of these, which we hereafter refer to as imputed earnings, is an independent measure of earnings in the previous year.[34] Since we are interested in change in earnings, we use the change in imputed earnings as the instrument for the change in reported earnings.

The two-equation system that we estimate by instrumental variables is

$$(2) \qquad \Delta Y_i = a + b\Delta Z_i + \mathbf{X}_i'\mathbf{d} + \mu_i$$

$$(3) \qquad \Delta C_i = \gamma + \beta\widehat{\Delta Y_i} + \mathbf{X}_i'\mathbf{d} + \nu_i,$$

where ΔZ_i is the instrument, $\mathbf{X}_i$ is the vector of covariates of equation 1, and $\widehat{\Delta Y_i}$ is the change in earnings predicted by equation 2.

This instrumental variables strategy will be valid if the measurement error in change in imputed earnings is uncorrelated with the measurement error in change in reported earnings. Note that the instrument will be invalidated only by correlated error in the changes, not in the levels. For example, if a family always underreports earnings, hours, and wages, the instrument is valid, because the correlated measurement errors will be eliminated when one takes differences. But if a family underreports earnings, hours, and wages in one year only and not in

33. Our PSID measure of hours is hours worked in the previous year. Our CEX hours measure is usual weekly hours worked times weeks worked in the previous year. Our PSID wage measure is actual hourly pay for hourly workers, and for salaried workers, reported current salary normalized by forty hours per week. We construct our CEX wage measure by dividing weekly pay by weekly hours of work. The CEX collects data on gross pay for the last pay period and the frequency of pay. Eighty-seven percent of our CEX sample are paid weekly or biweekly and another 10 percent are paid monthly, so that this earnings figure closely approximates earnings at the interview date. Most of the remaining 3 percent of respondents do not report frequency of pay, so we set their wages to missing. Note that the wage and hour variables are reported independently of annual earnings in both the PSID and the CEX, and thus constitute an independent measure of earnings.

34. For example, for an individual interviewed in April 1977, we construct imputed earnings with the product of hours worked in 1976 and wage in April 1977. In the PSID sample, we could instead use the wage rate at the point of the previous interview (in this example, April 1976). Doing so yields very similar results for our wage times hours instrument. We use the timing convention described above for consistency with the CEX, where it is the only approach possible, since we only have two observations on each individual.

other years, differencing will not eliminate the correlated measurement errors in reported and imputed earnings. With such a pattern of misreporting, measurement error is not eliminated from equation 3 and our estimated β would be biased toward zero.

The second concern is endogeneity through planned coincident changes in consumption and labor supply, as highlighted by Cochrane.[35] The direction of the bias to β from endogeneity is not obvious and depends on the complementarity or substitutability of leisure and consumption. This endogeneity should be mitigated, to some extent, by our use of a prime-age male sample, for which full-time work is the general activity, so that changes in labor supply may be largely exogenous. But we cannot rule out that year-to-year variation in hours is determined by the same factors that drive consumption decisions.

The third concern is that equation 1 assumes that the consumption smoothing process is linear. In fact, features such as liquidity constraints could give rise to a nonlinear process: individuals may be able to smooth losses that are less than existing wealth holdings but unable to borrow in order to smooth variation that exceeds ex ante asset levels. For this reason, different sources of earnings variation could have quite different effects, in terms of dollar change in earnings: smaller, higher frequency changes in earnings may influence consumption much less than larger, lower frequency shocks.

In order to address all three concerns, we use a second instrument for estimating equation 1: unemployment shocks. In particular, we create a dummy variable for becoming unemployed for more than one month. This measure is plausibly exogenous to consumption decisions and represents a major change in the earnings prospects of the head; on average, a head who becomes unemployed faces a 30 percent reduction in earnings. In addition, any measurement error in this indicator is likely to be independent of error in reported earnings. Thus, by comparing the effects of year-to-year changes in earnings with the effects of unemployment shocks, we can assess the sensitivity of our findings to endogeneity and nonlinearity in consumption smoothing. We find that year-to-year earnings variation and reductions in earnings due to unemployment have similar effects, suggesting that these empirical prob-

35. Cochrane (1991).

lems do not account for our finding of fairly comprehensive consumption smoothing.

Smoothing Variation in Earnings

This section discusses our findings on the ability of families to smooth year-to-year variation in earnings.

Results from the Panel Study of Income Dynamics

Table 2 shows the results from estimating equation 1 in the PSID by ordinary least squares (OLS). As discussed above, OLS estimates of β are likely to be biased toward zero by measurement error in the change in earnings. We present these results for comparison with the previous literature, which relies largely on OLS. We show results for three dependent variables: food, housing, and the sum of food and housing. We also report the elasticities implied by these regressions.

There is a highly significant effect of income changes on consumption changes, concordant with the previous literature rejecting full insurance. But the coefficient is quantitatively very small. Each dollar rise in the earnings of the head increases consumption of food by only 1 cent, and of food and housing by only 1.7 cents. Food consumption appears to be more elastic with respect to income changes than is housing consumption; a 10 percent rise in the earnings of the head raises food consumption by 0.53 percent, while it raises housing consumption by only 0.46 percent. The resulting elasticity of food plus housing consumption with respect to income is only 0.051.

The control variables show that the growth rate of food consumption declines and the growth rate of housing consumption rises with age. The growth rate of food consumption rises with education, but there is no significant effect of education on growth in housing consumption. There is a small negative effect on consumption growth of being married, but a large positive effect of becoming married. There are also strong effects of change in family size and change in food needs.

Table 3 reports instrumental variables estimates of equation 1 in the PSID, using as the instrument the change in imputed earnings (esti-

Table 2. Estimating Consumption Smoothing Using PSID Data, OLS Estimation[a]

Independent variable	Dependent variable		
	Food	Housing	Food plus housing
Change in earnings of head	0.0099	0.0068	0.0171
	(0.0014)	(0.0017)	(0.0025)
Age	−402.9	404.3	50.0
	(228.8)	(240.0)	(385.2)
Age^2	16.17	−16.10	−1.15
	(9.04)	(9.41)	(15.09)
Age^3	−0.279	0.268	0.070
	(0.154)	(0.159)	(0.255)
Age^4	0.0017	−0.0016	0.0001
	(0.0010)	(0.0010)	(0.0016)
Change in family size	421	52	463
	(37)	(28)	(55)
Change in children-to– family size ratio	81	−32	−47
	(119)	(115)	(187)
Change in food need[b]	0.0805	0.0330	0.1173
	(0.0358)	(0.0194)	(0.0524)
Dummy variables			
Black	−21	−26	−34
	(30)	(27)	(46)
High school graduate	19	−1	23
	(24)	(23)	(37)
College graduate	48	−18	31
	(30)	(30)	(47)
Married	−13	−68	−72
	(26)	(31)	(46)
Change in marital status[c]	311	573	869
	(60)	(80)	(114)
Implied elasticity[d]	0.053	0.046	0.051
Summary statistic			
N	43,812	34,311	27,484

Source: Authors' calculations based on data from the PSID.

a. The dependent variable is the annual change in expenditures in the given category. Regressions include the independent variables listed plus a full set of year dummies. The sample period is 1976–92; regressions involving food exclude 1988–89, and regressions involving housing exclude 1982 and 1988–89. Standard errors are shown in parentheses.

b. A PSID variable; see text for details.

c. Becoming married equals 1; becoming single equals −1; no change equals 0.

d. Elasticity implied by the coefficient on head's earnings, evaluated at variable means.

Susan Dynarski and Jonathan Gruber 251

Table 3. Comparing OLS and IV Estimates of Consumption Smoothing Using PSID Data[a]

	OLS method		IV method	
Dependent variable	Earnings coefficient	Implied elasticity[b]	Earnings coefficient	Implied elasticity[b]
Basic equations				
Food	0.0099	0.053	0.0381	0.205
	(0.0014)		(0.0066)	
Housing	0.0068	0.046	0.0241	0.163
	(0.0017)		(0.0075)	
Food plus housing	0.0171	0.051	0.0581	0.174
	(0.0025)		(0.0111)	
Equations with individual fixed effects[c]				
Food	0.0098	0.053	0.0378	0.203
	(0.0016)		(0.0078)	
Housing	0.0068	0.046	0.0269	0.182
	(0.0019)		(0.0090)	
Food plus housing	0.0168	0.050	0.0595	0.179
	(0.0028)		(0.0133)	

Source: Authors' calculations based on data from the PSID.
a. Coefficient is that on change in head's earnings from regression specifications like that described in table 2 and its notes. Standard errors are shown in parentheses. Instrumental variables (IV) column instruments change in earnings with change in imputed earnings, as described in the text.
b. Evaluated at variable means.
c. These equations add a person-specific fixed effect identifying each individual in the sample.

mated using wage at the interview and hours worked last year).[36] The OLS coefficients (from table 2) are included for comparison.

We find that instrumenting significantly raises the effect of income changes on consumption changes. Each dollar of income rise in this IV specification leads to an increase of 3.8 cents in food consumption and of 5.8 cents in food plus housing consumption. In elasticity terms, this is an elasticity of food consumption of 0.205, and of food plus housing consumption of 0.174. While significant, these effects remain fairly small. Thus, while one can reject full consumption insurance, the deviations from that benchmark are not substantively significant.[37]

36. The imputed earnings instrument has significant explanatory power. The R^2 of the first stage is 0.192, and the t statistic on the instrument is 20.94.
37. Note that our food plus housing coefficient need not equal the sum of the food and housing coefficients. This is because (1) the sample is changing across these regressions, due to missing data on food or housing expenditure; and (2) we censor separately the food, housing, and food plus housing variables. For this second reason, in the CEX

As discussed above, this is only one possible specification for identifying the transitory component of individual earnings. Another approach would be to include individual fixed effects in this changes model, measuring as transitory only deviations from a person-specific growth path. We show the results of this approach in the lower panel of table 3. In fact, these results are almost identical to those in the first panel. These findings imply that our CEX differences results would be robust to the inclusion of fixed effects. Therefore for the rest of the paper we present only the results of estimating equations that do not include individual fixed effects. We have replicated all of our PSID results with the inclusion of fixed effects and find that they are very similar in every case.[38]

Results from the Consumer Expenditure Survey

Table 4 reports the basic consumption smoothing estimates from the CEX. We show only the coefficients of interest, but these regressions include all the variables in equation 1 described above. We present results for both the OLS and the IV models, using imputed earnings as an instrument. The table includes each of our consumption subcategories in the CEX.

We begin by measuring the effect on food and housing consumption. The effects in the CEX are very similar to those in the PSID, albeit somewhat smaller. The OLS estimates indicate that a dollar change in earnings leads to a 0.4 cent change in food consumption and a 0.5 cent change in food plus housing consumption. The IV estimates yield a

---

sample the results for total consumption expenditure need not equal the sum of the results for nondurables and durables expenditure.

38. Lawrence Katz has pointed out to us that the tripling of the estimates between the OLS and the IV specifications is inconsistent with a simple measurement error explanation. As noted above, the measurement error in earnings changes in the PSID is estimated to be roughly 20 to 25 percent of the variation. This implies that our coefficient estimate should rise by a factor of only 1.25 when we instrument, if we are simply purging measurement error. One possible explanation for the larger rise, suggested to us by John Abowd, is that the types of events that induce variation in imputed earnings are somewhat different from the types of events that induce variation in actual earnings. If variations in imputed earnings were perceived as more permanent than movements in actual earnings, and if permanent changes were reflected more strongly in consumption (as given by the permanent income hypothesis), instrumenting would lead to a rise in the estimated coefficient. It seems unlikely that this process is playing a large role here, however, since imputed earnings is simply an independent measure of actual earnings.

Table 4. Estimating Consumption Smoothing Using CEX Data[a]

	OLS method		IV method	
Dependent variable	*Earnings coefficient*	*Implied elasticity[b]*	*Earnings coefficient*	*Implied elasticity[b]*
Food	0.0044 (0.0015)	0.026	0.0238 (0.0064)	0.142
Housing	0.0008 (0.0012)	0.006	0.0042 (0.0048)	0.029
Food plus housing	0.0053 (0.0022)	0.017	0.0339 (0.0089)	0.109
Nondurables	0.0344 (0.0058)	0.042	0.0893 (0.0237)	0.110
Durables	0.0329 (0.0112)	0.169	0.1727 (0.0047)	0.888
Total consumption	0.0680 (0.0130)	0.067	0.2440 (0.0550)	0.240
Utilities	0.0004 (0.0006)	0.005	0.0017 (0.0026)	0.021
Clothing	0.0058 (0.0013)	0.693	0.0111 (0.0053)	0.177
Entertainment	0.0073 (0.0022)	0.102	0.0013 (0.0091)	0.018
Vehicle maintenance and fuel	0.0034 (0.0017)	0.030	0.0016 (0.0072)	0.014
Home services	0.0028 (0.0015)	0.076	0.0224 (0.0063)	0.604
Alcohol and tobacco	0.0011 (0.0004)	0.047	0.0044 (0.0015)	0.188
Medical care and insurance	0.0013 (0.0008)	0.051	0.0022 (0.0034)	0.086
Other insurance	−0.0007 (0.0010)	−0.013	−0.0087 (0.0039)	−0.166
Contributions to others	0.0016 (0.0008)	0.048	0.0088 (0.0033)	0.266
Summary statistic				
N^c	19,155		12,875	

Source: Authors' calculations based on data from the CEX.

a. Coefficient is that on change in head's earnings from regression specifications like that described in table 2 and its notes, including a full set on month dummies. Standard errors are shown in parentheses. IV column instruments change in earnings with change in imputed earnings, as described in the text. The sample period is 1980–93.

b. Evaluated at variable means.

c. For equation involving total consumption.

Table 5. Estimating Consumption Smoothing: Food at Home versus Food Away from Home[a]

	PSID data		CEX data	
Dependent variable	*Earnings coefficient*	*Implied elasticity*[b]	*Earnings coefficient*	*Implied elasticity*[b]
Food at home	0.0225	0.156	0.0106	0.092
	(0.0054)		(0.0042)	
Food away from home	0.0215	0.540	0.0070	0.158
	(0.0034)		(0.0035)	

Source: Authors' calculations based on data from the PSID and the CEX.
a. Coefficient is that on change in head's earnings from regression specifications like that described in table 2 and its notes. Standard errors are shown in parentheses. Estimates are by IV and instrument change in earnings with change in imputed earnings, as described in the text. The PSID sample period is described in table 2, note a. The CEX sample period is 1980–93.
b. Evaluated at variable means.

coefficient on food plus housing of 0.034 and an elasticity of 0.109. Once again, we find that consumption smoothing is fairly complete.

The main advantage of the CEX data is that they allow one to expand the measures of consumption expenditure. That is, one can estimate a set of "dynamic Engel curves," tracing out how the consumption of different categories of goods changes with transitory variation in income.

The fourth row of table 4 considers the effects on total nondurables expenditures. Using our IV specification, we find that a dollar change in earnings results in an increase in nondurables expenditures of 9 cents; the elasticity is 0.110. It is striking that this elasticity is actually lower than the estimated elasticity for food consumption, given that the Engel curve for food is generally assumed to be relatively flat.

We address this point further in table 5, which decomposes food spending in both data sets into spending on food at home and away from home. We find that the absolute effect on spending on food away from home is roughly as large as that on food at home, despite the fact that spending on food away from home is only 20 to 25 percent of total food expenditure. As a result, the relatively large elasticity for food expenditures is driven by spending on food away from home; spending on food at home has an IV elasticity of only between 0.092 (in the CEX) and 0.156 (in the PSID), while spending on food away from home has an IV elasticity of between 0.158 and 0.540. Thus the elasticity of actual food consumption is low; it is the elasticity of food preparation services that drives the fairly large effects on total food expenditures.

The fifth row of table 4, however, shows a relatively large response for durables expenditures. Despite the fact that durables are only 11 percent of the consumption bundle on average, changes in earnings have a larger absolute effect on durables spending than on nondurables spending, according to the instrumental variables estimates. This is reflected in an elasticity that is eight times larger for durables than nondurables. Because of the high elasticity for durables, as the next row shows, the effect of earnings changes on total consumption is fairly large: for each dollar change in earnings, total consumption changes by 24 cents.

This finding confirms the notion that durables are, to some extent, savings; individuals absorb income variation, in part, by adjusting the timing of durables purchases. This raises the important and difficult question of how to combine the responses of durables and nondurables in computing the effective change in total consumption. On the one hand, if one simply adds these responses, one overstates the welfare implications of a drop in earnings, since the loss in utility caused by a decrease in durables purchases is presumably smaller than that caused by an equal decrease in other expenditures. On the other hand, by revealed preference, there is some welfare loss from delayed durables purchases. So the true change in consumption, as opposed to measured expenditures, lies somewhere between the effect on nondurables expenditures and the effect on total expenditures; exactly where in this range is a function of how one values the utility loss from altering the timing of durables purchases.

The remaining rows of table 4 examine the effect of earnings variation on the subcomponents of nondurables expenditures. Focusing on the IV model, the elasticities are largest for clothing, home services (repair and maintenance), alcohol and tobacco, and contributions to others. For clothing and home services, as for durables, the welfare loss from delayed purchase may be relatively small. For contributions to others, the estimates are consistent with an altruistic model, which posits that transfers between households will rise with the donor's income.[39]

39. See Cox (1987).

The elasticity of consumption with respect to income variation is smallest for entertainment, medical care and insurance, vehicle maintenance and fuel, and utilities. The estimate for other insurance purchases (for example, life and automobile insurance) is actually negative. This may reflect delayed automobile purchases, which are included in the durables category. But it is also consistent with a falling absolute coefficient of risk aversion; as individuals get richer, they feel less need for a given dollar of insurance.

To summarize, the results from both the PSID and the CEX show that there is a highly significant effect of income variation on consumption variation. This effect is quantatively small for nondurables purchases; of each dollar of earnings change, less than 10 cents is reflected in nondurables expenditures. The effect becomes more sizable, however, when one values durables purchases at their expenditure value. But even in this case, individuals are smoothing over 75 cents of each dollar of earnings change.

Changes in the Quantity and Price of Labor

One important issue raised by the discussion above (and by the permanent income hypothesis literature) is the differential impact of transitory and permanent income variation. Under the permanent income hypothesis, changes in earnings that are perceived as relatively permanent will have larger effects on consumption than will changes that are perceived as relatively transitory. As noted above, it is difficult to decompose earnings changes convincingly into their permanent and transitory components, but one crude approximation is to decompose year-to-year variation in labor earnings into two component sources of variation: changes in hours worked (the quantity of labor), and changes in wage rates (the price of labor). For our prime-age male sample, changes in hours are likely to be transitory, perhaps resulting from overtime or vacation. But changes in wages are likely to be relatively permanent, reflecting promotions or new job matches.

This contention is supported by previous work on the dynamics of earnings and hours. Henry Farber and Robert Gibbons find that wage residuals approximately follow a martingale process for younger workers, while John Abowd and David Card report substantial mean rever-

Table 6. Estimating Consumption Smoothing: Changes in Hours versus Changes in Wage[a]

| | Coefficient on head's earnings | | | |
| | Change in hours worked | | Change in wage | |
Dependent variable	PSID data	CEX data	PSID data	CEX data
Food	0.015	0.027	0.092	0.017
	(0.005)	(0.008)	(0.016)	(0.010)
Housing	0.010	0.005	0.040	0.004
	(0.005)	(0.006)	(0.015)	(0.007)
Food plus housing	0.016	0.031	0.128	0.030
	(0.008)	(0.011)	(0.025)	(0.014)
Nondurables	. . .	0.057	. . .	0.094
		(0.030)		(0.037)
Durables	. . .	0.091	. . .	0.207
		(0.058)		(0.073)
Total consumption	. . .	0.148	. . .	0.294
		(0.069)		(0.085)

Source: Authors' calculations based on data from the PSID and the CEX.
a. Coefficient is that on change in head's earnings from regression specifications like that described in table 2 and its notes. Standard errors are shown in parentheses. Change in earnings is instrumented either with the change in hours worked or with the change in hourly wage, as indicated. The PSID sample period is described in table 2, note a. The CEX sample period is 1980–93.

sion in hours of work.[40] We also find more persistence in wage changes, as compared with hours changes, in our PSID data.[41]

One can distinguish between these two sources of variation in a straightforward manner, by separating imputed earnings (wage times hours) into its two components: change in hours worked and change in the hourly wage rate. Separate instrumental variables estimations of equation 1 will then demonstrate the differential effects of these two sources of income variation on consumption.

The results of using these two instruments in the PSID are presented in table 6. The results show a striking difference between the effects of these two sources of variation. Earnings variation due to changes in hours has a relatively small effect on consumption, with each dollar of hours-induced earnings change producing only a 1.6 cent change in

40. Farber and Gibbons (1996); Abowd and Card (1989).
41. More specifically, regressing change in wages or hours on lagged changes, we find that the sum of the coefficients on the first three lags is −0.98 for hours, but only −0.75 for wages.

food plus housing consumption. But each dollar change in earnings due to change in wages corresponds to a 12.8 cent change in food plus housing consumption. That is, the effect of wage-induced change in earnings is eight times as large as the effect of hours-induced change in earnings. This is consistent with the notion that wage changes are relatively permanent, and that permanent changes have a larger effect on consumption.[42]

The results for the decomposition into hours and wages are not as robust across data sets as are our earlier findings, however. Table 6 also shows this decomposition for the CEX. For food and housing, the effect of hours-induced variation in earnings is actually larger than that of wage-induced variation. For nondurables and durables, the effect of wage-induced variation in earnings is roughly twice as large as that of hours-induced variation. Thus, while the direction is in accordance with the PSID, the magnitudes are not comparable. The reason for this inconsistency across data sets is not clear. Both hourly wage measures have limitations. The PSID measure is more precise for hourly workers, but less precise for salaried workers (since it is normalized by forty hours, rather than reflecting actual hours). Our PSID findings are fairly similar for hourly and salaried workers, however, so differential accuracy does not seem to be an important problem.

Nevertheless, the broad picture that is painted by these findings is consistent across the two data sets. There is clearly a much larger effect of wage variation than of hours variation. Yet individuals can smooth over 70 cents of each dollar in earnings changes due to changes in wages. Thus even in the case of wage variation, the vast majority of earnings variation is smoothed.

Upward and Downward Movements in Earnings

Another natural extension of this analysis is to consider asymmetric responses to upward and downward movements in earnings. If individuals face liquidity constraints and have low savings, they may be less able to smooth downward changes in earnings. We investigate this

---

42. An alternative interpretation is that the measurement error in hours is more highly correlated with the measurement error in earnings than is the measurement error in wages. But it seems unlikely that this would account for coefficient differences of the magnitude observed in the PSID.

Table 7. Estimating Consumption Smoothing: Earnings Increases versus Decreases[a]

| | Coefficient on head's earnings | | | |
| | Earnings increases only | | Earnings decreases only | |
Dependent variable	*PSID data*	*CEX data*	*PSID data*	*CEX data*
Food	0.035	0.018	0.041	0.035
	(0.010)	(0.035)	(0.011)	(0.011)
Housing	0.022	−0.007	0.026	0.017
	(0.011)	(0.007)	(0.012)	(0.008)
Food plus housing	0.046	0.018	0.070	0.056
	(0.017)	(0.013)	(0.018)	(0.016)
Nondurables	. . .	0.071	. . .	0.109
		(0.035)		(0.041)
Durables	. . .	0.051	. . .	0.346
		(0.069)		(0.081)
Total consumption	. . .	0.142	. . .	0.392
		(0.081)		(0.095)

Source: Authors' calculations based on data from the PSID and the CEX.

a. Coefficient is that on change in head's earnings from regression specifications like that described in table 2 and its notes. Standard errors are shown in parentheses. Estimates are by IV and instrument change in earnings with change in imputed earnings, as described in the text. The first two columns give coefficients on upward movements in predicted earnings (obtained from the first-stage regression); the final two columns show coefficients on downward movements. The PSID sample period is described in table 2, note a. The CEX sample period is 1980–93.

proposition in our instrumental variables framework by estimating our first-stage equation to generate predicted earnings, and dividing predicted earnings into its upward and downward components. We then include these components separately in our consumption model.[43]

The findings of this decomposition are presented in table 7. In the PSID, there is only slight evidence of a stronger effect of downward movements in earnings than of upward movements. For food plus housing, the coefficient on downward movements is roughly 50 percent larger than that on upward movements. In no case are the coefficients statistically distinguishable. In the CEX, the gap is similar for nondurables; while the effect on downward movements is roughly 50 percent larger, the estimates are not significantly different from each other. But for durables purchases, we do find a very large gap, indicating that the large effects for durables shown in table 4 appear to be driven mainly

43. This is equivalent to IV estimation done in two steps. In this context, our standard errors are somewhat understated, since we do not account for the two-step nature of the estimation (whereas our direct IV estimates correct the standard errors automatically). Given the very strong first-stage relationship between actual and imputed earnings, this understatement should be small.

by responses to downward movements in earnings. Thus families appear to smooth upward changes in earnings largely through other sources of insurance or saving, whereas downward changes are mainly reflected in reduced durables purchases.

The analysis thus far, particularly in the CEX, shows that earnings variation arising from most sources is reflected in families' consumption in only a very limited way. This naturally raises the question of *how* families smooth consumption against swings in the earnings of the head.

Sources of Consumption Insurance

There are three possible sources of insurance against idiosyncratic variation in the earnings of the head: nonhead earnings, nonlabor income, and saving. The key component of nonhead earnings is the labor supply of other family members; that is, other family members can increase their labor supply when the earnings of the head fall.

There are several sources of nonlabor income. One is increased receipts from government social insurance programs, such as unemployment insurance or workers' compensation. Another source is transfers from others to the family when income is transitorily low, which would be consistent with the altruistic model that finds support in the results above. A final source of nonlabor income is the tax system. A family's net income is automatically insulated from movements in the head's earnings through taxation: lower earnings imply lower payments of income and payroll taxes, so that the net fall in resources is smaller than the gross fall in the head's earnings.

The third source of consumption insurance is saving. In the standard permanent income hypothesis model, families use saving and dissaving to smooth consumption over changes in the employment status of the head. The results discussed in the previous section clearly reject the strong form of this hypothesis, since families are not using saving to smooth consumption fully. Nonetheless, a substantial proportion of the consumption smoothing that does occur may be through saving behavior.

We use a regression framework to measure the magnitudes of the three souces of family income smoothing for which we have data: wife's

Table 8. Estimating Sources of Family Income Smoothing[a]

	Coefficient on head's earnings	
Dependent variable	*PSID data*	*CEX data*
Wife's earnings	−0.016	−0.012
	(0.014)	(0.015)
Transfer payments		
Government	−0.122	−0.046
	(0.007)	(0.004)
Total	−0.145	−0.062
	(0.009)	(0.007)
Taxes paid	0.347	0.262
	(0.014)	(0.016)

Source: Authors' calculations based on data from the PSID and the CEX.
a. Coefficient is that on change in head's earnings from regression specifications like that described in table 2 and its notes. Standard errors are shown in parentheses. Estimates are by IV and instrument change in earnings with change in imputed earnings, as described in the text. The PSID sample period is as described in table 2, note a, but the regression involving taxes also excludes 1992. The CEX sample period is 1980–93.

earnings, transfer income, and taxes. For each source of income, we estimate an equation of the form

$$(4) \qquad \Delta I_i = \gamma \Delta Y_i + X_i' \phi + \epsilon_i,$$

where I_i is a given source of family income. The coefficient γ measures how much a source of family income insurance changes for each dollar change in the head's earnings (ΔY_i). Measurement error in ΔY_i will bias the estimate of γ toward zero; we therefore employ an instrumental variables strategy, using imputed earnings as the instrument. These estimates are reported in table 8.

RESPONSE OF WIFE'S EARNINGS. Both the CEX and the PSID measure the wife's labor income over the same time frame as the earnings of the head. The results presented in table 8 indicate that, in general, there is relatively little compensation for lost earnings through the earnings of the wife. In the PSID, the coefficient is small and insignificant. In the CEX, the coefficient is somewhat larger, but still insignificant. Thus, overall, we find that spousal labor supply plays only a small role in the smoothing of year-to-year earnings variation.

TRANSFER INCOME. In both data sets, transfer income is defined as government transfers, retirement income, and other sources of support that are not earned labor income or asset income. As table 1 shows, the mean of this variable is very similar across the two data sets. The results reported in table 8 indicate that transfer income plays a nontrivial role in consumption smoothing. In the PSID results, transfer income flows off-set 15 cents of each dollar lost due to earnings variation. The basic pattern is similar in the CEX, albeit with smaller coefficients. The table also shows that the majority of the response of transfer income comes through government transfers; private transfers account for, at most, one-quarter of the transfer estimates.

TAXES. A mechanical, but important, source of smoothing of earnings variation is taxation. Indeed, one justification that has been offered for a redistributive tax system is the provision of insurance against income variation.[44] Yet previous analyses of consumption smoothing have largely ignored taxes. The CEX reports the actual tax payments of households over the previous year, while the PSID calculates expected tax payments on the basis of the comprehensive income data in the survey.[45] We include both the income and the payroll tax payments of households. Payroll tax payments are reported in the CEX; for the PSID sample, we calculate them by applying the payroll tax schedule to household earnings.

The results presented in table 8 show a very important role for taxes. In the PSID, changes in tax burdens smooth 35 cents of each dollar of earnings variation. In the CEX, the coefficient is somewhat smaller, indicating smoothing of 26 percent. These coefficients can be interpreted as marginal tax rates.[46]

There are two possible reasons for the larger tax effects in the PSID. First, the PSID contains data for five years before the tax reforms of the early 1980s, which substantially lowered marginal rates (although the effect of the reforms was somewhat counteracted by a rising payroll tax rate over this period). Indeed, if we estimate our PSID models over the same sample period as the CEX, we find that the tax coefficients fall and are more similar to those that we estimate in the CEX, whereas there is no difference in other sources of consumption insurance. Second, self-reported taxes (as in the CEX) may respond less to changes

44. Varian (1980) bases this justification on permanent (cross-person) differences in income, not transitory (within-person) changes, but the same basic principles apply.
45. The PSID does not report tax payments for 1992, so we are unable to use the last year of our data for this exercise.
46. These coefficients are consistent with previous estimates of the average marginal tax rate in the United States. Barro and Sahasakul (1986) estimate year-by-year averages of the sum of federal income and payroll taxes. The average of their estimated rates for 1976 through 1983 (the last year in their data) is 0.348.

in reported earnings than do tax payments calculated directly on the basis of those reported earnings (as in the PSID).

IMPLIED SAVING RESPONSE. To summarize our findings for the three sources of consumption smoothing, we find in the PSID that roughly one-half of earnings changes are off-set by net income flows to the family; in the CEX, where the income data are probably less reliable, the offset is only 32 cents. Most of this offset arises from reduced tax payments, although some comes through increased government transfers.

Taken together with our consumption estimates, these findings imply that 25 to 40 percent of change in earnings from year to year is smoothed by saving. This estimate rises to about 40 to 55 percent if one includes durables expenditures as saving. Thus saving and off-setting sources of family income appear to play an almost equally important role in smoothing consumption. That is, there is an equal role for insurance through others (predominantly the government) and self-insurance through saving.[47]

Unemployment

Unemployment is a large, arguably exogenous, source of earnings variation. As such, earnings variation due to unemployment may be harder for households to smooth than that arising from the sources explored above, both because unemployment is unplanned and because its effects on earnings are large.[48] In fact, previous analyses have shown that unemployment is associated with a significant decline in consumption. But none have quantified the deviation from full smoothing due to unemployment. For each dollar of earnings loss due to unemployment, by how much does consumption fall?

47. We also investigate the differential response of transfers and taxes to upward and downward movements in earnings. As might be expected, transfers respond somewhat more strongly to downward movements, whereas taxes respond somewhat more strongly to upward movements; this is consistent with the redistributive structures of tax and transfer programs in the United States.

48. As noted above, the coefficient from regressions for the PSID and the CEX of the change in log earnings on our unemployment dummy (controlling for the year dummies and family characteristics used throughout the paper) yields sizable effects: unemployment lowers the earnings of the head by over 30 percent.

In this section we consider the effect of becoming unemployed on consumption. It is possible for unemployment to be somewhat anticipated; for example, individuals may be on regular temporary layoff. Our goal is to draw a sample for which unemployment appears unanticipated. In the PSID, we do so by contrasting the sample of workers who report at interview date t (for example, April 1978) that they had one month or more of unemployment last year (in this example, January 1997 to December 1977) with those who report no unemployment last year. We further condition the sample on both employment at interview date $t - 1$ (April 1977) and no unemployment during the year preceding that interview (January–December 1976). The dummy variable for unemployment therefore measures the transition from employment to unemployment for a sample that appears to be regularly employed ex ante, and thus for whom unemployment is not a regular event. In addition, by conditioning on employment at interview date $t - 1$, which is in the early spring, we generally capture unemployment spells occurring in the second half of the year, which is closer to the frame of reference for the consumption question.[49]

Our CEX measure is defined analogously. However, the CEX provides information not on weeks of unemployment, per se, but only on weeks without work. We therefore replace the condition of zero weeks of unemployment in the year preceding interview $t - 1$ with a condition of more than forty-eight weeks of employment in that year; and the condition of one month of unemployment in the year preceding interview t with a condition of fewer than forty-eight weeks of employment.

We estimate the response of consumption variation to earnings variation, using this dummy variable for unemployment as an instrument. In neither data set are we able to determine whether unemployment is due to voluntary or involuntary job separation. Thus, to the extent that quits are planned and reflected in consumption profiles, our estimates may understate the impact of exogenous job loss.[50] But for prime-age

---

49. In fact, our unemployment spells may be occurring before April 1977, since the question in April 1978 simply asks about unemployment during the previous year. That is, an individual may have been employed during all of 1976, unemployed during February 1977, and employed again by April 1977. But for individuals who report no unemployment during 1976 and employment in April 1977, it seems likely that any unemployment during 1977 occurred after April.

50. That is, quitters may lower their consumption in the previous period in antici-

Table 9. Estimating Consumption Smoothing for Earnings Losses due to Unemployment[a]

	Coefficient on head's earnings	
Dependent variable	*PSID data*	*CEX data*
Food	0.076	0.055
	(0.018)	(0.013)
Housing	0.027	0.006
	(0.017)	(0.010)
Food plus housing	0.088	0.067
	(0.027)	(0.018)
Nondurables	. . .	0.108
		(0.049)
Durables	. . .	0.129
		(0.097)
Total consumption	. . .	0.241
		(0.114)

Source: Authors' calculations based on data from the PSID and the CEX.
a. Coefficient is that on decrease in head's earnings from regression specifications like that described in table 2 and its notes. Standard errors are shown in parentheses. Estimates are by IV and instrument earnings loss with an unemployment dummy, as described in the text. The sample is confined to heads who experience an unanticipated period of unemployment in a given year. The PSID sample period is described in table 2, note a. The CEX sample period is 1980–93.

heads, a period of search of more than one month seems most likely to be associated with exogenous job loss, rather than a planned quit.

Basic Results

The results using the unemployment dummy as an instrument are presented in table 9. For most components of consumption, these estimates are very similar to those for general downward movements in earnings, shown in table 7. In the PSID, each dollar of earnings loss due to unemployment reduces food consumption by 7.6 cents, and food plus housing consumption by 8.8 cents; these effects are slightly larger than those in table 7. In the CEX, the pattern is similar. The effects are slightly larger for food and housing, and almost identical for total nondurables consumption; each dollar of unemployment-induced earn-

---

pation of having low income and, as a result, have a small consumption change when they quit.

ings loss lowers nondurables expenditure by 10.8 cents, as compared to 10.9 cents in table 7.[51]

As in the analysis above, the major impact of earnings variation is on durables expenditures. An employment-induced drop of one dollar in earnings produces a drop of 12.9 cents in durables expenditure. This is considerably smaller than the 34.6 cent drop in durables expenditure in response to general downward movement in earnings shown in table 7. As a result of this differential response of durables expenditures, the effect of earnings variation on total consumption is actually smaller for the case of unemployment (0.241) than for general downward movement in earnings (0.392).

Overall, though, we find that this very different instrumental variable produces results quite similar to those uncovered by our basic instrumental variables regressions, shown in tables 3 and 4. Nondurables expenditures change by about 10 cents for each dollar change in earnings and total expenditures change by less than 25 cents. This suggests that the previous findings are not badly biased by measurement error, endogeneity, or nonlinearities in consumption smoothing. But, once again, these results raise the question of how families smooth this large shock to the earnings prospects of the head.

Sources of Consumption Insurance

Table 10 extends the analysis of the sources of family income smoothing to unemployment. This is a particularly interesting case, since here is an explicit government insurance program—unemployment insurance—that is designed to deal with income variation due to unemployment.

In both the PSID and the CEX, we find that there are substantial (net) income flows offsetting the income loss from unemployment; the totals are similar, although the sources are quite different. In the CEX, there is a large offsetting response from spousal earnings to the income loss from unemployment; in the PSID, there is little response from spousal earnings. These CEX findings, however, are at odds with a

---

51. The similarity of these consumption responses may seem counterintuitive, since unemployment is a rather severe shock to earnings prospects. But, as discussed below, the government explicitly provides insurance against the income shock of unemployment. Thus, while the shock of unemployment may be severe, insurance against that shock is relatively complete.

Table 10. Estimating Sources of Family Income Smoothing in Response to Unemployment[a]

	Coefficient on head's earnings	
Dependent variable	PSID data	CEX data
Wife's Earnings	−0.022	−0.124
	(0.032)	(0.033)
Transfer payments		
Government		
Unemployment insurance	−0.220	−0.072
	(0.020)	(0.005)
Total government	−0.232	−0.104
	(0.024)	(0.008)
Total transfers	−0.258	−0.165
	(0.012)	(0.016)
Taxes paid	0.282	0.204
	(0.022)	(0.034)

Source: Authors' calculations based on data from the PSID and the CEX.
a. Coefficient is that on change in head's earnings from regression specification like that described in table 2 and its notes. Standard errors are shown in parentheses. Estimates are by IV and instrument earnings loss with an unemployment dummy, as described in the text. The sample is confined to heads who experience an unanticipated period of unemployment in a given year. The PSID sample period is described in table 2, note a. The CEX sample period is 1980–93.

large literature on the *added worker effect*, which finds that there is no strong effect of the husband's unemployment on the labor supply of the wife.[52]

By contrast, the response of transfer income is much larger in the PSID than in the CEX. While it is highly significant in both data sets, in the PSID we find that for each dollar lost in income due to unemployment, transfers rise by 26 cents. Most of this increase is through government transfers, in particular, through income flows from the unemployment insurance program. The finding of a 22 cent rise in unemployment insurance payments for each dollar of earnings lost through unemployment is sensible, in that unemployment insurance receipt rates among the unemployed are around 40 percent and the average replacement rate over this period averages roughly 50 percent.[53] The CEX results for transfers are much smaller. In both data sets, there is also a highly significant and sizeable response of tax payments.

52. See Gruber and Cullen (1996) for a review of this literature and some new evidence that confirms the absence of an added worker effect.
53. See Blank and Card (1991) on receipt rates, and Gruber (1997) on replacement rates.

Overall, we find that about 50 to 55 cents of each dollar of earnings loss due to unemployment is compensated by increased income flows, primarily through taxes and transfers. Taken together with our consumption estimates, this suggests that only 20 to 25 cents of each dollar of earnings loss due to unemployment is reflected in dissaving. Thus for unemployment-induced earnings variation, relative to earnings variation in general, there is a larger consumption smoothing role for transfers and a smaller role for saving.

Are Our Results Consistent with Wealth Holding?

One weakness of our analysis is that we do not have direct data on saving; instead, we define the saving response as a residual. This suggests that there is value in confirming our contentions in terms of actual wealth or saving. For example, our findings for unemployment imply that a sizeable share of the resulting income loss is financed by dissaving. However, this is potentially at odds with the well-known fact that most households in the United States have low asset holdings. This fact has particular salience, considering that the households where the head experiences unemployment are largely drawn from the lower end of the income distribution. Moreover, unemployed households are likely to face serious liquidity constraints when trying to borrow to finance the unemployment spell. Thus it is natural to ask whether household asset holdings are plausibly large enough to finance one-quarter of the loss in earnings due to unemployment.

This question is addressed elsewhere by Gruber, using data from the Census Bureau's Survey of Income and Program Participation (SIPP).[54] We use the data from this study, but add sample restrictions to match our PSID and CEX samples (males aged twenty to fifty-nine). The SIPP is a large, nationally representative survey, which follows a sample of roughly 15,000 households for a period of two to three years. Households are interviewed every four months and provide retrospective information on each of the previous four months, including weekly employment status information. At two points in each SIPP panel, households also provide an asset inventory. The advantage of the SIPP data, for our purpose, is that one can match asset holdings shortly before an unemployment spell with the precise income loss from that spell.

54. Gruber (1996b).

We use the sample of households for which the head, within one year of the wealth interview, experiences a job separation that results in unemployment of more than four weeks. We then compare the ex ante wealth holdings of those households to the ex post income loss due to the head's unemployment. The income loss is defined by taking the head's ex ante after-tax weekly earnings and multiplying by weeks of unemployment; we then add back the unemployment insurance benefits received during the spell. This will not account for other offsetting income flows from spousal labor supply or transfers other than unemployment insurance, but our PSID results show that these are small relative to the unemployment insurance and tax effects that are incorporated in the analysis.[55]

The adequacy of wealth holding to smooth consumption in the face of income loss is defined for two different concepts of wealth: gross liquid assets, which include interest-earning assets in banks and other institutions, household equity in stocks and mutual funds, and other assets, such as bonds and checking accounts; and total net worth, which is the sum of all household net assets, liquid and illiquid, including (in addition to those previously mentioned) equity in retirement savings accounts, homes, vehicles, and personal businesses. Which one of these is the appropriate concept for measuring the ability to finance consumption during unemployment is unclear. Liquid assets are easily accessed to finance income loss, whereas illiquid assets may be harder to tap. Nevertheless, there is only a small penalty for drawing down retirement savings, and those who have some equity in their residences may be able to take out a home equity loan, so focusing only on liquid assets may seriously understate the resources available to households.

The results of our calculations are reported in the top panel of table 11.[56] We present results for the median ratio of wealth to lost income, as well as the distribution of the sample across categories defined by wealth-to–income loss ratios as follows: wealth holdings that are less than 10 percent of the expected income loss, less than 25 percent, less

55. We compare wealth holding only to realized ex post income loss, not to ex ante expected income loss. Since the duration of unemployment is endogenous, this approach may bias upward our adequacy calculations, because those with low wealth will have relatively short spells.

56. These results include imputed wealth observations in the SIPP. Since imputation rates are much higher at higher wealth levels, excluding them would potentially skew the sample.

Table 11. Ratio of Wealth to Unemployment-Induced Income Loss, by Educational Attainment[a]

Wealth as share	Definition of wealth	
of income loss	Gross liquid assets	Net worth
Entire sample		
Median	0.35	6.35
Less than 0.10	0.37	0.17
Less than 0.25	0.46	0.20
Less than 0.50	0.54	0.23
Less than 1.00	0.64	0.28
High school dropouts		
Median	0.05	3.78
Less than 0.10	0.55	0.21
Less than 0.25	0.62	0.25
Less than 0.50	0.69	0.30
Less than 1.00	0.76	0.36
High school graduates		
Median	0.40	7.26
Less than 0.10	0.33	0.15
Less than 0.25	0.43	0.18
Less than 0.50	0.53	0.21
Less than 1.00	0.63	0.27
College graduates		
Median	1.24	7.11
Less than 0.10	0.16	0.15
Less than 0.25	0.23	0.16
Less than 0.50	0.32	0.18
Less than 1.00	0.45	0.21

Source: Author's calculations based on data from the Census Bureau's Survey of Income and Program Participation.
a. Each entry gives either the median wealth-to-income loss ratio or the share of the given subsample whose wealth holdings are less than the given share of their unemployment-induced income loss.

than 50 percent, and less than 100 percent. These categories are defined cumulatively, so that one minus the final row gives the share of the sample whose wealth is higher than their income loss.

Our results are consistent with the notion that assets are used to smooth about one-quarter of the income loss from unemployment. We find that the median household has gross liquid assets equal to 35 percent of its income loss from the unemployment spell, and that about one-half of households have assets greater than one-quarter of their income loss. Thirty-six percent of households have assets that are greater than their entire income loss. If one includes illiquid assets, wealth appears more than adequate to finance the kind of consumption smoothing that one observes in the PSID and the CEX. Thus our finding is not implausible, even if families cannot borrow.

Heterogeneity

Thus far, the analysis has considered the average effect of income variation on all male heads in our PSID and CEX samples. But there is reason to suspect considerable heterogeneity in the ability of families to smooth unemployment shocks. There is marked heterogeneity in wealth holding in the United States. As R. Glenn Hubbard, Jonathan Skinner, and Stephen Zeldes report, the median nonhousing wealth holdings of households headed by thirty- to thirty-nine-year-old high school dropouts is only one-sixth that of households headed by college graduates in the same age range.[57] This suggests that higher income households may be better able to smooth consumption. Yet, to the extent that government social insurance programs are means tested, or have redistributive benefits structures, there may be more scope for consumption smoothing among low-income households.[58] Thus an important question is whether there are differences in the ability to smooth income variation across households of different levels of wealth holding.

In order to examine heterogeneous responses to earnings variation, one must divide the sample by underlying ability to smooth consumption. Using actual wealth holdings for this purpose is problematic, however, for two reasons. First, wealth holding is endogenous to earnings variation. That is, if a family has low asset holdings, this may not imply that it is unable to smooth consumption, but rather that it has already drawn down its wealth to finance consumption smoothing. Second, while there is information on wealth holding for two points in time (1984 and 1989) in the PSID, there is no wealth information in the CEX.[59]

57. Hubbard, Skinner, and Zeldes (1995).
58. Indeed, Hubbard, Skinner, and Zeldes (1995) suggest the redistributive social insurance structure as an explanation for the skewed nature of asset holding. Gruber and Yelowitz (1997) offer empirical support for this contention, finding that means-tested health insurance under the medicaid program has a large crowd-out effect on wealth holding.
59. In theory, the final CEX interview collects data on wealth; in practice, these data are missing for most households.

We therefore consider heterogeneity by the educational attainment of the head. Education is strongly correlated with wealth holding, as noted above, but it is exogenous to the underlying income variation over our sample period (since we exclude students). We divide our data into three categories for this analysis: high school dropouts, high school graduates who have not completed college, and college graduates.

The correlation of education with wealth holding is also documented in table 11, which shows the ratio of asset holdings to income loss from unemployment by education category. There is clearly a skewed distribution of gross liquid asset holdings, which might be associated with differential ability to smooth consumption. The median household headed by a high school dropout who separates from his job has gross liquid assets amounting to only 5 percent of the resulting income loss; only 38 percent of these households have liquid assets greater than 25 percent of the income loss. By contrast, the median household headed by a college graduate who separates from his job has gross liquid assets 1.2 times the income loss, and over three-quarters of these households have assets greater than 25 percent of the income loss. The distribution of net worth, relative to income loss, is somewhat less skewed.

The relationship between unemployment-induced earnings variation and consumption, by education, is shown in table 12. The upper panel considers the effect of unemployment-induced earnings variation on consumption by educational group. In the PSID, we find that the effects are much larger among households headed by high school dropouts and graduates than among those headed by college graduates; there is essentially no effect of unemployment-induced earnings variation on the consumption of the highly educated. In the CEX, the pattern for food and housing consumption is flatter. For total nondurables, there is a larger effect on households headed by high school dropouts than among those headed by college graduates, but the difference is not large. There is an enormous difference, however, for durables expenditures: there is no effect of unemployment-induced earnings variation on the durables purchases of households headed by college graduates, whereas there is a 53 cent drop in the durables purchases of households headed by high school dropouts for each dollar reduction in earnings due to unemployment. Thus for total consumption expenditures, there is large heterogeneity by educational group.

Table 12. Estimating Responses to Unemployment-Induced Earnings Changes, by Educational Attainment[a]

	Coefficient on head's earnings					
	PSID data			CEX data		
Dependent variable	High school dropouts	High schoool graduates	College graduates	High school dropouts	High school graduates	College graduates
Expenditure						
Food	0.075	0.098	0.019	0.096	0.049	0.055
	(0.045)	(0.024)	(0.032)	(0.031)	(0.016)	(0.026)
Housing	0.077	0.024	−0.007	−0.008	0.007	0.017
	(0.043)	(0.023)	(0.028)	(0.018)	(0.013)	(0.020)
Food plus housing	0.091	0.126	−0.009	0.089	0.062	0.074
	(0.078)	(0.037)	(0.041)	(0.038)	(0.023)	(0.037)
Nondurables	. . .	. . .	. . .	0.197	0.079	0.129
				(0.103)	(0.062)	(0.097)
Durables	. . .	. . .	. . .	0.525	0.142	−0.079
				(0.197)	(0.132)	(0.180)
Total consumption	. . .	. . .	. . .	0.697	0.200	0.072
				(0.239)	(0.152)	(0.213)
Source of income smoothing						
Wife's earnings	−0.014	−0.006	−0.072	0.014	−0.094	−0.294
	(0.081)	(0.045)	(0.048)	(0.061)	(0.042)	(0.075)
Transfer payments Government Unemployment insurance	−0.301	−0.223	−0.138	−0.106	−0.079	−0.040
	(0.052)	(0.024)	(0.034)	(0.017)	(0.007)	(0.006)
Total government	−0.317	−0.254	−0.151	−0.166	−0.111	−0.056
	(0.062)	(0.031)	(0.042)	(0.030)	(0.011)	(0.009)
Total transfers	−0.338	−0.275	−0.148	−0.198	−0.184	−0.099
	(0.066)	(0.034)	(0.041)	(0.048)	(0.023)	(0.027)
Taxes paid	0.264	0.313	0.232	0.278	0.181	0.206
	(0.040)	(0.031)	(0.053)	(0.066)	(0.041)	(0.077)

Source: Authors' calculations based on data from the PSID and the CEX.
a. Coefficient is that on decrease in head's earnings from regression specifications like that described in table 2 and its notes. Standard errors are shown in parentheses. Estimates are by IV and instrument earnings loss with an unemployment dummy, as described in the text. The sample is confined to heads who experience an unanticipated period of unemployment in a given year. The PSID sample period is described in table 2, note a. The CEX sample period is 1980–93.

One potential problem with these findings is that the unemployment indicator may be capturing different types of shocks in the different educational groups. For example, the effect of unemployment-induced income variation on consumption may be larger for the lowest educational group because unemployment spells are more severe for this group, and consequently are perceived as more permanent in making consumption decisions. However, there is no evidence that unemployment spells are differentially severe across these groups. The average durations of unemployment spells within the three educational groups in the PSID are 15.3 weeks for high school dropouts, 14.3 weeks for high school graduates, and 13.8 weeks for college graduates. Similarly, examination of the effect of unemployment on earnings (the first stage of the two-stage least squares results in table 9) shows that the coefficients rise with education in the PSID (indicating that spells are actually more severe for the most educated) and are roughly equal in the CEX. Thus the differential consumption response to unemployment-induced income variation across educational groups shown in table 12 appears genuinely to reflect differential ability to smooth transitory income variation.

The fact that the effect of unemployment-induced earnings variation is larger for the lowest educational groups suggests that redistributive transfers are not offsetting underlying differences in wealth holding. Evidence on this proposition is shown in the lower panel of table 12, which documents the sources of consumption smoothing by educational group.

We find that transfers in response to unemployment-induced earnings variation are largest for the lowest educational group. This difference is driven by government transfers; nongovernment transfers appear to respond roughly equally across these groups. Off-setting these redistributive transfers, however, is a regressive response of spousal labor supply, particularly in the CEX. This may reflect the fact that the wives of the most educated have the highest potential spousal wages and commensurately greater ability to smooth earnings variation.[60] The tax

60. This finding is broadly consistent with the cross-sectional evidence of Juhn and Murphy (1997), who find that the wives of low-earning men who saw large declines in wages in the 1970s and 1980s did not earn more to off-set these declines. By contrast, they find a relative rise in earnings among the wives of high-earning men whose wages rose over this period.

Table 13. Comparing Responses to Unemployment, by Wealth Group[a]

	Coefficient on head's earnings	
Dependent variable	*Low wealth[b]*	*High wealth[b]*
Food	0.171	0.059
	(0.077)	(0.036)
Housing	0.061	0.026
	(0.050)	(0.036)
Food plus housing	0.255	0.084
	(0.109)	(0.052)

Source: Authors' calculations based on data from the PSID.

a. Coefficient is that on decrease in head's earnings from regression specifications like that described in table 2 and its notes. Standard errors are shown in parentheses. Estimates are by IV and instrument earnings loss with an unemployment dummy, as described in the text. The sample is confined to heads who experience an unanticipated period of unemployment in a given year. Sample period is 1985–92, excluding 1988–89.

b. Those in the bottom 75 percent of the wealth distribution in 1984.

c. Those in the top 25 percent of the wealth distribution in 1984.

effect is roughly equal across groups in both data sets, which is somewhat surprising, since marginal tax rates are, on average, higher for the more educated.

Our results therefore suggest important heterogeneity in the response of consumption to unemployment-induced earnings variation. For low-education heads, there is an enormous response of durables expenditures to earnings reductions through unemployment, and a large response of net government transfers as well; as a result, there is no implied smoothing through saving. This is consistent with the low asset holdings of this group. For college graduate heads, there is little consumption response to unemployment-induced earnings reductions, and a somewhat smaller role for government transfers than for the low-education group (although a larger role for spousal labor supply); for this group, dissaving offset roughly one-half of the earnings loss due to unemployment.

While cutting by education solves the problems noted above, it is a somewhat indirect approach to describing the effect of liquidity constraints. Therefore in table 13 we confirm our results for the educational groups by directly dividing our PSID data in terms of ex ante wealth holdings. We divide the post-1984 observations on the basis of their gross liquid asset levels in 1984; by using ex ante wealth, we hope to mitigate the dependence of wealth holding on unemployment.[61] We

61. However, this does not fully solve this problem if unemployment is serially correlated.

compare the top quarter of the wealth distribution to the bottom three quarters. The results are consistent with our findings by educational group: there is a much larger effect of income changes on consumption within the low-wealth group than within the high-wealth group.

Consumption Instability in the United States

Our findings from the microdata analysis of the previous sections suggest that families are fairly well able to smooth consumption against earnings variation. For nondurables consumption, we find that each dollar of earnings change leads to a change in consumption of less than 10 cents. Even when one adds durables expenditures, the total consumption response is only 25 cents for each dollar change in earnings.

In this section, we extend the aggregate analysis discussed at the start of this paper to describe time patterns in the variation of consumption. We follow the same approach as that described above, replacing head's earnings with food or food plus housing expenditures as the dependent variable. Figure 3 plots the time trends for variation in labor income, food consumption, and food plus housing consumption. This figure suggests two findings.

First, there is little countercyclicality in the variation of food consumption. There is more countercyclicality in the food plus housing series, but this may reflect cyclical asset pricing effects in the housing market that are not appropriately captured by the housing deflator.

Second, there is a secular rise in the variation of consumption. The proportional rise in the variation of food consumption is of almost exactly the same magnitude as that of head's earnings; over the entire period, food variation rises by 74 percent, while earnings variation rises by 76 percent. For food plus housing, the rise is smaller (43 percent), but still quite sizable. If we decompose the food series into spending on food at home and spending on food away from home, we find that the rise is driven by an increase in the variation of food at home; the variation of food away from home actually declines. Figure 4 shows the results using our fixed effects model. They are fairly similar; the rise in food plus housing variation over this period is roughly one-half as large as the rise in labor earnings variation.

The first finding, that consumption variation does not follow the

Figure 3. Variation of Earnings and Consumption Expenditures, 1970–91[a]

Variance

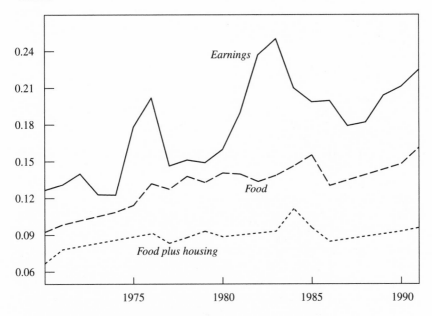

Source: Authors' calculations based on data from the PSID.
a. Figure plots, by year, the mean of the squared residuals produced in regressing changes in log earnings or consumption expenditure on the family characteristic controls and year dummies described in the text and used throughout the paper.

countercyclical pattern of earnings variation, is consistent with our micro-level evidence, which shows that individuals are largely able to smooth year-to-year variation in earnings. This point is made even more starkly in figures 5 and 6, which decompose the aggregate trend in earnings instability into its two components: variation in hours and variation in earnings per hour.[62] It is clear from these figures that the countercyclical pattern in earnings instability is driven by variation in hours of work, not in the wage rate. But in the microdata regressions we show that variation in hours of work is readily smoothed by house-

62. This is a literal decomposition of the earnings last year variable (using reported earnings divided by reported hours), so that earnings per hour is not our hourly wage instrument, which is an independent measure of wages. When we instead use our hourly wage instrument to compute this time series, the pattern is similar.

Figure 4. Variation of Earnings and Consumption Expenditures, Individual Fixed Effects Included, 1970–91[a]

Variance

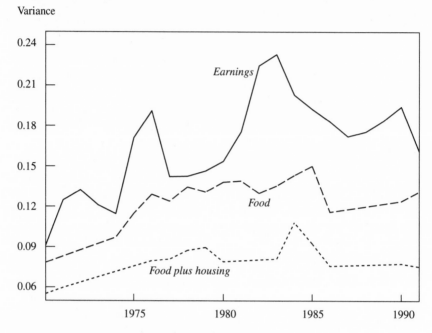

Source: Authors' calculations based on data from the PSID.
a. Produced by the same method as figure 3, except that this equation adds a person-specific fixed effect.

holds.[63] Thus it is not surprising that the variation of consumption does not display the countercyclicality seen in the variation of earnings.

The second finding, that variation in consumption is trending upward along with variation in earnings, is harder to reconcile with the micro-level evidence. The PSID data do indicate that there is a significant relationship between wage variation and consumption variation, and wage variation shows a upward trend in figures 5 and 6. But the magnitude of this relationship cannot explain the close parallel between consumption variation and earnings variation. In particular, for each 10 percent rise in the wage, there is a 1.13 percent rise in food consumption. This implies that the increased variation of the change in wages can explain less than 2 percent of the increased variation of the

63. Even variation through unemployment, which may be more meaningful when considering the cyclical pattern, is mostly smoothed.

Figure 6. Variation of Earnings, Hours Worked, and Wages, Individual Fixed Effects Included, 1970–91[a]

Variance

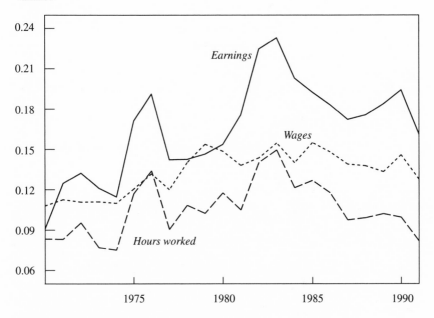

Source: Authors' calculations based on data from the PSID.
a. Produced by the same method as figure 5, except that this equation adds a person-specific fixed effect.

change in food consumption. As confirmation of this point, we plotted (not shown) the yearly squared residuals from an instrumental variables regression of change in consumption on change in earnings—the basic IV model from tables 3 and 4. Even after conditioning out the effect of earnings in this way, the variation of consumption rises virtually as fast as the absolute variation in consumption shown in figures 3 and 4.

Two additional pieces of evidence suggest that the time trends in earnings and consumption instability are not causally related. First, the time patterns of these series do not match. Three-quarters of the secular rise in earnings instability in the PSID occurs after 1980. But only 40 percent of the rise in food consumption instability and 10 percent of the rise in food plus housing consumption instability occur after 1980. Second, the patterns of these series by educational group do not match. If we disaggregate the earnings instability trends by educational group, we find a much smaller effect on college graduates than on lower

Figure 5. Variation of Earnings, Hours Worked, and Wages, 1970–91[a]

Variance

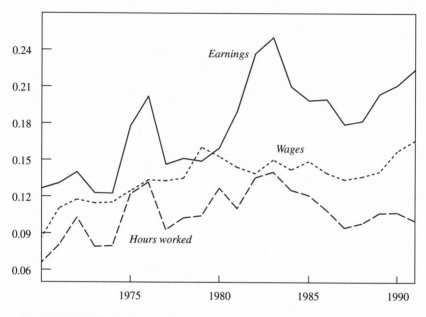

Source: Authors' calculations based on data from the PSID.

a. Figure plots, by year, the mean of the squared residuals produced in regressing changes in log earnings, log wages, or log hours worked on the family characteristic controls and year dummies described in the text and used throughout the paper.

educational groups. But if we disaggregate the consumption instability trends, we find a much larger effect on college graduates than on lower educational groups. Thus it does not appear that rising instability in earnings is driving the time-series pattern of consumption instability.

Are These Trends Spurious?

Given the lack of a causal link between rising variation in labor earnings and in consumption, a concern arises that one or both of these trends might be spurious. One possible source of a spurious change in the variation of consumption over time is change in family composition. But we include a detailed set of compositional controls in our regression and also limit our sample to families with male heads. If we further restrict the sample to heads with no change in marital status over the sample period, the results are similar: the magnitude of the rise in variation is smaller for both earnings and consumption (roughly, a 50 percent rise in both earnings and food consumption instability, rather than the 75 percent rise shown above), but the increases over time are of the same relative size. Thus change in family composition does not appear to be driving these trends.

Another potential concern is that our findings arise from increased early retirement among the old or weakening attachment to the labor force among the young, either of which could produce increasingly correlated changes in consumption and income. However, the time patterns in consumption and earnings are basically unchanged if we restrict our sample to males aged twenty-five to fifty-four, rather than twenty to fifty-nine.

Another concern is that the trends in both earnings and consumption might be driven by increasing measurement error in the PSID. The approach that we use in our aggregate time-series analysis is unable to distinguish true transitory movements from movements due to measurement error. As Gottschalk and Moffitt point out, there is no reason to think that measurement error in the PSID grew systematically worse over this period.[64] The fraction of interviews that is carried out by phone, for example, has remained constant (roughly 90 percent) since 1975. There has been a shift to computer-aided interviewing, but this did not begin until 1991. Nor should attrition from the PSID explain this finding, since we are using the sample weights.

The PSID does impute income and consumption for some households, but the imputation rate is relatively low. Over the sample period, on average, fewer than 3 percent of observations are imputed for any of our key variables. If the imputation rate is changing over time it could bias our time trends, since the distribution of imputed observations is presumably more compressed than the true distribution. However, there is little noticeable time trend in the imputation rate, with the exception of the first three years of the food consumption data, when it was relatively high. And if we reestimate our time trends excluding imputed values, the results are substantively unchanged.

Furthermore, if the quality of PSID interview data were simply deteriorating over time, one would expect that all dollar quantities would

---

64. Gottschalk and Moffitt (1994).

similarly show a pattern of rising instability. But this is not the case. If we plot variation in the earnings of other family members, for example, we see a secular decline in instability.

Thus we conclude that the time-series increase in the variation of both earnings and consumption is real, but that these two upward trends are not causally related. This raises the question of why the variation in consumption has increased over time. One possibility is that we are obtaining a misleading picture from our subcomponents of consumption. Unfortunately, we cannot test this hypothesis in the CEX, since the majority of the rise in consumption variation occurred in the 1970s, before our sample begins. Over the 1980s, the rise in variation of total consumption in the CEX is similar to that of food plus housing consumption in the PSID, but this is not a strong test, since both series are basically flat in these years.

Another possibility is that the dynamic of consumption smoothing has changed over time. Perhaps because of some change in the underlying process that determines earnings variation (for example, more severe unemployment spells), families may be increasingly unable to smooth earnings variation. But if we allow our microdata estimates to vary with time, we find no evidence of a linear time trend in the ability of families to smooth consumption.[65]

Conclusions

Earnings variation is a persistent and growing feature of the U.S. labor market. The past twenty years have seen a 76 percent rise in the earnings variation of male household heads. Key to interpreting the welfare implications of this growing earnings instability is understanding the extent to which earnings variation is translated into household consumption. We present a variety of evidence on the ability of families to smooth earnings variation in order to address this issue.

Our primary conclusion is that families are well able to smooth variation in the earnings of household heads. Our instrumental variables

65. In the PSID, there is a larger effect of unemployment-induced variation in earnings in later years, as is apparent from comparison of the post-1984 coefficients in table 13 with those in table 9. But the difference in effects over time is not large enough to explain our consumption time trend. Nor is this finding robust to the CEX.

estimates suggest that only roughly 10 percent of the variation in the head's earnings is translated into nondurables consumption. There is a large effect on durables expenditures, but it is difficult to draw strong welfare inferences from this finding without a clean measure of the consumption flow from durables. Our results are robust across both year-to-year variation in earnings and large exogenous movements in earnings due to unemployment.

We also find that the government is an important source of insulation against earnings variation for family consumption, through both transfers and—more important—taxes. For year-to-year variation in earnings, roughly half of the smoothing that is done by families is through government taxes and transfers and roughly half is through saving and dissaving. For earnings loss due to unemployment, transfers from the government are somewhat larger, so that saving plays a smaller role.

But our findings for unemployment point out important heterogeneity in the ability of families to smooth earnings losses. Consumption expenditures, particularly on durables, are much more responsive to unemployment-induced earnings reductions for low-education or low-wealth groups than for high-education or high-wealth groups. These differentials emerge despite a redistributive government transfer system that replaces a higher share of the earnings loss due to unemployment for lower income groups. These findings are consistent with the skewed nature of wealth holding across educational groups: the median high school dropout head of household who becomes unemployed has gross liquid assets of only 5 percent of the income loss from unemployment, while the median college graduate head has liquid assets that are 124 percent of the income loss.

We also present aggregate evidence on the variation of earnings and of consumption and report four key findings. First, we confirm the conclusion of Gottschalk and Moffitt that there has been a secular rise in earnings instability.[66] Second, we highlight the countercyclical nature of this instability, which is entirely driven by instability in hours of work. Third, we find that this countercyclical earnings instability is not reflected in consumption, which is consistent with our contention that individuals can smooth variation in their hours of work.

But we conclude with a puzzle. Despite the finding that earnings

66. Gottschalk and Moffitt (1994).

variation is largely smoothed, we find that there are parallel secular rises in the instability of earnings and of consumption. This suggests that some time-series mechanism is increasing the instability of consumption independent of earnings variation. An important priority for future work is to confirm and sort out the source of this rising instability in consumption.

Our findings raise two important issues for policy design. First, the government plays an important consumption smoothing role through both the tax and transfer systems. In particular, our results suggest that discussions of tax policy should not ignore the role of taxation as a consumption smoothing mechanism. In addition, while the wealth holdings of the unemployed appear adequate to finance one-quarter of their earnings reduction due to unemployment, families would be hard pressed to finance a much larger share. This suggests that the role of smoothing through taxes and transfers is particularly important for the unemployed. Yet this is a static comparison, which does not account for the fact that the earnings loss from unemployment might respond to the underlying tax and transfer scheme. Future work incorporating the dynamics of unemployment into calculations such as these could usefully inform policymaking in this area.

Second, the redistribution inherent in government transfers for unemployment is not sufficient to overcome the differential ability of households to smooth consumption over unemployment spells. The dramatic skewness in asset holding suggests that programs such as unemployment insurance could increase their value as total consumption insurance through further progressivity in the determination of benefits. Such increased progressivity would, once again, have implications for unemployment behavior that must be counterbalanced against the gains in consumption smoothing. But unless the elasticity of unemployment with respect to benefits is larger at low income levels, more redistribution would increase insurance without reducing incentives.[67]

---

67. A more radical alternative would be the asset testing of unemployment insurance benefits, but this might have important negative implications for asset accumulation. Powers (1996) and Gruber and Yelowitz (1997) document that asset holding is very responsive to asset testing through the aid to families with dependent children and medicaid programs.

Comments
and Discussion

Robert A. Moffitt: This paper by Susan Dynarski and Jonathan Gruber is a follow-up to, and extension of, a series of papers that Gruber has produced over the past few years addressing afresh the consumption smoothing and insurance effects of several public transfer programs.[1] In his paper on the unemployment insurance program, Gruber, improving on earlier work by Daniel Hamermesh, empirically examines whether the program smoothes consumption between periods of employment and unemployment and finds considerable evidence for smoothing.[2] In a greater departure from prior work, he studies whether the aid to families with dependent children (AFDC) program smoothes the consumption of women who experience the "event" of becoming a single mother (unmarried or divorced).[3] While a social insurance view of the AFDC program is not, by itself, a new idea, Gruber is the first to conduct a serious empirical examination of the program from this perspective. Janet Currie and Gruber examine the effect of the medicaid program on the health of babies in low-income families and find that it significantly reduces adverse outcomes.[4] Although the medicaid program, like AFDC, is not a traditional social insurance program, and although this study does not address consumption smoothing, it does reflect a more general interest in measuring the potential benefits of public programs rather than their disincentive effects, which have dominated the empirical literature on those programs.

1. The author would like to thank Christopher Carroll for a helpful discussion.
2. Gruber (1997); Hamermesh (1982).
3. Gruber (1996a).
4. Currie and Gruber (1996).

285

Dynarski and Gruber go far beyond a concern with the insurance effects of narrowly defined public transfer programs to ask whether there are general sources of insurance against shocks to income. Taking as their departure point a series of empirical studies that test whether risk pooling effectively eliminates cross-sectional variation in consumption changes in response to idiosyncratic income shocks—in particular, a paper by Cochrane—they seek to quantify the degree to which such insurance is present, by estimating the fraction of individual income variation that is smoothed away.[5] The most notable finding of the paper is that almost all income variation is smoothed. Their maximum estimate of the effect of a $1 change in head's earnings on family consumption, including spending on durables, is only 24 cents, implying that 76 cents is smoothed away. This estimate seems very high, as compared with the conventional wisdom that there is relatively little insurance against income shocks in the United States. Dynarski and Gruber conclude that familes are "fairly well able to smooth consumption in the face of variation in the heads' earnings." Dynarski and Gruber also find that smoothing occurs more due to an insurance effect arising from tax and government transfer payments than due to private transfers and the earnings of other family members, although there is a significant role for saving as well.

The authors' study is, in part, motivated by the findings of Gottschalk and myself that the transitory variation of earnings in the United States increased during the 1980s. They are to be commended for taking seriously the comment of Dickens concerning the welfare implications of such an increase.[6] More work needs to be done on both the source of that increase in variation and its effects on the consumption and labor market behavior of individuals and families. Dynarski and Gruber infer from their own results that the welfare implications of the increase in variation are not as unfavorable as might be expected, because consumption smoothing and insurance seem to be so effective in response to such transitory shocks.

I address three issues. The first concerns the prima facie plausibility of the amount of smoothing that Dynarski and Gruber find; the second concerns the interpretation of the estimates from the viewpoint of the

---

5. Cochrane (1991).
6. Gottschalk and Moffitt (1994); Moffitt and Gottschalk (1995); Dickens (1994).

permanent income hypothesis literature and the relationship of the authors' approach to the approaches in that literature; and the third concerns the puzzle in the time-series trends in income and consumption variation that they uncover.

The plausibility of the authors' results on smoothing depends, in part, on whether they are interpreted as arising from intertemporal smoothing—self-insurance—or from consumption insurance across individuals. I am not so bold as to attempt any statement of consensus on what the large empirical literature on the permanent income hypothesis has already shown, given the wide dispersion of estimates illustrated by Browning and Annamaria Lusardi.[7] However, it is fair to say that the conventional view is that there are relatively few opportunities for income insurance in the United States. For example, most negative earnings shocks are not compensated for by the unemployment insurance program, because they do not result in unemployment but are instead declines in earnings due to a change in jobs or the bad fortunes of a worker's employer. On average, the percent of income loss compensated by unemployment insurance equals the product of the fraction of income variation due to unemployment variation (that is, due to inflows and outflows from unemployment) and the replacement rate of the unemployment insurance program. My guess is that, at most, 10 percent of the variation of the year-to-year change in individual earnings is due to inflows and outflows from unemployment; and, if the replacement rate of the program is 0.50, as it is conventionally taken to be, this implies that smoothing of only 5 percent can arise from this source. Food stamps may be an important source of compensating income, but the participation rate in the program has never been more than 10 percent and has averaged closer to 8 percent over its history.[8] Yet Dynarski and Gruber find that as much as 12 percent of earnings variation, averaged over the entire population, is compensated by changes in government transfers (see table 8).

The authors find the tax system to be of greater importance for consumption smoothing; they find that as much as 35 percent of earnings variation is compensated by changes in tax burdens, implying that the average marginal tax rate in the United States is 0.35.[9] While such

7. See Browning and Lusardi (1996, table 5.1).
8. U.S. House of Representatives, Committee on Ways and Means (1996, p. 874).
9. In the PSID, the source of this estimate, taxes are calculated rather than actually

a rate could conceivably have occurred over the 1970s, and is consistent with some other calculations over that period, it is difficult to believe that the average marginal federal income tax rate today—averaged over the entire population—is so high, given the expansion of the Earned Income Tax Credit, the increase in the zero-tax threshold, and reductions in marginal rates embodied in the Tax Reform Act of 1986. It would have been helpful if Dynarski and Gruber had estimated separate replacement rates over time, for the increase in the transitory variation that Gottschalk and I find occurred primarily in the 1980s, when tax rates were lower. In addition, current policy should be based on current replacement rates, not historic ones.

Turning to the consistency of the authors' approach with that in the permanent income hypothesis literature, a major difference of this study is the emphasis on insurance and risk pooling. The authors are aware that considerable care is needed to separate insurance and risk-pooling effects from intertemporal mechanisms for consumption smoothing. A particularly clear discussion of the distinction is provided by Cochrane, who emphasizes that insurance is entirely a static—or cross-sectional—concept concerning interpersonal resource flows, holding aggregate output constant, whereas intertemporal smoothing, in theory, is an individual-specific mechanism for using saving and borrowing to smooth consumption flows over time (over a long enough time period, one could conceivably examine intertemporal smoothing on an individual-by-individual basis, without conducting any cross-sectional comparisons).[10] Dynarski and Gruber concede that it is difficult to separate consumption smoothing effects arising from insurance from the effects arising from intertemporal considerations, such as those suggested by the permanent income hypothesis literature, a point which has considerable importance. Ultimately, they decide to examine the effects of consumption smoothing from any source, and to take the simple approach of regressing contemporaneous consumption on contemporaneous earnings—though in first differences—as a type of reduced-form analysis that yields a coefficient reflecting smoothing in general.

A major difficulty with this position is that the specification that they assume is not a meaningful reduced form, in the usual sense. The

---

observed, which probably biases this coefficient upward. The estimate of 26 percent from the CEX may be more accurate.

10. Cochrane (1991).

authors mean to imply that their estimated coefficient is some average of smoothing from insurance and from intertemporal mechanisms, but their specification is inconsistent with those used in the permanent income hypothesis literature for measuring the latter; it is not measuring the same thing. In fact, the authors' equation 1 is most closely akin not to the permanent income hypothesis, but to the traditional Keynesian consumption function relating current income to current consumption.

The permanent income hypothesis literature is large.[11] In my reading, that literature provides at least five lessons for the Dynarski-Gruber study. The first is that a single, period-to-period change in income may contain a permanent shock arising from the presence of a random walk component in income. In the micro-level literature on earnings dynamics, Thomas MaCurdy, Abowd and Card, and Gottschalk and I all find evidence—also from the PSID—for a random walk in individual earnings in the United States.[12] To some extent, Dynarski and Gruber might welcome this source of bias because it would lead to a coefficient on earnings (ΔY) that is too large, whereas their study finds the coefficient to be smaller than expected. However, they instead seem to wish to interpret their coefficient as reflecting the effects of changes in permanent as well as transitory earnings, for they devote one section of their study to instrumenting actual earnings with hours worked (assumed to be transitory) and the hourly wage rate (assumed to be permanent). Leaving aside the issues of whether fluctuations in the wage rate can be taken as permanent—a position for which there is no obvious evidence—or fluctuations in hours of work can be taken to be transitory (what about permanent changes in health and work capacity?)—this section suggests that they take their estimates as partly reflecting the effects of permanent income on consumption. If so, that effect is not what is referred to as smoothing in the permanent income hypothesis literature, which is very explicit in interpreting smoothing as a response to unanticipated and transitory changes in income.

A second lesson relates to the possible presence of serial correlation in individual income or earnings. The major studies of the permanent income hypothesis—for example, Marjorie Flavin's work using aggre-

11. See Deaton (1992b) and Browning and Lusardi (1996).
12. MaCurdy (1982); Abowd and Card (1989); Moffitt and Gottschalk (1995).

gate data and Hall and Mishkin's using micro-level data—have gone to some pains to model the earnings or income process, assuming either autoregressive structures (as does Flavin), a combination of autoregressive and moving-average specifications (as do Hall and Mishkin), or these and a random walk as well.[13] Also, the three micro-level studies already referred to, which examine the earnings process but not consumption, find autoregressive structures of either order one or order two plus a moving-average component of order one in individual earnings. For this reason, most studies of the permanent income hypothesis include some form of lagged ΔY to guarantee that the contemporaneous ΔY is measuring unexpected shocks. Because Dynarski and Gruber do not include such lags, it is possible that their coefficient is, in part, picking up the effects of lagged shocks. A leading possibility, for example, is that consumption has been adjusted at some point in the past and that current consumption appears not to change in response to current changes in income because the adjustment has already taken place. More generally, current consumption should not respond to expected changes in income, but only to unexpected shocks; this is one of the key points of the permanent income hypothesis literature.

A third lesson is the more general point that it is, ultimately, difficult to avoid the need to model the dynamics of the earnings process in one way or another in order to isolate the components of income change that are permanent or transitory, or those that are expected or unexpected. Although making that distinction can be quite difficult and can be sensitive to specification, as the authors argue, in its absence the coefficient on the contemporaneous change in income is virtually impossible to interpret and, as already noted, is very far from corresponding to the effect of smoothing as that term is ordinarily used.

A fourth lesson from the permanent income hypothesis literature concerns the importance of measurement error in earnings, an issue examined at some length by Dynarski and Gruber. However, the instruments that they use for last year's earnings—their key regressor— are last year's hours of work and the current hourly wage rate at the

---

13. Flavin (1981); Hall and Mishkin (1982). An additional issue is that Dynarski and Gruber examine the effect of the earnings of the head—rather than family earnings— on family consumption, so that if the earnings of other family members are experiencing movements correlated with those of the head, the authors' estimated coefficient proxies some unknown change in family earnings.

time of the survey. The authors argue that because these three variables come from different questions on the survey, they are independent and free of correlated measurement error. Unfortunately, this is not sufficient to guarantee the absence of such correlation. For example, if the respondents in the survey are trying to be even halfway internally consistent—and let us hope that they are, in general!—then last year's earnings should be arithmetically a function of last year's hours of work, and measurement error in the latter should generate measurement error in the former. The contemporaneous wage rate is a stronger variable, because it is separated by a period of time from that covered by the earnings question, but how much of the measurement error is eliminated by this separation depends largely on the source of that error. For example, a respondent's omission of casual or informal earnings or of income from a second job (which should be reported but may not be) is likely to be made both last year and currently.

A fifth lesson concerns the importance of precautionary—buffer-stock—saving, which has been the focus of much of the recent research on the permanent income hypothesis. For example, Christopher Carroll finds in a simulation study that a simple model of buffer-stock saving can generate marginal propensities to consume out of transitory income that are in line with the empirical literature.[14] Taking Dynarski and Gruber's estimates at face value, the portion of income smoothed by saving might arise from this source. Yet the interpretation is very different if this is a major source of the smoothing that Dynarski and Gruber find, because it has significant welfare implications. For example, if precautionary saving rises with the variation of transitory income, there is a welfare loss associated with that change that is missed by the examination of consumption smoothing.

This brings me to my final remark, concerning the puzzle posed by the data showing an increase in consumption variation over time, which, if the cross-sectional smoothing result is true, should not have occurred in response to the increase in transitory income variation. The authors' figures are intriguing, and they are to be credited for being the first to show time trends in consumption variation matched up with those for income. Dynarski and Gruber argue that the two trends may not be causally related, but an alternative explanation is that the cross-

14. Carroll (1997, p. 28).

sectional smoothing coefficient found in their microdata analysis is a mixture of permanent and transitory consumption responses of various kinds, and that the mixture has changed over time. Put differently, it suggests that the structure of the relationship that the authors estimate may have changed over time, a hypothesis which could readily be examined with their model. In addition, their finding that the growth in consumption variation was greater in the 1970s than in the 1980s, exactly the reverse of the timing of the growth of variation in earnings, might be traceable to an increase in precautionary saving in the 1980s. There is much additional work to be done to explore this interesting set of issues.

Gary Burtless: The proposition examined in this paper would astonish most noneconomists. Susan Dynarski and Jonathan Gruber take seriously the idea that families can insure completely against variability in the earnings of their principal breadwinners. According to the full insurance hypothesis, individual consumption should not vary in response to idiosyncratic shocks in that individual's wealth or earnings. The existence of a variety of risk-sharing institutions and arrangements permits individuals and their families to smooth consumption fully in the face of individual-specific fluctuations in earnings. These arrangements allow consumption to remain constant, even when the breadwinner's wages take a nose dive.

While most noneconomists will be skeptical of this theory, many economists find it attractive. At least a few find the evidence for it persuasive.[1] The basic idea is similar to, although not quite the same as, that behind the permanent income—or life-cycle consumption—hypothesis. According to that theory, far-sighted workers rationally plan consumption over a full lifetime. In doing so, they take account of the likely path of their labor earnings as they age and prudently accumulate savings in anticipation of their retirement. Any transitory deviations in earned income will be smoothed by additions to or subtractions from household savings. Changes in the flow of earnings that are expected to be permanent will cause breadwinners to recalibrate their lifetime consumption plans in order to stay within their lifetime budget constraints.

---

1. See, for example, Mace (1991) and Cochrane (1991).

The full insurance hypothesis goes beyond the permanent income model in one important respect. It assumes that workers and their families smooth consumption in the face of *all* idiosyncratic fluctuations in income, even those that are expected to be permanent. The permanent income model makes a clear distinction between unanticipated changes in flows of income that can be expected to last and changes that are only temporary. An unexpected income improvement that is permanent, such as an earnings gain associated with a promotion, will have a much bigger impact on the worker's consumption than an improvement that is only temporary, such as a one-time bonus for outstanding job performance. According to the full insurance hypothesis, however, neither of these kinds of earnings changes should affect the flow of consumption, so long as they are idiosyncratic to the individual earner.[2] Individual consumption should only be affected if the income fluctuation reflects an economywide change.

In estimating the permanent income model, the trick is to distinguish between changes that are thought to be temporary and those that are expected to be permanent. Making this distinction is not easy for the typical consumer; making it accurately is impossible for the econometrician. Economists have invested great ingenuity in plausibly separating out transitory and permanent income changes in order to estimate their different effects. In the full insurance model, it is not necessary to make this distinction, but the statistician must instead distinguish between income changes that are idiosyncratic to the individual and those that reflect permanent economywide movements.

Dynarski and Gruber emphasize another distinction between the full insurance and permanent income models. They suggest that the latter relies on self-insurance against earnings fluctuations (through saving and borrowing), whereas the former also considers interpersonal transfers, for example, across extended families and through social insurance. This will come as a surprise to many economists who have worked within the permanent income—or life-cycle consumption—framework. Martin Feldstein argues strongly for a version of the life-cycle model in which anticipated social security retirement benefits fully or partially offset private retirement saving. Hubbard, Skinner, and Zeldes offer a version in which, for a sizable minority of households, asset-tested

2. This follows from the model as presented in Mace (1991) and Cochrane (1991).

transfer programs erode the incentive to save.[3] In these life-cycle models, choices about the level and timing of household saving are made in light of incentives created by the social insurance and public assistance systems. The observed pattern of wealth accumulation is a predictable consequence of the design of those systems. Workers accumulate too little private wealth to finance their own retirement because they anticipate receiving social security pensions. Workers with low lifetime earnings accumulate proportionately less precautionary savings than workers with high wages because unemployment insurance and means-tested transfer programs offer them better protection when their earnings decline than is available to high-income workers. Table 12 offers indirect support for this theory. Workers with low educational attainment (and low expected earnings) have less net worth or liquid assets in relation to typical earnings loss due to unemployment than do workers with greater educational attainment.

The authors take the full consumption insurance model seriously, but they do not take it literally. They play down the importance of statistically rejecting the implications of full consumption insurance. With a large enough and good enough data set, the hypothesis that consumption is invariant to idiosyncratic movements in the earnings of the principal breadwinner would certainly be rejected. The authors focus instead on the more interesting question of how far actual consumption deviates from its predicted path under full insurance, and they closely examine the mechanisms that permit consumption to remain much more stable than earnings.

The paper offers a good introduction to the subject of consumption smoothing. It treats several interesting aspects of the issue in ingenious ways. Its conclusions rely on evidence drawn from two data sets rather than one, as is usual. This difference is particularly important. Poor data is the Achilles's heel of research in this area. Few data sets offer reliable measures of consumer income, and almost none provides good information about consumption. Dynarski and Gruber note that between 15 and 30 percent of the cross-sectional variation in earnings in the PSID is due to measurement error. Between 20 and 25 percent of the variance in the first difference of earnings in the CPS is apparently due to measurement error. It seems inevitable that measurement error in

---

3. Feldstein (1974); Hubbard, Skinner, and Zeldes (1994).

income will bias most studies toward a finding of full consumption smoothing, unless respondents' errors in reporting consumption are correlated with their errors in reporting income. Using two data sets rather than one does not eliminate this source of bias, but it assures us that the findings are not due to idiosyncratic measurement problems in a single data source.

It is natural to ask whether the authors confirm or reject the hypothesis of full consumption insurance. If they reject the model, how far does the actual path of consumption deviate from its predicted path under full consumption smoothing? My interpretation of the paper is that they reject it, but do not think deviations from full smoothing are particularly large, except in special circumstances. Their basic results (in tables 2–4) imply that families do not succeed in smoothing consumption fully. In both their PSID and their CEX samples, and under both the OLS and IV specifications, the authors statistically reject the hypothesis of full consumption insurance.

Whether the practical difference between actual consumption smoothing and full smoothing is large or small depends on the statistical specification that one favors. The OLS estimates imply much lower responsiveness of consumption to earnings changes than do the IV estimates. Although the authors appear to favor the latter, there is no clear explanation for the large differences between the results under the two specifications.

Assuming that the IV estimates are more accurate, how should one interpret the findings? The authors state in their introduction and again in their conclusion that families are "well able" to smooth consumption in the face of fluctuations in the earnings of the male breadwinner. They report that the average estimated elasticity of food consumption with respect to male earnings ranges between 0.142 (in the CEX) and 0.205 (in the PSID). The average elasticity of total consumption is 0.240, and that of nondurables consumption is 0.110. It is important to consider one's benchmark in assessing whether these deviations from full consumption smoothing are large or small. In comparison with the change in gross male earnings, these changes in consumption seem modest.

But male earnings represent only part of household income. If male earnings account for 70 percent of household income, a 1 percent reduction in male earnings will represent a loss of just 0.7 percent of family income (assuming other sources of family income remain unchanged). This means that a 1 percent reduction in family income (caused by a 1.4 percent reduction in male earnings) reduces food consumption by between 0.2 and 0.3 percent, reduces total consumption by 0.34 percent, and reduces nondurables consumption by 0.16 percent. In addition, earned income is taxed under a progressive schedule. Thus a 1 percent change in gross earnings causes less than a 1 percent change in after-tax income from employment. For example, if the average tax on earned income is 15 percent, while the marginal tax is 30 percent, a 1 percent rise in gross earned income will increase net earnings by just 0.82 percent. Stated another way, gross earnings must increase by 1.21 percent to produce a 1 percent gain in net earned income. By implication, a 1 percent increase in *net* family income (produced by a 1.7 percent increase in *gross* male earnings) will boost food consumption by between 0.25 percent and 0.35 percent, will increase total consumption by 0.42 percent, and will raise nondurables consumption by 0.19 percent.

These estimates of the implied elasticity of consumption with respect to net family income are not intended to be exact. Exact calculations require more information than is provided in the paper. Rather, they show that the reported elasticities may understate the responsiveness of household consumption to changes in after-tax family income. In a naive model of household consumption, spending in each period is financed entirely out of income received in the period. Actual consumption does not come close to following this model; but neither does it come close to following the full consumption insurance model. This suggests to me that the welfare loss associated with increased earnings variability is sizable.

Results in the paper suggest that a large part of consumption smoothing is attributable to changes in government transfers and tax payments, and much of the remainder may be the result of changes in household saving. It is interesting to consider how consumption smoothing would be affected if government transfers or taxes were reduced. If consumers are rational and far-sighted, they will off-set the loss of government insurance by increasing their accumulation of savings. Whether they will boost saving enough to fully offset the loss of government insurance is an empirical question. Government insurance for prime-age men has declined over the past two decades. The fraction of new job losers who collect unemployment insurance benefits dropped by about 20 percent between 1980 and 1985. Also, the after-tax value of these benefits fell when compensation payments, which were once tax free, became fully taxable between 1978 and 1987. Marginal income tax rates were reduced, particularly for high-wage earners, as a result of changes to the tax law passed in 1981 and 1986. On the one hand, the reductions in unemployment compensation and marginal tax rates has meant that changes in gross male earnings are more fully reflected by equivalent changes in net family incomes. On the other hand, male earnings have become a less important component of family income as wives' earnings have become more important.

Near the end of the paper, Dynarski and Gruber present evidence that both variation in male earnings and variation in family consumption have increased over time. They find these parallel increases puzzling. The increase in consumption variation is much larger than can be accounted for by the increase in the variation of male earnings, in light of the fact that families are largely successful in smoothing the variation in the earnings of the male breadwinner. The parallel increases in consumption and in earnings variation suggest that families are less successful in smoothing consumption than was the case in the 1970s. Not only is earnings variation greater than it once was, but some source of consumption insurance that was available to families in the 1970s is weaker than it once was.

General discussion: Ben Bernanke reinforced a point made by both discussants, that the paper does not distinguish sharply between smoothing and insurance as explanations for the observed insensitivity of consumption to income changes. He suggested that it would have been useful to estimate directly the response of individuals' consumption to aggregate income and test whether that response is significantly greater than their response to idiosyncratic changes in their own income, as it should be with full insurance. Robert Hall added that the appropriate benchmark for testing the insurance model is the response implied by a simple permanent income model, rather than zero. A larger response than that implied by the permanent income model would suggest a failure such as liquidity constraints, while a smaller response would suggest a role for interfamily transfers. Hall also agreed with the discussants that it was difficult to interpret the results without making a better distinction between transitory and permanent shocks. Gruber responded that the paper did not fully test the permanent income hypothesis, because such a test requires a full specification of transitory and permanent shocks, which depends crucially on what procedure is used to distinguish these shocks. He observed that while the equations being estimated should be interpreted as reduced-form equations, the procedures used were consistent with some common identification assumptions. One such assumption is that age and education affect permanent income; the variation remaining after conditioning on these is labeled transitory. Since the regressions in the paper include most of these variables on the right-hand side, these effects should be captured. Another common identifying assumptions is that all mean-reverting shocks are transitory. But transitory shocks may largely reflect measurement error, which the paper handles by the use of instrumental variables.

Robert Shiller questioned the implicit assumption that the relevant horizon for smoothing or insurance was one year. Conceptually, one can argue that the relevant horizon for insurance is an individual's lifetime, although, with just twenty-two years of PSID samples and thirteen from the CEX, the data for testing a model with such assumptions is not available. He also observed that the limited response of consumption to annual changes may reflect, in part, the difficulty of adjusting consumption rather than insurance. Having children in private schools or owning an expensive house are consumption decisions that cannot be quickly changed. The results may simply indicate that habits and consumption commitments are important.

John Abowd doubted that the two measures of earnings used in the paper actually have independent measurement errors. He suggested other ways to investigate the importance of measurement error in the PSID and CEX, such as looking at the within-quarter variation in the CEX and cross-year variation in the PSID. Lawrence Katz suggested it might be useful to concentrate on specific groups that would be expected to have quite different resources for smoothing the effects of income variation, such as college graduates and high school dropouts. Gruber replied that they had explored differences between some groups. They were baffled by the finding that the highest educational group, whose earnings variability had risen least, had the greatest increase in consumption variability. But other comparisons were more in line with expectations: those in the top quartile of the wealth distribution smoothed the effect of becoming unemployed much more than those in the lowest quartile.

George Borjas cautioned against drawing policy conclusions from the estimated importance of government programs in smoothing shocks. In the absence of such programs, either the wage structure or the saving behavior of individuals might be quite different. Katz said that the paper had changed his view of which government programs are most important in helping people to smooth income shocks. While unemployment insurance and welfare help in smoothing transitory shocks, longer-term programs, such as the Earned Income Tax Credit, are needed to help the less educated workers who have taken the largest permanent earnings losses in the past twenty years. Hall speculated that the paper's finding of a change in the character of consumption and earnings dynamics could be explained by a trend away from short unemployment spells toward longer spells as a result of displacement. The recent Bureau of Labor Statistics survey shows that displacement has remained at very high levels following the 1990 recession. Since the consequences of permanent job loss have been estimated at 1.2 years of earnings, this may explain the change in the response of consumption.

References

Abowd, John M., and David Card. 1989. "On the Covariance Structure of Earnings and Hours Changes." *Econometrica* 57(2): 411–45.

Altonji, Joseph G., and Aloysius Siow. 1987. "Testing the Response of Consumption to Income Changes with (Noisy) Panel Data." *Quarterly Journal of Economics* 102(2): 293–328.

Altug, Sumru, and Robert A. Miller. 1990. "Household Choices in Equilibrium." *Econometrica* 58(3): 543–70.

Attanasio, Orazio, and Steven J. Davis. 1996. "Relative Wage Movements and the Distribution of Consumption." *Journal of Political Economy* 104(6): 1227–62.

Barro, Robert J., and Chaipat Sahasakul. 1986. "Average Marginal Tax Rates from Social Security and the Individual Income Tax." *Journal of Business* 59(4, part 1): 555–66.

Blank, Rebecca M., and David E. Card. 1991. "Recent Trends in Insured and Uninsured Employment: Is There an Explanation?" *Quarterly Journal of Economics* 106(4): 1157–89.

Bound, John, and Alan B. Krueger. 1991. "The Extent of Measurement Error in Longitudinal Earnings Data: Do Two Wrongs Make a Right?" *Journal of Labor Economics* 9(1): 1–24.

Browning, Martin, and Thomas Crossley. 1996. "Unemployment Insurance Benefit Levels and Consumption Changes." Unpublished paper. McMaster University.

Browning, Martin, and Annamaria Lusardi. 1996. "Household Saving: Micro Theories and Micro Facts." *Journal of Economic Literature* 34(4): 1797–855.

Burgess, Paul L., and others. 1981. "Changes in Spending Patterns Following Unemployment." Unemployment Insurance Occasional Paper 81–3. Washington: Unemployment Insurance Service.

Carroll, Christopher D. 1997. "Buffer-Stock Saving and the Life Cycle/ Permanent Income Hypothesis." *Quarterly Journal of Economics* 112(1): 1–55.

Cochrane, John H. 1991. "A Simple Test of Consumption Insurance." *Journal of Political Economy* 99(5): 957–76.

Cox, Donald. 1987. "Motives for Private Income Transfers." *Journal of Political Economy* 95(3): 508–46.

Currie, Janet, and Jonathan Gruber. 1996. "Saving Babies: The Efficacy and Cost of Recent Changes in the Medicaid Eligibility of Pregnant Women." *Journal of Political Economy* 104(6): 1263–96.

Cutler, David M., and Lawrence F. Katz. 1991. "Macroeconomic Performance and the Disadvantaged." *BPEA, 2:1991*, 1–61.

Deaton, Angus. 1992a. "Saving and Income Smoothing in Côte d'Ivoire." *Journal of African Economics* 1(1): 1–24.

———. 1992b. *Understanding Consumption*. Oxford: Clarendon.

Dickens, William T. 1994. "Comment." *BPEA, 2:1994*, 262–67.

Duncan, Greg J., and Daniel H. Hill. 1985. "An Investigation of the Extent and Consequences of Measurement Error in Labor-economic Survey Data." *Journal of Labor Economics* 3(4): 508–32.

Dynarski, Mark, and Steven M. Sheffrin. 1987. "Consumption and Unemployment." *Quarterly Jourrnal of Economics* 102(2): 411–28.

Farber, Henry S., and Robert Gibbons. 1996. "Learning and Wage Dynamics." *Quarterly Journal of Economics* 111(4): 1007–47.

Feldstein, Martin S. 1974. "Social Security, Induced Retirement, and Aggregate Capital Accumulation." *Journal of Political Economy* 82(5): 905–26.

Flavin, Marjorie A. 1981. "The Adjustment of Consumption to Changing Expectations about Future Income." *Journal of Political Economy* 89(5): 974–1009.

Friedman, Milton. 1957. *A Theory of the Consumption Function*. Princeton University Press.

Garcia, René, Annamaria Lusardi, and Serena Ng. 1997. "Excess Sensitivity and Asymmetries in Consumption: An Empirical Investigation." *Journal of Money, Credit, and Banking* 29(2): 154–76.

Garner, Thesia I. 1993. "Consumer Expenditures and Inequality: An Analysis Based on Decomposition of the Gini Coefficient." *Review of Economics and Statistics* 75(1): 134–38.

Gertler, Paul, and Jonathan Gruber. 1997. "Insuring Consumption Against Illness." Unpublished paper. Massachusetts Institute of Technology (April).

Gottschalk, Peter, and Robert Moffitt. 1994. "The Growth of Earnings Instability in the U.S. Labor Market." *BPEA, 2:1994*, 217–54.

Gruber, Jonathan. 1996a. "Cash Welfare as a Consumption Smoothing Mechanism for Single Mothers." Working Paper 5738. Cambridge, Mass.: National Bureau of Economic Research (September).

———. 1996b. "The Wealth of the Unemployed: Levels, Distribution, and Utilization." Unpublished paper. Massachusetts Institute of Technology (September).

———. 1997. "The Consumption Smoothing Benefits of Unemployment Insurance." *American Economic Review* 87(1): 192–205.

Gruber, Jonathan, and Julie Berry Cullen. 1996. "Spousal Labor Supply As Insurance: Does Unemployment Insurance Crowd Out the Added Worker Effect?" Working Paper 5608. Cambridge, Mass.: National Bureau of Economic Research (June).

Gruber, Jonathan, and Aaron Yelowitz. 1997. "Public Health Insurance and

Private Savings.'' Unpublished paper. Massachusetts Institute of Technology (April).

Hall, Robert E., and Frederic S. Mishkin. 1982. "The Sensitivity of Consumption to Transitory Income: Estimates from Panel Data on Households." *Econometrica* 50(2): 461–81.

Hamermesh, Daniel. 1982. "Social Insurance and Consumption: An Empirical Enquiry." *American Economic Review* 72 (1): 101–13.

Hayashi, Fumio. 1985. "The Effect of Liquidity Constraints on Consumption: A Cross-Sectional Analysis." *Quarterly Journal of Economics* 100(1): 183–206.

Hayashi, Fumio, Joseph Altonji, and Laurence Kotlikoff. 1996. "Risk-Sharing Between and Within Families." *Econometrica* 64(2): 261–94.

Hubbard, R. Glenn, Jonathan Skinner, and Stephen P. Zeldes. 1994. "Expanding the Life-Cycle Model: Precautionary Saving and Public Policy." *American Economic Review, Papers and Proceedings* 84(2): 174–79.

———. 1995. "Precautionary Saving and Social Insurance." *Journal of Political Economy* 103(2): 360–99.

Juhn, Chinhui, and Kevin M. Murphy. 1997. "Wage Inequality and Family Labor Supply." *Journal of Labor Economics* 15(1, part 1): 72–97.

Karoly, Lynn A., and Gary Burtless. 1995. "Demographic Change, Rising Earnings Inequality, and the Distribution of Personal Well-Being, 1959–1989." *Demography* 32(3): 379–405.

Lusardi, Annamaria. 1996. "Permanent Income, Current Income, and Consumption: Evidence from Two Panel Data Sets." *Journal of Business and Economic Statistics* 14(1): 81–90.

MaCurdy, Thomas. 1982. "The Use of Time Series Processes to Model the Error Structure of Earnings in a Longitudinal Data Analysis." *Journal of Econometrics* 18(1): 83–114.

Mace, Barbara J. 1991. "Full Insurance in the Presence of Aggregate Uncertainty." *Journal of Political Economy* 99(5): 928–56.

Mariger, Randall P., and Kathryn Shaw. 1993. "Unanticipated Aggregate Disturbances and Tests of the Life-Cycle Consumption Model Using Panel Data." *Review of Economics and Statistics* 75(1): 48–56.

Moffitt, Robert, and Peter Gottschalk. 1993. "Trends in Covariance Structure of Earnings in the United States: 1969–1987." Unpublished paper. University of Wisconsin (April).

———. 1995. "Trends in the Autocovariance Structure of Earnings, 1967–1987." Unpublished paper. Johns Hopkins University.

Morduch, Jonathan. 1995. "Income Smoothing and Consumption Smoothing." *Journal of Economic Perspectives* 9(3): 103–14.

Nelson, Julie A. 1994. "On Testing for Full Insurance Using Consumer Expenditure Survey Data: Comment.'' *Journal of Political Economy* 102(2): 384–94.

Paxson, Christina H. 1992. ''Using Weather Variability to Estimate the Response of Savings to Transitory Income in Thailand.'' *American Economic Review* 82(1): 15–33.

Powers, Elizabeth. 1996. ''Does Means-Testing Welfare Discourage Saving? Evidence from the National Longitudinal Survey of Women.'' Unpublished paper. Federal Reserve Bank of Cleveland.

Slesnick, Daniel T. 1992. ''Gaining Ground: Poverty in the Postwar United States.'' *Journal of Political Economy* 101(1): 1–38

Townsend, Robert M. 1994. ''Risk and Insurance in Village India.'' *Econometrica* 62(3): 539–91.

———. 1995. ''Consumption Insurance: An Evaluation of Risk-Bearing Systems in Low-Income Economies.'' *Journal of Economic Perspectives* 9(3): 83–102.

U.S. House of Representatives. Committee on Ways and Means. 1996. *Background Material and Data on Programs within the Jurisdiction of the Committee on Ways and Means: 1996 Green Book*. WMCP 104–14, 104 Cong., 2 sess. Government Printing Office.

Varian, Hal. 1980. ''Redistributive Taxation as Social Insurance.'' *Journal of Public Economics* 14(1): 49–68.

Zeldes, Stephen P. 1989. ''Consumption and Liquidity Constraints: An Empirical Investigation.'' *Journal of Political Economy* 97(2): 305–46.

BRENT R. MOULTON
Bureau of Labor Statistics

KARIN E. MOSES
Bureau of Labor Statistics

Addressing the Quality Change Issue in the Consumer Price Index

THE FINAL REPORT of the Advisory Commission to Study the Consumer Price Index (CPI) represents the most influential critique of the CPI in decades.[1] This report, in conjunction with a number of other reviews of CPI bias, has focused the attention of policymakers and economists on the limitations of price index numbers, in particular, and of other measures of economic activity, more generally.[2] The commission's estimate of overall bias in the CPI is 1.1 percent per year, of which 0.4 percent is attributed to the failure of the fixed weight index to account for consumer substitution as relative prices change, 0.1 percent is attributed to failure to account for discount stores and other innovations in retailing, and 0.6 percent is attributed to inadequate measurement of improvements in quality and of new goods. In contrast to the commission's estimates of substitution bias, which have been relatively uncon-

The authors thank Katharine Abraham, Barry Bosworth, Kenneth Dalton, Claire Gallagher, John Greenless, Zvi Griliches, Charles Hulten, Patrick Jackman, Paul Liegey, Jeffrey Madrick, Marshall Reinsdorf, David Richardson, Kenneth Stewart, Jack Triplett, and Marybeth Tschetter for comments on an earlier draft. Thanks also to Bill Cook, Royce Buzzell, Cristine Jackson, Keith Waehrer, and Joseph Chelena for help in locating data. The opinions expressed in this paper are those of the authors and do not represent an official policy of the Bureau of Labor Statistics or the views of other BLS staff.

1. See U.S. Senate, Committee on Finance (1996). The members of the advisory commission were Michael J. Boskin (chair), Ellen R. Dulberger, Robert J. Gordon, Zvi Griliches, and Dale Jorgenson.

2. Other recent reviews of CPI bias include Baker (1996), Congressional Budget Office (1994), Diewert (1996), Klumpner (1996), Lebow, Roberts, and Stockton (1994), Moulton (1996), Shapiro and Wilcox (1996), U.S. Senate, Committee on Finance (1995), and Wynne and Sigalla (1994).

troversial, the estimates of quality and new goods bias have been criticized by several economists.[3]

There are two general categories of quality errors: failure to detect a change in quality and failure to make the appropriate adjustment for a change that has been detected. The new products bias can also be considered in two forms: failure to include new products in the sample without long lags and failure to include the consumer surplus generated by a new product.[4] In contrast to the quality bias, which can, in principle, go in either direction, the new product bias is theoretically known to be an upward bias (although it may be offset to some extent by the downward bias that occurs when a product disappears).

Many discussions of quality bias have begun with the premise that much quality change goes undetected, that such quality change is predominantly improvement, and that the result is an upward bias of the index. We concur with Jack Triplett that this is of doubtful validity as a general proposition, although it may hold true in specific cases.[5] The data collectors and commodity analysts at the Bureau of Labor Statistics

3. For example, Abraham (1997a, 1997b), Baker (1997), Bosworth (1997), Hulten (1997), and Triplett (1997) suggest that the quality bias estimate may be too large, whereas Diewert (1997, p. 95) describes the commission's estimates as "perhaps a bit conservative."

4. These are not actually separate biases, since the consumer surplus generated by the new good should, in principle, include the value generated by any price decline early in the product's life cycle. The case of the new good may be treated in the theory of the cost of living index by using the reservation price of the item; that is, the price at which the consumer's demand for the item is just equal to zero. (See Hicks, 1940; Rothbarth, 1941; and Hausman, 1997.) Let P_{tn} represent the price of the new good after introduction and $P_{t-1,n}^{*}$ represent its reservation price before introduction. Let the prices of the other $n - 1$ goods be $p_t = (P_{t1}, P_{t2}, \ldots, P_{t,n-1})$, and similarly for p_{t-1}. The constant-utility cost of living index, I, evaluated at the period t level of expenditures is

$$I(p_t, P_{tn}, p_{t-1}, P_{t-1,n}^{*}, u_t) = y_t / e(p_{t-1}, P_{t-1,n}^{*}, u_t),$$

where the expenditure function gives the minimum amount of expenditures, $y = e(p, P_n, u_t)$, needed to achieve the level of utility, u_t, that arises from the corresponding indirect utility function. The cost of living index is related to the equivalent variation, EV, by

$$I(p_t, P_{tn}, p_{t-1}, P_{t-1,n}^{*}, u_t) = y_t / (y_t - EV).$$

The equivalent variation is negative in this case, because the introduction of the new good is a welfare improvement. If the share of the new item is small relative to total spending, the equivalent variation will closely approximate the ordinary Marshallian consumer surplus. The bias from omitting the new good in the index calculation is approximately equal to the ratio of consumer surplus to total expenditure.

5. Triplett (1971).

(BLS) work from checklists that are designed to provide detailed product descriptions—for example, they include model numbers. In general, quality changes are well detected for most commodities. The possibility of undetected quality change is presumably more important for services, especially complex, knowledge-based services, such as professional medical services and higher education. Quality adjustments are made for services, but gradual improvements or declines in quality may not be adequately detected by data collectors. For example, the CPI checklist for local telephone services provides for adjustments for special features such as call waiting, but not for gradual improvement in sound quality or gradual deterioration in the convenience of scheduling installation appointments. Changes in general retail services, such as the installation of credit card scanners at checkout counters or the disappearance of helpful salespersons, are generally not captured by the BLS checklists either.

In many cases, the CPI methods do detect quality change. Then the issue of quality error revolves, in part, around the adequacy or inadequacy of the quality adjustment methods used in constructing the index. It appears to be widely held that quality improvements are pervasive and that the BLS does very little to account for them. An alternative point of view, however, is that the BLS methods of adjusting for quality change already attribute a great deal of price change to quality improvement, so that any remaining quality bias could be either negative or positive. Consequently there is an important need, which we attempt to address in this paper, to develop useful measures of the amount of quality adjustment now applied by the BLS in constructing the CPI. However, such measures do not, by themselves, provide direct evidence of quality bias in either direction. The best test of quality bias is careful analysis of the data, item by item. Only a few item categories have received such detailed analysis. The advisory commission has reviewed available research and, in some cases, conducted its own analysis.

The problems associated with bringing new goods into the CPI samples have been highlighted in many recent studies.[6] Over the past two decades, the BLS has adopted procedures to bring new products into the sample more promptly, beginning in 1978 with a shift to probability-

---

6. For example, Berndt, Griliches, and Rosett (1993) demonstrate the importance of keeping the sample up to date for prescription drugs, and Hausman (1997) examines the potential consequences of the long lag in including cellular telephone service.

based methods for selecting samples. Subsequently, the regular reselection of samples (currently, at five-year intervals) was introduced. From 1999, the BLS will have the capability to schedule sample rotations more frequently for selected categories of items, which should further enhance its capacity to capture new goods.

In this paper, we first review the discussion of quality and new goods in the commission's report. We then review BLS procedures for making quality adjustments in the CPI and discuss how these might give rise to quality change bias. Finally, we examine the quality adjustments that occur when CPI sample items change or need to be replaced because of sample attrition. We provide estimates of the quality and price changes, both implicit and explicit, associated with those replacements.

Quality and New Products in the Advisory Commission's Report

In its analysis of the quality change and new products biases, the advisory commission classifies the CPI into twenty-seven major categories of items and gives a separate bias estimate for each. This is the first systematic analysis, category by category, of quality bias in the CPI, and it is a noteworthy accomplishment. In general, the commission's approach to the problem of producing an overall assessment of bias seems sensible, and this type of structure will likely prove to be useful in the future. Hereafter, following the commission, we sometimes use the term "bias" without distinguishing between new product and quality change bias.

The advisory commission's estimates of bias by category are shown in table 1. Of the twenty-seven categories, the commission assigns eight a quality bias of zero: fuels, housekeeping supplies, housekeeping services, other private transportation, public transportation, health insurance, entertainment services, and tobacco. It assigns each of the remaining nineteen categories an estimated bias that is positive; that is, the commission concludes that price change is overstated because quality change is understated. For six of these nineteen categories (appliances, including electronic; prescription drugs; professional medical services; hospital and related services; entertainment commodities; and personal care) the advisory commission reviewed existing studies of bias in the price trends of specific items to draw inferences about likely

**Table 1. Advisory Commission's Estimates of Quality and
New Product Bias in the CPI**
Percent

Item category	Share in CPI	Estimated bias at annual rate[a]
Food and beverages		
Total	17.33	. . .
Food at home, other than produce	8.54	0.30
Fresh fruits and vegetables	1.34	0.60
Food away from home	5.89	0.30
Alcoholic beverages	1.57	0.15
Housing		
Total	41.35	. . .
Shelter	28.29	0.25
Fuels	3.79	0.00
Other utilities, including telephone	3.22	1.00
Appliances, including electronic	0.81	5.60
Other housefurnishings	2.64	0.30
Housekeeping supplies	1.12	0.00
Housekeeping services	1.48	0.00
Apparel and upkeep		
Total	5.52	1.00
Transportation		
Total	16.95	. . .
New vehicles	5.03	0.59
Used cars	1.34	0.59
Motor fuel	2.91	0.25
Other private transportation	6.15	0.00
Public transportation	1.52	0.00
Medical Care		
Total	7.36	. . .
Prescription drugs	0.89	2.00
Nonprescription drugs and medical supplies	0.39	1.00
Professional medical services	3.47	3.00
Hospital and related services	2.26	3.00
Health insurance	0.36	0.00
Entertainment		
Total	4.37	. . .
Commodities	1.98	1.20
Services	2.39	0.00
Other goods and services		
Total	7.12	. . .
Tobacco, smoking products	1.61	0.00
Personal care	1.17	0.90
Personal and educational expenses	4.34	0.20
Total	100.00	0.61

Source: U.S. Senate, Committee on Finance (1996, table 2).
a. Biases are estimated over different periods, all of which end in 1996.

bias for related but unstudied items within the category. These six categories are important in the commission's accounting for quality bias, since the appliance category and the three medical care components together account for roughly half of the estimated quality and new products bias.

For another four of the nineteen categories with positive estimated bias (shelter, apparel and upkeep, new vehicles, and used cars), the commission either conducted original research or presented detailed, back-of-the-envelope calculations of the sources of bias.

For the other nine of the nineteen categories (food at home, other than produce; fresh fruits and vegetables; food away from home; alcoholic beverages; other utilities, including telephone; other house furnishings; motor fuel; nonprescription drugs and medical supplies; and personal and educational expenses), in the absence of empirical research or data, the commission simply describes potential sources of bias and gives an estimate of the magnitude of bias. The following assessment of bias due to new products and variety for the category of food at home is typical:

> There is little if any published evidence on the food category, other than [Jerry] Hausman's . . . attempt to establish the value for the introduction of a new variety of breakfast cereal. Perhaps more important than new varieties of packaged goods has been a wave of technological improvements that has greatly increased the variety of fresh fruits and vegetables available in the typical supermarket during the winter months, and a trend toward more services provided in supermarkets, eliminating the need to travel to small specialty shops, especially fresh fish markets and deli counters preparing fresh-cooked food. How much would a consumer pay to have the privilege of choosing from the variety of items available in today's supermarket instead of being constrained to the much more limited variety available 30 years ago? A conservative estimate of the value of extra variety and convenience might be 10 percent for food consumed at home other than produce, 20 percent for produce where the increased variety in winter (as well as summer farmers' markets) has been so notable, and 5 percent for alcoholic beverages where imported beer, microbreweries, and a greatly improved distribution of imported wines from all over the world have improved the standard of living.[7]

In several places, the report characterizes the commission's specific

7. U.S. Senate, Committee on Finance (1996, p. 28).

estimates of bias as "conservative," but it generally is not clear why this is believed to be so. The commission's standard, the cost of living index, is defined as a function of consumer preferences, so it is reasonable to ask whose preferences are being described and how they are assessed. Economists bring to the measurement of preferences expertise in the use of methods for drawing inferences about preferences from market data on observed consumer choices. It is therefore appropriate to ask what sort of analytical method or framework commission members used to determine their point estimates of bias.

We consider the commission's bias estimates for selected item categories, sometimes presenting simple back-of-the-envelope calculations based on available, though often incomplete, data. We find that most of our calculations imply significantly smaller estimates of bias than those of the advisory commission. We do not intend that these estimates be interpreted as a complete response to the commission's estimates of bias and are aware that our conclusions could be altered by further analysis. We view them, rather, as starting points for analysis; their advantage over some of the commission's estimates is that they are based on data or assumptions about consumer behavior—such as demand elasticities—that, at least in principle, can be tested.

Fresh Fruits and Vegetables

The quote cited above indicates that the advisory commission attributes a bias of 20 percent over the period 1967–96 due to increased seasonal availability and variety. It is reasonable to think that, to the extent that consumers value the increased seasonal availability of produce, they will consume more of it. Our analytical framework is to consider the "November strawberry" to be a new good, distinct from the "June strawberry," and measure the consumer surplus associated with the new good.[8]

Among the various methods that have been proposed for incorporating new goods in a cost of living index, Jerry Hausman's suggestion of calculating the consumer surplus from a linearized demand is particularly easy to apply to back-of-the-envelope calculations.[9] Hausman's

8. See Diewert (1983).
9. Hausman (1997) refers to his linearized method as a "lower bound" on the consumer surplus, but it is unclear to us whether the conditions for the method to be a lower bound—that is, a convex demand curve—necessarily hold in all cases.

linearized method implies that the percentage bias of the price index from failure to incorporate the consumer surplus from a new good, n, is approximately

$$(1) \qquad\qquad \text{bias} = -0.5 \times S_n/\delta_n,$$

where S_n is the percentage expenditure share of the new good after introduction and δ_n is its price elasticity of demand. Thus the calculation of consumer surplus and bias can be inferred from information on the expenditure share, which is often readily available, and the elasticity of demand, which can be estimated or inferred from elasticity estimates for similar goods.[10]

New varieties or seasonal availability of fresh fruits and vegetables face many substitutes, not only from other fresh produce, but also from frozen fruits and vegetables. We assume a value of -1.0 for δ_n. Under these assumptions, equation 1 implies that the increased consumption of new seasonal items and varieties as a share of current fruit and vegetable consumption would need to be quite large—about 40 percent of 1996 expenditures—to be consistent with the advisory commission's estimated index bias of 20 percent.[11]

Table 2 presents U.S. Department of Agriculture data on changes in per capita consumption of fresh fruit from 1975 to 1995. The change in consumption is shown, somewhat unconventionally, as a percentage of 1995 consumption, because the shares in equation 1 refer to current period consumption. As the advisory commission observes, per capita consumption of many fruits has indeed increased substantially over this period: in particular, limes, cranberries, grapes, kiwifruit, mangos, papayas, and strawberries. Despite these large increases, however, most of these items continue to represent a small percentage of overall fruit consumption, so that the total increase in per capita fruit consumption as a share of 1995 consumption (measured in pounds) is only 14 percent. The largest absolute increase in consumption of fruit is that for bananas. We are confident that there was no important improvement in seasonal availability of bananas and that there were only minor

10. If a new variety fully replaces an old one, the consumer surplus calculation should deduct the lost surplus of the disappearing variety from the surplus gained from the new variety.

11. Ideally, one would examine monthly consumption data to isolate seasonal changes in consumption, but such data do not appear to be available.

Table 2. Per Capita Consumption of Fresh Fruits, by Type, 1975–95
Units as indicated

| | Pounds per capita | | | Change, 1975–95 | |
| | | | | As percentage of | In |
Type of fruit	1975	1985	1995	1995 consumption	pounds
Citrus					
Oranges and temples	15.9	11.6	12.3	− 29.6	− 3.6
Tangerines and tangelos	2.6	1.5	2.0	− 27.9	− 0.6
Lemons	2.0	2.3	2.9	32.1	0.9
Limes	0.2	0.6	1.2	81.7	1.0
Grapefruit	8.4	5.5	6.0	− 38.4	− 2.3
Total	29.0	21.5	24.4	− 18.9	− 4.6
Noncitrus					
Apples	19.5	17.3	18.9	− 3.0	− 0.6
Apricots	0.1	0.2	0.1	20.0	0.0
Avocados	1.2	1.8	1.4	10.9	0.2
Bananas	17.6	23.5	27.4	35.6	9.8
Cherries	0.7	0.4	0.2	− 187.5	− 0.5
Cranberries	0.1	0.1	0.3	53.3	0.2
Grapes	3.6	6.8	7.6	52.7	4.0
Kiwifruit	. . .	0.1	0.5	. . .	. . .
Mangos	0.2	0.4	1.1	85.8	1.0
Peaches and nectarines	5.0	5.5	5.4	8.5	0.5
Pears	2.7	2.8	3.4	19.4	0.7
Pineapples	1.0	1.5	1.9	46.6	0.9
Papayas	0.2	0.2	0.4	56.8	0.2
Plums and prunes	1.3	1.4	0.9	− 41.5	− 0.4
Strawberries	1.8	3.0	3.8	52.1	2.0
Total	55.1	65.1	73.5	25.0	18.4
Total	84.1	86.5	97.9	14.1	13.8

Source: U.S. Department of Agriculture (1996a, table F-29).

increases in consumption of new varieties of bananas over this period. In addition, consumption of apples did not change significantly and consumption of oranges decreased. We wonder whether the use of apples for baking may have decreased during this period, masking a possible increase in the consumption of raw apples.

We do not attempt to calculate the overall bias using equation 1 because doing so would require average price or expenditure data for each of the detailed categories, which we have not been able to assemble. As mentioned above, under Hausman's model and our earlier assumptions, to be consistent with the commission's bias estimate consumption of new varieties and seasonal items would need to increase by about 40 percent over thirty years, which annualizes to 25 percent over the twenty years for which we have data. If increased consumption of seasonal varieties was relatively unimportant for apples, bananas, and citrus fruits, which, according to the Consumer Expenditure Survey (CEX) of the Bureau of Labor Statistics, together represent 61 percent of dollar expenditures on fresh fruit in 1995, it would be difficult for increased seasonal consumption of the other fruits to produce an estimated bias as large as the commission proposes.

Table 3 shows changes in consumption of vegetables from 1972 to 1995. Unlike the data for fruit, the data for vegetables show important increases in consumption for many items and thus appear, at first glance, to be consistent with the advisory commission's estimates of bias. Under the assumptions stated above, our consumer surplus calculations indicate that for the commission's estimate to hold, the growth in consumption over thirty years would need to be about 40 percent of current consumption, which annualizes to 29 percent over the twenty-three years for which we have consumption data. This is, in fact, very close to the overall increase over this period: 27 percent. We are skeptical, however, about concluding that the increase in consumption derives entirely from improved seasonal availability. A BLS food specialist, Bill Cook, has suggested that the increase in seasonal availability of fresh vegetables mostly occurred before 1985, as evidenced by a 1984 internal BLS study showing that 91 percent of the CPI price quotes for the "other fresh vegetables" category were by then available year round.[12] Table 3 shows, however, that almost half of the increase in consumption of fresh vegetables occurred after 1985. Part of the increase appears to have been driven by shifts in preferences, perhaps as a response to improved knowledge about the health benefits of fresh vegetables.

Shelter

Because rent and owners' equivalent rent have a very large weight in the index, any quality bias in shelter is particularly important. Con-

12. Internal memorandum from William L. Weber to Dan Ginsburg, U.S. Bureau of Labor Statistics, May 25, 1984.

Table 3. Per Capita Consumption of Fresh Vegetables, by Type, 1972–95

Units as indicated

| | Pounds per capita | | | Change, 1972–95 | |
| | | | | As percentage of | In |
Type of vegetable	1972	1985	1995	1995 consumption	pounds
Asparagus	0.4	0.5	0.6	33.3	0.2
Broccoli	0.7	2.6	3.2	78.1	2.5
Carrots	6.5	6.5	10.1	35.6	3.6
Cauliflower	0.8	1.8	1.3	38.5	0.5
Celery	7.1	6.9	6.4	− 10.9	− 0.7
Sweet corn	7.8	6.4	7.8	0.0	0.0
Bell peppers	2.4	3.8	5.8	58.6	3.4
Onions	10.7	13.6	17.7	39.5	7.0
Tomatoes	12.1	14.9	16.6	27.1	4.5
Cabbage	8.5	8.8	9.1	6.6	0.6
Spinach	0.3	0.7	0.6	50.0	0.3
Cucumbers	3.0	4.4	5.6	46.4	2.6
Artichokes	0.4	0.7	0.4	0.0	0.0
Snap beans	1.5	1.3	1.6	6.3	0.1
Eggplant	0.4	0.5	0.4	0.0	0.0
Escarole or endive	0.6	0.4	0.2	− 200.0	− 0.4
Garlic	0.4	1.1	2.1	81.0	1.7
Lettuce					
Head	22.4	23.7	21.6	− 3.7	− 0.8
Leaf or romaine	. . .	3.3	6.0	. . .	. . .
Watermelon	12.3	13.5	15.9	22.6	3.6
Cantaloupe	7.0	8.5	9.9	29.3	2.9
Honeydews	1.0	2.1	2.4	58.3	1.4
All others	0.8	0.8	0.7	− 14.3	− 0.1
Total	107.1	126.8	146.0	26.6	38.9

Source: U.S. Department of Agriculture (1996b, table 14).

sequently the section on shelter is one of the most detailed in the advisory commission's report and includes many citations to data about changes that have occurred in the characteristics of housing. In our opinion, however, the commission's analysis of the data on shelter is misleading and its conclusions on bias are invalid.

The commission's reasoning is, essentially, as follows. Over the period 1976–93, the median rent increased about 1 percent per year faster than the CPI rent index. This fact might suggest that the quality adjustments embedded in the index are substantial. According to the advisory commission, however, these quality adjustments remain in-adequate because of a supposed dramatic increase in average apartment size: "From the evidence we have examined, we believe that 20 percent is a low-end estimate of the increase in the average size of apartments [between 1976 and 1993], which would support the conclusion that the average rent per square foot has increased no faster than the CPI."[13] In addition, the commission estimates that other improvements, including "appliances, central air conditioning, and improved bathroom plumbing, and other amenities," amount to 10 percent over the past forty years, giving a net upward bias of 0.25 percent per year. Several observers have pointed out that rents generally increase less than proportionally to apartment size, which implies that the advisory commission's proportional adjustment for apartment size overstates the increase in rents. A more fundamental problem, however, is that the commission's factual premise—that average apartment size increased by 20 percent from 1976 to 1993—is clearly wrong. Although data giving an exact measure of the growth in size of rental units since 1976 are not available, one careful examination of data from several sources concludes that the increase was probably about 6 percent; that is, the commission's estimate is too high by, roughly, a factor of three.[14] This estimate is based on the following evidence:

—The American Housing Survey, conducted by the Census Bureau, has published the median size of single detached and mobile home rental units since 1985. From 1985 to 1993, the median unit size increased by 2.2 percent, an average of less than 0.3 percent per year.[15]

—The Energy Department's Residential Energy Consumption Survey collected data on the average square feet of housing units over the period 1980–93. Although these data are based on smaller samples than the American Housing Survey, the trend is the same. The Energy Department data show a 3.5 percent increase in the average size of all rental units from 1980 to 1993; that is, about 0.3 percent per year.[16]

—In order for the average size of rental units to have increased as rapidly as the advisory commission claims, the average size of newly constructed apartments would need to be much larger than the average size of existing apartments. Data comparisons indicate that newly con-

13. U.S. Senate, Committee on Finance (1996, p. 30).

14. Moulton (1997).

15. U. S. Department of Commerce and U.S. Department of Housing and Urban Development (1985, 1993; table 2-3).

16. U.S. Energy Information Administration (1980, table 9; 1993, table 3.4).

structed apartments were not, in fact, much bigger than existing apartments over the period 1976–93.

After adjusting for the advisory commission's overstatement of the increase in apartment size and taking account of several other measurement issues, a small downward bias is more plausible than the upward bias claimed in the report.[17]

Appliances, including Electronic

The commission's estimate of bias for appliances—5.6 percent per year—is the largest of its estimates. It is also probably the best documented. A number of academic and government studies develop hedonic quality adjustment models and find upward quality bias for personal computers, television, video equipment, and other items in this category. Hedonic methods are already being applied in the Producer Price Index (PPI), for personal computers and peripherals. Matthew Shapiro and David Wilcox describe substitution bias as harvesting "low hanging fruit," pointing out that there are generally accepted methods for removing substitution bias.[18] We view the application of hedonic methods to the appliances category as harvesting the low hanging fruit of the quality bias problem, and the BLS is currently developing such methods and improved sampling of new products within this category.

Apparel and Upkeep

The advisory commission's estimates of bias for apparel and upkeep are based on a recent study by Robert Gordon that compares the CPI apparel indexes with indexes constructed from prices in the Sears catalog.[19] In addition to noting the obvious difference in data sources, we would point out an important methodological difference between the Gordon study and the CPI. By contrast with CPI methods, Gordon measures year-to-year price changes only for apparel items that remain identical from year to year. Many BLS studies find that price change tends to occur when new varieties or fashions are introduced.[20] Gor-

17. See Moulton (1997).
18. Shapiro and Wilcox (1997).
19. Gordon (1996).
20. See, for example, Triplett (1971), Armknecht (1984), Armknecht and Weyback (1989), Liegey (1993, 1994), and Reinsdorf, Liegey, and Stewart (1996).

don's method of analysis would exclude these price increases; in essence, it attributes any price increases associated with the introduction of new fashion lines entirely to quality improvement. In BLS terminology, the price changes would be "linked out." Empirical evidence that Gordon's study may link out too much price change is provided by the fact that his index for women's apparel, where fashion changes and implied item substitutions are most common, shows no increase from 1984 to 1993, whereas his indexes for men's, boys', and girls' apparel increase between 14 percent and 17.5 percent over the period.

Furthermore, the apparel and upkeep category seems to be particularly sensitive to an issue that may affect several of the commission's estimates of bias; because of their volatility, apparel prices may have been affected by so-called formula bias and lower-level substitution bias.[21] Part of the method that BLS adopted in 1995 and 1996 to correct the problem of formula bias has, for other reasons, been applied to many of the apparel indexes since 1989. The rate of growth of the apparel and upkeep component of the CPI has obviously been affected by these changes. In addition, simulations of possible lower level substitution bias using a geometric mean index formula indicate that apparel and upkeep may also be particularly affected by lower-level substitution bias.[22] It is unclear whether the advisory commission avoided double counting when sorting through these various sources of bias to produce its estimate of quality bias.[23]

New Vehicles

In the case of automobiles, the advisory commission makes one of its few methodological recommendations with respect to quality adjustment: it recommends that the BLS should price cars and other durables using a cost of services ("user cost" or "leasing equivalence") approach. This is an important recommendation that will require significant research to evaluate. However, the suggestion seems, in part, to be motivated by a misinterpretation of BLS quality adjustment procedures. The advisory commission report states that the CPI has not

21. The advisory commission emphasizes these two separate sources of bias (U.S. Senate, Committee on Finance (1996, sect. 4).
22. Moulton and Smedley (1995).
23. See Baker (1997).

taken into account "the increased service lifetime of the typical new car." [24] Although it is true that the CPI does not adjust directly for changes in the average service lifetime of automobiles, many adjustments have been made for improvements that are related to durability. Without a major, detailed study it is impossible to know whether the CPI adjustments related to durability fully account for the increased lifespan of the typical car, but to attribute the entire increase in automobile service life to unmeasured quality bias clearly involves some double counting.

Motor Fuel

For the motor fuel category, the advisory commission attributes "a small upward bias of 0.25 percent per year to the CPI for ignoring the convenience and time-saving contribution of automatic credit-card readers built into gasoline pumps." [25] Because the commission applies this estimate over a ten-year period, the estimate of the cumulative bias from this source amounts to 2.5 percent. [26] Our approach to measuring the consumer surplus created by pay-at-the-pump credit card technology is to attempt to value the saving in time. Suppose that paying at the pump saves two minutes per fill-up, and that the customer's time is valued at $18 per hour (average total compensation per hour for all workers in private industry was $17.49 in 1996). Then the value of paying at the pump is 60 cents per fill-up. Assuming that ten gallons are purchased, the quality bias for the customer who pays at the pump is 6 cents per gallon, or roughly 4.5 percent of the cost of a gallon of gasoline.

Since this service is of value only to the customers who use it, one must next determine the approximate percentage of gasoline purchasers

24. U.S. Senate, Committee on Finance (1996, p. 35).
25. U.S. Senate, Committee on Finance (1996, p. 36).
26. We also note that the report does not address possible unmeasured decline in retail services, such as the introduction of fees for providing air for tires at some service stations. In addition, the advisory commission incorrectly assumes that the CPI does not make quality adjustments for air pollution mandates and, agreeing with this supposed BLS practice, makes no bias adjustment for the mandates itself. Since BLS does, in fact, make cost-based adjustments for motor fuel pollution mandates, the commission presumably should have counted these as downward bias (see U.S. Bureau of Labor Statistics, "Quality Adjustment for Gasoline," *CPI Detailed Report*, January 1995, p. 8).

who use pay-at-the-pump technology. Although we have not found direct information on this percentage, the September 1996 issue of the trade journal *National Petroleum News* reports that 28 percent of the retail facilities operated by thirteen oil companies had installed pay-at-the-pump technology as of 1996.[27] Since many of the customers at these stations do not use credit cards, we attempt to find the percentage of gasoline customers who do so. We have not found published information, but an industry source has told us that roughly 35 percent of sales are made through credit cards.

A naive estimate of the proportion of sales using pay-at-the-pump technology would thus be 10 percent (28 percent × 35 percent). However, there are at least three reasons why this estimate is too low: first, pay-at-the-pump technology was doubtless first targeted at high-volume sites in areas with high credit card usage; second, the availability of the technology induces customers to make more use of credit cards; and third, the technology is spreading rapidly, so that even estimates published in September 1996 will understate current availability. Consequently we take 25 percent as our estimate of the percentage of customer sales made with pay-at-the-pump technology at the end of 1996. Under these assumptions, we calculate the cumulative index bias from neglecting the benefits of this technology as approximately 1.1 percent (4.5 percent × 25 percent), which is less than half of the advisory commission's estimate.

Medical Care

The advisory commission's estimate of bias in the medical care component of the index appears to have been largely based on just two recent empirical studies—one concerning the treatment of cataracts and the other concerning heart attacks—both of which identify large quality improvements that are missed in the calculation of the CPI.[28] Although there have been enormous improvements in medical technology over time, we are not convinced that these two examples should be considered representative of the unmeasured quality advances in the treatment of medical conditions in general.

27. "Pay-at-the-Pump Shows Solid Growth in '90s," *National Petroleum News*, September 1996, p. 22.

28. The two studies cited by the commission are Shapiro and Wilcox (1996) and Cutler and others (1996).

Without necessarily endorsing the advisory commission's estimate of bias, we agree that BLS methods are not likely to capture fully the quality improvements that have occurred in medical services. Adjustment for quality change in this component is the most challenging in the index. The BLS has recently taken steps to address some of the problems in measuring price change for medical care. In January 1995 it changed the method of pricing prescription drugs when generic alternatives become available to reflect the research of Zvi Griliches and Iain Cockburn.[29] For hospital services, in January 1997 the CPI adopted the practice, already used in the PPI, of pricing courses of treatment (as represented by bundles of services on selected patient bills) rather than individual medical inputs. These measures do not overcome the difficult measurement issues in these categories, but BLS is actively pursuing further research.

Cellular Telephone Service

The CPI does not currently include cellular telephone service in its sample—this item will be added to the market basket during the January 1998 update. Although the advisory commission's report is unclear as to the extent that the commission counts cellular phones in its estimate of bias for telephone service, a recent study by Hausman concludes that the bias from late introduction and uncounted consumer surplus is large.[30] His analysis overstates the magnitude of the bias, however, because it is based on data that include business use, which is not within the scope of the CPI.

The share of total *consumer* expenditure going to cellular telephone service in 1995, according to the Consumer Expenditure Survey, is 0.088 percent. Hausman's estimate of its price elasticity is -0.5. Since his data predominately represent business users and we think that consumers are more price sensitive than businesses, his elasticity estimate may be smaller than our ideal number. Nevertheless, applying the CEX expenditure share and his elasticity estimate to equation 1, we calculate the cumulative bias in the CPI from failure to include cellular telephones as 0.088 percent ($-0.5 \times 0.088 / -0.5$) through 1995. Applied over a

29. Griliches and Cockburn (1994).
30. Hausman (1997).

322   Brookings Papers on Economic Activity, 1:1997

five-year period, this represents a bias of a little less than 0.02 percent per year.

We would not say that 0.02 percent per year is a small number, nor that the delay in including cellular telephones is justified. To the contrary, in our experience, any bias that affects the "all items" index by 0.02 percent per year should be considered large. We do, however, think that showing that missing consumer surplus in one of the most important new products in recent years produces a bias of roughly this magnitude helps to explain why we consider many of the larger numbers that appear in the advisory commission's report implausible.

Summary

The above discussion does not cover all the components of bias, and we do not attempt to give our own estimate of quality bias. For two major components—medical care and appliances—we agree with the advisory commission that the evidence of upward bias due to quality and new goods is convincing. We also agree that new products contribute an upward bias to many components of the index, though we think that the commission and others have overstated the magnitude of this bias. However, there are many important components of the index—including shelter, apparel and upkeep, and new vehicles—for which we have not seen convincing evidence of upward bias and, in some circumstances, think it possible that the methods used by the BLS may overadjust for quality change.

In the case of appliances, the availability of substantial academic research together with the recently announced CPI budget initiative and research projects currently being conducted by BLS staff suggest that the quality biases can be corrected relatively soon.[31] As noted above, the BLS has also made improvements to the medical care indexes, but the quality adjustment problems in this component are difficult, and progress may come slowly.

CPI Methods for Addressing Quality Change

The methods for collecting data for the CPI were designed to identify and adjust for quality changes.[32] The BLS selects sample items by

31. On the CPI budget initiative, see Abraham (1997b).
32. New products are usually "linked" into the sample through the regular (cur-

probability methods, so that the items that are repriced each month are representative of consumer purchases. Each item is described in detail on a checklist, to ensure that identical items are compared for price while they remain in the sample. Each time the price data are collected, the data collector compares the item with the detailed description to see if any of the characteristics of the item have changed. If, during the monthly (or bimonthly) price collection, the exact sample item has become permanently unavailable at that outlet, the data collector selects a similar item as a replacement. This item replacement process is the focus of our analysis in the remainder of this paper.

After an item has been replaced, a BLS commodity analyst examines the descriptions of the old and new versions of the item to determine which quality adjustment procedure is to be applied. These methods were developed to be applied in an environment in which 80,000 sample prices are collected and processed each month, of which roughly 4 percent represent item replacements. These item replacements are much more important than may be suggested by the 4 percent monthly attrition rate, however. Approximately 30 percent of all sample items scheduled to remain in the sample for the full year (that is, not scheduled for regular sample rotation) need to be replaced at some time during the year. Detailed explanations of the various methods used by BLS to adjust for quality changes due to item replacements are available elsewhere; here, we give a heuristic description.[33]

COMPARABLE ITEMS. In some cases, the commodity analyst examines the differences between the two specifications and determines that the change has not resulted in a significant change in quality, so that the

---

rently, five-year) rotation of samples, although some new products may enter through the sample replacement procedures described below. Current CPI procedures do not generate a reduction in the cost of living from the consumer surplus attributable to new products.

33. Recent papers that give detailed descriptions of the methods currently used for quality adjustment include Armknecht, Lane, and Stewart (1997) and Reinsdorf, Liegey, and Stewart (1996).

The terminology used to describe the various methods of handling item substitutions is not standardized. We follow Armknecht and Weyback (1989). The advisory commission (U.S. Senate, Committee on Finance, 1996) and Gordon (1990) use different terminology: ''direct comparison'' instead of ''comparable,'' ''linking'' instead of ''overlap method,'' and ''deletion'' instead of ''link method;'' the commission's report omits the relatively new method of class-mean imputation.

Figure 1. Comparable Items

Price

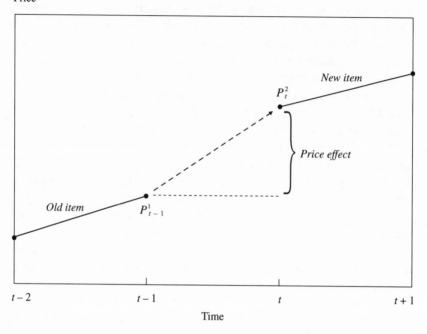

$t-2$ $t-1$ t $t+1$

Time

prices of the old and new versions can be directly compared. Let $P^1_{t-1,i}$ denote the price in the previous period ($t - 1$) of the old version (denoted by superscript 1) of item i, and P^2_{ti} denote the price in the current period (t) of its new version (superscript 2). As shown in figure 1, this method counts the entire price change, $P^2_{ti}/P^1_{t-1,i}$, as part of inflation; that is, no quality difference is attributed to the new version of the item. These comparable replacements would typically involve versions of an item that differ by minor changes in styling or other minor differences in characteristics that do not reflect quality.

OVERLAP METHOD. This method is used when prices of both the old and the new versions are available during an overlap period, so that the difference in price levels can be used as an estimate of the difference in quality. As shown in figure 2, the pure price change (or "price effect") before period t is measured by the price change of the old version, and the price change after period t is measured by the price change of the new version. It is relatively uncommon to have prices for

Figure 2. Overlap Method

Price

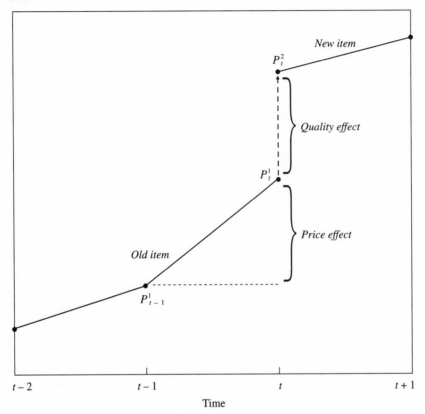

an item and its replacement during an overlap period, but an aggregate version of the overlap method is used when an entire CPI component sample is replaced during sample rotation. Both the old and new samples are collected during an overlap period, t, and the old sample is used to measure the price change from $t - 1$ to t, while the new sample is used to measure the price change from t to $t + 1$.

LINK METHOD. The disappearance of an item is typically not detected until the item is no longer available at the sample outlet, so prices of the old and new versions are not available concurrently. Consequently the overlap method cannot be used to estimate the portion of the price difference that is attributable to inflation and the portion that is attrib-

Figure 3. Link Method and Class-Mean Imputation

Price

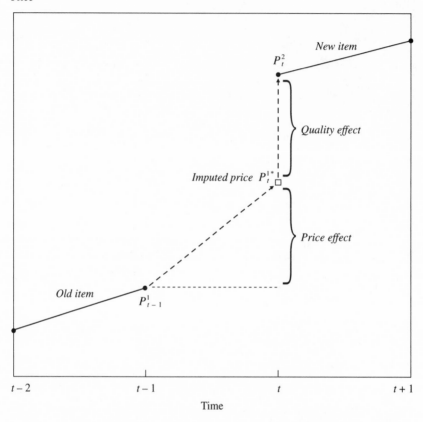

utable to quality change. Each item is part of a stratum of similar goods. When an item vanishes, the link method first calculates the rate of inflation for its stratum during that month, omitting the item from the calculation of price change. Suppose, for example, that the inflation rate for the other goods in the stratum is 2 percent, but that the replacement version of the item, when it appears, costs 5 percent more than the earlier version. As illustrated in figure 3, the link method effectively assumes that of that 5 percent, 2/5 is due to the overall rise in the price of goods and the other 3/5 is due to an improvement in quality. Note that the estimated quality change is essentially a residual in this calculation.

CLASS-MEAN IMPUTATION. This method was introduced to the CPI new cars index in 1989 and to other items in 1992.[34] Like the link method, class-mean imputation also imputes a price change and treats the quality change as a residual. In this case, however, the price change is imputed from a set of similar items that are classified as comparable replacements or are directly adjusted for quality change. This method is based on the assumption that the rate of inflation when a new model of an item replaces an earlier model is different from the inflation rate when the model does not change.

DIRECT QUALITY ADJUSTMENT. These methods are applied when there is information available with which to directly estimate the dollar value of the change in quality. Sometimes (in particular, in the cases of new and used cars and motor fuel) manufacturers provide information on the cost of the quality improvement. In other cases, the hedonic method is used to estimate the relationship between price and quality by regressing price on characteristics of the goods. The coefficients of these regressions are then used to infer the value of changes in characteristics of the goods in the sample. The CPI has used hedonic methods since 1988 for calculating the effects of depreciation and other housing characteristics on rent, and since 1991 for calculating quality changes in apparel. Figure 4 illustrates a direct quality adjustment, in which an adjustment is made to the period $t - 1$ price of the old item for the estimated value of the quality improvement embedded in the new item.

Potential Errors in Quality Adjustment

In cases when a change in characteristics is observed but the replacement is classified as comparable, it is possible that small, unmeasured quality changes are incorrectly attributed to price change. The advisory commission concludes that this leads to upward bias because "most goods tend to undergo steady improvement."[35] This conclusion does not necessarily follow from its premise, however, because replacements are not randomly classified as comparable. Suppose, for example, that the value of the relative change in quality that occurs with item replacement is uniformly distributed between -25 percent and 75 percent, and that all quality changes smaller than 25 percent are classified as

34. Armknecht, Lane, and Stewart (1997); Reinsdorf, Liegey, and Stewart (1996).
35. U.S. Senate, Committee on Finance (1996, p. 25).

Figure 4. Direct Quality Adjustment

Price

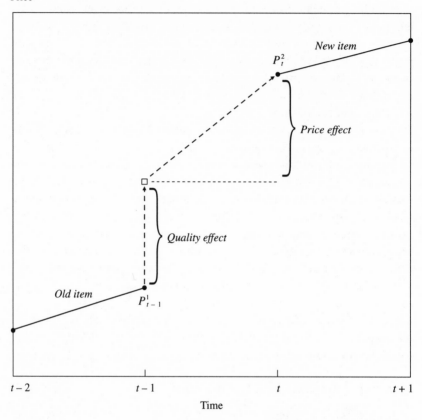

Time

comparable. In this case, the average bias of the comparable items is zero, even though the average quality change for all replacement items is 25 percent.

The advisory commission's report argues that "when a new model is introduced that is more expensive than an old model, but it gains market share, we can conclude that it was superior in quality to the old model by more than the differential in price between the two."[36] This statement suggests that the bias resulting from use of the link and overlap methods is necessarily upward. We agree with this reasoning

36. U.S. Senate, Committee on Finance (1996, p. 24).

in regard to major new goods and the most significant improvements in quality.[37]

The commission does not mention, however, that in many cases the increase in price exceeds the differential in quality, so that the link and overlap methods may result in downward bias. This is especially likely to occur when a model change involves a modest improvement in quality, perhaps combined with changes in fashion or style. Triplett describes this situation:

> During a period of rising prices, if a price change and a change in the varieties in retailers' stocks are both imminent, sellers at all levels are likely to try to arrange both changes to coincide, rather than putting them into effect separately. If this occurs, prices of unchanged varieties are not moving parallel to those of the new varieties encountered. Because price increases coincide with substitution, deletion of the price quotation misses some of the true price change. Thus, when prices are rising, this method of handling quality change tends to bias the index downward.[38]

Considerable BLS research, especially in the apparel and upkeep category, has found empirical evidence of such downward bias.[39]

Direct quality adjustments are also potentially subject to bias in either direction. On the one hand, adjustments based on manufacturers' estimates of cost may underadjust for quality if, as the advisory commission says, they miss "quality improvements achieved by those firms which supply better materials and inputs to producers of final goods."[40] Griliches, on the other hand, has suggested a potential bias in the opposite direction: "I am concerned that by basing such adjustments largely on data furnished by manufacturers and on 'producer costs' [the BLS] may wind up overestimating 'quality change,' accepting as 'improvements' expenditures which consumers may not interpret as such."[41] Well-specified hedonic models probably represent the most robust method currently used by BLS, but it is well known that errors

---

37. Studies of price change for computers have consistently found that hedonic methods result in greater price declines than matched model (that is, linking) methods; see, for example, Cole and others (1986) and Berndt, Griliches, and Rappaport (1995).

38. Triplett (1971, p. 185). Triplett (1990) presents a mathematical analysis of this case.

39. See Armknecht (1984), Armknecht and Weyback (1989), Liegey (1993, 1994), and Reinsdorf, Liegey, and Stewart (1996).

40. U.S. Senate, Committee on Finance (1996, p. 26).

41. Griliches (1971, p. 11).

in hedonic model specification can lead to errors of quality adjustment in either direction. We conclude that the sign of any quality bias is almost never known a priori, but must be determined empirically.

Decomposing Price and Quality Changes

The present study, modifying a methodology developed by Paul Armknecht, decomposes the relative price difference between old and new items for each item replacement during 1995 into a pure price change (that is, the part of the price difference that is counted as inflation in the CPI) and the implied quality change.[42] In this study, we analyze item replacements that take place in 171 strata of nonshelter items.[43]

Methods of Decomposing Quality Change

The CPI can be written as a weighted average of price ratios for the sample items:

$$(2) \qquad I_{t,t-1} = \sum_i W_{t-1,i} R_{t,t-1,i},$$

where $I_{t,t-1}$ is the relative change of the index from $t-1$ to t, $W_{t-1,i}$ is the weight of sample item i, which depends in a complicated way on the sampling and past price history of the item relative to other items, and $R_{t,t-1,i}$ is the relative price change of the sample item. In the case of a continuously priced item, the relative price change is simply the ratio of its price in period t to its price in period $t-1$; that is, $R_{t,t-1,i} = P_{ti}/P_{t-1,i}$. For a replacement item, the value of the price relative depends on the method used to adjust for quality. We decompose total price change as measured in the CPI into a price change derived

42. Armknecht (1984) applies the methodology to CPI item substitutions that occurred during 1983, and Armknecht and Weyback (1989) analyze item substitutions that occurred during 1984. Since this method is applied solely to quality changes arising from item substitutions, any changes in the average quality of items in the sample that occur for other reasons, such as sample replacement, are omitted.

43. We exclude twenty-three unpriced strata, four health insurance strata, rent, owners' equivalent rent, household insurance, postage, babysitting, care of invalids in the home, used cars, automobile finance charges, and sports vehicles.

from replacement items and a price change derived from continuously priced items:

$$(3) \qquad I_{t,t-1} = \sum_{\substack{\text{unchanged}\\\text{items}}} W_{t-1,i} \frac{P_{ti}}{P_{t-1,i}} + \sum_{\substack{\text{replacment}\\\text{items}}} W_{t-1,i} R_{t,t-1,i}.$$

In the case of replacement items, we define the total (unadjusted) relative price change between the old version (denoted by superscript 1) and the new version (superscript 2) of item i as $T_{t,t-1,i} = P_{ti}^2/P_{t-1,i}^1$. Then the portion of the total relative price change that is used in the CPI calculation is $R_{t,t-1,i}$, the "pure price relative," and the remaining portion is $A_{t,t-1,i}$, the quality adjustment:[44]

$$(4) \qquad T_{t,t-1,i} = R_{t,t-1,i} A_{t,t-1,i}.$$

Within the category of replacement items, we further decompose price changes by method of quality adjustment used. Finally, for each method of quality adjustment, we decompose the overall price difference between the old item and the new item into a price change component and a quality difference component.

COMPARABLE ITEMS. The pure price relative for comparable replacements and continuously priced items is the entire price change:

$$(5) \qquad R_{t,t-1,i} = T_{t,t-1,i} = P_{ti}^2/P_{t-1,i}^1.$$

The quality is assumed not to change in these cases.

OVERLAP METHOD. For noncomparable replacements with overlap prices (that is, prices in the same time period for both varieties of the item), the assumed quality ratio is the contemporaneous price differential between varieties and the price relative is the change in the price of the old variety:

$$(6) \qquad A_{t,t-1,i} = P_{ti}^2/P_{ti}^1,$$

$$(7) \qquad R_{t,t-1,i} = P_{ti}^1/P_{t-1,i}^1.$$

A common application of the overlap method in the CPI involves creating an artificial full price for a sale-priced item to avoid recording a

---

44. Equation 4 presents the multiplicative version of the decomposition. The additive version sets $A_{t,t-1,i}^* = T_{t,t-1,i} - R_{t,t-1,i}$, and defines the "pure price effect" as $R_{t,t-1,i} - 1$ and the "quality effect" as $A_{t,t-1,i}^*$.

large quality change when the sale- priced item is replaced by a full-priced item. Consequently the price effects appear to be surprisingly large. This artificial overlap, or "return from sale," method is currently being replaced by other methods.[45]

LINK METHOD AND CLASS-MEAN IMPUTATION. Under both of these methods, the implicit quality change is the differential between the price of the new variety and the imputed price of the old variety, $P_{ti}^{1}{*}$, and the pure price relative is the differential between the imputed price and the previous price of the old variety:

$$(8) \qquad\qquad A_{t,t-1,i} = P_{ti}^{2}/P_{ti}^{1}{*},$$

$$(9) \qquad\qquad R_{t,t-1,i} = P_{ti}^{1}{*}/P_{t-1,i}^{1}.$$

As described above, the two procedures differ in their methods of imputation.

DIRECT QUALITY ADJUSTMENT. Under these methods, the quality effect is the ratio of the measured value of the quality difference between the two varieties, $D_{t-1,i}$, to the price of the old item. The price effect is the differential between the price of the new variety and the price of the old variety, adjusted for the quality difference:

$$(10) \qquad\qquad A_{t,t-1,i} = 1 + (D_{t-1,i}/P_{t-1,i}^{1}),$$

$$(11) \qquad\qquad R_{t,t-1,i} = P_{ti}^{2}/(P_{t-1,i}^{1} + D_{t-1,i}).$$

Once the price effect and the quality effect for each priced item have been identified, the contribution to the total price change of the pure price changes resulting from each type of quality adjustment can be summed, using the same weights as in equations 2 and 3 for each type of replacement:

$$(12) \qquad\qquad \text{price effect} = \sum_{i} W_{t-1,i}(R_{t,t-1,i} - 1).$$

The sum of the price effects for each type of replacement and the price effect of unchanged items equals the change of the price index.

---

45. Return from sale processing is described by Armknecht and Weyback (1989, p. 114).

Aggregating Quality Adjustments

Aggregation of the quality adjustments to obtain an aggregate quality effect is complicated by two features of these data. First, because quality adjustment may be triggered by the attrition of items as well as changes in their characteristics, the measure of quality change must account for the effects of sample turnover as well as changes that are made to existing products. When an item is no longer available, the price collector attempts to select a similar replacement item; but when no similar item is available at the outlet, a dissimilar item may be selected—for example, the sample price of a piano lesson might be replaced by that of a violin lesson. This type of sample turnover can, in some cases, lead to quality adjustments that are very large, either up or down. Given the enormous variety of items priced by the CPI and the large number of item replacements, there is no simple way to define and screen out replacements that involve substantially dissimilar items. We attempt to eliminate all cases involving data errors or simple changes in units or quantities—for example, repackaging, such as the replacement of the price of a contract for ten piano lessons with one for twenty lessons—before aggregating the quality adjustments. Further effects of sample turnover may be alleviated by truncating some of the outlying quality adjustments.

A second issue affecting aggregation is the asymmetry (skewness) of the distribution of $A_{t,t-1,i}$. We expect the median of the distribution to be near one, but the distribution is bounded below at zero for downward quality adjustments and is unbounded for upward quality adjustments. This suggests that in estimating the "average," or central, tendency of the quality changes, it may be appropriate to aggregate using the logarithms of $A_{t,t-1,i}$. The theory for aggregating measures of quality change for individual items to an overall measure of quality change has not been fully worked out. We have identified some cases for which arithmetic aggregation as used in Laspeyres indexes may be appropriate—for example, when quantity consumed is not correlated with quality—and other cases for which logarithmic aggregation is most appropriate—for example, when quantity consumed declines in proportion to quality. The data that would be needed to test these alternative assumptions, however, are not readily available.

We have one important caveat. The present analysis is an attempt to provide some descriptive measures of the quality adjustments that occur due to item replacement, as part of the CPI data collection process. For several reasons, it would be inappropriate to interpret them as measuring the rate of improvement in the quality of goods and services in the economy. They will miss some quality changes that are captured in other phases of the CPI data collection process, in particular, those reflected in the regular sample rotations. Furthermore, the replacement item selected by the data collector may not be the same as the substitute item selected by the consumer in response to the change or disappearance of the original item. It is entirely possible that consumers systematically substitute higher or lower quality items than those selected by BLS data collectors.

We examine both an additive measure and a logarithmic measure of aggregate quality change. The additive version is exactly analogous to equation 12, using the additive quality adjustments defined above in note 44:

$$(13) \qquad \text{additive quality effect} = \sum_i W_{t-1,i} A^*_{t,t-1,i}.$$

Note that the sum of the price effect and the additive quality effect has a simple interpretation: it is the index change that would have been calculated if the unadjusted price relative, $T_{t,t-1,i}$, had been used in place of the pure price relative, $R_{t,t-1,i}$, in equation 3.

The logarithmic version is

$$(14) \qquad \text{logarithmic quality effect} = \sum_i W^g_i \ln A_{t,t-1,i},$$

where the weights are those that are appropriate for the geometric mean index form.[46] The logarithmic version treats upward quality adjustments symmetrically with equal proportionate downward quality adjustments, so, under certain assumptions, it may better reflect the "typical" quality change.

As mentioned earlier, outliers might largely be the result of sample turnover. To deal with this problem, we consider two truncation rules, both of which are symmetric around zero in the logarithm of the quality

---

46. In particular, the weights used for the geometric mean index are not proportional to $P_{t-1,i}$, in contrast to the additive "modified Laspeyres index" form that is currently used in the U.S. CPI. For details, see Moulton and Smedley (1995).

changes.[47] Method A removes from the calculation any $A_{t,t-1,i}$ greater than 5 or less than 0.2 (ln P_t/P_{t-1} = ±1.61). Method B is more stringent and removes any $A_{t,t-1,i}$ greater than 2 or less than 0.5 (ln P_t/P_{t-1} = ±0.69).

Rates of Item Replacement in 1983, 1984, and 1995

One can examine changes in BLS quality adjustment methods by looking at rates of various types of sample replacement methods. Table 4 compares the percentage of each type of item replacement in the period 1983–84, as studied by Armknecht and Donald Weyback, with the percentage in 1995.[48] There have been important changes. Although the total percentage of price quotes that were replacements in 1995 (3.9 percent) is about the same as during 1983–84, the percentage of item replacements declined within food and beverages, apparel and upkeep, entertainment, and other goods and services, and increased within medical care. The overall rate of replacement did not fall along with the components, because of a shift in sample composition away from food and beverages and toward apparel and upkeep.

The percentage of replacements classified as comparable, relative to all quotes, has increased substantially, from 1.7 percent in 1984 to 2.5 percent in 1995. That increase can probably be attributed, first, to major efforts to redesign checklists so that BLS field staff are more likely to select directly comparable replacement items; and second, to hedonic studies which have indicated that some item characteristics have little effect on prices, so that products with different levels of those characteristics can be treated as comparable in quality. These changes demonstrate, furthermore, that the use of hedonic regression analysis within the CPI program has had effects beyond the direct quality adjustments presented in the final column of table 4.

The use of the overlap and link price methods have both declined substantially over this period, since many replacement items that were formerly thought to require these methods are now either treated as comparable or adjusted using direct quality adjustment or class-mean

---

47. The distribution of the logarithm of quality changes is not centered exactly at zero, but is close enough to zero that the truncation is approximately symmetric in the logarithms.

48. Armknecht and Weyback (1989).

Table 4. Product Replacements, by Item Category and Replacement Method, 1983, 1984, and 1995

Percentage of all quotes in item category

Item category[a]	Year	Total	Replacement method				
			Comparable items	Overlap method	Link method	Class-mean imputation	Direct quality adjustment
All items studied	1983	3.85	1.56	0.23	1.74	. . .	0.32
	1984	3.95	1.70	0.23	1.71	. . .	0.30
	1995	3.90	2.54	0.05	0.57	0.32	0.41
Food and beverages	1983	1.81	0.52	0.04	1.25	. . .	0.00
	1984	1.93	0.52	0.08	1.33	. . .	0.00
	1995	1.63	0.84	0.02	0.73	0.00	0.03
Housing	1983	4.25	2.21	0.22	1.67	. . .	0.15
	1984	4.83	2.67	0.21	1.72	. . .	0.22
	1995	4.83	3.56	0.05	0.44	0.64	0.14
Apparel and upkeep	1983	17.34	7.15	2.69	7.46	. . .	0.03
	1984	17.59	7.80	2.43	7.27	. . .	0.09
	1995	11.10	8.50	0.20	0.24	1.10	1.06
Transportation	1983	6.72	3.13	0.06	1.35	. . .	2.18
	1984	5.80	3.02	0.07	0.96	. . .	1.74
	1995	6.69	3.60	0.00	0.27	0.76	2.05
Medical care	1983	2.22	0.65	0.03	0.91	. . .	0.64
	1984	2.19	0.80	0.03	0.99	. . .	0.38
	1995	3.91	2.33	0.08	0.80	0.00	0.69
Entertainment	1983	4.61	1.92	0.23	2.28	. . .	0.18
	1984	6.08	2.85	0.26	2.70	. . .	0.27
	1995	3.47	2.05	0.03	0.45	0.61	0.33
Other goods and services	1983	3.30	1.44	0.06	1.64	. . .	0.17
	1984	3.99	1.94	0.08	1.56	. . .	0.40
	1995	2.01	1.23	0.05	0.43	0.09	0.20

Source: 1983 data are from Armknecht (1984); 1984 data are from Armknecht and Weyback (1989); and 1995 data are authors' calculations from unpublished CPI data.

a. The following price quotes are excluded from the studies: under housing, residential rent and homeowners' equivalent rent (all years) and household insurance, postage, babysitting, and care of invalids (1995); under transportation, used cars (all years) and automobile finance charges (1995); under medical care, health insurance (all years); and under entertainment, magazines, periodicals, and books (1983, 1984) and sports vehicles, including bicycles (1995).

imputation. The newer class-mean imputation method is now used nearly as much as direct quality adjustment. Within the apparel and upkeep category, the use of direct quality adjustment has increased greatly.

Effects of Item Replacements on Price Change in the CPI

Table 5 shows the contribution of each type of item replacement to the overall price change during 1995. The change of the CPI for the items in this table was 2.16 percent. Of this, 1.09 percent is attributable to replacement items and 1.07 percent is attributable to continuously priced items—that is, items for which monthly or bimonthly price comparisons involve no replacement. The total price change due to replacement items is further decomposed by type of replacement: 0.60 percent comes from comparable items, 0.10 percent from items that were adjusted for quality change using the overlap method, 0.02 percent from items adjusted using the link method, 0.18 percent from items adjusted by class-mean imputation, and 0.19 percent from items treated with direct quality adjustment.

Many readers of an earlier draft of this paper were surprised by the large aggregate price effect attributable to the 4 percent of price quotes that are replacement items. The main reasons for this appear to be the tendency of manufacturers to increase prices coincident with introduction of new models or fashions and the tendency of retailers to discount prices before dropping an item.[49] The return of the discount price of a disappearing item to the full price of the replacement item is included in the price effect.

Table 5 also provides evidence of changes in BLS procedures for handling replacements, especially in the apparel and upkeep and new

---

49. For example, 28 percent of the overall price change in 1995 is attributable to comparable items, although these account for only 2.5 percent of all collected prices. Such a large price effect would seem to imply an unrealistically large price change for each comparable replacement. The resolution of this puzzle lies in the fact that prices are collected monthly or bimonthly, so that after the replacement has occurred, the same item will be reclassified as an unchanged item. Suppose, for example, that the prices of new cars are collected monthly, that a replacement occurs once during the year for each car in the sample, that the price of each car increases by 3 percent when the replacement occurs, and that no other price changes occur during the year. One of twelve monthly price collections involves an item replacement, so replacement items account for about 8 percent of collected prices, but they account for all of the price change.

Table 5. Pure Price Effects of Unchanged and Replacement Items, 1983, 1984, and 1995
Percentage point contribution

Item category[a]	Year	All quotes	Unchanged items	Replacement items					
				Total	Comparable items	Overlap method	Link method	Class-mean imputation	Direct quality adjustment
All items studied	1983	2.99	1.16	1.83	0.62	0.89	0.12	...	0.20
	1984	3.40	0.14	3.26	1.37	1.38	0.16	...	0.35
	1995	2.16	1.07	1.09	0.60	0.10	0.02	0.18	0.19
Food and beverages	1983	2.64	2.41	0.23	0.14	0.06	0.03	...	0.00
	1984	3.73	3.14	0.59	0.26	0.22	0.12	...	0.00
	1995	2.08	1.94	0.14	0.04	0.05	0.04	0.00	0.01
Housing	1983	2.26	1.63	0.63	0.27	0.32	0.03	...	0.01
	1984	3.00	1.90	1.10	0.57	0.43	0.03	...	0.06
	1995	2.06	1.31	0.75	0.53	0.05	0.01	0.18	-0.02
Apparel and upkeep	1983	2.94	-21.10	24.04	8.31	14.41	1.26	...	0.06
	1984	1.95	-39.62	41.57	17.49	22.73	1.45	...	-0.10
	1995	0.21	-7.20	7.41	4.68	0.90	-0.01	0.89	0.95
Apparel commodities	1983	2.53	-25.78	28.31	9.80	17.02	1.49	...	0.00
	1984	1.42	-47.59	49.01	20.57	26.75	1.71	...	-0.02
	1995	0.15	-8.07	8.22	5.19	1.00	-0.02	0.99	1.06

Transportation	1983	1.51	0.58	0.93	0.00	0.00	0.09	. . .	0.84
	1984	2.09	0.07	2.02	0.62	0.03	0.12	. . .	1.24
	1995	1.19	0.08	1.11	0.31	0.00	0.00	0.33	0.47
New vehicles	1983	3.22	−2.01	5.23	0.31	−0.03	0.32	. . .	4.63
	1984	2.51	−6.11	8.62	1.04	0.04	0.27	. . .	7.26
	1995	1.91	−1.62	3.53	0.60	0.00	0.00	0.97	1.97
Medical care	1983	7.95	7.70	0.25	0.20	0.00	0.03	. . .	0.02
	1984	6.83	6.50	0.33	0.25	0.03	0.06	. . .	−0.02
	1995	3.73	3.70	0.03	−0.04	0.00	0.01	0.00	0.06
Entertainment	1983	3.73	2.62	1.11	0.40	0.30	0.23	. . .	0.18
	1984	4.28	2.09	2.19	0.68	0.82	0.47	. . .	0.22
	1995	3.44	2.87	0.57	0.27	0.07	0.04	0.08	0.10
Other goods and services	1983	7.95	7.14	0.81	0.58	0.06	0.12	. . .	0.05
	1984	6.07	4.51	1.56	0.92	0.13	0.03	. . .	0.47
	1995	4.18	3.69	0.49	0.40	0.02	0.01	0.01	0.04

Source: 1983 data are from Armknecht (1984); 1984 data are from Armknecht and Weyback (1989); and 1995 data are authors' calculations from unpublished CPI data.
a. Some items excluded: see table 4, note a for details.

Table 6. Percentage of Overall Pure Price Effect Due to Replacements, 1983, 1984, and 1995

Percent

Year	All items studied[a]	All items studied less apparel[a]
1983	61	20
1984	96	34
1995	50	31

Source: 1983 data are from Armknecht (1984); 1984 data are from Armknecht and Weyback (1989); and 1995 data are authors' calculations from unpublished CPI data.

a. Some items excluded; see table 4, note a for details.

vehicles categories. In both of these categories, retailers tend to discount the prices of items that are about to disappear. For apparel and upkeep, in 1995 and 1983–84 the negative pure price effect for unchanged items nearly cancels out the positive pure price effect for quotes with replacements. The magnitude of these differences, however, is much smaller in 1995 than in 1983–84. This reflects a decline in the use of the overlap method, which was often associated with large positive price effects in connection with returning sale prices to regular prices before making a quality adjustment. Likewise for new vehicles in 1995, the negative pure price effect for unchanged quotes was almost half of the positive pure price effect for replacement quotes.

Table 5 shows that the imputation of pure price change by the link method results in very small pure price effects. This is the consequence of imputing price changes from the average of price changes for all other items within the stratum. In strata where noncomparable replacement items were adjusted for quality change by the link method, the quotes that were not replaced apparently show relatively little average price change.

One noticeable difference between the results for the two periods is that in 1995 replacement items contributed only 50 percent of the pure price change for all items studied, whereas in 1984 replacement items contributed 96 percent. The source of the large difference between these ratios appears to be change in the methodology applied to replacements in apparel and upkeep. When price effects for apparel and upkeep are excluded from the study, the overall effect of replacement remains more stable across the periods studied. Table 6 shows the percentage of overall pure price effect due to replacement items for all CPI items studied versus the percentage for all items studied less apparel.

The average price change that occurs with each replacement event is also of interest. Table 7 shows the mean period-to-period pure price change, weighted by the weights that were applied in calculating the aggregate contributions to price change. These are simple percentage changes that have not been converted to an annual rate, and this calculation mixes some quotes that are priced monthly with others that are priced bimonthly.[50] The average pure price change attributed to each replacement is 2.51 percent for comparable items, 0.34 percent for the link method, 5.17 percent for class-mean imputation, and 2.66 percent for direct quality adjustment. The overlap method, which is usually applied when the item is discounted, has a much larger average pure price increase: 28.0 percent.

Measures of Quality Change

As discussed above, there are a number of problems with aggregating our data on quality adjustments by item to arrive at an aggregate quality effect. Table 8 presents the results from six alternative methods of aggregation, together with the contributions to each aggregate from the different forms of quality adjustment applied to individual items. The first column of data, presenting the full-sample arithmetic aggregation, shows an aggregate quality effect of 1.76 percent during 1995.[51] This implies that if all item replacements that were adjusted for quality change by other methods had been treated as comparable, the inflation

50. It would be inappropriate to convert these changes to an annual rate because, for a given sample item, the replacement event typically occurs only once during the year.

51. An earlier draft of this study, which has now been widely cited, reported the difference as 2.56 percent (these results are available from the authors, upon request). In that draft of the paper we noted, however, that some of the measured "quality change" might include substitutions that were done for reasons other than ordinary quality changes, in particular, changes in units of measurement and other kinds of simple repackaging. In this version, we have dropped these kinds of substitutions as well as those involving data corrections from the measured quality change, to the extent that we have been able to screen them out. Certain issues remain as to whether all of the "quality" in our revised measure is appropriately designated as quality change. We discuss some of these issues below and produce several alternative measures of quality change.

Table 7. Mean Monthly or Bimonthly Pure Price Change, by Item Category and Replacement Method, 1995[a]

Percent

Item category	All quotes	Unchanged items	Comparable items	Replacement items			
				Overlap method	Link method	Class-mean imputation	Direct quality adjustment
All items studied	0.23	0.12	2.51	28.00	0.34	5.17	2.66
Food and beverages	0.20	0.19	0.38	28.39	0.42	0.00	1.05
Housing	0.20	0.14	1.68	13.30	0.32	3.89	-1.98
Apparel and upkeep	0.03	-1.03	7.87	68.32	-0.47	12.39	17.18
Apparel commodities	0.02	-1.17	8.33	68.33	-0.61	12.40	17.81
Transportation	0.13	0.01	1.05	27.29	0.00	3.96	1.90
New vehicles	0.26	-0.25	3.52	0.00	-0.07	4.48	3.28
Medical care	0.50	0.51	-0.19	0.04	0.19	0.00	1.46
Entertainment	0.40	0.35	1.93	53.46	1.33	2.52	2.42
Other goods and services	0.38	0.34	3.57	3.75	0.60	2.79	1.82

Source: Authors' calculations from unpublished CPI data.

a. For all quotes and for unchanged items, table reports mean of monthly and bimonthly pure price changes. For replacement items, table reports mean pure price change per replacement event.

rate for these items during 1995 would have been 3.92 percent instead of 2.16 percent.[52] Although this arithmetic aggregation measure is appropriate for this calculation, the alternative measures shown in the table, which exclude outliers or use logarithmic aggregation, give substantially different estimates that, under certain cirumstances, may be more appropriate indicators of the aggregate quality effect.

For the arithmetic aggregation, the quality effect for all replacement items drops from 1.76 percent without any truncation to 1.10 percent with truncation method A and to 0.54 percent with truncation method B.[53] The drop in quality effects is concentrated in replacements that use the link method and class-mean imputation; replacements using direct quality adjustment are hardly affected. Apparently, direct quality adjustments are not applied in cases that result in outlying quality adjustments.

As discussed above, to answer the question "What is the size of the typical quality adjustment made with CPI item replacements?", logarithmic aggregation may be appropriate.[54] As shown in table 8, without truncation the aggregate logarithmic quality effect is 0.44 percent. Under truncation method A the logarithmic aggregate quality effect is 0.40 percent. Under truncation method B, it drops to 0.28 percent. Each of the methods of quality adjustment, except the overlap method, contribute to the total effect under all six aggregation formulas, although the contributions of the link method and class-mean imputation are greatly reduced by truncation and the use of logarithms.

The results from the logarithmic version suggest that the quality change accounted for by BLS item replacement procedures are especially concentrated in the transportation and apparel and upkeep categories. Without truncation, the logarithmic quality effects are 1.35

52. The quality effect that we measure for 1995 is higher than the effects reported for 1983 (1.11 percent) and 1984 (1.23 percent). As noted above, the quality effects are sensitive to outliers, changes in units, and so forth. We have not been able to determine the extent to which Armknecht (1984) and Armknecht and Weyback (1989) control for these problems, so comparisons of measured quality effects between their studies and ours may be misleading.

53. For the arithmetic aggregation, the proportion of noncomparable replacements that are truncated is 2.2 percent under method A and 11.5 percent under method B. For logarithmic aggregation, the proportion is 1.3 percent under method A and 10.4 percent under method B.

54. Note that this question is distinct from that answered by arithmetic aggregation: "What would be the effect on CPI inflation of not applying quality adjustment methods?"

Table 8. Measured Quality Effects, by Item Category and Replacement Method, 1995[a]

Percentage points[b]

Item category	Replacement method	Additive quality effect[c]			Logarithmic quality effect[c]		
		No truncation	Method A	Method B	No truncation	Method A	Method B
All items studied	Overlap method	0.00	0.00	0.00	-0.01	-0.01	-0.01
	Link method	0.99	0.55	0.23	0.21	0.18	0.10
	Class-mean imputation	0.66	0.43	0.21	0.15	0.14	0.10
	Direct quality adjustment	0.11	0.12	0.10	0.08	0.09	0.08
	Total	1.76	1.10	0.54	0.44	0.40	0.28
Food and beverages	Overlap method	-0.01	-0.01	-0.01	-0.02	-0.02	-0.01
	Link method	1.40	0.62	0.35	0.14	0.10	0.08
	Class-mean imputation	…	…	…	…	…	…
	Direct quality adjustment	0.01	0.01	0.00	0.00	0.00	0.00
	Total	1.39	0.62	0.34	0.12	0.09	0.07
Housing	Overlap method	0.05	0.03	0.00	0.01	0.01	-0.01
	Link method	0.88	0.77	0.19	0.34	0.25	0.09
	Class-mean imputation	0.57	0.47	0.28	0.06	0.02	0.07
	Direct quality adjustment	0.06	0.07	0.00	0.01	0.02	-0.01
	Total	1.57	1.33	0.47	0.42	0.31	0.15
Apparel and upkeep	Overlap method	-0.02	0.00	0.00	-0.03	-0.03	0.00
	Link method	0.50	0.48	0.37	0.26	0.21	0.16
	Class-mean imputation	2.62	2.43	0.61	0.97	0.94	0.29
	Direct quality adjustment	0.27	0.34	0.29	0.15	0.15	0.15
	Total	3.37	3.25	1.27	1.35	1.26	0.61
Apparel commodities	Overlap method	-0.02	0.00	0.00	-0.03	-0.03	0.00
	Link method	0.59	0.56	0.44	0.33	0.27	0.21
	Class-mean imputation	2.90	2.69	0.68	1.08	1.04	0.33
	Direct quality adjustment	0.30	0.37	0.32	0.16	0.16	0.17
	Total	3.77	3.64	1.44	1.54	1.44	0.70

Transportation	Overlap method	0.00	0.00	0.00	0.00	0.00	0.00
	Link method	0.33	0.35	0.22	0.16	0.25	0.17
	Class-mean imputation	0.44	0.44	0.40	0.21	0.28	0.27
	Direct quality adjustment	0.36	0.36	0.36	0.35	0.35	0.36
	Total	1.13	1.16	0.98	0.72	0.89	0.79
New vehicles	Overlap method	..	..	..	..	..	..
	Link method	0.19	0.19	0.19	0.15	0.15	0.15
	Class-mean imputation	0.97	0.96	0.87	0.71	0.71	0.64
	Direct quality adjustment	0.56	0.56	0.56	0.54	0.54	0.54
	Total	1.71	1.71	1.61	1.40	1.40	1.33
Medical care	Overlap method	0.00	0.00	0.00	0.00	0.00	0.00
	Link method	2.53	0.52	0.14	0.44	0.11	0.05
	Class-mean imputation	..	..	..	..	..	..
	Direct quality adjustment	-0.02	-0.02	-0.02	-0.03	-0.03	-0.03
	Total	2.51	0.50	0.13	0.41	0.08	0.01
Entertainment	Overlap method	-0.03	-0.03	0.00	-0.04	-0.04	-0.04
	Link method	0.67	0.55	0.16	0.10	0.22	0.07
	Class-mean imputation	4.09	0.76	0.31	0.36	0.06	0.12
	Direct quality adjustment	0.06	0.06	0.06	0.05	0.05	0.05
	Total	4.79	1.34	0.52	0.47	0.30	0.20
Other goods and services	Overlap method	0.00	0.00	0.00	0.00	0.00	0.00
	Link method	0.62	0.38	0.09	-0.01	0.04	0.06
	Class-mean imputation	0.02	0.02	-0.02	-0.01	-0.01	-0.03
	Direct quality adjustment	-0.04	-0.04	-0.02	-0.06	-0.06	-0.03
	Total	0.60	0.36	0.05	-0.09	-0.04	0.00

Source: Authors' calculations from unpublished CPI data.

a. Missing values indicate that given method is not used for given item category.

b. Entries are expressed as percentage point contributions to quality effect in item category–specific CPI.

c. Method A truncates observations when quality increases or decreases by a factor of 5 or more; method B truncates when quality changes by a factor of 2 or more. See text for further details on different methods of aggregation and truncation.

Table 9. Mean Monthly or Bimonthly Quality Change, by Item Category and Replacement Method, 1995[a]
Percent

Item category	Replacement method	Mean additive quality change[b]			Mean logarithmic quality change[b]		
		No truncation	Method A	Method B	No truncation	Method A	Method B
All items studied	Overlap method	0.92	0.73	-0.75	-1.67	-1.37	-1.65
	Link method	30.39	11.58	5.45	4.27	3.68	2.36
	Class-mean imputation	18.62	12.44	6.79	4.19	3.94	3.16
	Direct quality adjustment	1.59	1.68	1.44	1.19	1.22	1.16
	Total noncomparable replacements	14.26	7.07	3.68	2.74	2.51	1.85
Food and beverages	Overlap method	-8.77	-3.75	-4.17	-10.58	-8.09	-5.38
	Link method	28.65	6.17	3.71	1.35	0.98	0.80
	Class-mean imputation	...	...	...	...	...	...
	Direct quality adjustment	0.77	0.77	0.19	0.39	0.39	0.08
	Total noncomparable replacements	26.16	5.65	3.33	1.08	0.77	0.64
Housing	Overlap method	12.34	6.99	-1.36	2.96	2.96	-1.56
	Link method	36.99	21.82	6.15	9.24	7.16	2.95
	Class-mean imputation	12.31	10.34	7.28	1.20	0.46	1.86
	Direct quality adjustment	5.05	5.49	0.41	0.86	1.68	-0.94
	Total noncomparable replacements	20.38	13.78	5.52	4.16	3.14	1.70
Apparel and upkeep	Overlap method	-1.15	0.34	0.24	-1.57	-1.57	-0.24
	Link method	17.55	16.88	16.03	9.49	7.63	7.47
	Class-mean imputation	36.46	36.92	13.43	13.03	13.04	6.04
	Direct quality adjustment	4.84	6.15	5.35	2.52	2.52	2.69
	Total noncomparable replacements	19.96	20.07	9.42	7.59	7.23	4.18
Apparel commodities	Overlap method	-1.15	0.34	0.24	-1.57	-1.57	-0.24
	Link method	20.19	19.47	18.89	11.70	9.70	9.70
	Class-mean imputation	36.45	36.92	13.42	13.03	13.03	6.04
	Direct quality adjustment	5.01	6.39	5.55	2.61	2.61	2.79
	Total noncomparable replacements	20.64	20.79	9.90	7.97	7.61	4.50

Transportation	Overlap method	...	...	...	...	...	...
	Link method	15.36	14.16	9.17	6.05	9.82	6.83
	Class-mean imputation	5.34	5.37	4.97	2.47	3.36	3.24
	Direct quality adjustment	1.46	1.46	1.46	1.43f	1.43	1.43
	Total noncomparable replacements	3.35	3.25	2.78	2.00	2.48	2.22
New vehicles	Overlap method	...	...	...	...	...	...
	Link method	4.39	4.39	4.39	3.41	3.41	3.41
	Class-mean imputation	4.47	4.45	4.06	3.23	3.23	2.96
	Direct quality adjustment	0.94	0.94	0.94	0.90	0.90	0.90
	Total noncomparable replacements	2.00	1.99	1.89	1.62	1.62	1.54
Medical care	Overlap method	...	...	...	...	...	...
	Link method	61.82	13.46	4.24	10.57	2.76	1.37
	Class-mean imputation	...	...	...	...	...	...
	Direct quality adjustment	-0.44	-0.44	-0.44	-0.86	-0.86	-0.86
	Total noncomparable replacements	28.31	5.82	1.54	4.57	0.87	0.16
Entertainment	Overlap method	...	...	...	...	...	...
	Link method	19.94	16.39	5.63	3.10	6.62	2.58
	Class-mean imputation	124.76	24.19	12.59	10.28	1.88	4.64
	Direct quality adjustment	1.45	1.45	1.45	1.24	1.24	1.24
	Total noncomparable replacements	43.83	12.43	5.55	4.28	2.72	2.08
Other goods and services	Overlap method	...	...	...	...	...	...
	Link method	27.25	17.31	6.07	-0.58	1.86	4.15
	Class-mean imputation	4.70	4.70	-6.52	-3.81	-3.81	-9.08
	Direct quality adjustment	-1.84	-1.84	-1.00	-3.06	-3.06	-1.65
	Total noncomparable replacements	11.48	6.97	1.08	-1.75	-0.75	-0.06

Source: Authors' calculations from unpublished CPI data.

a. Table reports mean quality change per replacement event. Missing values indicate fewer than twenty replacement events.

b. Method A truncates observations when quality increases or decreases by a factor of 5 or more; method B truncates when quality changes by a factor of 2 or more. See text for further details on different methods of aggregation and truncation.

percent for apparel and upkeep and 0.72 percent for transportation, as compared to 0.12 percent for food and beverages, 0.42 percent for housing, 0.41 percent for medical care, 0.47 percent for entertainment, and −0.09 percent for other goods and services. Under truncation method B, the quality effects drop to 0.61 percent for apparel and upkeep, 0.15 percent for housing, 0.01 percent for medical care, 0.20 percent for entertainment, and 0.00 percent for other goods and services.

The mean quality change is presented in table 9. The typical quality adjustment is larger for the link method and class-mean imputation than for direct quality adjustment, and is negative for the overlap method. Again, the largest average quality adjustments tend to occur in the apparel and upkeep category.

Conclusions

The advisory commission and others who have analyzed the measurement of quality change and new products in the CPI have identified a number of areas in which the methods used by the BLS still require attention. The BLS has made a series of modifications to take better account of quality change, but further improvements clearly are needed in some components of the index. For certain important categories of items considered by the advisory commission, it would be difficult to argue that the CPI does not overstate the rate of price change. In other cases, however, any bias seems likely to be considerably smaller than the advisory commission has estimated and, in certain cases, it could even be negative.

The results of our decomposition of price differences between old and new items into quality and price changes are somewhat ambiguous. The arithmetic method of calculating these changes demonstrates that the quality adjustment methods have a profound effect on measured price change; they cause the measured price change of the CPI to be reduced by 1.76 percentage points for the items studied. The logarithmic method indicates a range of 0.28 to 0.44 percent for quality change, which we consider to be a significant amount of quality adjustment.

Our measurements of quality effects do not provide direct evidence of quality bias in a particular direction. They do show that any quality bias could go in either direction, either through inadequate quality adjustment (as emphasized by the advisory commission) or through excessive quality adjustment by the application of the link method to items with rising prices. Avoiding both downward and upward bias should be of concern to the Bureau of Labor Statistics.

Comments and Discussion

Robert J. Gordon: In some past eras, there was a military atmosphere to debates between the Bureau of Labor Statistics and those academics who were doing research on price measurement. The BLS was harrassed and besieged, as if in a medieval fortress, throwing hot oil from the parapets at the academics who were attacking with bows and arrows, battering rams, and other tools of their trade.

The dialogue over the past two years between the CPI commission (of which I was a member) and the BLS has been very different. The BLS generously hosted several meetings at its offices, in which its procedures were explained to us at a fine level of detail, and we subsequently met a number of times off-site, as our findings and recommendations began to come together. BLS officials were open in their recognition that there are many problems in the CPI; they worked with us to identify the nature of the problems and potential solutions and they have generally welcomed the attention that the commission and its final report has directed to the need for more investment in the quality of government statistics, both the CPI and more broadly.

Our report acknowledges that some of the best research on the issues that we address has been produced within the BLS, and indeed, the whole issue of formula bias—now relabeled lower-level substitution bias—has come to light because of pathbreaking research at the BLS by Marshall Reinsdorf, by himself initially and more recently with Brent Moulton. Our report has a long reference list, and it is striking how many of the citations are to studies by current or former employees of the BLS.

350

In turn, this paper by Moulton and Karin Moses is generous to our report, calling it "the most influential critique of the CPI in decades." Indeed, comparisons are inevitable between ours and the famous Stigler commission report of 1961. Some contrasts between our commission and the Stigler commission provide useful background for those evaluating our report and the subsequent criticisms of it, in this paper and elsewhere. The reports have one thing in common: Zvi Griliches was involved in both. They have several important differences. Our report concerns only the CPI, while the Stigler report covered the PPI and agricultural price indexes as well. The Stigler commission did not produce any numerical estimate for bias in any of the price indexes reviewed, whereas our mandate included providing a point estimate of the overall bias in the CPI. A final and important difference, in the context of the present discussion, is that the Stigler commission had a substantial budget to commission new research studies, including Griliches's famous paper on hedonic price indexes for automobiles, whereas ours had no budget at all (except for travel expenses).[1] We did our best to assemble all the relevant existing research by academics, BLS insiders, and others, but we did not have any research support for conducting new studies.

The CPI commission's report arrives at an overall bias estimate of 1.1 percent, consisting of two main parts. Almost half (0.5 percent) involves upper- and lower-level substitution bias and outlet substitution bias. This estimate seems to be uncontroversial and to be widely accepted; indeed, it may be too conservative, for reasons mentioned below. The other portion (0.6 percent) is our estimate of the bias due to inadequate adjustment for quality change and inadequate allowance for the introduction of new products—we did not separate the quality change and new product sources of bias, but treated them together.

As Moulton and Moses emphasize, our approach to the problem of quality change differs from past evaluations. Previously, it had been common to take available research on a limited number of CPI commodities, multiply the bias figures for those commodities by their weight in the CPI, and take the product as the estimate of the overall quality change bias in the CPI, assuming that all categories for which research was not available had a bias of exactly zero. We rejected that

1. Griliches (1961).

approach: "The evaluation that the rest of the CPI is unbiased represents an extreme one-sided answer to the question as to whether the components of the CPI subject to relatively little research are biased. They may be as likely to be subject to the average rate of bias of those components which have been subject to careful research as to no bias at all." Further, "because the magnitude of quality change bias differs so much across product categories, any overall evaluation of the magnitude of quality change bias must be conducted 'down in the trenches,' taking individual categories of consumer expenditure, assessing quality change bias for each category, and then aggregating using appropriate weights."[2]

Moulton and Moses do not object to our "down in the trenches" approach to the problem. Indeed, they state that "this is the first systematic analysis, category by category, of quality bias in the CPI, and it is a noteworthy accomplishment." However, as indicated, the analysis was conducted without research staff or a research budget. Inevitably, there is a back-of-the-envelope quality to some of the estimates. But Moulton and Moses recognize that "the commission's approach to the problem of producing an overall assessment of bias seems sensible, and this type of structure will likely prove to be useful in the future." They concur with us that the quality change problem is usefully viewed as a matrix—our report plugged numbers into many slots of the matrix, and some of those numbers are better than others. As some of the weaker numbers come under scrutiny, more solid numbers will emerge, and the matrix will be continuously updated. Some of Moulton and Moses's findings suggest that some of our bias estimates may be too high, and I suggest, for other reasons, that some are too low.

Before discussing the substance of this paper, I want to emphasize some broader issues of relevance to the debate over bias in the CPI. To start with, there is the question of whether estimates of quality change bias are inevitably too "subjective" and "judgmental" to be taken seriously. One response is that quoted above from our report: it is just as subjective to assume that every CPI category not subject to careful research has a zero bias as to extrapolate research-based estimates from one category to another. Another response is that it is better to be imprecisely right than precisely wrong. Even though one can never

2. U.S. Senate, Committee on Finance (1996, p. 22).

precisely measure the value of the invention of the video-cassette recorder or the jet airplane, one can use the economist's toolbox to estimate the size of consumer surplus triangles. We know that the size of these triangles is positive, or, in the language of this paper, the bias due to the failure to value the invention of new products inherently must be positive.

In addition, there are three reasons to suspect that the commission's overall estimate of a 1.1 percent CPI bias is too low for the period 1995–96 and one reason to suspect that at some point in the past the bias may have been much smaller, or even negative.

The first reason that the bias may be too low is that we did not quantify any of the numerous intangible aspects of quality change, such as the improved safety and lighter weight of home power tools and the improved quality of stereo sound and television pictures, among many others. Second, with the exception of food and beverages, motor fuel, and personal banking, we did not attempt to make any estimate of the consumers surplus triangles created by the invention of new goods and services.

The third reason concerns the growing divergence between the inflation rate as measured by the CPI and by the chain-weighted personal consumption expenditures (PCE) deflator. In the four quarters ending in 1995:4, and again in 1996:4, these measures differed by 0.7 percentage point, with the CPI growing faster. In an unpublished study conducted by the BLS and Bureau of Economic Analysis, fully 0.35 percentage point of the difference over the period from mid-1994 to mid-1996 was attributable to weighting differences; the PCE deflator uses much more current weights and also places much higher weights on medical care and personal computers than does the CPI. This number is much higher than our estimate of 0.15 for upper-level substitution bias, an important reason why our overall bias estimate may be too low. Much of the remaining difference between the CPI and PCE deflator arises because the latter uses the PPI rather than CPI for medical care (the PPI apparently goes part but not all of the way to an outcome-based, rather than an input-based, approach to pricing medical care) and because it registers a much faster decline in the price of personal computers.

If one were to accept the PCE deflator treatment of upper-level weighting, medical care prices, and computer prices, one would start with a 0.7 percent upward bias in the CPI over the two years 1995–96. But the PCE deflator still incorporates the lower-level substitution bias, the outlet substitution bias, and at least 0.4 percent of our 0.6 percent estimate of quality change bias. The sum of 0.7, 0.4, and 0.4 provides an alternative estimate of an upward bias of 1.5 percent in the CPI.

Could the bias in the CPI have been smaller in the past, and perhaps in the opposite direction? This possibility emerges from the "Nordhaus paradox." If one takes the bias in the CPI as 1 or 1.5 percent and extrapolates this rate back two centuries, the implied level of per capita income in today's prices is so low that it would not be sufficient to keep a person alive on a diet consisting solely of potatoes, without leaving anything over for clothing and shelter. At some point in the past, the bias must have been lower. One will never detect bias, or lack of it, for data from the nineteenth and early twentieth centuries, because it is based on academic research by pioneers such as Dorothy Brady, Ethel Hoover, and Albert Rees, who essentially used all the information available. However, as the commission reports, the back-of-the-envelope technique that I used to quantify the shelter bias in the CPI from 1976 to 1993 suggests a severe downward bias for shelter between 1920 and 1976, and this may have been important enough to create a downward bias in the overall CPI for much of that period.[3]

Turning to the present paper, it is really two papers. The first part provides a critique of some of the numbers in the commission's quality change matrix. The second part provides valuable information quantifying the frequency and extent of quality change adjustments in the current CPI. Let me discuss the second part first.

For most categories in the CPI, the extent of current quality adjustments is irrelevant to an assessment of the treatment of quality change in the commission's report, simply because most of our estimates of quality change bias are valid independent of how the BLS arrives at its estimates of price change or the extent to which its adjustments for quality change are large or small. Most of our bias estimates are based on the collection of price data from independent sources and the careful quality adjustment of those data. The difference between these quality-adjusted independent price indexes and the corresponding CPI indexes (however they are adjusted for quality change) forms the basis of our

3. U.S. Senate, Committee on Finance (1996, p. 31).

estimates of bias. We use such independent sources of price data in our bias estimates for shelter, appliances, radio-television, personal computers, apparel, public transportation, prescription drugs, and medical care. Estimates derived from these categories are extrapolated, sometimes partially rather than fully, to other housefurnishings, nonprescription drugs, entertainment commodities, and personal care.

Only in the few remaining cases do we add a bias estimate to a CPI category in which there are already quality adjustments, rather than computing the bias estimate indirectly by subtracting an independent estimate from the CPI estimate for that category. These categories are food and beverages, other utilities, new and used cars, motor fuel, and personal expenses.

Moulton and Moses previously estimated that the BLS made adjustments that reduced the rate of inflation in the CPI by about 2.6 percent in 1995. In the present revised version of their paper, this number has shrunk to 1.76 percent. Using logarithmic aggregation and excluding "outliers"—commodity pairs for which the implicit price-quality change is two-fold or greater (which are simply noncomparable pairs and are not likely to reflect what we had in mind by the concept of quality change)—the number shrinks to a mere 0.3 percent. At this point, the argument loses any quantitative significance.

But it is still instructive to discuss this argument, since it illustrates the substantive difficulties and the problems of communication in this field. Most of the reported "quality adjustment" by the BLS (1.65 percent out of the 1.76 percent that includes outliers) comes from "linking" procedures or class-mean imputation, in which a missing item is replaced by another. No judgment at all is made about the quality differential between the new and old items. The price change during the link period is imputed, by using either the inflation rate in the overall CPI or that of other commodities in the particular class. These adjustments are the consequence of the BLS sampling procedures, which focus on pricing a very specific item in a particular store and city. There are thousands upon thousands of such commodities in the market, but only a small fraction of them is in a particular store at any time. The pricing agent has to deal with rapid turnover and high probability of stockout. Roughly one out of three items disappear sometime during the year and have to be replaced by a different item in the same general class: a larger versus a smaller package of yogurt, a blue raincoat versus a black one, a refrigerator with a freezer at the bottom rather than at the top. But this churning is not what we had in mind by ''quality change,'' which rather involves the appearance of new and improved goods, such as the increased variety and freshness of vegetables and fish due to improved transport facilities and the globalization of trade, or the substitution of laporascopic procedures for gallstone operations, and so on.

This brings me to the first part of Moulton and Moses's paper. Much of this is solid, and I accept some of it. To quantify what is at stake, recall that the commission's estimate of quality change and new product bias is 0.61 percent annually for the period 1995–96. Of this, 0.31 percent comes from appliances, radio-television, personal computers, drugs, and medical care, all of which Moulton and Moses accept at face value. Their analysis of fruits, vegetables, shelter, and motor fuel is very helpful. But these categories together only account for 0.08 point of our 0.61 percent.

On apparel, Moulton and Moses do not actually come up with a quantitative reason to doubt the commission's estimate of a 1.0 percent bias. This estimate is based on the difference between my Sears catalogue estimate of apparel prices for the four major subdivisions of apparel and the corresponding four categories of the CPI. That difference was 1.92 percent, and we cut it down to 1.0 percent just to be conservative. But recall that during the last decade of the Sears catalogue, the company was losing market share to new competitors like Wal-Mart, so the Sears apparel index probably overstates the rate of inflation actually experienced by consumers who are free to choose where to shop.

On motor vehicles, our bias estimate is based solely on the increase in durability. I agree that some unknown part of the increase in durability has already been taken into account in the CPI. But going in the other direction is an enormous improvement in the quality of new vehicles, as measured by the J. D. Power survey of initial defects, as well as by the *Consumer Reports* questionnaire, which registers a decline in defects by a factor of 3 over the past two decades. Decreased frequency of repairs is not adequately taken into account in the CPI, so the paper's discussion does not convince me that our bias estimate for motor vehicles is too high.

Moreover, while Moulton and Moses's helpful discussion of certain categories does reduce our overall quality change bias estimate slightly, not all new research goes in this direction. For the television category, the commission took my estimate of a 3.3 percent bias over the period 1973–83, the final decade in my earlier study.[4] I have recently updated that work with a new study of the prices of three different sizes of television sets over the period 1984–97, using annual evaluations in *Consumer Reports* that allow one to hold constant not only picture size, but also such features as picture-in-picture, stereo capability, and the number of input-output channels, among others. The annual rate of price decline for television sets in the CPI over these years is 3.0 percent and in my index is 11.1 percent, for an upward bias in the CPI of 8.1 percent, in contrast to the 3.3 percent that we assumed. Yet even this much larger rate of bias is understated. Some features have improved in ways that could not be taken into account, such as picture and sound quality and the number of cable channels that could be received. Perhaps more important, my study fails to take into account a significant increase in reliability: the median percentage of sets repaired in their first five years decreased from 19 percent in 1986 to 6 percent in 1997.

To conclude, Moulton and Moses have contributed a very useful discussion suggesting that several of the commission's estimates of bias are too high. I contribute four reasons why they are too low: failure to include intangible quality improvements, failure to include the consumer surplus contribution of new products for most categories, the divergence between the CPI and the personal consumption expenditures deflator, and new research on television sets that suggests the possibility of similarly large biases in other products involving electronics.

The road to solid estimates of quality change bias is long and arduous. I am pleased that the journey down that road has become such a fruitful partnership between academic research and research within the government agencies producing numbers that are crucial ingredients in virtually every measure of American economic performance and well-being.

Barry P. Bosworth: This an interesting and obviously timely paper. It has two major parts; the first responds to portions of the CPI advisory commission's report that deal with the issue of quality change; and the

---

4. See Gordon (1990).

second provides a new empirical analysis of the frequency and extent of product substitutions in the CPI for the years 1983, 1984, and 1995.

Very little is said about the portions of the commision's report that focus on the issue of substitution bias. I think that is because the authors basically agree with the commission's suggestion that the methodology of the CPI should be changed from the current Laspeyres index to some superlative index that would yield a closer measure of the cost of living—in effect, following the recent methodological changes to the national accounts. The only real question is the speed with which the change will be implemented.

The role of quality change is far more controversial, however. The commission alleges that current BLS procedures fail adequately to capture improvements in quality, and that the result is an overestimate of annual inflation of about 0.6 percentage point. Moulton and Moses challenge the notion of a pervasive bias in the treatment of quality change. The first portion of their paper provides a useful response to the report—the commission's analysis itself seems somewhat biased in ignoring the potential for overstating the quality change. In combination, the two statements provide a more comprehensive discussion of a difficult issue, but they are largely confined to a war of anecdotes. I am skeptical of alternative indexes based on catalogues or *Consumer Reports,* when there is no way of determining the relevant quantity weights. The amount of research that actually bears on the issue is very limited.

Thus the really significant contribution comes in the second part of the paper, where the authors present some data on the decomposition of the total price change for items in the CPI sample into a quality change component and a pure price change component. While some of the public debate presents the issue as an argument over whether there are or are not quality improvements, the question is, more accurately, whether quality change is greater or less than the BLS estimates. Since it has never really been known how much quality change is captured in the BLS procedures, it difficult to determine if it is too much or too little. A study of the actual BLS adjustments is a crucial starting point.

It is evident that this paper is very much a study in progress, and to draw any conclusions from the analysis at this point may be hazardous. First, the data are derived from situations in which it was necessary to substitute for one of the items in the sample. These substitutions occur for a wide variety of reasons other than a change in the quality characteristics of the surveyed item. The authors have tried to exclude those substitutions that result from simple changes in the units in which an item is sold, but there remain a large number of substitutions that do not involve the introduction of a new model. However, one could possibly argue that differences in price levels for those substitutions that result from the simple disappearance of an item might be randomly distributed. In the event of a substitution, the data collector is instructed to search for a close substitute, but there may be no particular tendency to chose an item that is more or less costly. Thus the mean change would be dominated by situations involving the introduction of a new model.

The paper classifies substitutions according to the different techniques that the BLS uses to factor out the quality change, ranging from comparable substitutions (when there is no difference in quality between old and new items) to direct adjustment for the quality component. The major issues arise with respect to the link method. Consider two extreme views of the process by which firms introduce changes in price and quality. On the one hand, if quality changes are typically introduced in a continuous process that is uncorrelated with price changes, it seems reasonable to believe that the BLS procedures may miss some part of the quality change: small differences would be overlooked. On the other hand, if firms tend to save up price and quality changes and incorporate them in a new model, the timing of price and quality changes are correlated and the BLS link procedures would tend to eliminate nearly all of the price difference between the old and new items and overstate the amount of quality change. Concern about just such a practice was a primary reason why the BLS adopted direct adjustment for the automotive market; and Moulton and Moses provide a nice example of the same phenomenon for women's clothing. The use of the link method is probably responsible for some of the CPI's failure to capture price declines fully in areas of rapid innovation, such as consumer electronics.

This paper finds that substitutions occur very frequently: if one assumes that all items are priced monthly, the typical item will require a substitution within a two-year period. However, in 1995 two-thirds of the substitutions were deemed comparable and hence were not adjusted for quality change. This is a sharp increase from 1983–84 and supports the commission's view that small changes in quality are overlooked. One should also worry that in two-thirds of those cases with a quality adjustment, the adjustment was derived from the link method or its close equivalent, class-mean imputation.

The data arrayed in table 5 also highlight the important role of subjective judgements in the classification of substitutions as comparable or noncomparable. If the data collector cannot find the item and reports the price of a substitute item, the analyst has to decide if it is comparable or noncomparable. The distinction is critical. If the substitute item is ruled to be noncomparable, nearly all of the price change is linked out. If it is ruled comparable, there is a relatively large contribution to the overall estimate of inflation. Yet if the items are so comparable, why are the price increases so large?

Moreover, the large category of items with no substitutions (96 percent of the total) represents a surprisingly small part of the overall price increase: only about one-half. If the BLS counts improvements as price increases, why does the category of nonsubstitutions not account for a larger portion?

At first glance, the data indicate that current BLS procedures account for a surprisingly large amount of quality improvement: 1.76 percent in 1995, according to table 8. The authors go on, however, to raise some serious questions about their estimate of the mean quality change; in particular, they show that it is very sensitive to extreme values. As shown in table 8, the mild truncation of method A—a loss of 2 to 3 precent of the sample—reduces the mean estimate of the quality change component from 1.76 to 1.10. The tighter distribution of method B—representing an 11 percent loss—reduces it to 0.54. Why do these restrictions have the greatest effect in the category of food and beverages, where it should be possible to find very close substitutes? One might expect a large role for extreme values in the cases of medical care and entertainment, because of the heterogeneous nature of those categories. The logarithmic aggregation probably provides a better adjustment for extreme values in the ratio of new to old prices: it reduces the estimated mean quality change to 0.4 percent.

If the data from item substitutions are to provide useful insights into the issue of quality change in the CPI, more work needs to be done to understand the nature of the substitutions and the reasons for some of the large changes. I would hope that the BLS would expand on this type of analysis and make it a regular part of an annual review of the CPI. One needs to know more about the factors that influence the decision to classify an item as comparable or noncomparable; and some further classification is needed for those substititutions for which the link method is used to adjust for quality change.

General discussion: William Nordhaus raised an issue about the purpose of indexing and how that relates to the construction of the CPI. He noted that improved life expectancy was a quality improvement discussed by the commission's report in connection with pricing medical costs. Valuing this improvement with numbers conventionally used by environmentalists for the price of life would attribute a substanatial increase in living standards over the past thirty years to health care (market and nonmarket). While it may be appropriate to take that into account in indexing the tax system, he questioned whether the annuity benefits of social security recipients indexed to the CPI should be reduced simply because they are living longer. Katharine Abraham expanded on Nordhaus's point, noting similar quandaries with medical procedures that deliver better outcomes, even without increased longevity. Should the government be saying to social security recipients that they will not be compensated for the full price of operations just because those operations are now better? She believed that such a policy might be difficult for the average citizen to accept. Some other suggested adjustments, such as for the utility coming from greater variety of products available to consumers raise similar questions. How can it be explained to voters that the price level has really dropped because of increased variety, even if no price has fallen?

Abraham further observed that while substitution bias and outlet substitution bias are important problems, there is room for disagreement about how much to change present procedures. Although switching to geometric mean aggregation makes sense in many categories where price changes lead to item substitution, she argued that it should not become universal. In prescription drugs, for instance, although drugs for treating ulcers have declined in price relative to those for treating heart conditions, one should not expect significant substitution between them, and geometric mean aggregation would not be appropriate. She was skeptical about outlet bias, which is difficult to measure because buying at different stores involves different services and amenities. She added that the bias arising from the emergence of new outlets could even go in the opposite direction than usually assumed: consider a case where discount stores move into an area, people shift away from traditional stores, and, in order to compete, the traditional stores cut back on staffing and other services. The CPI could then pick up the fall in prices due to the entry of discount stores, without picking up any of the deterioration in the quality of service at the traditional stores. Gordon replied that much of the actual outlet substitution has not been from high-service to low-service outlets, but from inefficient self-service stores, such as Sears, to more efficient ones, such as Wal-Mart.

James Duesenberry noted the great difference between the historical BLS approach, which focused on pricing a list of items over time, and the commission's approach, which looks for ways to measure how people are better off as a consequence of new products and quality changes. The ambitious approach taken by the commission calls attention to the problems of using one index for a diverse population, because it highlights the fact that whether people are made better off depends on which group is being referenced. From the perspective of upper-middle income people like those on the commission, the prices of computers and televisions that can get 150 channels are important. But people relying on social security, who tend not to own computers or get cable television, are more interested in items like rent and food.

Robert Hall questioned Duesenberry's assertion that television sets were relatively unimportant for those lower in the income distribution and was convinced that Gordon's television data identified a large CPI bias in this category. Television sets are constantly being upgraded, in which case the replacement is noncomparable, and so almost all the price decline has been taken out by BLS methodology. Moulton replied that a hedonic study of televisions and some other items is underway. While he would quibble over some points in Gordon's analysis, he agreed with the direction of the bias for television sets. But he noted that since televisions account for only 0.3 to 0.4 percent of the consumer market basket, their relative importance is small.

Several participants offered other specific instances of bias in the CPI data. Hall explained that the CPI prices long distance telephone calls by tabulating the regular tariff rates that the long distance companies report, even though many customers are switching to lower-priced plans. The problem here is not with quality changes, but rather, is just the failure to check what prices people actually pay. He calculated that according to the CPI, everyone is paying about 30 cents a minute, whereas the aggressive consumer nowadays pays only 10 cents a minute and the average customer pays 14 cents a minute. Although automobiles have undoubtedly become more rust-resistant and more reliable, Jack Triplett expressed reservations about the assertions by the CPI commission and Gordon that these quality improvements are missed by the CPI. Automobile manufacturers submit costs of quality changes to the BLS, and from Triplett's work at the BLS, he reported that they seldom overlooked quality changes. In fact, manufacturers tried to attribute too much price change to quality improvements—he recalled arguing with one car company about whether taking the "90" and "100" off of the speedometer was an improvement—leading to a downward bias in the CPI. He reasoned that whether the CPI, on balance, is biased upward or downward can only be determined by looking at hundreds of procedural details. Finally, reflecting on these examples of specific items in the index, Nordhaus reasoned that real progress could not be made via "war by anecdotes." As an alternative approach, he recommended that the BLS and outside experts draw a probability sample of detailed CPI components and, on the basis of in-depth study, develop an estimate of the bias (positive or negative) in each of those components. Then, using the weights that guided the initial sample selection, it would be a straightforward matter to estimate the bias in the overall CPI, as well as a confidence interval for same. David Wilcox agreed that Nordhaus's suggestion was a good one, but urged that it be taken as a model for how the BLS should be organized permanently: the BLS should review all of the components of the CPI on a rotating basis (say, once every ten years). Achieving this objective might require both administrative reorganization and the commitment of substantial additional resources, but it would pay significant dividends in terms of improvement in the index.

References

Abraham, Katharine G. 1997a. "The CPI Commission: Discussion." *American Economic Review, Papers and Proceedings* 87(2): 94–95.

————. 1997b. "Testimony before the Senate Finance Committee." 105 Cong., 1 sess., February 11.

Armknecht, Paul A. 1984. "Quality Adjustment in the CPI and Methods to Improve It." In *American Statistical Association, Proceedings of the Business and Economic Statistics Section.*

Armknecht, Paul A., Walter F. Lane, and Kenneth J. Stewart. 1997. "New Products and the U.S. CPI." In *The Economics of New Goods*, edited by Timothy F. Bresnahan and Robert J. Gordon. University of Chicago Press.

Armknecht, Paul A., and Donald Weyback. 1989. "Adjustments for Quality Change in the U.S. Consumer Price Index." *Journal of Official Statistics* 5(2): 107–23.

Baker, Dean. 1996. "The Overstated CPI—Can It Really Be True?" *Challenge* (September–October): 26–33.

————. 1997. "Does the CPI Overstate Inflation? An Analysis of the Boskin Commission's Report." Unpublished paper. Washington: Economic Policy Institute (March).

Berndt, Ernst R., Zvi Griliches, and Neal J. Rappaport. 1995. "Econometric Estimates of Price Indexes for Personal Computers in the 1990's." *Journal of Econometrics* 68(1): 243–68.

Berndt, Ernst R., Zvi Griliches, and Joshua G. Rosett. 1993. "Auditing the Producer Price Index: Micro Evidence from Prescription Pharmaceutical Preparations." *Journal of Business and Economic Statistics* 11(3): 251–64.

Bosworth, Barry P. 1997. "Testimony before the Senate Finance Committee." 105 Cong., 1 sess., February 11.

Cole, Roseanne, and others. 1986. "Quality-Adjusted Price Indexes for Computer Processors and Selected Peripheral Equipment." *Survey of Current Business* 66(1): 41–50.

Congressional Budget Office. 1994. "Is the Growth of the CPI a Biased Measure of Changes in the Cost of Living?" CBO Paper. Congressional Budget Office (October).

Cutler, David M., and others. 1996. "Are Medical Prices Declining?" Working Paper 5750. Cambridge, Mass.: National Bureau of Economic Research (September).

Diewert, W. Erwin. 1983. "The Treatment of Seasonality in a Cost of Living Index." In *Price Level Measurement: Proceedings from a Conference Sponsored by Statistics Canada*, edited by W. E. Diewert and C. Montmarquette. Ottawa: Statistics Canada.

————. 1996. "Comment on CPI Biases." *Business Economics* 31(2): 30–35.

————. 1997. "The CPI Commission: Discussion." *American Economic Review, Papers and Proceedings* 87(2): 95–96.

Gordon, Robert J. 1990. *The Measurement of Durable Goods Prices*. University of Chicago Press.

————. 1996. "The Sears Catalog Revisited: Apparel and Durable Goods." Unpublished paper. Northwestern University (April).

Griliches, Zvi. 1961. "Hedonic Price Indexes for Automobiles: An Econometric Analysis of Quality Change." In *The Price Statistics of the Federal Government*. New York: National Bureau of Economic Research.

————. 1971. "Introduction: Hedonic Price Indexes Revisited." In *Price Indexes and Quality Change: Studies in New Methods of Measurement*, edited by Zvi Griliches. Harvard University Press.

Griliches, Zvi, and Iain Cockburn. 1994. "Generics and New Goods in Pharmaceutical Price Indexes." *American Economic Review* 84(5): 1213–32.

Hausman, Jerry. 1997. "Cellular Telephone, New Products, and the CPI." Unpublished paper. Massachuetts Institute of Technology (February).

Hicks, J. R. 1940. "The Valuation of the Social Income." *Economica* 7(May): 105–24.

Hulten, Charles R. 1997. "Quality Change in the CPI." Federal Reserve Bank of St. Louis *Review* (forthcoming).

Klumpner, Jim. 1996. "Fact and Fancy: CPI Biases and the Federal Budget." *Business Economics* 31(2): 22–29.

Lebow, David E., John M. Roberts, and David J. Stockton. 1994. "Monetary Policy and 'The Price Level.'" Unpublished paper. Board of Governors of the Federal Reserve System (July).

Liegey, Paul R. Jr. 1993. "Adjusting Apparel Indexes in the Consumer Price Index for Quality Differences." In *Price Measurements and Their Uses*, edited by Murray F. Foss, Marilyn E. Manser, and Allan H. Young. University of Chicago Press.

————. 1994. "Apparel Price Indexes: Effects of Hedonic Adjustment." *Monthly Labor Review* 117(5): 38–45.

Moulton, Brent R. 1996. "Bias in the Consumer Price Index: What Is the Evidence?" *Journal of Economic Perspectives* 10(4): 159–77.

————. 1997. "Issues in Measuring Price Changes for Rent of Shelter." Paper prepared for Conference on Service Sector Productivity and the Productivity Paradox. U.S. Bureau of Labor Statistics, April 11.

Moulton, Brent R., and Karin E. Smedley. 1995. "A Comparison of Estimators for Elementary Aggregates of the CPI." Unpublished paper. U.S. Bureau of Labor Statistics (June).

Reinsdorf, Marshall B., Paul Liegey, and Kenneth Stewart. 1996. "New Ways of Handling Quality Change in the U.S. Consumer Price Index." Working Paper 276. U.S. Bureau of Labor Statistics (November).

Rothbarth, E. 1941. "The Measurement of Changes in Real Income under Conditions of Rationing." *Review of Economic Studies* 8: 100–07.

Shapiro, Matthew D., and David W. Wilcox. 1996. "Mismeasurement in the Consumer Price Index: An Evaluation." In *NBER Macroeconomics Annual 1996*, edited by Ben S. Bernanke and Julio J. Rotemberg. MIT Press.

———. 1997. "Alternative Strategies for Aggregating Prices in the CPI." Federal Reserve Bank of St. Louis *Review* (forthcoming).

Triplett, Jack E. 1971. "Quality Bias in Price Indexes and New Methods of Quality Measurement." In *Price Indexes and Quality Change: Studies in New Methods of Measurement*, edited by Zvi Griliches. Harvard University Press.

———. 1990. "Hedonic Methods in Statistical Agency Environments: An Intellectual Biopsy." In *Fifty Years of Economic Measurement: The Jubilee of the Conference on Research in Income and Wealth*, edited by Ernst R. Berndt and Jack E. Triplett. University of Chicago Press.

———. 1997. "Measuring Consumption: The Post-1973 Slowdown and the Research Issues." Federal Reserve Bank of St. Louis *Review* (forthcoming).

U.S. Department of Agriculture. 1996a. *Fruit and Tree Nuts: Situation and Outlook Report*. FTS-278. Department of Agriculture, Economic Research Service.

———. 1996b. *Vegetables and Specialties: Situation and Outlook Yearbook*. VGS-269. Department of Agriculture, Economic Research Service.

U.S. Department of Commerce and U.S. Department of Housing and Urban Development. Various years. *American Housing Survey for the United States*. Current Housing Report H150. Department of Commerce.

U.S. Energy Information Administration. Various years. *Housing Characteristics*. Department of Energy.

U.S. Senate. Committee on Finance. 1995. *Consumer Price Index*. Hearings before the Committee on Finance. S. Hrg. 104-69, 104 Cong., 1 sess. Government Printing Office.

U.S. Senate. Committee on Finance. 1996. *Final Report of the Advisory Commission to Study the Consumer Price Index*. S. Prt. 104-72, 104 Cong., 2 sess. Government Printing Office.

Wynne, Mark A., and Fiona D. Sigalla. 1994. "The Consumer Price Index." Federal Reserve Bank of Dallas *Economic Review* (2d quarter): 1–22.

RUDIGER DORNBUSCH
Massachusetts Institute of Technology

Brazil's Incomplete Stabilization and Reform

SINCE THE INITIATION of the Real Plan in July 1994, after a decade of failed stabilizations, Brazil has made dramatic progress. Figure 1 makes the point forcefully: starting from hyperinflation levels, inflation has been under control for the past three years and there is no sign of it coming back. But the stabilization program is unconventional and this raises doubts about its eventual success. Brazil has big budget deficits, large real appreciation, and a large and growing external deficit; there has been a major increase in real wages and incomplete progress on broad-based economic reform. These conditions recall the many failed programs of Latin America, including Brazil's own Cruzado Plan of 1986.

Will Brazil stay the course and return to the high growth rates that it experienced in the 1960s and 1970s and that are common in Asia? Or will it continue with makeshift policies that lead to increased vulnerability and stand in the way of such dramatic improvements as have occurred in Chile and are now underway in Argentina? In particular, how will Brazil handle the significant real appreciation, growing external deficits, and incomplete structural reform? With politics seeming always to take the front seat, will there ever be a good time to attend to these important issues, which stand in the way of economic improvement?

If Brazil fails to make dramatic improvements, it is very unlikely that it will experience a Mexican-style collapse or a pervasive loss of confidence. There are 150 million Brazilians, and they are relentless optimists. Beyond that, trade controls, a more rapid crawling peg, a

I am indebted to Francesco Giavazzi, Ilan Goldfajn, Eustaquio Reis, and William Cline and members of the Brookings Panel for helpful suggestions. Drausio Giacomelli was very helpful with research assistance.

Figure 1. CPI Inflation, Monthly Rates, 1992–97ᵃ

Percent per month

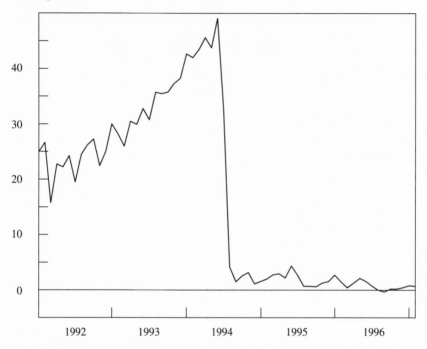

Source: Author's calculations based on data from International Monetary Fund (IMF), *International Financial Statistics*, various issues.

a. Sample period is January 1992 to February 1997. Data are monthly; tic marks correspond to January.

devaluation, or all three together, would easily avoid the worst. But Brazilians will say, ''Why be pessimistic at all? With high productivity growth and an improved distribution of income, Brazil could provide a new model by getting ahead on all fronts.'' Perhaps it will. But more likely not, and so the stabilization strategy is just giving Brazil more time—perhaps a lot of time—to procrastinate on growth policies.

The issue is not the possibility of near-term collapse, but that policies and performance are unnecessarily disappointing. Since the 1990–92 recession there has been an upturn, and growth is now running at 3.0 to 4.5 percent. But that is still far from the performance of Brazil in 1960–80 or the more recent experience of emerging economies from Chile to Malaysia. The current strategy of income redistribution and

Figure 2. Real Per Capita GDP, 1963–96

Index, 1963 = 100

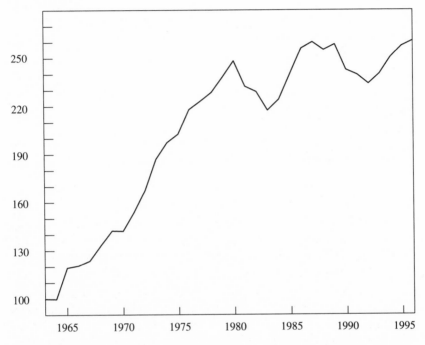

Source: Author's calculations. Data for 1963–94 are from IMF, *International Financial Statistics*, various issues. For 1995–96, GDP data are from J. P. Morgan, *Emerging Markets: Economic Indicators*, April 4, 1997; and population data are estimated by the author.

making do will not translate into the sustained high growth rates that are the hallmark of successful stabilization and reform. In fact, the external deficit and the government's inability or unwillingness to bring down the budget deficit increasingly distort incentives and undermine stability.

Looking Back: Growth, Inflation, and Many Failed Stabilizations

In the mid-1970s, Brazil had every right to expect extraordinary performance. Figure 2 shows the country's rapid growth in per capita

Table 1. Macroeconomic Performance, 1965–97
Percent

Period	Growth rate[a]	Inflation rate[b]	Current account balance[c]
1965–79[d]	5.9	30	−3.0
1980–93[d]	0.3	423	−1.4
1993	2.3	2,149	0.0
1994	4.2	2,669	−0.2
1995	2.7	23	−2.5
1996	1.5	10	−3.2
1997[c]	2.3	7	−4.0

Source: Author's calculations. Data for 1965–94 are from IMF, *International Financial Statistics*, various issues; and for 1995–97, from J. P. Morgan, *Emerging Markets: Economic Indicators*, April 4, 1997.
a. Percent change in real GDP per capita.
b. Percent change in CPI.
c. As a percentage of GDP.
d. Annual average.
e. Forecast.

income, which had been higher than in almost any other country for over a decade. The Brazilian model had been successful and showed no sign of running out of steam. The country had mastered living with inflation and import substitution. A mixed economy with a very dynamic public sector provided a successful growth strategy, and high growth contained the problems of income distribution that might otherwise have surfaced.[1] The "Washington consensus" was nowhere in sight, and Brazil was getting ahead in the wrong lane.

Brazil's depressing experience over the past fifteen years stands in sharp contrast to that of the preceding decades. Table 1 presents some statistics on Brazil's economic performance since 1965. It has always had some inflation, but in the late 1980s inflation soared to unprecedented levels. More striking, Brazil has experienced high growth rates for much of the postwar period. Over 1950–80, growth averaged 7.1 percent per year. With average population growth at 2.7 percent over that period, real per capita GDP almost quadrupled.[2] At the beginning of the 1980s, Brazil held great promise as an emerging economy, with a track record of growth and the expectation of exceptionally strong performance. Nothing of that has materialized: Brazil remains the coun-

1. See Bacha (1977), Cardoso and Fishlow (1990), and Malan and Bonelli (1977).
2. See Cardoso and Fishlow (1990).

try of the future. But after the disillusionment, the completion of reform and stabilization offer a chance to return to strong performance.

Brazil is rightly famous—and infamous—as a model of living with inflation. A system of comprehensive and effective indexation, ranging from the labor market to public sector prices and from the exchange rate to financial markets, has ensured that inflation is relatively stable and financial markets can function, preventing money from being driven offshore. The system was perfected during the military regime in the late 1960s to center on ex post inflation with infrequent readjustment. Initially, indexation adjustments to wages were made annually, so that price shocks would be substantially diluted rather than quickly turned into a price-wage spiral. Moreover, since the exchange rate rule made no allowance for external inflation, there was a built-in real depreciation effect.[3] As a result, external balance problems were never significant. Indeed, until the late 1970s the military regime did succeed in avoiding macroeconomic problems and, through indexation, preventing significant misalignments in relative prices and capital flight.

Figure 3 shows the Brazilian inflation rate from the stabilization implemented by the military regime in the mid-1960s to the eve of the Cruzado Plan, the most gloriously failed heterodox stabilization. Brazil's claim to living well with inflation goes back to the late 1960s and early 1970s, when inflation was moderate—20 to 30 percent—quite stable and even declining slightly. In combination with very high growth, stability and prosperity seemed unproblematic.

The oil shocks of the 1970s changed this picture. Brazil was a major importer of oil. At the outset, increases in the domestic prices of oil products were postponed and the external deficits occasioned by the higher prices and the lack of adjustment were financed in the emerging debt market. Prudently, the government practiced long-term borrowing. Had the oil shock been transitory, all might have ended well, but the second oil shock made it clear that there would be no early relief. A large external deficit led to accumulating debt. The United States's battle against inflation in the early 1980s made external financing precarious. Passing on the oil price increases to the domestic market, with

---

3. See Simonsen (1984, 1986) for an extensive discussion of the indexation arrangements written from the perspective of the early 1980s, giving a glimpse of the problem and no little indication of what was to come.

Figure 3. CPI Inflation, Annual Rates, 1965–84[a]

Percent per year

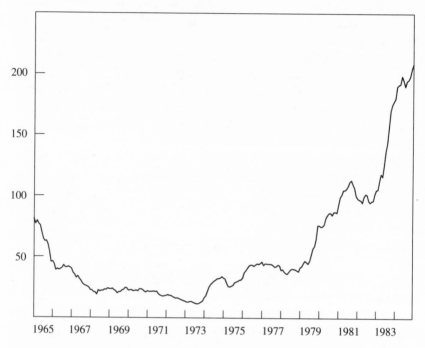

Source: Author's calculations based on data from from IMF, *International Financial Statistics*, various issues.
a. Sample period is January 1965 to December 1984. Data are monthly at annual rates; tic marks correspond to January.

its comprehensive indexation, doubled the rate of inflation from about 40 percent in the mid-1970s to 98 percent in 1982. Moreover, the frequency of indexation adjustments was increased from once a year to every six months, which, substantially accommodated by passive money, increased the inflation rate even further. The debt crises cut short the opportunities for external rollover and deficit finance. The party was over and Brazil was on its way to extreme inflation and stagnation.

In the face of full domestic indexation of wages and the exchange rate, oil price increases became wage increases, which, in turn, led to another and higher round of price inflation.[4] To reduce the average real

4. See Simonsen (1984, 1986) for the mechanics of supply shocks in the context of indexation.

wage between indexation adjustments, which reset wages, the rate of inflation had to increase, producing a more substantial erosion of real wages over the wage cycle. Monetary policy accommodated this process. Annual inflation surpassed 100 percent in the early 1980s; but even then, it seemed relatively stable.

In hindsight, there was a steady acceleration with wide swings in the month-to-month inflation rate. Because inflation depressed real wages, the system of annual wage increases gave way to semiannual raises and then to progressively more frequent increases. The inflation rate accelerated and the inflation stability of the early 1970s was lost. By 1985, inflation had surpassed 200 percent, with no prospect of subsiding.

Brazilian economists have long recognized that in a setting of full, compulsory indexation, orthodox monetary restraint is not a satisfactory answer to inflation. The idea that inflation has inertia, by virtue of the indexation law and practice, implies the need for an alternative stabilization strategy, namely, ''heterodoxy.'' The issue is not only to control demand, but, more important, to coordinate a stop to wage and price increases, which feed on one another. The ill-fated Cruzado Plan of 1986 was designed to accomplish this. The plan gave central place to a coordinated incomes policy, including cutting back wage increases, partial adjustment of wage contracts that had not yet been adjusted, and vigorous enforcement of price controls. Inflation would be killed overnight; euphoria would ensue. Since Brazil's inflation was not the outcome of inflationary money creation—the government was perfectly able to finance itself in the capital market—it was altogether plausible to use the stopping of the wage-price process as the central disinflationary measure. It was not plausible, however, to take advantage of the prevailing calm by immediately stepping up demand with a major expansion. The boom was short-lived, price controls became binding, and markets became distorted. (The government ultimately had to use the air force to round up cattle that were being withheld from the market.) Not surprisingly, the episode ended in a wave of corrective inflation. By late 1987, Brazilian inflation was running at nearly 400 percent and rising.

The Cruzado Plan is of interest because it highlights the basic conception of inflation in Brazil: inflation is sui generis, characterized by the inertia of an implicit or explicit indexation scheme and the resulting inability of restrictive monetary policy to promote disinflation rather than recession. The plan also highlights Brazil's low threshold for pain. Implementation of a restrictive demand policy to reinforce the incomes policy was never considered; to the contrary, demand was actually stimulated. The failure of subsequent stabilization programs has much to do with these two points.

The following years were marked by repeated unsuccessful attempts to stop inflation. Each stabilization was shortly followed by another round of inflation, with successively higher peaks. Most introduced a new money or at least skipped a few zeros, but each plan had its own name and its own special features: some did not specify any measures at all, others called for the freezing and inflationary erosion of all nominal assets, all had some particular mechanism to disarm inflation inertia. There was the Cruzado Plan, Cruzado 2, the Plan Bresser, the Summer Plan, the Collor Plan, Collor 2, and finally the Real Plan (named after the new currency that it introduced), which is still in place and, though incomplete, may be the lasting solution to Brazil's inflation.

The Real Plan uses neither wage-price controls nor the confiscation of assets. And in the Brazilian context, a sharp contraction of demand was also out of the question. Recognizing that even without extreme inflation rates inertia and coordination were major problems, the architects of the plan had to devise some way to bring wage- and price-setting into a noninflationary regime. This time, rather than readjusting all contracts to coordinate a simultaneous disinflation, they chose an elaborate move into a unified reference value. Wages were converted into this unit of account in March 1994, at their average over the previous four months, thus avoiding inflationary erosion. Once converted, wages were indexed on an annual basis for another year. The unit of account, in turn, was linked to the dollar, and when the stabilization formally began, it became the new currency—the real—at a parity of one to one.

In the immediate aftermath of stabilization, the new money appreciated against the dollar by nearly 15 percent, reinforcing the disinflation. However, over the next year, various forms of wage adjustment sharply raised wages. Just as under the previous stabilization plans, disinflation was incomplete and there was no assurance that it would continue.

Poststabilization Tensions

Once inflation had been brought down by the shift into a new money, several critical developments followed. Key features are highlighted here, some of which are discussed in more detail below.

—The exchange rate was fixed at one to one on the dollar as Brazil emerged from the transition period. Then the real appreciated significantly against the dollar between 1994 and 1996, reinforcing the disinflationary effect of the monetary reform. Depending on the measure— wages, the consumer price index (CPI), or manufactured goods prices—the appreciation was between 3 and 76 percent. With excessive real appreciation, as evidenced by Brazil's trade problems, the initial slipping of the real followed by the implementation of a crawling peg have created a relatively stable, though strongly appreciated, real exchange rate.

—A huge increase in real wages occurred in the process of shifting to the new money. This increase was the product of a combination of factors, including deliberate wage policy, indexation, some inertia being carried over into the new money, and real appreciation. One statistic suffices to illustrate the magnitude of the change: the real income of the bottom 50 percent of the income distribution rose by 35 percent over 1993–95.

—A very rapid rise in industrial production and a shift to large external deficits were driven by the return of credit and real wage growth. The risk of reigniting inflation persuaded the government to raise real interest rates to extremely high levels (just as in Germany in 1925). In 1995, real interest rates averaged over 40 percent; bankruptcy was pervasive and a large number of banks were destroyed. But as a disinflation strategy, it worked.

—The high interest rates not only slowed growth and significantly increased the problems of the banks, but also led to very large capital inflows. Foreign exchange reserves increased from $32 billion in December 1993 to $52 billion in December 1995; by late 1996, they had risen to $59 billion.

—A significant deterioration of the external balance resulted from import trade liberalization in the early 1990s, strong demand, and real appreciation. From near equilibrium in 1992, the external balance had moved to a deficit of $24 billion by 1996, and it is still rising.

Table 2. Median Real Monthly Wage Income, by Income Group, 1990–95
September 1995 reais, except as indicated

Income group	1990	1993	1995	Percent change, 1993–95
Bottom 10 percent	29	23	42	83
Bottom 50 percent	96	86	116	35
Top 10 percent	1,707	1,648	2,044	24

Source: Author's calculations based on data from the PNAD, a household survey conducted by the Instituto Brasileiro de Geographia e Economia (IBGE).

Real Wages and Real Income

The stabilization has been a massive political success not only because there is no longer any inflation, but also because there have been substantial gains in real income for all workers, and in particular, the poor. This section reviews the basic facts on real wages, income distribution, and the reduction of poverty in the aftermath of stabilization.

In the years 1990–92, per capita GDP was falling. The year of the stabilization, 1994, as well as 1995, were characterized by strongly rising GDP per capita. But beyond the growth in output, a lot happened on the side of real wages. In São Paulo, for example, real wages increased by 26 percent between 1993 and 1996.[5] The real minimum wage also increased significantly. The minimum wage plays a key role in the Brazilian economy; it directly affects the 21 percent of the labor force estimated to work below the minimum wage, and is also a benchmark wage for the formal sector. Rodrigo Reis Soares shows that the minimum wage exerts a significant influence on real earnings. Moreover, the reduction in inflation reduced the inflationary erosion of the real wage over the indexation cycle.[6]

The gain in real wages has led to a major redistribution of income in Brazil. Household survey evidence shows both a rise in real wages overall and a rise in the relative wages of low-income workers.[7] Table 2 shows the distribution of real wage changes. While real labor income has increased for every decile of the distribution, the average

5. See *Conjuntura Econômica*, various issues.
6. See Neri, Considera, and Pinto (1996), Reis Soares (1997), and Rocha (1996a).
7. Data are from tabulations reported in Instituto Brasiliero de Geographia e Economia (IBGE) (1995).

real wage of those in the bottom 10 percent nearly doubled between 1993 and 1995. And the relative position of the poorest group has risen dramatically: between 1993 and 1995, the ratio of those in the top 10 percent wage to that of those in the bottom 10 percent declined from 72 to 49.[8]

The same phenomenon occurred under the Cruzado Plan. In 1986 the real median income of the poorest group briefly recorded an increase of 77 percent, but this did not last in either absolute or relative terms. Price controls provided a temporary stabilization that ended in a blowout.[9]

The real wage gains and their distribution can also be considered in terms of the issue of poverty. This is a central issue in Brazil, where income distribution is extraordinarily bad, even by third world standards.[10] In the decades preceding the Real Plan, the income distribution had grown steadily worse: in the 1960s the income share of the poorest 60 percent was 25 percent and by the 1990s it had fallen to only 16.3 percent. Over the same period, the share of the richest 10 percent increased from 39.7 to 49.7 percent.[11] The Real Plan—taken together with other domestic developments, including growth, the restoration of bank credit, and improvements in agriculture—has led to a dramatic improvement in poverty.[12] The real wage gains and increased employment moved almost 13 million people over the poverty line during the first year of the plan. The proportion of poor in the population fell to the levels during the Cruzado Plan, a decade earlier. The data are

8. It seems reasonable to ask how real wages could increase so substantially. The answer is that the share of labor in Brazil's GDP is actually very low: about 30 to 35 percent, according to oral tradition (no estimates from the income side are available).

9. Brazil's heterodox stabilization under the Cruzado Plan followed a path very similar to that of Peru in the mid-1980s, under Alain Garcia: a big hike in wages, fixed exchange rates, a boom, and a big bust.

10. Deininger and Squire (1996) show that the ratio of the top quintile to the bottom quintile of the income distribution, averaged over 1960–89, is 23 for Brazil, exceeded only by Armenia (24), Honduras (28), and Guinea-Bissau (29). For Chile, this ratio is 14, and the average for East Asia is 7.

11. See Bonelli and Ramos (1992, table 1, p. 5).

12. For a discussion of the evolution and measurement of Brazilian poverty, including in the context of the Real Plan, see Rocha (1996a, 1996b), Neri, Considera, and Pinto (1996), and Sonia Rocha, "Crise, Estabilizção, e Pobreza—1990 a 1995," *Conjunctura Econômica*, January 1997, pp. 22–26.

impressive: between 1990 and 1995, the total number of poor declined from 42 million to only 30.4 million, and the fraction of poor, from 30 percent to only 21 percent.[13]

The real wage gains and their favorable effects on the income distribution actually understate the extent to which the situation has improved for workers.[14] The disappearance of the inflation tax on real balances accounts for some increase in real income, as does the elimination of the variation of real income within the adjustment cycle. It is important to recognize that the restoration of credit that always comes with a reduction of inflation also raises the standard of living.

Consumption boomed soon after the plan was initiated. Credit expansion reinforced the spending impact of the rise in real wages.[15] The share of consumption in GDP rose to 82.1 percent, in contrast to an average of 77 percent over the period 1980–94. The only time in the past fifteen years when consumption reached similar levels was 1986, the year of the Cruzado Plan; indeed, the share was virtually identical at that time—82.3 percent. The comparison is uncomfortable.

A major rise in real wages is a feature common to many countries that have undergone stabilization programs, in Latin America and elsewhere. To the extent that real wage increases and a consumption boom have ultimately led to the failure of several stabilizations, or at least to difficulties, this must be held out as a prospect for Brazil.[16] As discussed, the Real Plan has been successful in creating growth with an improved income distribution. Real wage gains have been significant across the board, and in the bottom half of the distribution, in particular. The obvious question is how to make these effects last. Alternatively, one could ask what is the other side of the coin of the gains in real wages and income. If these gains are coupled with external borrowing and overvaluation, then caution is important, because this stabilization may not last long enough—as the Cruzado Plan did not—to increasingly

13. See Sonia Rocha, "Crise, Estabilizção, e Pobreza—1990 a 1995," *Conjunctura Econômica*, January 1997, p 26.
14. Even before the introduction of the Real Plan, Cardoso, Paes de Barros, and Urani (1995) had noted the adverse impact of certain macroeconomic conditions—in particular, inflation—on income distribution.
15. Real credit to consumers expanded by 98.7 percent in the period July 1994 to July 1996; see *Conjuntura Econômica*, various issues.
16. See Kiguel and Liviatan (1992), Dornbusch, Goldfajn, and Valdés (1995), and Rebelo and Vegh (1995).

and rapidly translate into reforms and the resulting advances in productivity. At best it is a prepayment on reform, at worst, an unaffordable consumption boom.

The Real Exchange Rate

In the aftermath of the Mexican collapse, the real exchange rate has come to assume a special place in judging the success of a stabilization program. Even though other factors contributed to the massive meltdown in Mexico—for example, shortening of debt, dollarization, expansionary credit policy—the large real appreciation played a major role in setting the scene for a crisis.[17] Going beyond the Mexican case, Ilan Goldfajn and Rodrigo Valdés provide a detailed study of large real appreciations worldwide.[18] For a cross-section of ninety-three countries, they do not find a single case of a real appreciation of 35 percent or more (adjusted for trend and fundamentals) that did not ultimately result in a major depreciation. And even for somewhat more moderate real appreciation, they find that the probability of a large real depreciation is very substantial.

It is important therefore to ask where Brazil stands in this regard. The issue of real appreciation inevitably arises, because the Brazilian data are very striking. As always, interpretations differ. Analyzing the industrial price index for São Paulo relative to Brazil's trading partners since the inception of the Real Plan, Edmar Bacha concludes that there was a modest real appreciation of 6 percent by mid-1996. The Instituto de Economia do Setor Público (IESP) reports a real exchange rate in industry and shows roughly the same results. Eliana Cardoso investigates a broad range of indexes to conclude that, by some measures, real appreciation has been as high as 40 percent under the Real Plan. Alfonso Pastore and Maria Pinotti likewise find evidence of substantial real appreciation.[19]

Goldman Sachs uses a model-based approach to determine fundamental exchange rates as benchmarks for judging over- or undervaluation. Based on this model, by February 1997 the real was overvalued

17. See Dornbusch, Goldfajn, and Valdés (1995) and also Sachs, Tornell, and Velasco (1996).
18. Goldfajn and Valdés (1996).
19. Bacha (1996); Instituto de Economia do Setor Público, *Indicadores IESP* 6(58), January–February 1997; Cardoso (1996); Pastore and Pinotti (1996).

Figure 4. Two Indicators of Currency Overvaluation, 1992–96ᵃ

Index, January 1992 = 100

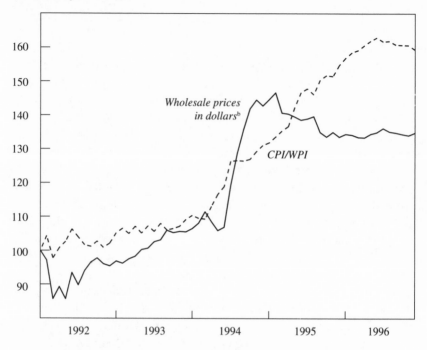

Source: Author's calculations based on data from from IMF, *International Financial Statistics*, various issues.
a. Sample period is January 1992 to December 1996. Data are monthly; tic marks correspond to January.
b. Wholesale price index divided by index of nominal exchange rate (real to dollar).

by 19.1 percent. Gustavo Franco, one of the leading architects of the Real Plan, rejects the hypothesis of overvaluation on the grounds that Brazil is in an unprecedented situation, for which past data are not relevant; the present combination of high productivity growth, an open economy, and stable money is unique in Brazil's history.[20]

Figure 4 presents two indicators of overvaluation for Brazil. One series is the Brazilian wholesale price index, deflated by the real-to-dollar exchange rate; that is, wholesale prices in dollars. This measure shows an increase of about 25 percent over January 1994, before the adoption of the Real Plan. However, it makes no adjustment for prices in dollars of goods in competitor countries, whether Argentina, with its

20. Ades (1996); Franco (1996).

Figure 5. J. P. Morgan Real Effective Exchange Rate, 1977–97ᵃ

Index, 1990 = 100

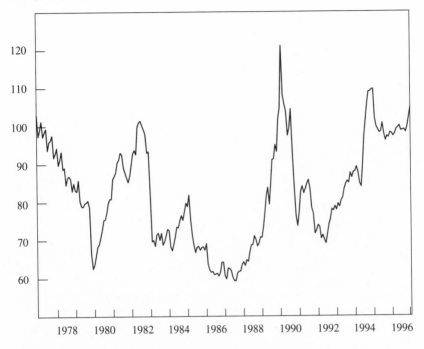

Source: J. P. Morgan currency index database, available on J. P. Morgan's worldwide web page.
a. Effective exchange rate index based on nonfood wholesale prices. Sample period is January 1977 to February 1997. Data are monthly; tic marks correspond to January.

increased price level, or Europe and Japan, where prices in dollars have fallen sharply in the past several years.

The other series in figure 4 shows the ratio of the Brazilian consumer price index to the wholesale price index. This serves as a rough proxy for the price ratio of nontradables to tradables. By this measure, the relative price ratio has risen by almost 50 percent since early 1994. This represents an extraordinary shift in relative prices, as could be expected from the large shifts in income distribution and real wages discussed above.

Figure 5 reports the J. P. Morgan real effective exchange rate since January 1977.[21] A rise in this index represents a real appreciation. By

21. During periods of high inflation, measurement of real exchange rates is poor

Table 3. Alternative Measures of the Real Exchange Rate, 1993–96
Index, 1990 = 100

Real exchange rate measure	1993	1994	1995	1996
CPI/WPI	114	129	154	172
Exchange rate indexes[a]				
J. P. Morgan, nonfood wholesale prices	82	95	101	97
IPEA, manufactured goods prices	82	89	94	92
Fundap, industrial goods prices	89	96	98	97
Fundap, CPI	82	93	112	120
IPEA, wages	107	139	196	245

Source: CPI and WPI data are from IMF, *International Financial Statistics*, various issues. J. P. Morgan data are from the J. P. Morgan currency index database, available on J. P. Morgan's worldwide web page. IPEA data are provided directly from the Instituto de Pesquisa Econômica Aplicada. Fundap data are from Instituto de Economia do Setor Público, *Indicadores IESP* 6(58), January–February 1997.

a. Indexes are constructed so that an increase represents an appreciation of the real. Effective exchange rate indexes are deflated as indicated.

this measure, the real exchange rate has been quite high for over two years, its level matched only by brief episodes on the eve of the Collor Plan and the 1982 debt crisis. This time series illustrates how hard it is to decide on a benchmark for assessing the real appreciation. Compared with the average for the period 1980–94—when Brazil's performance deteriorated—the current real effective exchange rate has appreciated by 35 percent. Of that, 5 percent is due to the very recent rise in the value of the dollar relative to European currencies and the yen. Table 3 reports several real exchange rate measures, including trade-weighted (effective) exchange rates, all of which show some real appreciation.

The possibility that this real appreciation represents an overvaluation arouses concern because large real appreciations have almost invariably ended in external crises. The problem accumulates over time and induces a growing external deficit. The exchange rate becomes unsustainable whenever events undercut the rollover of debt and the financing of current account deficits. Even without an actual crisis, overvaluation cuts into growth and in this fashion signals its unsustainability.

Large real appreciation, without fundamental support, involves increased vulnerability and, for that reason, makes a country more prone to crisis. When and how the crisis comes about depends on the particular circumstances. For example, a political reversal could break a pattern

because wage and price data are not synchronized. The bias is systematic, in that the relevant price is understated (because of reporting lags) and consequently the reported real exchange rate is overdepreciated relative to the true rate.

of continuity and credibility and lead to a sell off; a bout of easy money would hasten such a crisis, a fragile banking system with foreign currency exposure would magnify the collapse, and a liquid debt structure would accelerate and magnify the collapse. Financial considerations are all important in interpreting specific events, but must not be misconstrued as the primary or sole source of a collapse.

Before a crisis, there is little agreement on what is a misaligned real exchange rate. Because of that disagreement, real appreciation can run its course. But theory can help to predict what should happen to equilibrium relative prices. If an economy undergoes reform, specifically, significant trade opening and restructuring that reduces employment and hence leads to a decline in the equilibrium wage in dollars, real appreciation is the wrong development. The basic point is that reforms that reduce employment, at least in the medium term, in themselves create an overriding presumption that real depreciation is necessary.

Brazil has opened trade very substantially. Quotas have been almost completely abandoned, and the average tariff fell from 51 percent to only 14 percent between 1988 and 1994.[22] Import penetration in manufacturing has increased sharply. Imports as a percentage of apparent consumption rose from 4.4 in 1989 to 15.5 in 1995.[23]

Economic reform—trade liberalization, deregulation, restructuring, privatization and government downsizing, opening the capital account—has two important impacts. First, by improving resource allocation, its raises productivity and hence the long-run economic prospects of the economy.[24] This effect might best be summarized as an increase in the valuation of equity in those industries that benefit from liberalization; and it is not unambiguous, because opening will trim the scope for collusive profits and hidden subsidies. Nevertheless, in combination, the reform measures invariably make the economy more attractive to outside investors and hence raise the valuation of assets.

Second is the impact of the reform measures on labor. In the long run, it is plausible that a country that uses its resources more effectively

22. See Cardoso (1996) and Abreu, Carneiro, and Werneck (1996).
23. See Mesquita Moreira and Correa (1996, table 2). It is interesting to note that there is no commensurate rise in the ratio of exports to production. Although this ratio did rise over the period 1989–95, it did so only from 10.1 to 14.9 percent. It is the differential opening on the import side that is of interest here.
24. This point is central to the discussion in Franco (1996).

and puts itself in a position to attract foreign investment will also pay higher real wages. But that is definitely not the case in the short run, before the reallocation of resources is substantially underway and investment in new plant and equipment is realized. In fact, in the short run the *equilibrium* wage in dollars must fall. Thus stock prices and equilibrium wages in dollars (or the exchange rate) are likely to move in opposite directions.

Despite the argument that trade liberalization calls for real depreciation and a decline in wages in dollars, one cannot presume that in a live situation involving a complex set of reforms, including a return to the world capital market, this must actually happen. In fact, I have shown that exactly the opposite can take place: real wages rise and the real exchange rate appreciates. But that precisely highlights the tension. In the labor market, the reforms call for wages in dollars to fall in order to accommodate the reduction in labor demand in the government sector and in import-competing businesses that face unprecedented competition. Yet wages in dollars are driven up by the dominant effect of capital inflows.

There are two ways in which such a situation might arise without incurring short-term employment problems. In one case, a boom in physical investment uses labor in the implementation process and, over the longer term, creates new jobs in the domestic goods and export sectors at unchanged or even increased wages. It is conceivable that this could be accomplished by pervasive deregulation and increased efficiency in public finance, or improved market access abroad. The expansion of exports due to the elimination of a host of implicit taxes, for example, would be sufficient. The more antiexport bias there is in the initial system, the better the chance that reform will pay for itself in the labor market, without any need for wage cuts and depreciation. In the typical distorted economy, though, exports have long received special attention and anti-import bias has increasingly been superimposed. In such a case, the overwhelming presumption is that there will be wage cuts and depreciation.

Measures to increase the profitability of exports, including, for example, privatizing ports and allowing access to imported intermediate goods at reduced tariffs, can translate into substantial export expansion. But such expansion is not often large enough to absorb the excess labor generated by the reforms. Even though exports expansion is strong, unemployment is high. To a significant extent, depreciation and the reform of labor market institutions are substitutes; without either, unemployment is certain to rise. Even with credible reform, it takes a very long time to realize the investment required to expand net exports and the high growth needed to absorb the excess labor.

Deflation does not come quickly and hence the economy is trapped in a situation of high unemployment. Lower levels of wages and prices in dollars are the most effective solutions to the problem, although one can always find some other reforms that might help. Argentina is a good case in point: widespread restructuring and real appreciation have caused unemployment to rise to nearly 20 percent, and investment is not booming. The wage in dollars must fall in order to help create employment. Given the fixed exchange rate, that means deflation, which, in this case as always, is painful and hence slow.

The alternative way to accommodate deregulation, restructuring, and trade liberalization is by means of a domestic spending boom. The Diaz Alejandro effect—a short-run rise in real demand—and access to the world capital market will both push in this direction, and fiscal expansion can help. But a spending boom is clearly only a short-term solution. After a year or two, as productivity gains take hold and the spending effect wears off, unemployment increasingly becomes a problem. Moreover, this is unlikely to be an economy in which resources are reallocated to export expansion and import substitution, but rather, one that overspends on imports and neglects to build the jobs on the trade front that ultimately support high wages. As a result, in the longer run major imbalances arise. The other side of the coin, a large external deficit, reflects the availability of "cheap" imports, a high level of domestic demand, and easy financing in the world market. When financing suddenly stops, the corrective depreciation is substantial.

When trying to explain why a particular real exchange rate is not overvalued, governments often point to productivity gains. They note that reforms have translated into vastly improved opportunities for firms; as a result, firms are competitive, even at a significantly appreciated real exchange rate. This argument needs scrutiny for two reasons. First, why is there real appreciation if firms are so much more efficient? Real wages may rise without a deterioration in unit labor costs. But a rise in prices in dollars would suggest that productivity improvements are not dominant, and for that reason, competitiveness is lost. Typi-

Table 4. Change in Industrial Production, Employment, and Productivity, 1970–95
Percent per year

Period	Production	Employment	Productivity
1970–80	9.0	6.5	2.4
1980–90	−0.2	−0.4	0.2
1990–95	2.1	−5.1	7.5

Source: Considera (1996, table 1, p. 41).

cally, it is not possible to find a price index that focuses uniquely on international competitiveness, and yet it is often inappropriate to refer instead to export growth rates. More likely than not, both imports and exports are rising at double-digit rates and net exports are deteriorating.

Second, at a more fundamental level, large productivity gains may simply mean high unemployment. If firms shift to increasingly capital-intensive technology and their investment predominantly takes the form of capital deepening and shifting to higher quality using imported intermediate goods, the labor market problem remains. Quite a few firms succeed and give the impression that it is possible to live with almost any exchange rate, but that is no answer to the problems of the labor market, the domestic economy, or the financial sector.

Table 4 reports trend growth rates of Brazilian productivity over the period 1970–95. Claudio Considera, from whom these data are taken, cautions that the measurement of productivity may be flawed because of difficulties in measuring value added.[25] Even so, it is evident that if firms adjust to a high real exchange rate, the issue of how to sustain full employment remains. Budget deficits and a shift in the income distribution toward labor are, at best, temporary solutions. In Brazil's case, the large real appreciation reflects the redistribution of income and is accommodated by the rise in spending that has followed from strong wage increases and budget expansion. Unemployment has not yet risen precipitously, but the tension is already present both in the labor market and in the external balance.

The Budget Issue

The budget deficit is among the more important unresolved issues in the aftermath of Brazil's stabilization. Table 5 reports annual budget

25. Considera (1996).

Table 5. Budget Balances and Public Debt, 1991–96
Percent of GDP

	Annual balance[a]				
	Primary budget[b]		*Operational budget*[c]		
Year	*Total*	*Federal*	*Total*	*Federal*	*Accumulated debt*
1991	3.0	0.8	1.5	0.3	43.5
1992	2.3	1.3	−2.2	−0.8	42.8
1993	2.6	1.4	0.3	0.0	36.4
1994	4.3	3.0	0.5	1.6	28.5
1995	0.3	0.6	−4.8	−1.6	31.7
1996	−0.7	0.4	−3.9	−1.7	35.1

Source: Data are provided directly by the Central Bank of Brazil, the Brazilian Ministry of Finance, and Garantia.
a. Positive numbers indicate surplus.
b. Excludes interest payments.
c. Includes inflation-adjusted interest.

balances and public debt for Brazil over the period 1991–96. The melting down of debt under the Collor freeze helped to improve the budget by cutting debt service. However, the very high real interest rates of 1995 have restored much of that debt. The operational budget deficit, which reflects substantial state deficits rather than federal deficits, is not so large as to create a financing problem for Brazil. But in conjuction with the still high levels of debt, it will certainly make a new spell of high interest rates troublesome. It is also clear that the deficit is too large and sticky for major reforms to wipe out soon. Thus, if there is a problem, the budget deficit and the debt will make it worse—possibly much worse. Without a problem, in a growing economy the deficit will not push up the debt ratio dramatically. From that point of view, gradual deficit reduction is a plausible strategy.

Brazil's public finances are attracting the most attention in financial markets. Efforts to promote higher national saving and financial stability must focus on the budget. Nevertheless, the real exchange rate issue seems more serious. Even countries without fiscal problems experience currency crises—for example, Mexico.

To What Extent Has Brazil Reformed?

Brazil has a history of pervasive statism, from public sector enterprises to trade protection, from administered labor markets to price management in oligopolistic sectors. The surprise is just how well Brazil did when it was doing well. In emerging economies around the world, the race is on to reform, downsize the state, and strive for openness as a means of improving productivity and gaining access to external resources. How well is Brazil doing, compared to other countries? The answer is unambiguous: not very well. A number of surveys report on reform. Whether their approach is broad or highly specific, they all conclude that Brazil is among the slow or incomplete reformers.

One survey that ambitiously covers the world is conducted by the Heritage Foundation and the *Wall Street Journal*.[26] The topics covered include trade, taxation, government intervention, monetary policy, foreign direct investment, the banking sector, wages and prices, property rights, regulation, and black markets. The scores range from 1 (free) to 5 (repressed). Brazil is placed ninety-fourth out of 150 countries, with a score of 3.35, which falls in the category of "mostly not free." In this survey, Brazil performs as well, or poorly, as Mexico, better than Venezuela (3.60), but worse than Pakistan (3.10). It ranks far worse than Chile (2.25) and South Korea (2.45), and even than Argentina (2.65)—which, like Brazil, is penalized by the survey's use of long-term rather than recent inflation data.[27]

Another survey of reform performance is provided by the Inter-American Development Bank.[28] It covers a comprehensive set of indicators of structural reform, including the external sector, tax policy, financial policy, privatization, labor market regulation, and the pension system. Countries are assessed, according to a four-fold system, as early or late reformers and slow or fast reformers. Brazil emerges as a late and slow reformer, as do Venezuela and Mexico.[29] Argentina and Chile, by contrast, are early and fast reformers.

The World Economic Forum (under the direction of Jeffrey Sachs), evaluates a group business survey on a number of indicators—giving special weight to openness, financial and labor markets, budgets, and regulation—to form a "competitiveness" index for forty-nine coun-

26. Holmes, Johnson, and Kirkpatrick (1997).
27. The emphasis on a history of low inflation, as opposed to a recent episode that remains on probation, is appropriate because so many stabilization programs have failed.
28. Inter-American Developent Bank (1996) and Lora (1997).
29. See Lora (1997, p. 19).

tries.[30] In this horse race, Brazil ranks as number 48, one position behind Venezuela and far behind Mexico (33) and Chile (18), and is trailed only by Russia.

Economic Freedom of the World, 1975–95 is an annual assessment of economic freedom issued by a group of market-oriented institutes.[31] For a group of 103 countries, an index summarizes four sets of criteria: money and inflation, government operation and regulation, takings and discriminatory taxation, and restraints on international exchange. Over the period 1993–95, Brazil ranks as number 97. The report concludes that "Brazil's policies conflict with economic freedom in almost every area."[32]

The American Express Bank provides a score card for a group of forty-three developing countries.[33] Using the criteria of macroeconomic stability, human capital, market orientation, export orientation, and investment, countries are sorted into five groups, according to their degree of "tiger-ness" (in allusion to the Asian "tiger" economies). Those in the top group are "confirmed tigers" and those in the bottom group are "stragglers." Brazil, which scores 30 out of 100 points, is placed in the next-to-last group, as an "emerging tiger." Within this group it ranks last, tied with Zimbabwe. Of the entire sample, only Pakistan and Nigeria have lower scores than Brazil and are classified as stragglers.

Brazil has brought down inflation and its performance is certainly not among the worst of reformers worldwide. But this summary of surveys shows that Brazil is, at best, in the middle of the field and, by all accounts, is a reluctant and tardy reformer.

The Policy Problem

The problem facing Brazil's policymakers can be summarized in a simple diagram that focuses on the social objective of high real wages,

30. For a discussion of the index, see Jeffrey D. Sachs, "Why Good Policy Matters," *World Link*, July–August, pp. 8–9.
31. Gwartney, Lawson, and Block (1996).
32. Gwartney, Lawson, and Block (1996, p. 125).
33. Grice (1997).

Figure 6. The Latin Triangle

Wage in dollars

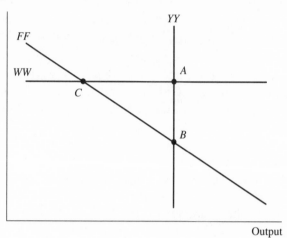

Output

Source: Author's model, as described in text.

the target of full employment, and the constraint of limited external deficits. Figure 6 shows three schedules. Along and above *WW*, the wage in dollars, and hence the real wage, is at least at its minimum acceptable level. But the real wage affects competitiveness, as do the levels of demand and output. Along *FF*, the external balance reaches its target level. Points above and to the right of *FF* correspond to unacceptable deficits. Finally, points to the left of *YY* represent unemployment (informality), while points to the right of *YY* correspond to overheating.

The diagram is deliberately drawn to highlight a policy conflict. At *B* there is full employment and external balance, but the real wage is unacceptably low; this might be called the International Monetary Fund equilibrium. At *A* the real wage is politically acceptable and there is full employment, but the deficit is too large. I call this the Latin equilibrium; it is the typical overborrowing equilibrium. Finally, at *C* there is unemployment with the target real wage. This represents the familiar retrenchment in response to external deficits, but in a situation where devaluation is not acceptable. It is typical of the year before an election, just before expansion starts.

The obvious solution is to break out of the overdeterminacy by means of a boost to productivity: workers can have their jobs, their real wages, and their competitiveness, all at the same time. But if productivity does not grow, or if improvements are predominantly labor saving, protection would be an alternative course of action. As would borrowing, in the hope that the situation would sort out in time. Neither alternative is good economic policy.

How Vulnerable Is Brazil?

As noted above, it is very unlikely that Brazil will suffer the fate of Mexico. There are good reasons why Brazil is a very different story. In particular, there is no single point of acute vulnerability, and policymakers operate with maximum flexibility. *Jogo de cintura* and *jeitinho* are essential concepts of Brazilian policymaking, consistency is not.[34] Other points in Brazil's favor are as follows:

—Brazil has not promised anything, is performing beyond expectations, and keeps alive hopes for doing more in the future. No firm line has been drawn and no date has been set as decisive. Hence there is no cause for disillusionment, and that is a great source of stability.

—Brazil has no explicit inflation target or nominal exchange rate commitment. As a result, the government has been able to move to a crawling peg exchange rate to avoid further real appreciation. That leaves the question of whether there is overvaluation, but it eliminates the prospect of a nominal anchor that will gradually and inevitably sink the ship.

—Brazil has $60 billion in foreign exchange reserves. When problems come and speculators attack, reserves are never enough—neither in Britain nor in Mexico—but high reserves deter attacks in the first place. Moreover, it is unlikely that the Brazilian government would just stand by and watch, or even accommodate a fall in reserves, as did its Mexican counterpart.

—There is political continuity. President Cardoso, who is considered a reformer, is expected to seek and win reelection in 1998, on the basis of the record of low inflation. Optimists will interpret the reelection as

---

34. These terms defy translation; loosely, they refer to getting around rules and bureaucracy in order to get things done.

a mandate to "continue" reforms. And it will encourage the market to believe that there will not be any exchange rate experiments.

—Notwithstanding the recovery from the 1995 slowdown, inflation is not picking up. As a result, there is no need for a renewed slowdown and the attendant political risk to the popularity of President Cardoso.

—Brazil does not have an external financing problem and there is none in sight, as yet. The current account deficit, although rising, is less than $30 billion, far below that of Mexico as a share of GDP. So far, external financing has been possible with declining interest rates. A substantial portion of the deficit is being financed by direct investment, so that liquidity issues are commensurably less salient.

—If the external balance were to become a problem, controls could mitigate it. In fact, some of the liberalization measures of the early 1990s have already been reversed.

—Significant public sector assets have yet to be privatized. Their privatization will not only provide budget revenues, but can also be a source of external financing. More broadly, it will foster Brazil's reputation as being in a reformist mode.

From this list, one must conclude that Brazil will be able to hold on to stabilization and go forward, with moderate reform and much financing . . .? But it cannot hold on forever. Since the basic policy mix is bad and reform is slow, growth performance and financial stabilization will wear thin. Ultimately, that would create sufficient vulnerability that even Brazil might face, if not a speculative attack, at least an attrition of capital inflows. The fact that this point may be far off must not encourage the view that Brazil can wait to complete its program of stabilization and reform.

In discussing the possible overvaluation of the real, Franco recognizes that large current account deficits—for example, the 6 to 7 percent of GDP in Mexico in 1994—are perilous.[35] He further emphasizes that it does not make sense for emerging economies to aim to eliminate their deficits. His golden mean is 3 percent, large enough to take advantage of world capital markets and small enough to avoid risk. Brazil is very likely to leave that safe place during 1997, unless the government either imposes more trade restrictions or slows down demand. Forecasts for the current account deficit in 1998, the election year, now run to 5

35. Franco (1996).

percent of GDP. There is a conflict between external stability and domestic growth; with a strongly appreciated real exchange rate, options narrow and risks increase. If reform is to pave the way for Brazil's future, reform must come soon and forcefully.[36]

Conclusion

To date, Brazil's stabilization has been limited to lowering inflation, while real wages have been raised dramatically and the real exchange rate has been allowed to appreciate significantly. The public celebrates the end of inflation, but in fact it is celebrating the large rise in real incomes, which it associates with the end of inflation rather than with real wages and a real exchange rate that are potentially unsustainable.

There is pervasive evidence that good economic policy leads to high growth. Good economic policy not only comprises a set of institutions, raging from a lean government to functioning open markets, it also includes high rates of saving and investment. In Brazil, the rate of saving is low and so is the rate of investment. Figure 7 shows that the share of investment in GDP (in constant prices) is currently barely 16 percent and has been low for a decade. If the consumption boom should give way to saving and investment, and to reform in the fast lane, the Real Plan will have been a brilliant platform for a dramatic shift in Brazilian performance.

But if, as is more likely, muddling along continues to be the rule—with the real appreciation limiting the profitability of industry, external finance taking center stage, the macroeconomy being played to assure President Cardoso's reelection in 1998, and so forth—Brazil cannot expect to move to the 7 to 9 percent growth rate that routinely characterize successful emerging economies. The country is still celebrating the success at reducing inflation; but it is time to start thinking about how to realize sustained high growth.

Capital markets do not reliably provide a stable bridge for wages to rise ahead of investment and jobs. It might appear possible, in the short run, to spend the income ahead of investment and output expansion by

36. Paulo Rabelo de Castro rightly emphasizes the need for the widening and deepening of reform; "Brazil Needs More Than the Real Plan for Growth," *Wall Street Journal*, November 29, 1996, p. A7.

Figure 7. Investment as a Share of GDP, 1960–95ª

Percent

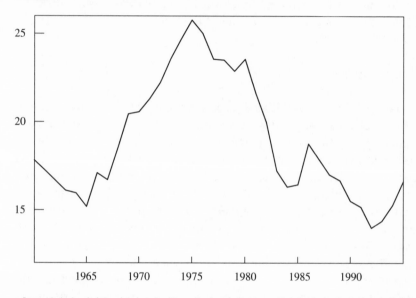

Source: Author's calculations based on Brazilian national accounts data provided directly by the Instituto de Pesquisa Econômica Aplicada (IPEA).
a. Calculated using constant prices.

borrowing to finance deficits, but this almost always results in a crisis. Even with international capital mobility, the way to get ahead is to put the horse in front of the cart. Successful reformers have gone slow on consumption spending; they have emphasized competitiveness, saving, and investment as means of implementing the opportunities opened up by economic reform. A real appreciation strategy, while seemingly helpful in terms of inflation, invariably derails the growth process. The real exchange rate is a key component of success, as the case of Chile bears out.[37] If Brazil does not shift to reform and saving, the Real Plan will prove to be nothing but another botched populist stabilization plan.

37. See Dornbusch and Edwards (1994) and Williamson (1996).

Comments and Discussion

William R. Cline: I like Dornbusch's paper. I agree with most of it. My comments seek to push the implications somewhat further and to take a few exceptions.

This is an important paper. It clarifies Dornbusch's views on Brazil. Last summer the financial press had Dornbusch sounding the alarm. He had been among the few—certainly, he was the most conspicuous—to predict the Mexican peso crisis, so his new warnings on Brazil seemed significant. Now, however, one can breathe a sigh of relief that the Dornbusch rating system has upgraded Brazil from "crash" to "muddle through."

Dornbusch's central conclusions are, first, that Brazil cannot reach its growth potential without further reform. I agree with that. Second, however, he seems to place exchange rate depreciation at the top of the list of reforms needed and fiscal adjustment somewhat below that. I would certainly reverse that order of priority. Moreover, it would be helpful if the paper pursued the substance of how to reduce the real exchange rate without destabilizing the success on inflation.

The key issues of the paper are these: First, it suggests that there was a golden era of high growth in the 1960s and 1970s. I think that it is important to note, however, that there were severe imbalances in that growth, especially in the 1970s. In fact, I published a book with Brookings in February 1981 that refers to Brazil's strategy for responding to the 1970s oil shock as "aggressive," with expansionary policy, in-

395

creased protection, and higher borrowing. This left "burdensome external debt that will inhibit future efforts at high growth."[1]

Second, the paper states that the Real Plan is the first potentially successful stabilization plan. I think that Dornbusch's evaluation is broadly valid, pending further reform. And the plan certainly has an elegant design. Its main problem, in my view, has been the inadequate fiscal adjustment. This, in turn, has necessitated excessively tight money. A consequence is excessively high real interest rates, which, in the context of an abundant international capital market, mean large capital inflows in response to interest arbitrage. Large capital inflows, in their turn, drive the widening of the current account deficit. The challenge is to reduce these imbalances, and there has been some progress. For example, the real interest rate has fallen substantially in the past year, and there has been some success in curbing excess demand.

The third issue that the paper raises is real exchange rate appreciation. The real exchange rate has indeed increased. The Institute of International Finance estimates that the exchange rate deflated by relative wholesale prices has increased by 15 to 20 percent under the Real Plan. It seems to me that this is probably more germane than the up to 60 percent real appreciation suggested by some other measures. Is even 15 to 20 percent real appreciation too much? It is important to keep in mind that before the Real Plan, the current account was in balance. There was a zero external deficit, which is excessively low for a large developing country.

There is the question of the appropriate current account target. Dornbusch cites Gustavo Franco as preferring a figure of 3 percent of GDP. That kind of magnitude has considerable merit. Suppose that one wanted the external debt to stabilize at 40 percent of GDP. It would take a current account deficit of about 3 percent of GDP, on the one hand, and real growth of about 5 percent plus a rise in world dollar prices of about 3 percent, on the other, to be compatible with that target. From this example, 3 percent might be appropriate; the current account deficit of about $24 billion last year is at about that level.

Brazil's export base, however, is relatively weak, because this is a large and inherently relatively closed economy. Recent work confirms economists' previous expectations that exports are particularly relevant

1. Cline (1981, p. 133).

in analyzing the sustainability of the current account deficit.[2] Mexico's current account deficit, as a fraction of exports of goods and services, was 50 percent before the peso crisis. By the same measure, Brazil's current account deficit this past year was 40 percent. So, there may not be as much comfort from the low fraction of GDP as one would like to think. These numbers suggest that a current account deficit of around $30 billion is starting to get into a zone in which one has to be very careful.

In sum, I tend to agree that the real exchange rate appreciation is a potential source of vulnerability. The questions are, on the one hand: how much vulnerability does it pose? And on the other: what to do about it?

I would note, by the way, that the "Tequila effect" of early 1995 was beneficial to Brazil because without that shock in the capital markets, policymakers would not have undertaken demand-curbing measures, and so the external imbalance would have become even wider.

Fourth, the paper says that there will be no collapse in Brazil like the Mexican peso crash. Again, I agree. One reason is that Brazil has no comparable commitment to a quasi-fixed exchange rate. Another reason is that its $60 billion of reserves have considerable protection from a fast runoff because they have minimum term limits. Their most volatile component is the so-called CC-5 accounts, which are, basically, bank deposits and have already been drawn down. Brazil's so-called trade credit is probably exaggerated by speculative flows, but when and if they start to run off, the authorities are quite capable of very carefully scrutinizing whether these credits were, in fact, for trade.

Dornbusch is right. Brazilian pragmatism means that interventions will be taken if necessary, and that the government is unlikely to stand by and witness an utter collapse in the name of adherence to a rigid ideological position on an exchange rate peg. The most eloquent evidence for this so far is the increase in protection for automobiles in 1995.

The fifth issue raised by the paper is wages. It is very encouraging that the wage data show a sharp increase in low-end wages that reduces the poverty index. Is this sustainable? I would point out that much of this increase must be due to the elimination of the inflation tax, rather

2. See Milesi-Ferretti and Razin (1996).

than official wage policy. There are also some statistical questions. The São Paulo wage survey is perhaps affected by the fact that restructuring has shaken out the lower wage workers from the sample, which may tend to exaggerate wage increases.

I guess I do disagree with Dornbusch's proposition that theory says that when a country reduces tariffs, it must also lower wages. It seems to me that this advice may be prudent as a transitory measure, but it does not follow as a steady state. If one believes that lower tariffs increase real output and if one asserts that lower tariffs require lower wages, one must be arguing that trade liberalization requires a redistribution of income away from labor to capital. I see no reason to propose this. Indeed, the Stolper-Samuelson theory would say that for Brazil, with its factor endowments, trade liberalization should have just the opposite effect. In terms of policy, one would be hesitant to recommend trade liberalization if, somehow, it would inevitably result in a major concentration of income.

I think that the problem is that this is a partial-equilibrium approach. A general-equilibrium approach would take cognizance of the fact that protection biases production toward the domestic market. Once protection is reduced, producers have an incentive to reallocate their output toward the export market. In this context, while Dornbusch points to the sharp increase in import penetration, I would also note a substantial increase in exports of almost 25 percent from 1993 to 1996.

Yes, perhaps Brazil did go too far. The decision to increase the minimum wage sharply was probably a populist excess. The minimum wage affects all pensioners, as well as those earning at that level and below. But there has been some correction lately: in 1996 government employees received a zero wage increase.

Sixth, there is the issue of fiscal imbalance. The flavor of the paper, to my taste, somewhat downplays the need for fiscal adjustment. It does say some favorable things about Argentina. But in comparison with Brazil, Argentina has had a similar problem of an initial rise of the real exchange rate; the principal difference is that Argentina has had a more impressive fiscal adjustment. So, in some sense, it is difficult to both be more in favor of the Argentinean case and, at the same time, place more emphasis on the real exchange rate than on fiscal adjustment, as the paper seems to do.

Part of the problem is the traditional measures that are used. Because

Brazil had such high inflation in the past, people have grown accustomed to using the operational deficit, which excludes the inflationary component of interest payments. But with Brazil now approximating more normal levels of inflation, by international standards, one needs to look also at the nominal deficit. The nominal deficit was 7 percent of GDP in 1995 and 6 percent last year. The paper says that the operational deficit is "not so large." I think that in his oral presentation Dornbusch laid greater emphasis on the need for fiscal adjustment, which makes more sense to me.

Just one technical comment. In the oral presentation, Dornbusch said that there is no sign of budget correction for 1997. I think that, formally, the budget calls for a cut in the operational deficit from 4 percent to 2.5 percent of GDP.

The last issue is saving and investment. It is right to emphasize the need for higher saving and investment; one simply cannot expect to achieve 8 percent growth with saving at less than 20 percent of GDP. I would note the link to the country's fiscal posture. The fiscal deficit is an important source of dissaving, and it is no accident that the high-growth Asian countries typically have zero fiscal balances or fiscal surpluses. Moreover, it is not quite accurate to say that growth has been solely consumption based. Certainly, in 1994 and 1995 the growth in investment exceeded that in consumption.

In sum, the paper seems to say that it is essential to depreciate the real exchange rate at this point because it has become overvalued. There should be gradual fiscal adjustments and more reform, although the paper is rather vague on the substance of the additional reform.

For my part, I would emphasize, first, aggressive fiscal adjustment; for example, through constitutional reform that eliminates, or makes more flexible, civil service tenure and overcomes the serious problem of excessive revenue-sharing with the states.

Second, I would pursue gradual real depreciation, rather than anything more ambitious. This raises the operational question of how to adjust the exchange rate without destabilizing the success in reducing inflation. The paper is silent on this issue. One can imagine a sharp devaluation; and it seems likely that a devaluation of 15 or 20 percent or more would, in fact, go a long way toward destabilizing the progress against inflation.

By contrast, some modest acceleration of the crawl, which currently is 0.5 percentage point per month, more or less, to something like 0.8 or 0.9 percent per month, sustained over two or three years could have a fairly good chance of success. The authorities could even cite the recent rise of the dollar against the yen and the deutsche mark as the motivating force for such a change; they could say appropriate words about exchange rate baskets, and so forth. It might also be necessary to increase interest rates somewhat to assure that there is not a sudden pressure on reserves in the face of an accelerated crawl.

In the Brazilian context, it seems quite possible that this kind of a shift could be accomplished without provoking an equal, off-setting increase in domestic prices. Brazilian expectations, it seems to me, are less sensitive to the exchange rate than most; Brazilians have tradition- ally looked inward at the domestic economy, rather than to the dollar. They are the exact opposite of the Argentineans in this regard. Argen- tina's experience of hyperinflation without indexation made its public acutely aware of the exchange rate, so that a sharp devaluation of the Argentinean peso would likely have severe inflationary consequences.

Finally, what does the international capital market imply for the feasibility of muddling through? Currently, this market is extremely abundant. It seems quite easy to finance a current account deficit of $25 billion to $30 billion, especially given the large direct investment associated with privatization. If U.S. interest rates increase by no more than, say, 50 basis points, there is no obvious reason to expect a sharp change in that outlook.

Overall, however, it seems to me that there is little doubt that Brazil should move on fiscal reform. At the very least, it needs to avoid further real appreciation of the exchange rate. It also needs to increase saving, and to limit external borrowing as the source of growth.

General discussion: Benjamin Friedman asked Dornbusch how Brazil had achieved such a large rise in real wages, particularly at the bottom of the income distribution, given that GDP growth in the 1990s had been so modest. He noted that real wages have risen for each decile of the income distribution, so that it was not a case of redistribution among wage earners. Dornbusch explained that Brazil has the most unequal distribution of income in the world, after Honduras, and so it was possible to make the poor richer without making the rich poor. The biggest gains have been for the lowest income earners, but their wages were so low that a doubling could easily be covered by most firms. More broadly, there has probably been some erosion of the profit share. Current data are not accurate, but in the 1980s the wage share was as low as 32 percent, so there was ample room for it to expand while maintaining adequate returns to capital generally. Only the firms with heavy exposure to international trade would be badly hurt, and indeed, firms in sectors such as textiles and automobiles are going bankrupt.

William Brainard pointed out that this hypothesis would not explain how the stock market could increase by 30 percent. But Dornbusch noted that Brazil's stock market is only now catching up to the bull market in emerging market stocks. William Branson observed that if wages were only 30 percent of income, a 12 percent rise in real GDP and 40 percent growth in real wages would not reduce the nonwage part of GDP at all, presumably leaving ample room for overall profits to rise. Branson added that the large current account deficit of around 50 percent of exports could raise worries about currency depreciation having substantial *J*-curve effects, and thus pose credibility problems for a policy of depreciation.

References

Abreu, Marcelo de P., Dionisio D.Carneiro, and Rogerio L. F. Werneck. 1996. "Brazil: Widening the Scope for Balanced Growth." *World Development* 24(2): 241–54.

Ades, Alberto. 1996. "GSDEEMER and STMPIs: New Tools for Forecasting Exchange Rates in Emerging Markets." Goldman Sachs *Economic Research* (October).

Bacha, Edmar L. 1977. "Issues and Evidence on Recent Brazilian Economic Growth." *World Development* 5(1 and 2): 47–67.

———. 1996. "Plano Real: Uma Segunda Avaliação." Unpublished paper. Rio de Janeiro: Universidad Federal de Rio de Janeiro (UFRJ) (July).

Bonelli, Regis, and Lauro Ramos. 1992. "Income Distribution in Brazil: Longer Term Trends and Changes in Inequality Since the Mid–1970s." Discussion Paper 288. Rio de Janeiro: Pontifícia Universidade Católica de Rio de Janeiro, Department of Economics.

Cardoso, Eliana A. 1996. "Brazil's Macroeconomic Policies and Capital Flows in the 1990s." Unpublished paper. International Monetary Fund (October).

Cardoso, Eliana A., and Albert Fishlow. 1990. "The Macroeconomics of the Brazilian External Debt." In *Developing Country Debt and Economic Performance*, vol. 2, *Country Studies*, edited by Jeffrey D. Sachs. University of Chicago Press.

Cardoso, Eliana A., Ricardo Paes de Barros, and Andre Urani. 1995. "Inflation and Unemployment as Determinants of Inequality in Brazil: The 1980s." In *Reform, Recovery, and Growth: Latin America and the Middle East*, edited by Rudiger Dornbusch and Sebastian Edwards. University of Chicago Press.

Cline, William R. 1981. "Brazil's Aggressive Response to External Shocks." In *World Inflation and the Developing Countries*, by William R. Cline and Associates. Brookings.

Considera, Claudio Monteiro. 1996. "Globalização, Produtividade e Emprego Industriais." *Boletim Conjuntural* 35(October): 41–42. Rio de Janeiro: Insituto de Pesquisa Econômica Aplicada (IPEA).

Deininger, Klaus, and Lyn Squire. 1996. "A New Data Set Measuring Income Inequality." *World Bank Economic Review* 10(3): 565–91.

Dornbusch, Rudiger, and Sebastian Edwards. 1994. "Exchange Rate Policy and Trade Strategy." In *The Chilean Economy: Policy Lessons and Challenges*, edited by Barry P. Bosworth, Rudiger Dornbusch, and Raúl Labán. Brookings.

Dornbusch, Rudiger, Ilan Goldfajn, and Rodrigo O. Valdés. 1995. "Currency Crises and Collapses." *BPEA, 2:1995*, 219–93.

Rudiger Dornbusch 403

Franco, Gustavo H. B. 1996. "A Inserção Externa e o Desenvolvimento" Unpublished paper. Central Bank of Brazil (June).

Goldfajn, Ilan, and Rodrigo O. Valdés. 1996. "The Aftermath of Appreciations." Working Paper 5650. Cambridge, Mass.: National Bureau of Economic Research (July).

Grice, Kevin. 1997. "Becoming a 'Tiger' Economy." American Express Bank Economics for Investment (March): 2–5.

Gwartney, James D., Robert Lawson, and Walter Block. 1996. Economic Freedom of the World, 1975–95. Vancouver: Fraser Insitute.

Holmes, Kim R., Bryan T. Johnson, and Melanie Kirkpatrick, eds. 1997. 1997 Index of Economic Freedom. Washington: Heritage Foundation.

Instituto Brasileiro de Geographia e Economia (IBGE). 1995. "Sintese de Indicadores da Pesquisa Nacional Por Amostra de Domicilios." Rio de Janeiro: Instituto Brasileiro de Geographia e Economia.

Inter-American Development Bank. 1996. Economic and Social Progress in Latin America: 1996 Report. Washington: Inter-American Development Bank.

Kiguel, Miguel A., and Nissan Liviatan. 1992. "The Business Cycle Associated with Exchange Rate-Based Stabilizations." World Bank Economic Review 6(2): 279–305.

Lora, Eduardo. 1997. "Una Década de Reformas Estructurales en América Latina: Qué se ha Reformado y Cómo Medirlo?" Unpublished paper. Inter-American Development Bank (February).

Malan, Pedro S., and Regis Bonelli. 1977. "The Brazilian Economy in the Seventies: Old and New Developments." World Development 5(1 and 2): 19–45.

Mesquita Moreira, Maurício, and Paulo Guilherme Correa. 1996. "Abertura Comercial e Indústria: O Que se Pode Esperar O Que se Vem Obtendo." Discussion Paper 49. Rio de Janeiro: Banco Nacional de Desinvolvimento Económico e Social (BNDES).

Milesi-Ferreti, Gian Maria, and Assaf Razin. 1996. "Current-Account Sustainability." Princeton Studies in International Finance 81. Princeton University, Department of Economics (October).

Neri, Marcelo, Claudio Considera, and Alexandre Pinto. 1996. "Crescimento, Desigualidade e Pobreza: O Impacto da Estrabilização." Seminar paper 28/96. Rio de Janeiro: Insituto de Pesquisa Econômica Aplicada (IPEA) (November).

Pastore, Alfonso Celso, and Maria Cristina Pinotti. 1996. "Inflação e Estabalização: Algumas Lições da Experiência Brasileira." Unpublished paper. Universidad de São Paulo (USP) (April).

Rebelo, Sergio, and Carlos A. Vegh. 1995. "Real Effects of Exchange-Rate-Based Stabilization: An Analysis of Competing Theories." In NBER Mac-

roeconomics Annual 1995, edited by Ben S. Bernanke and Julio J. Rotemberg. Cambridge, Mass.: National Bureau of Economic Research.

Reis Soares, Rodrigo. 1997. "Um Modelo Econometrico Para O Mercade de Trapalho Brasileiro." Unpublished paper. Rio de Janeiro: Insituto de Pesquisa Econômica Aplicada (IPEA).

Rocha, Sonia. 1996a. "Poverty Studies in Brazil: A Review." Discussion Paper 398. Rio de Janeiro: Insituto de Pesquisa Econômica Aplicada (IPEA) (January).

———. 1996b. "Renda e Pobreza: Os Impactos do Plano Real." Discussion Paper 439. Rio de Janeiro: Insituto de Pesquisa Econômica Aplicada (IPEA) (December).

Sachs, Jeffrey D., Aaron Tornell, and Andrés Velasco. 1996. "The Collapse of the Mexican Peso: What Have We Learned?" *Economic Policy* 22: 13–56.

Simonsen, Mario Henrique. 1984. "Inflation and Anti-Inflationary Policies in Brazil." *Brazilian Economic Studies* 8: 1–36.

———. 1986. "Indexation: Current Theory and the Brazilian Experience." In *Inflation, Debt, and Indexation*, edited by Rudiger Dornbusch and Mario Henrique Simonsen. MIT Press

Williamson, John. 1996. *The Crawling Band as an Exchange Rate Regime: Lessons from Chile, Colombia, and Israel.* Washington: Institute for International Economics.